Modelling Techniques for Financial Markets and Bank Management

Contributions to Management Science

Marida Bertocchi · Enrico Cavalli
Sándor Komlósi (Eds.)

Modelling Techniques for Financial Markets and Bank Management

With 42 Figures

Physica-Verlag

A Springer-Verlag Company

Series Editors
Werner A. Müller
Peter Schuster

Editors
Professor Marida Bertocchi
Professor Enrico Cavalli
Department of Mathematics, Statistics,
Informatics and Applications
University of Bergamo
Piazza Rosate 2
I-24129 Bergamo, Italy

Professor Sándor Komlósi
Department of Management Science
Faculty of Business and Economics
Janus Pannonius University Pécs
Rákóczi út 80
H-7622 Pécs, Hungary

ISBN 3-7908-0928-4 Physica-Verlag Heidelberg

CIP-Kurztitelaufnahme der Deutschen Bibliothek
Modelling techniques for financial markets and bank management/Marida Bertocchi... (ed.). – Heidelberg: Physica-Verl., 1996
  (Contributions to management science)
  ISBN 3-7908-0928-4
NE: Bertocchi, Marida [Hrsg.]

SPIN 10533495   88/2202-5 4 3 2 1 0 – Printed on acid-free paper

Foreword

The XVIth meeting of the Euro Working Group on Financial Modelling was held from November 24 to 27th 1994 in Pécs, Hungary. The Conference was hosted by the Regional Centre of the Hungarian Academy of Sciences and co-organized by the Faculty of Business and Economics, Janus Pannonius University, Pécs.

The XVIIth meeting of the Euro Working Group on Financial Modelling was held from May 31 to June 3rd 1995 in Bergamo, Italy. The Conference was hosted by the University of Bergamo and co-sponsored by the Department of Mathematics, Statistics, Informatics and Applications, University of Bergamo, and by Fondazione "Pro Universitate Bergomensi".

Bergamo's meeting started with a 1-day tutorial on recent operational research tools applied to Finance. The tutorial was sponsored by the Med-Campus Program on Banking and Finance, coordinated by the University of Cyprus, involving also members of the Euro Working Group on Financial Modelling.

In the first part of Bergamo's meeting, three invited lectures were given by Prof. Alexander Malliaris from Loyola University in Chicago, Prof. Jitka Dupacova from Charles University in Prague and Prof. Stavros Zenios from University of Cyprus.

This volume contains selected refereed papers from the participants of these two meetings.

The papers cover a wide collection of topics, ranging from corporate financial management, banking, to game, neural network, rough set approaches applied to finance and financial market models. Both the conceptual or theorical and empirical aspects are explored. A special emphasis is given on up-to-date modelling techniques for a better understanding of financial market and bank management.

We give a brief summary of the collected works.

Alexander Malliaris and Jerome Stein develop a non linear dynamic model, a chaotic map, to explain the relation between asset price volatility, speculation and errors made by the traders. Testing of the model shows that the randomness in the time series sequence of price changes cannot be rejected.

Jitka Dupacová presented an application of postoptimality analysis for stochastic programming to problems arising in portfolio management. She identifies several key input data of portfolio management that are known, at best, with some probabilistic distribution and she presents models for analyzing the sensitivity of the solution of a portfolio optimizer to "out of sample" data.

Maria Elena De Giuli and Umberto Magnani deal with properties of perfect-matching problems. They study the behaviour of optimal primal and dual solutions depending on changes of the right-hand-sides and interpret these results in light of selected economic applications.

Paolo Falbo, Silvana Stefani and Marco Frittelli show how mean reversion hypothesis can be applied to describe the dynamic of commodity futures prices. An empirical investigation on cotton futures prices is provided. It is shown how is possible to select trading strategies which offer higher expected returns linked to lower risk.

Giorgio Calcagnini and Rita D'Ecclesia examine whether a standard framework for deriving asset demands and asset sustitutability can explain observed relative holdings of various asset classes in the Italian market. Despite the non satisfactory results for the Italian market, the paper outlines some of the problems with standard portfolio models when confronted with data. Further improvements will be provided in a future work.

Adriana Gnudi presents empirical evidence of the appropriateness of a multinomial model for the evolution of the interest rates term structure in the Italian market.

Elisabetta Allevi models transaction costs through a concave function of the amount traded and suggests possible application of the model.

Andrea Resti's paper addresses the question of the difference between parametric and non-parametric assessments of the efficiency of a set of banks. It is shown, using a common panel of 270 Italian banks, that the two techniques do give similar results.

Thomas Hartman and James Storbeck focus on the subject of efficiency of a bank, showing how to use Data Envelopment Analysis to analyze the efficiency of different layers that build the bank's structure and network and for assessing the degree of managerial ability present at each level of the structure.

Kari Takala and Matti Viren's paper deals with the relation between bankruptcy and indebtedness, real interest rates and asset prices. It analyzes the macroeconomic determinants of bankruptcies as well as the consequences of business failures for the financial markets.

Damiano Carrara and Enrico Cavalli focus on the problem of bankruptcy prediction in the textile manifacturing sector. They compare the predictive capability of the linear discriminant analysis approach with the feed-forward artificial neural network approach. Experimental results on a small sample of companies identify some interesting performance of the neural network approach.

Salvatore Greco, Silvestro Lo Cascio and Benedetto Matarazzo introduce the use of a relatively new approach, the rough set, to the modelling of information imperfection in financial modelling. Results on the Italian stock markets confirm the efficiency of rough set analysis as learning tool for investors.

Gianfranco Gambarelli' paper deals with the use of Banzhaf-Coleman power index in case where a shareholder needs to evaluate the outcome of a potential take-over bid by knowing, a priori, how the configuration of a major share holding would change.

Michael Page documents an extensive simulation to assess the effectiveness of statistical tests used to validate the Arbitrage Pricing Theory models.

Jozsef Varga suggests the use of modified statistic tests for randomness in multiple financial time series. The adequacy of the suggested approximations are checked by simulation experiments.

Margherita Cigola and Paola Modesti deal with a Skew-Symmetric Bilinearity (SSB) model to describe a very large class of preference relationship. They give a probabilistic interpretation for the SSB utility in the sense that preference, described by a pairwise comparison to a third random variable, can be estimated by a set of bets on the possible outcomes.

Luisa Tibiletti provides a syntethic analysis of the relevant notion of proper risk aversion and proposes a sufficient condition to guarantee it.

Marida Bertocchi and Enrico Cavalli, Bergamo, Italy.
Sándor Komlósi, Pécs, Hungary.
December 1995

Contents

Financial Modelling: From Stochastics to Chaotics and Back to Stochastics[1]

A. G. MALLIARIS[2] and JEROME L. STEIN[3]

[2] Department of Economics, Loyola University Chicago, Chicago, Illinois 60611, USA.

[3] Department of Economics, Brown University, Providence, Rhode Island 02912, USA.

Abstract. In this paper we argue that the stochastic paradigm of asset prices has prevented us from understanding market behavior because most of the variance of the variables of economic interest is often attributed to random shocks. One implication of the tests of the Efficient Market Hypothesis is that most of the variation in prices is due to our ignorance of the underlying structure. As an alternative to the stochastic methodology we propose an economic interpretation of the most famous chaotic map called the Lorenz system. We briefly describe the major characteristic of this chaotic system and we also use financial data for its empirical testing.

Keywords. Stochastics, Chaos, Lorenz System, Econometric System, Estimation.

1. Introduction

The early observation by Holbrook Working (1934), that certain sensitive commodity price differences tended to be largely random, eventually directed researchers to seek theories for such a statistical phenomenon. Paul Samuelson (1965) developed the Efficient Market Hypothesis (EMH) to rationalize the random walk behavior, whereby the current price p(t) fully reflects all relevant information. Since the flow of information between now and the next period cannot be anticipated, price changes in an efficient market are serially uncorrelated.

Neither the EMH nor the numerous statistical studies about random walk investigate the analytical properties or characteristics of the information set beyond the assumption of the existence of a probability space (Ω, F, P). The flow of real world information is then modelling as a process of random sampling, at certain time

---

[1] We are thankful to Henry Wen-herng King, Dimitrios Bouroudzoglou and Raffaella Cremonesi for extensive computations. An earlier version of this paper was presented at the EUROPEAN WORKING GROUP ON FINANCIAL MODELLING, June 1-3, 1995 at the University of Bergamo, ITALY. We are very grateful to Professor Marida Bertocchi for the invitation to participate and to two anonymous referees for constructive criticisms.

intervals, from such an arbitrary space. Furthermore, because sampling is random, the EMH claims that price changes are also random. In other words the statistical notion of a random sample from an information set during a given time interval is connected by the EMH to the economic notion of unpredictable price changes.

In section 2 we argue that the stochastic paradigm of asset prices has prevented us from understanding market behavior to such an extent that most of the variance of the variables of economic interest are attributed to random shocks, that is, the error term. This is just a euphemism for ignorance. The implication of the tests of the EMH is that most of the variation in prices is due to our ignorance of the underlying structure. To contrast the stochastic approach to modelling financial markets with the alternative of chaotic modelling, we offer in section 3 an economic interpretation of the Lorenz system. This is the best known three-dimensional chaotic system whose time trajectories look like random when they are actually fully deterministic and converge to a strange attractor. Some important properties of this chaotic system are presented in section 4. In section 5 we use financial data to estimate econometrically the various parameters of the Lorenz system. Our conclusion are summarized in the last section.

2. Stochastic Modelling

During the past twenty years, the EMH has been refined analytically, mathematically and statistically. The concept of information was made precise. The notion of random walk was generalized to martingales and Itô processes; and numerous sophisticated statistical tests were employed to test the theory. Moreover, a very large literature developed concerning the statistical distribution of the changes in spot or futures prices: are they normal, or are they leptokurtic and if leptokurtic, how fat are the tails? The theoretical foundations underlying these studies are not always clear. It was not surprising to find that along with numerous studies confirming market efficiency, there were many rejecting it, and that there is no agreement concerning the statistical distribution functions of price changes. Nevertheless, the most convenient and widely acceptable paradigm postulates that returns are normally distributed which means that asset prices follow lognormal distributions. Both modern portfolio theory and the Black-Scholes methodology of pricing derivative assets are founded on such a paradigm.

The randomness of asset price changes hypothesized by the EMH naturally leads to questions about the behavior of the variance of such changes. If price changes are induced by changes in information, can shocks in fundamental factors affecting the economy explain the observed price volatility? Or, is the variance of price changes due to other factors? This topic is exposited in Shiller (1989), known as volatility tests and efficient markets. This literature documents that prices are too volatile and although this evidence does not imply rejection of the EMH, it raises the crucial question: what factors other than fundamental shocks could explain such evidence of high volatility. Among several such factors, speculation has received special attention.

The topic of speculation and price volatility has been studied at both the theoretical and the empirical level. In an efficient market, since price changes are unpredictable, speculation should not be profitable. Milton Friedman (1953) argued that profitable speculation reduces the price variance. This insight has generated many empirical papers which examined the profitability of speculation. However, it was shown in Hart and Kreps (1986), that his conclusion only follows under special conditions, and that plausible models can be developed explaining excess volatility by the speculative behavior of noise traders.

There are additional reasons why the stochastic approach should be reevaluated. First, when asset price researchers postulate that tomorrow's expected price is equal to today's actual price, they readily acknowledge that these models are not suitable for prediction or theoretical explanation. Put differently, the influence of the postulated random shock dominates the importance of the independent variables; and because such a shock is necessarily theoretically unpredictable, so is the value of the dependent variable.

Secondly, stochastic models typically discourage active economic policy or regulation designed to improve market performance. This is a consequence of the unpredictability of future shocks. Randomness does not render itself to a clear diagnosis of market behavior or understanding of the relation between changes in the fundamentals and economic performance.

3. Chaotic Dynamics

This state of events has led researchers to investigate a key question: Is there a nonlinear deterministic methodology, as an alternative to the stochastic approach of the EMH, which generates a time series sequence of price changes that appear random when in fact such a sequence is nonrandom ?

Numerous expository articles such as Brock (1988), Baumol and Benhabib (1989), and Boldrin and Woodford (1990) have appeared that use various single variable chaotic maps as a metaphor to illustrate the intellectual possibilities of the deterministic approach.

We wish to go beyond these illustrations and explain the behavior of volatility in a nonlinear dynamical system that establishes a relationship of such asset volatility to speculation and to Bayesian learning processes followed by the traders. In other words, we show in this section how nonlinear dynamics, as an alternative to linear stochastic models, can clarify the relation between price variability and speculation, and also explain why the empirical studies of the time series properties of asset prices are ambiguous and inconclusive.

Consider three key variables: price volatility, speculation and errors made by traders. We propose a model of three differential equations that relate these three variables. This model is known in the dynamical systems literature as the Lorenz equations. This system is perhaps the most famous chaotic map in the mathematical literature of dynamical systems and has been studied extensively for its remarkable properties. See for example Sparrow (1982).

Let x denote excess volatility of a given financial variable. For example x may denote the excess volatility of the futures price of corn. Volatility is given the standard definition of the annualized standard deviation of returns. Note that we wish to model excess volatility defined as the volatility of the price of an asset less the volatility of fundamentals. In the example of the volatility of the futures price of corn we substract the volatility of corn inventories which accounts for a measure of the volatility of fundamentals.

Malliaris and Stein (1995) develop a detailed economic model to derive

$$(3.1) \qquad dx/dt = s(-x + y)$$

which says that changes in the excess volatility of an asset depend on two factors: first, the level of excess volatility and also the volatility of Bayesian errors by traders, denoted by y.

Equation (3.2) describes the dynamics of the Bayesian error. The Bayesian error depends upon the noisiness of the system and the average costs of sampling by the market participants. The latter depends upon the types of people attracted to the market. Moreover, given the noisiness of the system, the volatility of the Bayesian error converges as time increases. Equation (3.2) is one specification of this process.

$$(3.2) \qquad dy/dt = x(r - z) - y$$

Equation (3.2) above involves a parameter r and three financial variables: x, y and z. Recall that x denotes excess volatility of the price of a financial asset while y denotes the volatility of the average Bayesian error. This error is measured as the difference between the subjective estimate of the price today and the objective price at the expiration of the futures price. The third variable z is a measure of excess speculation.

Holbrook Working (1949) and Ann Peck (1985) have developed a measure of excess speculation which they refer to as the z index. It measures the amount of speculation in excess of what is necessary to accommodate the hedgers. This index can be expressed as

$$z = 1 + Ss/Hs, \qquad \text{if } Hs > Hl; \text{ or}$$
$$z = 1 + Sl/Hl, \qquad \text{if } Hs < Hl,$$

where Ss=short speculation, Hs=short hedging, Sl=long speculation and Hl=long hedging. For example if z=1, then speculation is minimal. Insofar as a rise in z is

due to the entrance of more small traders, the price variance will rise. If the rise in z
is due to the entrance of more large commercial and non-commercial traders, price
variance will decline.

Equation (3.2) states that, given excess volatility x and the amount of excess
speculation z, the variance of the Bayesian error will converge. If x and z are zero,
$dy/dt = -y$, i.e. the Bayesian error converges to zero.

The variance of the Bayesian error is driven by a term related to the noisiness of
the system and an amount of speculation, of the form $x(r - z)$. The noisiness of the
system increases price variance in thin markets, if there is a small amount of
speculation $(r > z)$, but as speculation increases $(z > r)$ then the variance of the Bayesian
error decreases. The logic of the term $x(r-z)$ is that in thin markets, where there is little
speculation $(r > z)$, slight changes in hedging pressure produce large changes in the
futures price. Moreover, when there is a low level of speculation the information set
of the speculators is small: the speculators in total have taken small samples from the
information set. When there is a lot of speculation $(z > r)$, then there is a considerable
number of speculators who operate in a Bayesian manner, and take large samples from
the information set, as described in Stein, (1992), so that the variance of the sample
mean around the population mean (concerning the fundamentals) is low and the market
on average is better informed.

Equation (3.3) states again that speculation tends to be stabilizing. Given the
noisiness of the system and the Bayesian error, the amount of speculation converges
to xy/b. The logic here is that speculation is induced by profits to speculators and the
noisiness of the system. The profits of speculators converge, given xy, and are driven
to zero when xy=0.

(3.3) $dz/dt = -bz + xy$

This is an extremely rich system in its implications for the time series of price
changes and amounts of excess speculation. There are three crucial parameters (b,s,r),
where r is the most important. Parameter b reflects the speed of convergence of excess
speculation to zero. Hence b reflects how speculation affects profits or losses which
in turn induce entry or exit of non-commercials into speculative markets. Parameter
s reflects the speed of convergence of the volatility to a constant, if the Bayesian errors
are given.

Parameter r (which is $d(dy/dt)/dx$ when y=0) reflects the critical amount of excess
speculation such that speculation is stabilizing. As the noisiness of the system increases,
the variance of the Bayesian error will change depending upon the composition of the
induced excess speculation, z. If $z < r$, the market is thin, the speculators are dominated
by noise traders, and the variance of the Bayesian error rises. But if $z > r$, then there
is a broad market of speculators who are dominated by rational traders. Then more
noise induces more rational speculators who take samples from the information set and

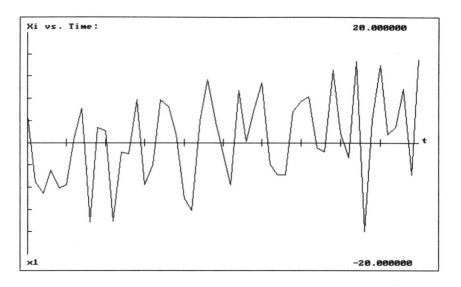

Figure 1

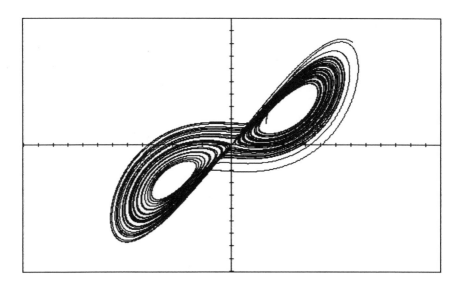

Figure 2

accelerate the process of price discovery. Denote r as the critical amount of speculation.

4. Analysis of the Lorenz System

The dynamics of the system depend upon the critical amount of speculation (r) relative to the speeds of convergence (b,s). Almost anything is possible in this system, depending upon the specification of the parameters: asymptotic stability or strange attractors as a special case of chaotic dynamics . A strange attractor is a closed, simply connected region, containing the origin (equilibrium point), such that the vector field is directed everywhere inwards on the boundary. Chaotic dynamics are produced when:

(i) $r > r^*$ and (ii) $s > 1 + b$, where (iii) $r^* = s(s+b+3)/(s-b-1)$.

Thus we may say that chaotic dynamics are produced when
(iv) $r > r^* > 0$.

There is an economic interpretation of condition (iv), based upon (i)-(iii). First, notice that speculation is stabilizing when it exceeds r, in equation (3.2). Broad markets with a lot of speculation reduce the variance of the Bayesian error, as seen in equation (3.2).   Second, notice the amount of speculation is stable because of the first term in (3.3). There is a critical value of r. If the actual value of parameter r exceeds r^*, then condition (i) for chaos is satisfied. If $z > r > r^*$, that is speculation z exceeds r which (is stabilizing in (3.2)) exceeds r^*, condition (i) is satisfied.

Third: parameter b in (3.3) reflects the speed of convergence of speculation to zero; and parameter s in (3.1) reflects the speed of convergence of the variance of price changes. Condition (ii) for chaos is that the speed of convergence of speculation to zero should not be too large: it must be less than s-1. For example, column (a) is a set of parameters which yield a strange attractor; and columns (b) and (c) produce asymptotic stability.

parameters	strange attractor	asymptotic stability	
	(a)	(b)	(c)
b	1	1	4
s	5	5	5
r	15	14	15

There are important economic implications of this analysis, for the questions and issues raised in the introduction. First, if the economic model were as described by (3.1)-(3.3), then the pattern of the variables would change qualitatively as a result of "slight" changes in parameter values. Compare column (a) with the other two columns.

Second, when the parameters satisfy condition (iv) above, the variables do not follow random walks, but are constrained by the strange attractor. This is a pleasing result to the economist who does not like the random walk conclusion that the variable could end up anywhere. Within the strange attractor, the behavior of the variables seem random.

Third, the behavior of the variables within the strange attractor are qualitatively dependent upon the initial conditions. Each set of initial conditions will generate a different trajectory within the strange attractor. Therefore, without perfect knowledge of the system, it is impossible to predict the movement of the variables except to say that it lies within the strange attractor SA*. Instead of the old concept of equilibrium as a point, we may have a different concept: the equilibrium as a set SA*. The solution stays within the set SA*, but its behavior in that set is unpredictable without perfect knowledge of initial conditions; and its behavior with the equilibrium SA* seems almost indistinguishable from random.

As an illustration of the above discussion consider the Figure 1 depicting the first 100 simulated observations of the x variable of our model. An inspection of this graph may lead an efficient market hypothesis advocate to proclaim that random walk holds. However, this graph is generated by our system of deterministic differential equations.

Examine Figure 2. It clearly demonstrates the existence of a strange attractor for x. Obviously, this illustration is not a mathematical proof since the phase diagram is based on only 5000 observations. Nevertheless, there seems to be a clear pattern which also holds for the other two variables.

5. Testing the Chaotic System: Back to Stochastics

Recall that we propose that price volatility, price errors and speculation are dynamically interrelated in the system (3.1)-(3.3).

In our estimation we approximate the system above by

(5.1) $$x_t - (1-s)x_{t-1} - s\,y_{t-1}$$

(5.2) $$y_t - x_{t-1}(r - z_{t-1})$$

(5.3) $$z_t - (1-b)z_{t-1} + x_{t-1}\,y_{t-1}\ .$$

Before we discuss econometric estimation we need to describe our data and the definition of the three variables. We have weekly (Friday) settlement futures prices, open interest, and volume of trading contracts mid 1990 to mid 1991 (around 52 observations for each variable) for the three most important agricultural contracts traded at the Chicago Board of Trade: soybeans, corn and wheat.

We define volatility as the annualized standard deviation of actual prices during the

Table 5.1

	Values of coefficients from system estimation:			
	$x_t = [1 - c(1)]\, x_{t-1} + c(1)\, y_{t-1}$			
	$y_t = x_{t-1}\, [c(2) - z_{t-1}]$			
	$z_t = [1 - c(3)]\, z_{t-1} + x_{t-1}\, y_{t-1}$			

Commodity	Period	c(1)	c(2)	c(3)
Corn	Jul.-Dec. 1990	0.0470 (1.6219)*	-5.0957 (-21.9658)	-358.7827 (-2.5248)
Corn	Jan.-May 1991	-0.0182 (-0.7405)	-5.2891 (-14.9401)	-20.0286 (-2.4418)
Corn	Mid'90-Mid'91	0.0253 (1.2582)	-5.1519 (-26.6335)	-204.1049 (-2.6126)
Soybeans	Jul.-Dec. 1990	0.0096 (0.3487)	-2.1558 (-8.8256)	-351.1682 (-0.8964)
Soybeans	Jan.-May 1991	-0.0048 (-0.1498)	2.6764 (-12.6192)	-78.3869 (-3.1661)
Soybeans	Mid'90-Mid'91	0.0053 (0.2536)	-2.3642 (-14.0872)	-207.2729 (-1.2827)
Wheat	Jul.-Dec. 1990	0.0769 (2.7245)	-298.3307 (-3.5635)	-13.0968 (-11.3333)
Wheat	Jan.-May 1991	0.0012 (0.0411)	-5.6681 (-3.5442)	1.9839 (0.7788)
Wheat	Mid'90-Mid'91	0.0589 (2.7715)	-235.8173 (-4.1789)	-12.4531 (-14.2118)

*NOTE: t-statistics are in parentheses.

Table 5.2

Wald Coefficient Tests

Model 1:
$x_t = [1 - c(1)] \, x_{t-1} + c(1) \, y_{t-1}$
$y_t = x_{t-1} \, [c(2) - z_{t-1}]$
$z_t = [1 - c(3)] \, z_{t-1} + x_{t-1} \, y_{t-1}$

Parameter Restriction Null Hypotheses	Commodity	Period	χ^2	Probability
Restriction 1 $C(1)=0$	Corn	Mid 90 - Mid 91	5.0422	0.0803
	Soybeans	Mid 90 - Mid 91	0.0643	0.7997
	Wheat	Mid 90 - Mid 91	7.6817	0.0055
Restriction 2 $C(1)=0$ $C(2)=0$	Corn	Mid 90 - Mid 91	709.5517	0.0000
	Soybeans	Mid 90 - Mid 91	213.1050	0.0000
	Wheat	Mid 90 - Mid 91	26.7233	0.0000
Restriction 3 $C(1)=0$ $C(2)=1$	Corn	Mid 90 - Mid 91	1011.527	0.0000
	Soybeans	Mid 90 - Mid 91	432.7341	0.0000
	Wheat	Mid 90 - Mid 91	26.8786	0.0000
Restriction 4 $C(1)=0$ $C(2)=0$ $C(3)=0$	Corn	Mid 90 - Mid 91	862.2086	0.0000
	Soybeans	Mid 90 - Mid 91	230.2828	0.0000
	Wheat	Mid 90 - Mid 91	250.9293	0.0000
Chaotic Hypotheses	Corn	Mid 90 - Mid 91	87962.36	0.0000
Restriction 1 $C(1)=-5$ $C(2)=15$ $C(3)=-1$	Soybeans	Mid 90 - Mid 91	58169.94	0.0000
	Wheat	Mid 90 - Mid 91	57297.17	0.0000
Restriction 2 $C(1)=-5$ $C(2)=14$ $C(3)=-1$	Corn	Mid 90 - Mid 91	86543.85	0.0000
	Soybeans	Mid 90 - Mid 91	57738.92	0.0000
	Wheat	Mid 90 - Mid 91	57296.38	0.0000
Restriction 3 $C(1)=-5$ $C(2)=15$ $C(3)=-4$	Corn	Mid 90 - Mid 91	87951.31	0.0000
	Soybeans	Mid 90 - Mid 91	58170.07	0.0000
	Wheat	Mid 90 - Mid 91	57177.25	0.0000

past ten weeks (i.e. we use a sample of 10 weekly data to compute a historical standard deviation which is then annualized). The errors are annualized differences between the current futures price today and the futures at the expiration of the contract. When both the futures price of the nearby contract and the cash price converge to become equal, the traders' errors are zero. Finally, we compute the degree of speculation as 1-[open interest/volume]. This definition could be improved if we had daily data about large hedging and speculative positions.

The results are presented in Table 5.1. We use seemingly unrelated regression system estimation method. Because our system is nonlinear, the residuals are recalculated and the residual covariance matrix is updated. Estimation of (5.1)-(5.3) is performed on

$$(5.4) \qquad x_t = [1 - c(1)] \, x_{t-1} + c(1) \, y_{t-1} + \varepsilon_1$$

$$(5.5) \qquad y_t = x_{t-1} \, [c(2) - z_{t-1}] + \varepsilon_2$$

$$(5.6) \qquad z_t = [1 - c(3)] \, z_{t-1} + x_{t-1} \, y_{t-1} + \varepsilon_3$$

and is repeated until convergence is achieved. This technique is asymptotically full information maximum likelihood.

The system in (5.4)-(5.6) is estimated three times for each of the three commodities: corn, soybeans and wheat. First, it is estimated for the second half of 1990, then for the first half of 1991 and finally for the entire sample period. With minor exceptions, the coefficients appear stable, but diagnostics indicate that the model is poorly specified. The appropriateness of our model can be judged by the set of graphs in Figures 3, 4 and 5, where model and actual values are presented for volatility as the dependent variable.

The null hypothesis for a "strange attractor" would be conditions (i)-(iii) above. The random walk hypothesis requires that $c(1)=0$. To have a strange attractor coefficient $r=c(2)$ must exceed unity. A week test is whether coefficient $c(1)=0$, and $c(2)$, which estimates r, is significantly greater than unity. These are necessary conditions.

The results presented in Table 5.1 reject the "strange attractor". In all cases coefficient $c(2)$ which estimates r is negative and hence does not exceed unity. In the cases of corn and soybeans, coefficient $c(1)$ is not significantly different from 0. Thus, it is compatible with the random walk, and not the strange attractor hypothesis. The case of wheat generally rejects random walk, $c(1)>0$, but also rejects the strange attractor case.

Table 5.2 presents the results of Wald tests based upon Table 5.1. We are most concerned with price volatility, variable x. The sample period that we focus upon in the text is the longest period mid 1990 to mid 1991. Restriction $c(1)=0$ and $c(2)=0$

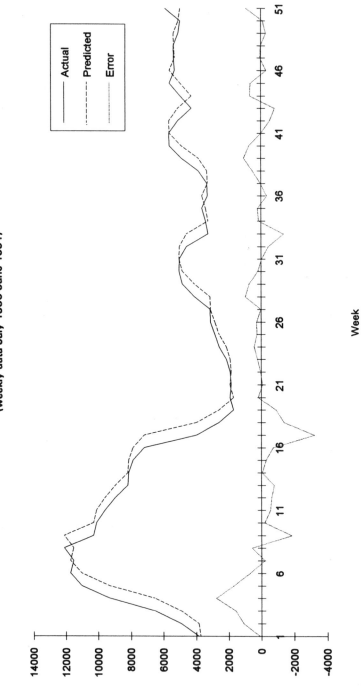

Figure 3: Actual and Predicted Price Volatility in Corn Futures Contracts, using coefficients from Table 5.1
(weekly data July 1990–June 1991)

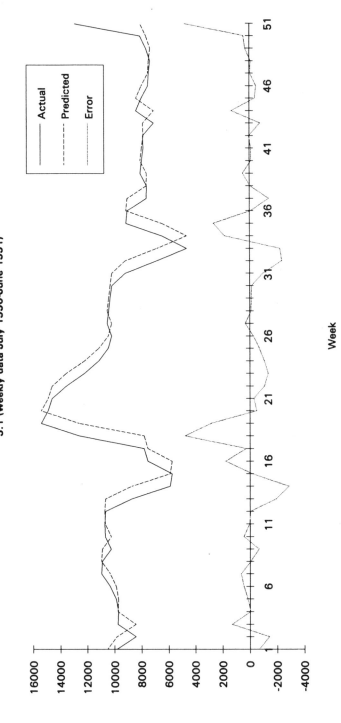

Figure 4: Actual and Predicted Price Volatility in Soybeans Futures Contracts, using coefficients from Table 5.1 (weekly data July 1990–June 1991)

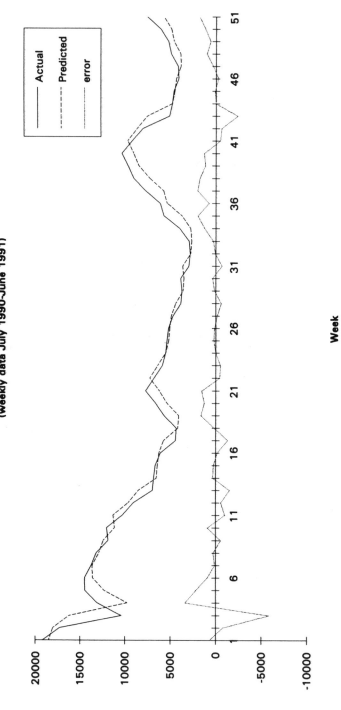

Figure 5: Actual and Predicted Price Volatility in Wheat Futures Contracts, using coefficients from Table 5.1
(weekly data July 1990–June 1991)

would mean that the variance in time t just depends upon its lagged value. However, this restriction is rejected. This means current price variability is not equal to its past value plus an error term, and that past Bayesian error y(t-1) does influence price variability.

Our results suggest that although the theoretical model that we developed is capable of generating a chaotic time series as a special case, the fitted model yields parameter values which support in seven out of nine cases the random walk and in the remaining two cases our deterministic model gives better results than the random walk.

6. Conclusions

In this paper we offer a rapid evaluation of the efficient market hypothesis as a theory which claims that the random arrival of relevant information is fully reflected in asset prices. Because information is random so are also prices.

Brock, Hsieh and LeBaron (1991) offer an extensive evaluation of the EMH and empirical evidence that asset prices are not always purely random. Often asset prices appear to be random but once rigorously tested by various techniques of chaotic dynamics are found not to be random. Our goal in this paper is to hypothesize that three important economic variables are related in a particular way described by the chaotic system known as the Lorenz equations.

The three variables we consider are excess asset price volatility, volatility of errors and degree of speculation. The financial formulation that we offer of the Lorenz equations extends the random walk paradigm by replacing errors terms by nonerror variables. Thus the Lorenz equations transform the random walk paradigm into a fully determinist system. This system exhibits a rich variety of trajectories depending on the values of its parameters.

The econometric system estimation of our hypothesized Lorenz model however does not yield coefficient values that would allow us to claim chaotic dynamics. The rejection of the Lorenz system by the data, in most but not all cases, does not mean that researchers should not continue developing models of chaotic dynamics. However, one must realize that despite the numerous shortcomings of the stochastic approach, it remains at the present time, the dominant methodology.

REFERENCES

Baumol, William and J. Benhabib (1989), Chaos: Significance, Mechanism and Economic Applications. *Journal of Economic Perspectives*: 3, 77-105.

Boldrin, M. and M. Woodford (1990), Equilibrium Models Displaying Endogenous Fluctuations and Chaos. *Journal of Monetary Economics*: 25, 189-222.

Brock, William A., David A. Hsieh and Blake Le Baron (1991), *Nonlinear Dynamics, Chaos and Instability: Statistical Theory and Economic Evidence*. Cambridge, Massachusetts. MIT Press

Brock, William A. (1988), Nonlinearity and Complex Dynamics in Economics and Finance, in *The Economy as an Evolving Complex System*, SFI Studies in the Sciences of Complexity. Addison-Wesley Publishing Company.

Friedman, Milton (1953), The Case for Flexible Exchange Rates, in *Essays in Positive Economics*, University of Chicago Press.

Hart, O. and D. Kreps (1986), Price Destabilizing Speculation. *Journal of Political Economy*: 94, 927-52.

Malliaris A.G. and J.L. Stein (1995), "Micro Analytics of Price Volatility", Working Paper, Department of Economics, Loyola University of Chicago, Chicago, Illinois.

Peck, Anne (1985), The Economic Role of Traditional Commodity Futures Markets in Anne E. Peck (ed.) *Futures Markets: Their Economic Role*. Washington, DC., American Enterprise Institute.

Samuelson, P. (1965), Proof that Properly Anticipated Prices Fluctuate Randomly, *Industrial Management Review*: 6, 41-49.

Shiller, R, (1989), *Market Volatility*, The MIT Press, Cambridge, MA.

Sparrow, C. (1982), *The Lorenz Equations: Bifurcations, Chaos and Strange Attractors*. New York. Springer-Verlag.

Stein, Jerome (1992), Cobwebs, Rational Expectations and Futures Markets. *Review of Economics and Statistics*: 74, 127-34.

Working, Holbrook (1934), A Random-Difference Series for Use in the Analysis of Time Series. *Journal of the American Statistical Association*: 29.

--------------------(1949), Investigation of Economic Expectations. *American Economic Review*: 39.

Uncertainty about Input Data in Portfolio Management

Jitka Dupačová[1]

Department of Probability and Mathematical Statistics, Charles University,
186 00 Prague, Czech Republic

Abstract. Selected techniques suitable for postoptimality and sensitivity analysis for the optimal value of portfolio management problems based on incompletely known input data are presented. The discussed problems involve Markowitz mean-variance model with estimated expected returns (Section 2), the effect of inclusion of additional scenarios in bond management problems (Section 3) and a treatment of incomplete knowledge of liabilities (Section 4).

Keywords. Markowitz model, bond portfolio management, stochastic programs, scenarios, incomplete information, sensitivity, postoptimality

1   Introduction

The complexity of financial problems, the necessity to capture the dynamic features of the decision processes and to hedge against future uncertainties had been recognized already since the fifties. The uncertainties can be modeled in various ways, including chaos or fuzzy concepts; we shall deal with discrete time stochastic models. The present level of knowledge together with the existing efficient computer technologies allow for designing and application of realistic stochastic optimization models that can support financial decisions: Various relatively simple immunization and dedication models for management of bond portfolios (see e.g. Dahl et al. (1993) or Zipkin (1992) and references ibid.) or the static mean-variance model of Markowitz (1959) can be replaced by more complex multi-period and multistage stochastic programs that reflect better the increasing complexity of the financial decision problems in uncertain environment and that are able to adapt to specific features of new financial instruments; see e.g. Bradley and Crane (1972), Cariñho et al. (1994), Dembo (1993), Dempster and Ireland (1988), Golub et al. (1995), Hiller and Eckstein (1993),

---

[1]Supported by the Grant Agency of the Czech Republic under grant No. 402/93/0631

Typeset by $\mathcal{A}_{\mathcal{M}}\mathcal{S}$-TEX

Holmer et al. (1993), Hutchinson and Zenios (1991), Kusy and Ziemba (1986), Mulvey (1994b), Mulvey and Vladimirou (1992), Shapiro (1988). The random factors that enter these models concern the returns and prices, the evolution of interest rates (e.g., Bradley and Crane (1972), Dempster and Ireland (1988)) and exchange rates (Huoponen (1994)), holding period returns of callable bonds (Holmer, Yang and Zenios (1993)), future liabilities (Nielsen and Zenios (1992)) or external cashflows (Kusy and Ziemba (1986)), prepayments of mortgages (Kang and Zenios (1992)), lapse behavior of policyholders (Asay et al. (1993), future inflation (Mulvey (1994a)), etc. The stochastic models do acknowledge the stochastic nature of the data but they are exposed to another level of uncertainties - the incomplete knowledge of the probability distributions or of their parameters and its impact on the optimal decisions and on the optimal value. It is the level and the quality of the input information about the distribution of stochastic parameters that may be a source of problems for many practical purposes. Merely the acceptance of this fact is a step forward and it has resulted in interesting simulation studies, e. g., Chopra and Ziemba (1993), Holmer et al. (1993), Kusy and Ziemba (1986), or into changes of the model (Mulvey et al. (1995)).

We shall introduce selected approaches suitable for analysis of results of financial decision models solved under *uncertainty about the stochastic input*. Even when these approaches seem to be cast for a specific model and/or specific assumptions, e.g., for the mean-variance Markowitz model in Section 2, for influence of including additional scenarios in Section 3 or for incomplete knowledge about distribution of future liabilities in Section 4, there is an open possibility of their exploitation under other quite disparate circumstances; see also Dupačová and Bertocchi (1995).

2   Markowitz mean-variance model

From the point of view of optimization, an application of Markowitz mean-variance model in selection of optimal portfolio of risky assets can be reduced to solution of the following parametric quadratic program

(1)
$$\text{maximize} \quad \lambda m^\top x - x^\top V x$$

on a simple nonempty convex polyhedral set $\mathcal{X}$, e.g.,

$$(2) \qquad \mathcal{X} = \left\{ \mathbf{x} \in R_+^n \,|\, \mathbf{Ax} \leq \mathbf{b} \right\}$$

One assumes that the vector $\mathbf{m}$ of expected returns and the positive definite matrix $\mathbf{V}$ of their variances and covariances are known whereas the positive scalar parameter λ can be chosen according to the investor's attitude towards risk.

The optimal solution $\mathbf{x}(\mathbf{m}, \mathbf{V}; \lambda)$ and the optimal value $\varphi(\mathbf{m}, \mathbf{V}; \lambda)$ of (1), (2) depend on $\mathbf{m}, \mathbf{V}$ (and on the chosen value of λ, of course) and at the same time, one can hardly assume full knowledge of these input values. The impact of errors in expected returns, variances and covariances on the optimal return φ of the obtained portfolio was investigated, e.g., in Chopra and Ziemba (1993): The program (1), (2) was solved repeatedly with perturbed selected input parameters, ceteris paribus, and the cash equivalent loss was computed for each run. The results of this simulation study indicate that the errors in expected values are more important than those in the second order moments. The parametric study of Best and Grauer (1991) points out that the errors in expected returns influence essentially the composition of the resulting portfolio whereas the portfolio returns are less sensitive.

Inspired by the cited results we shall deal with sensitivity analysis of the optimal composition of the portfolio and of the optimal return on the input values of the expected returns $\mathbf{m}$ of the risky assets; we shall complement results based on parametric programming by *stochastic sensitivity analysis*. The variance matrix $\mathbf{V}$ and the parameter λ will be kept fixed and they will not be indicated in our denotation of the optimal value and of the optimal solution of (1), (2).

The set of feasible solutions $\mathcal{X}$ of the quadratic program (1), (2) can be decomposed into finitely many relatively open facets that are identified by indices of the active constraints; interior of $\mathcal{X}$ and vertices of $\mathcal{X}$ are special cases of these facets. The parametric space R^n of vectors $\mathbf{p} := \lambda \mathbf{m}$ can be also decomposed into finitely many disjoint stability sets linked with the facets by the requirement that for all $\mathbf{p}$ belonging to a stability set, the optimal solutions $\mathbf{x}(\mathbf{p})$ of the quadratic program (1), (2) lie in the same facet. It is possible to prove (see Bank et al. (1982), Guddat (1976)) that $\mathbf{x}(\mathbf{p})$ is linear on each stability set and differentiable on its interior. If, however, $\mathbf{p}$ belongs to the boundary of a stability set, $\mathbf{x}(\mathbf{p})$ looses the differentiability property and it is only directionally differentiable. The optimal value function $\varphi(\mathbf{p})$ is piecewise linear - quadratic convex function of $\mathbf{p}$. Thanks to the assumption of $\mathbf{V}$ positive definite (implies that the strong second order sufficient condition is fulfilled), φ is differentiable on the whole parameter space provided that the vectors of coefficients of the active constraints of (2) are linearly independent; see e. g. Fiacco (1983), Theorem

2.4.5. These results explain the observed cases of a relative stability of the optimal value and of an extremal sensitivity of optimal solutions on small changes of the vector **m** of expected returns: Whenever the initial value of **p** = λ**m** belongs to the boundary of a stability set arbitrarily small changes in **m** can cause transition to one of the neighboring stability sets. It means not only that some other assets are included into portfolio, but different small changes can cause transition to different stability sets and as a result, the composition of the optimal portfolio is regarded unstable. At the same time, the change of the maximal value of (1) is small for small changes of **m**. Notice that similar situations are not excluded in case of changes of the parameter λ (i.e., when tracing the mean-variance efficient frontier) but they are more easy to take in as the changes concern only a scalar parameter. There exist some generalizations of the cited results to the case of **V** positive semidefinite and bounded $\mathcal{X}$, hovewer, the fact that from the point of view of quadratic programming there might be multiple optimal solutions indicates clearly the limitations.

A simple clarifying example. Consider a simple quadratic program

$$\max \left\{ p_1 x_1 + p_2 x_2 - \frac{1}{2}x_1^2 - x_1 x_2 - x_2^2 \right\}$$

on the set $\mathcal{X} = \{x_1, x_2 | x_1 \geq 0, x_2 \geq 0, x_1 + x_2 \leq 1\}$.

The set $\mathcal{X}$ can be decomposed into relatively open facets $\Sigma_1, \ldots, \Sigma_7$, see Figure 1. The corresponding stability sets $\sigma(\Sigma_k), k = 1, \ldots, 7$ for parameters p_1, p_2 are drawn on Figure 2.

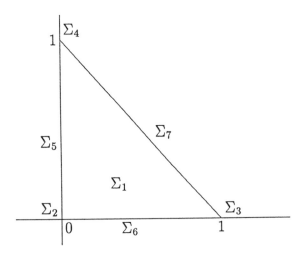

Figure 1. Set of feasible solutions $\mathcal{X}$

Now consider $p_1 = p_2 = 1$. For this parameter value, the optimal solution is the vertex Σ_3, however, a small change of parameter values causes moving the optimal solution into the adjacent facets Σ_6 or Σ_7 or into the interior Σ_1 of $\mathcal{X}$. The corresponding changes of the optimal value and of the first component of the optimal solution are illustrated for fixed $p_1 = 1$ and $p_2 \geq 0$ on Figure 3.

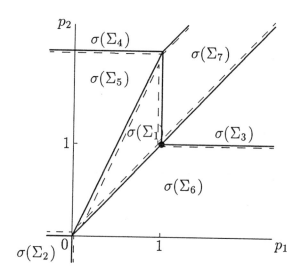

Figure 2. Stability sets

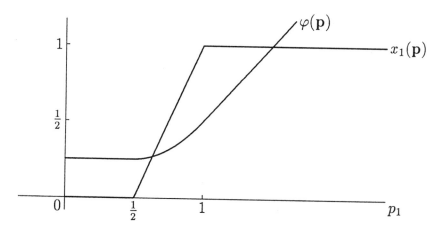

Figure 3. $\varphi(\mathbf{p})$ and $x_1(\mathbf{p})$ for $p_2 = 1$

Differentiability of φ allows in addition description of the approximate probability distribution of the optimal returns of the portfolio that are based on estimates of the true expected returns $\mathbf{m}$ obtained by a known appropriate statistical method. Such results are useful for constructing approximate confidence intervals for the true optimal value of the portfolio.

Theorem. Assume that $\mathbf{V}$ is positive definite and that the linear independence condition is fulfilled at the point of the true optimal solution $\mathbf{x}(\mathbf{m})$ of (1), (2). Let $\mathbf{m}^\nu$ be an asymptotically normal estimate of the true expectation $\mathbf{m}$,

$$(3) \qquad \sqrt{\nu}\,(\mathbf{m}^\nu - \mathbf{m}) \sim \mathcal{N}\,(0, \Sigma)$$

Then the optimal values $\varphi(\mathbf{m}^\nu)$ are asymptotically normal

$$(4) \qquad \sqrt{\nu}\,(\varphi(\mathbf{m}^\nu) - \varphi(\mathbf{m})) \sim \mathcal{N}\left(0, \nabla\varphi(\mathbf{m})^\top \Sigma \nabla\varphi(\mathbf{m})\right)$$

This type of results was presented in Dupačová (1984) and the statistical technique behind is nothing else but asymptotic normality of differentiable functions of asymptotically normal vectors, see e.g. Serfling (1980). It seems difficult to apply it as the variance matrix of the distribution (4) depends on the unknown expectation $\mathbf{m}$. However for ν large enough the result holds true with gradients computed at the estimated expectations and with the sample variance matrix Σ^ν. Hence, one has to calculate the gradient of the optimal value of the portfolio at the estimated expectation $\mathbf{m}^\nu$. Well known results from parametric programming (e. g. Fiacco (1983)) imply that

$$\nabla\varphi(\mathbf{m}^\nu) = \nabla_\mathbf{m}\left(\lambda \mathbf{m}^{\nu\top}\mathbf{x} - \mathbf{x}^\top\mathbf{V}\mathbf{x}\right)$$

computed at the optimal solution $\mathbf{x}(\mathbf{m}^\nu)$, i.e.,

$$\nabla\varphi(\mathbf{m}^\nu) = \lambda\mathbf{x}(\mathbf{m}^\nu)$$

and the final applicable result is

$$(5) \qquad \sqrt{\nu}\,(\varphi(\mathbf{m}^\nu) - \varphi(\mathbf{m})) \sim \mathcal{N}\left(0, \lambda^2\mathbf{x}(\mathbf{m}^\nu)^\top \Sigma^\nu \mathbf{x}(\mathbf{m}^\nu)\right)$$

where Σ^ν is the sample counterpart of the variance matrix Σ.

If for instance $\mathbf{m}^\nu$ equals the arithmetic mean of ν observed independent vectors of assets returns and if the assumptions of the Markowitz model hold true (i.e., the observed returns come from populations characterized by the fixed mean value $\mathbf{m}$ and the variance matrix $\mathbf{V}$) we get easily that $\mathbf{V} = \Sigma$. Accordingly, the approximate 2σ confidence interval for the true maximal value $\varphi(\mathbf{m})$ of the quadratic objective function (1) (for fixed λ and $\mathbf{V}$) is

$$\varphi(\mathbf{m}^\nu) \pm 2\lambda\sqrt{\nu^{-1}\mathbf{x}(\mathbf{m}^\nu)^\top \mathbf{V}\mathbf{x}(\mathbf{m}^\nu)}$$

Substitution for $\varphi(\mathbf{m}^\nu)$ gives the final form of the approximate confidence interval for the true maximal value $\varphi(\mathbf{m})$

$$(6) \quad \lambda \mathbf{m}^{\nu\mathsf{T}}\mathbf{x}(\mathbf{m}^\nu) - \mathbf{x}(\mathbf{m}^\nu)^\mathsf{T}\mathbf{V}\mathbf{x}(\mathbf{m}^\nu) \pm 2\lambda\sqrt{\nu^{-1}\mathbf{x}(\mathbf{m}^\nu)^\mathsf{T}\mathbf{V}\mathbf{x}(\mathbf{m}^\nu)}$$

The precision of the point estimate of $\varphi(\mathbf{m})$ based on the observed mean returns $\mathbf{m}^\nu$ depends on the sample size ν and also on the value of λ: for equal sample sizes, $\varphi(\mathbf{m}^\nu)$ is more precise for small λ, i.e., for a risk-averse investor.

3   Postoptimality with respect to scenarios in bond portfolio management

Let us consider now a stochastic programming model for management of portfolio of fixed income securities, called bonds for brevity. The main purpose of the portfolio management is to maximize utility of the final wealth and, depending on the specific field of investment activities, to fund the prescribed or uncertain future payments or just to protect the value of the overall portfolio. Similar problems arise in the context of management of one purpose investment funds, mutual funds, pension funds, investments of insurance companies, etc. In contrast to the problem of a dedicated portfolio selection (see e.g. Hiller and Eckstein (1993), Shapiro (1988)), we allow for an *active* trading strategy. The prices of bonds and sometimes also the coupon cashflows f_t are driven by the assumed evolution of the interest rates: Given a sequence of equilibrium future forward short term interest rates r_t valid for the time interval $(t, t+1], t = 0, \dots, T$ the fair price of the j-th bond at time t equals the total cashflow generated by this bond in subsequent time instances discounted to t:

$$(7) \qquad P_{jt}(\mathbf{r}) = \sum_{\tau=t+1}^{T} f_{j\tau} \prod_{h=t}^{\tau-1} (1+r_h)^{-1}$$

where T is greater or equal to the time of maturity.

   In reality, however, the sequence of the future short term forward rates that determines the prices (7) is not known, the sequences of interest rates are prescribed ad hoc or modeled in a probabilistic way (cf. Black et al. (1990), Cox et al. (1985), Ho and Lee (1986), etc.). We shall consider a discrete distribution, say P, of S possible vectors $\mathbf{r}$ of interest rates concentrated with probabilities $p_s > 0 \quad \forall s, \quad \sum_s p_s = 1$ at points $\mathbf{r}^s \in R^T, s = 1, \dots, S$ called *scenarios*; this is the input information which is used to build the model discussed in this Section.

We shall mostly use the notation introduced in Golub et al. (1995):

$j = 1, \ldots, J$ are indices of the considered bonds and T_j the dates of their maturities;

$t = 0, \ldots, T_0$ is the considered discretization of the planning horizon;

b_j denote the initial holdings (in face value) of bond j;

b_0 is the initial holding in riskless asset;

f_{jt}^s is cashflow generated from bond j at time t under scenario s expressed as a fraction of its face value;

L_t is liability due at time t;

x_j / y_j are face values of bond j purchased / sold at the beginning of the planning period, i.e., at $t = 0$;

z_{j0} is the face value of bond j held in portfolio after the initial decisions x_j, y_j have been made.

The first stage decision variables x_j, y_j, z_{j0} are nonnegative and

$$(8) \qquad y_j + z_{j0} = b_j + x_j \quad \forall j$$

For to be able to fund the future liabilities or to protect the value of the portfolio, the manager is allowed to use the cashflows f_{jt}^s and he can also rebalance the portfolio by further trading within the given set of bonds, he can reinvest his surplus and he can borrow money. The purchasing and selling prices per unite of face value of bond j at $t = 0$ are known for all j; we shall denote them by ζ_{j0} and ξ_{j0}, respectively. These prices include transaction costs. They are used to express the condition on conservation of the initial holding of the riskless asset

$$(9) \qquad y_0^+ + \sum_j \zeta_{j0} x_j = b_0 + \sum_j \xi_{j0} y_j$$

where the auxilliary nonnegative variable y_0^+ denotes the surplus.

The selling and purchasing prices of bonds at future time periods are obtained for each of scenarios from (7) (with $T \geq T_j \forall j$) by substracting or adding fixed transaction costs and spread. These prices are denoted by ξ_{jt}^s and ζ_{jt}^s and they can be further modified by inclusion of a multiplicative factor (risk or option adjusted premium) or by addition of the option adjusted spread in the discounting terms for to distinguish among various risk classes; for a more detailed discussion and additional references see e.g. Worzel et al. (1994) and Mulvey and Zenios (1994) respectively.

The constraints on conservation of holdings in each bond at each time period and for each of scenarios are similar to (8)

$$(10) \qquad z_{jt}^s + y_{jt}^s = z_{j,t-1}^s + x_{jt}^s \quad \forall j, s \quad \text{and} \quad t = 1, \ldots, T_0$$

where $x^s_{jt}, y^s_{jt}, z^s_{jt}$ denote the face value of bond j purchased, sold, held in the portfolio at time $t, t = 1, \ldots, T_0$ under scenario s and we have constraints on rebalancing the portfolio at each time period in the form

(11)
$$\sum_j \xi^s_{jt} y^s_{jt} + \sum_j f^s_{jt} z^s_{j,t-1} + (1 + r^s_{t-1}) y^{+s}_{t-1} + y^{-s}_t =$$
$$L_t + \sum_j \zeta^s_{jt} x^s_{jt} + (1 + \delta + r^s_{t-1}) y^{-s}_{t-1} + y^{+s}_t \quad \forall s \quad \text{and} \quad t = 1, \ldots, T_0$$

The optimization problem consists in maximization of the expected utility of the final wealth

(12)
$$\sum_s p_s U(W^s_{T_0})$$

subject to nonnegativity constraints on all variables and subject to constraints (8)–(11) with

(13)
$$W^s_{T_0} = \sum_j \xi^s_{j T_0} z^s_{j T_0} + y^{+s}_{T_0} - \alpha y^{-s}_{T_0} \quad \forall s$$

The multiplier α should be fixed according to the problem area: $\alpha = 0$ seems to be appropriate for protection of portfolio whereas funding a pension plan assumes repeated application of the model with rolling horizon and values $\alpha > 1$ take into account the debt service in the future.

Depending on the nature of the solved problem, other random factors that influence the prices and the cashflows can be included, such as the prepayment rates for mortgage backed securities (cf. Kang and Zenios (1992)), values of call options (Holmer, Yang and Zenios (1993)), credit and default risks, etc. Also the nature of liabilities can rank from fixed prescribed or planned external outflows (or inflows) to liabilities whose values depend on various external random factors such as mortality rates.

Thanks to the possibility of reinvestments and of unlimited borrowing, the problem has always a feasible solution. The existence of optimal solutions is quaranteed for a large class of utility functions that are *increasing and concave* what will be assumed henceforth. Moreover, due to strict inequalities $\xi^s_{jt} < \zeta^s_{jt} \quad \forall j, t, s, \quad \delta > 0$ and for $\alpha > 1$, the optimal solutions fulfil the following conditions

$$y_j x_j = 0 \quad \forall j$$
$$y^s_{jt} x^s_{jt} = 0 \quad \forall s, j \quad \text{and} \quad t = 1, \ldots, T_0$$
$$y^{+s}_t y^{-s}_t = 0 \quad \forall s \quad \text{and} \quad t = 1, \ldots, T_0$$

whose interpretation is straightforward: For to maximize the gain one has to *avoid unnecessary trading and borrowing*.

In this way, we obtain a large scale deterministic program with a concave objective function and numerous linear constraints. The main outcome is the optimal value of the objective function (the maximal expected utility of the final wealth) and the optimal values of the first-stage variables x_j, y_j (and z_{j0}) for all j. We can view it as an output of our model that depends on the input given by the set of considered bonds and their characteristics (initial prices and cashflows), by their initial holdings, by the scheduled liabilities and by the used scenarios of evolution of interest rates and their probabilities.

Given the values of the first-stage variables x_j, y_j and z_{j0} for all j, the maximal contribution of the portfolio management under scenario s to the value of the objective function (12) is obtained as the utility U of the maximal value of the wealth $W_{T_0}^s$ attainable for scenario s subject to constraints (10) on conservation of holdings for all j, t, constraints (11) on rebalancing the portfolio for all t and subject to nonnegativity conditions. Denoting by $\mathbf{x}, \mathbf{y}, \mathbf{z}$ the vectors of the first-stage variables and by $U^s(\mathbf{x}, \mathbf{y}, \mathbf{z})$ the maximal contribution of the subsequent decisions under scenario s to the total objective function (12), we can rewrite (8) – (13) in the following form:

(14)
$$\text{maximize} \sum_s p_s U^s(\mathbf{x}, \mathbf{y}, \mathbf{z})$$

subject to conditions

(8)
$$y_j + z_{j0} = b_j + x_j \quad \forall j$$

(9')
$$b_0 + \sum_j \xi_{j0} y_j - \sum_j \zeta_{j0} x_j \geq 0$$

$$x_j \geq 0, \quad y_j \geq 0, \quad z_{j0} \geq 0 \quad \forall j$$

We shall analyze now the sensitivity of the optimal value of (14) on the selected scenarios of interest rates. This is an important task for several reasons. One of them, sensitivity of bond prices on the interest rate changes, is well known. At the same time, we face certain arbitrariness in constructing the probability distribution of the interest rates; there are scenarios designed only by experts or required by local authorities (cf. New York State regulation # 126 requires evaluation of bonds for 7 specific scenarios) and those based on the binomial lattice techniques (e.g., Black et al. (1990), Ho and Lee (1986)) or on continuous stochastic models (e.g. Cox et al. (1985)). Moreover, inclusion of one arbitrary scenario into the problem (8)–(13) means, besides for evaluation of the corresponding prices and cashflows, inclusion of $T_0 J$ constraints (10) and T_0 constraints (11). The size of the resulting problem grows rapidly with the number of included scenarios. For the sake of the numerical tractability of the solved problem one cannot include all scenarios, has to select some of them using ad hoc reasoning or some more or less sofisticated sampling procedures (e.g. Zenios and Shtilman (1993)). A natural question is that of *influence of additional or out-of-sample scenarios on the output based on a manageable sample of scenarios.* There exist numerical experiments based on repeated runs of the solver for a modified input and on simulation of the performance for out-of-sample scenarios, cf. Holmer et al. (1993); we shall complement them by postoptimality and sensitivity results using techniques developed for scenario based stochastic programs (cf. Dupačová (1995a,b)). Another important problem - the impact of the sampling strategy - has been treated in Dupačová and Bertocchi (1995).

Inclusion of other, "out-of-sample" scenarios means to consider a convex mixture of two probability distributions: P that is carried by the initial sample and Q carried by the out-of- sample scenarios, indexed by $S + 1, \ldots, S + S'$ that occur with probabilities $q_s > 0, s = 1, \ldots, S', \sum_s q_s = 1$. Let λ denote the parameter that gives the distribution

$$P_\lambda = (1 - \lambda)P + \lambda Q, \quad 0 \leq \lambda \leq 1$$

carried by the pooled sample. The fixed initial distribution P gives the optimal value $\varphi(P)$ and optimal first-stage solutions $\mathbf{x}(P), \mathbf{y}(P), \mathbf{z}(P)$ of (14). The contaminating distribution Q gives the optimal value $\varphi(Q)$ of the objective function $\sum_{s=1}^{S'} q_s U^{S+s}(\mathbf{x}, \mathbf{y}, \mathbf{z})$ based on the S' out-of-sample scenarios. The optimal value for the pooled sample $\varphi(P_\lambda) := \varphi(\lambda)$ is a finite convex function on $[0,1]$ and according to Gol'shtein (1970), its value at $\lambda = 0$ equals $\varphi(P)$ and its derivative at $\lambda = 0^+$ equals

$$(15) \qquad \varphi'(0^+) = \max_{\Psi(P)} \sum_{s=1}^{S'} q_s U^{S+s}(\mathbf{x}, \mathbf{y}, \mathbf{z}) - \varphi(P)$$

where $\Psi(P)$ denotes the set of the optimal first-stage solution for the initial distribution P (for details see Dupačová (1995b)). Using convexity of φ, we get bounds for the optimal value $\varphi(P_\lambda)$ for the pooled sample:

$$(16) \quad \varphi(P) + \lambda\varphi'(0^+) \leq \varphi(P_\lambda) \leq (1 - \lambda)\varphi(P) + \lambda\varphi(Q) \quad \forall \ 0 \leq \lambda \leq 1$$

If there is a *unique* optimal first-stage decision $\mathbf{x}(P), \mathbf{y}(P), \mathbf{z}(P)$ for the original probability distribution P, it means that for all $\lambda \in [0, 1]$

$$(17) \quad (1 - \lambda)\varphi(P) + \lambda \sum_{s=1}^{S'} q_s U^{S+s}(\mathbf{x}(P), \mathbf{y}(P), \mathbf{z}(P)) \leq$$

$$\varphi(P_\lambda) \leq (1 - \lambda)\varphi(P) + \lambda\varphi(Q)$$

In case of *multiple optimal decisions*, the left hand side of (17) computed at any of these optimal decisions provides a lower bound for the left hand side of (16).

If, for instance, P is carried by S equally probable scenarios (sampled from a given population) and Q is carried by other S' equally probable scenarios sampled from the same population, it is natural to fix λ in such a way that the pooled sample consists of $S + S'$ equally probable scenarios, again. It means that

$$\lambda = S'(S + S')^{-1}$$

Hence, the bounds for the optimal value based on the pooled sample of size $S + S'$:

$$(18) \quad \frac{S}{S + S'}\varphi(P) + \frac{1}{S + S'}\sum_{s=1}^{S'} U^{S+s}(\mathbf{x}(P), \mathbf{y}(P), \mathbf{z}(P)) \leq$$

$$\varphi(P_\lambda) \leq \frac{S}{S + S'}\varphi(P) + \frac{S'}{S + S'}\varphi(Q)$$

The additional numerical effort consists thus in general in solving one additional program

$$\text{maximize} \sum_{s=1}^{S'} q_s U^{S+s}(\mathbf{x}, \mathbf{y}, \mathbf{z})$$

subject to (8), (9') and nonnegativity constraints of the same form but for another discrete distribution, Q, carried by the S' out-of-sample scenarios to obtain $\varphi(Q)$ and in computing one value of the objective function

$$\sum_{s=1}^{S'} q_s U^{S+s}(\mathbf{x}(P), \mathbf{y}(P), \mathbf{z}(P))$$

i. e., the value of the expected utility of the original optimal first-stage solution attainable for the distribution carried by the additional scenarios. Notice that one or both of the above values are computed naturally also in empirical studies on influence of out-of-sample scenarios. The technique we have suggested in this Section provides a solid base for a better exploitation of the information included in these values.

4   Incomplete information about liabilities

As the next type of problem we shall assume that the interest rate scenarios have been fixed and we shall turn attention to liabilities. In the bond management model (8)– (13), the liabilities L_t were modeled as the amounts to be paid at the time t which are known in advance. This assumption, however, need not be realistic for instance in management of pension funds, portfolios of insurance companies, etc. We shall assume now that the liabilities are random, *independent of random interest rates*. The objective function (the expected utility of the final wealth) assumes the form

$$(19) \qquad E_\omega \sum_s p_s U^s(\mathbf{x}, \mathbf{y}, \mathbf{z}; \mathbf{L}(\omega))$$

where, similarly to (14), $U^s(\mathbf{x}, \mathbf{y}, \mathbf{z}; \mathbf{L}(\omega))$ denotes the maximal contribution of portfolio management for fixed first-stage decisions, given scenario $\mathbf{r}^s$ of interest rates and a realization $\mathbf{L}(\omega)$ of liabilities.

We shall further assume that the probability distribution of $\mathbf{L}(\omega)$ is not known completely. Using the available information, we shall try to get bounds on the optimal value of (19) subject to (8), (9') and nonnegativity constraints.

As the first step, it is easy to realize that under our assumptions about the utility function U, the individual terms $U^s(\mathbf{x}, \mathbf{y}, \mathbf{z}; \mathbf{L}(\omega))$ in the objective function (19) are concave in the right-hand sides L_t (see (11)) that can be taken as parameters when evaluating the maximal final wealth under scenario $\mathbf{r}^s$ for fixed feasible first-stage variables $\mathbf{x}, \mathbf{y}, \mathbf{z}$. It means that the Jensen's inequality provides an upper bound for the objective function (19)

$$E_\omega \sum_s p_s U^s(\mathbf{x}, \mathbf{y}, \mathbf{z}; \mathbf{L}(\omega)) \le \sum_s p_s U^s(\mathbf{x}, \mathbf{y}, \mathbf{z}; E_\omega \mathbf{L}(\omega))$$

The corresponding upper bound for the *optimal* value of (19) subject to constraints on the first-stage variables equals

$$\max \sum_s p_s U^s(\mathbf{x}, \mathbf{y}, \mathbf{z}; E_\omega \mathbf{L}(\omega))$$

Hence, *replacing the random liabilities by their expectations in the bond management problem leads to overestimating the maximal expected gain.*

The lower bound can be based on the Edmundson - Madansky inequality (Madansky (1960)) if, in addition, for each t the random liabilities L_t are known to belong to finite intervals, say $[L'_t, L''_t]$. The general formula, however, is computationally expensive unless the objective function is separable in individual liabilities, which is not our case. A trivial lower bound can be obtained by replacing all liabilities by their upper bounds L''_t; this bound will be rather loose. Another possibility is to assume a special structure of liabilities (their independence, Markovian property, etc.) in which case the lower bound can be simplified provided that the objective function remains concave with respect to the random variables used to model the liabilities. Accordingly, let us assume that

$$\mathbf{L}(\omega) = \mathbf{Ga}(\omega)$$

with a given matrix $\mathbf{G}$ of the size $T_0 \times I$ and $a_i(\omega)$, $i = 1, \ldots, I$ mutually independent random variables with known expectations $E_\omega a_i$ and known supports $[a_i', a_i'']$ $\forall i$. Accordingly, the individual objective functions

$$U^s(\mathbf{x}, \mathbf{y}, \mathbf{z}; \mathbf{L}(\omega)) = U^s(\mathbf{x}, \mathbf{y}, \mathbf{z}; \mathbf{G}\mathbf{a}(\omega)) := \tilde{U}^s(\mathbf{x}, \mathbf{y}, \mathbf{z}; \mathbf{a}(\omega))$$

are concave in $\mathbf{a}(\omega)$.

For I small enough, the following string of inequalities valid for each of scenarios $\mathbf{r}^s$ and for all feasible first-stage solutions can be useful:

$$(20) \quad E_\omega U^s(\mathbf{x}, \mathbf{y}, \mathbf{z}; \mathbf{L}(\omega)) = E_\omega \tilde{U}^s(\mathbf{x}, \mathbf{y}, \mathbf{z}; \mathbf{a}(\omega)) \geq$$

$$\lambda_1 E_\omega \tilde{U}^s(\mathbf{x}, \mathbf{y}, \mathbf{z}; a_1', a_2(\omega), \ldots, a_I(\omega)) \quad +$$

$$(1 - \lambda_1) E_\omega \tilde{U}^s(\mathbf{x}, \mathbf{y}, \mathbf{z}; a_1'', a_2(\omega), \ldots, a_I(\omega)) \geq$$

$$\sum_{\mathcal{I} \subset \{1, \ldots, I\}} \prod_{i \in \mathcal{I}} \lambda_i \prod_{i \notin \mathcal{I}} (1 - \lambda_i) \tilde{U}^s(\mathbf{x}, \mathbf{y}, \mathbf{z}; \mathbf{a}_\mathcal{I})$$

where the components of $\mathbf{a}_\mathcal{I}$ equal a_i' for $i \in \mathcal{I}$ and a_i'' for $i \notin \mathcal{I}$ and

$$\lambda_i = \frac{a_i'' - E_\omega a_i}{a_i'' - a_i'} \quad \forall i$$

The lower bound for the maximal expected utility (19) based on inequalities (20) can be thus obtained by solving the corresponding stochastic program based on $2^I S$ scenarios.

For instance for *pension funds* it is natural to assume that $\mathbf{G}$ is a lower triangular matrix: The liabilities L_1 to be paid at the end of the first period are known with certainty and their portion, say, δL_1 corresponds to unrepeated payments (e. g., final settlements or premiums) whereas the remaining main part of L_1 will be paid also in the subsequent period (continuing pensions). The liabilities $L_2(\omega)$ to be paid at the end of the period 2 can be modeled as

$$L_2(\omega) = (1 - \delta)L_1 + a_2(\omega)$$

etc. Moreover, it is possible to assume that $a_i(\omega)$ are mutually independent so that (20) is a valid and tight lower bound that applies in the case that the intervals $[a_i', a_i'']$ $\forall i$ and the expectations $E_\omega \mathbf{a}$ are known.

References

Asay, M. R., P. J. Bouyoucos and A. M. Marciano, 'An economic approach to valuation of single premium deferred annuities', in: *Financial Optimization* (Zenios, S. A., ed.), Cambridge University Press, 101–131.

Bank, B., J. Guddat, D. Klatte, B. Kummer and K. Tammer, 1982, *Non-Linear Parametric Optimization*, Akademie Verlag, Berlin.

Best, M. J. and R. R. Grauer, 1991, 'Sensitivity analysis for mean-variance portfolio problems', *Management Science* 37, 980–989.

Black, F., E. Derman and W. Toy, 1990, 'A one-factor model of interest rates and its application to treasury bond options', *Financial Analysts Journal*, 33–39.

Bradley, S. P. and D. B. Crane, 1972, 'A dynamic model for bond portfolio management', *Management Science* 19, 139–151.

Cariño, D. R., T. Kent, D. H. Meyers, C. Stacy, M. Sylvanus, A. L. Turner, K. Watanabe and W. T. Ziemba, 1994, 'The Russell - Yasuda Kassai model: An asset/liability model for a Japanese insurance company using multistage stochastic programming', *Interfaces* 24, 29–49.

Chopra, V. K. and W. T. Ziemba, 1993, 'The effect of errors in means, variances and covariances on optimal portfolio choice', *J. Portfolio Mgt.* 19, 6–11.

Cox, J. C., J. E. Ingersoll Jr. and S. A. Ross, 1985, 'A theory of term structure of interest rates', *Econometrica* 53, 385–407.

Dahl, H., A. Meeraus and S. A. Zenios, 1993, 'Some financial optimization models: I. Risk management', in: *Financial Optimization* (Zenios, S. A., ed.), Cambridge University Press, 3–36.

Dembo, R. S., 1993, 'Scenario immunization', in: *Financial Optimization* (Zenios, S. A., ed.), Cambridge University Press, 290–308.

Dempster, M. A. H. and A. M. Ireland, 1988, 'A financial expert decision system', in: *Math. Models for Decision Support* (Mitra, B., ed.), NATO ASI Series, Vol. F48. Springer, Berlin, 415–440.

Dupačová, J., 1984, 'Stability in stochastic programming with recourse - Estimated parameters', *Math. Progr.* 28, 72–83.

Dupačová, J., 1995a, 'Postoptimality for multistage stochastic linear programs', *Annals of Oper. Res.* 56, 65–78.

Dupačová, J., 1995b, 'Scenario based stochastic programs: Resistance with respect to sample', to appear in *Annals of Oper. Res.*

Dupačová, J. and M. Bertocchi, 1995, 'Management of bond portfolios via stochastic programming – Postoptimality and sensitivity analysis', to appear in *System Modelling and Optimization*, Proc. of the 17-th IFIP Conference, Prague (Doležal, J. and J. Fidler, eds.), Chapman and Hall.

Fiacco, A. V., 1983, *Introduction to Sensitivity and Stability Analysis in Nonlinear Programming*, Academic Press, New York.

Gol'shtein, E. G., 1970, *Vypukloje Programmirovanie. Elementy Teoriji*, Nauka, Moscow. [Theory of Convex Programming, *Translations of Mathematical Monographs* 36, American Mathematical Society, Providence RI, 1972].

Golub, B., M. R. Holmer, R. McKendall, L. Pohlman and S. A. Zenios, 1995, 'A stochastic programming model for money management', to appear in

EJOR.

Guddat, J., 1976, 'Stability in convex quadratic parametric programming', *Math. Operationsforsch. u. Statist.* 7, 223–245.

Hiller, R. S. and J. Eckstein, 1993, 'Stochastic dedication: Designing fixed income portfolios using massively parallel Benders decomposition', *Management Science* 39, 1422–1438.

Ho, T. S. Z. and S.-B. Lee, 1986, 'Term structure movements and pricing interest rates contingent claims', *J. Finance* 41, 1011–1129.

Holmer, M. R., D. Yang and S. A. Zenios, 1993, 'Designing callable bonds using simulated annealing', Report 93-07-02, Decision Sciences Department, The Wharton School, Univ. of Pennsylvania, Philadelphia.

Holmer, M. R., R. McKendall, C. Vassiliadou-Zeniou and S. A. Zenios, 1993, 'Dynamic models for fixed-income portfolio management under uncertainty', Report 93-11-01, Decision Sciences Department, The Wharton School, Univ. of Pennsylvania, Philadelphia.

Huoponen, T., 1994, 'Stochastic optimization of a multi-currency bond portfolio', WP–94–98, IIASA, Laxenburg.

Hutchinson, J. M. and S. A. Zenios, 1991, 'Financial simulations on a massively parallel connection machine', *Internat. J. Supercomputer Applic.* 5, 27–45.

Kang, P. and S. A. Zenios, 1992, 'Complete prepayment models for mortgage-backed securities', *Management Science* 38, 1661–1685.

Kusy, M. I. and W. T. Ziemba, 1986, 'A bank asset and liability management model', *Oper. Res.* 34, 356–376.

Madansky, A., 1960, 'Inequalities for stochastic programming problems', *Management Science* 6, 197–204.

Markowitz, H. M., 1959, *Portfolio Selection: Efficient Diversification of Investments*, Wiley, New York.

Mulvey, J. M., 1994a, 'Generating scenarios for the Towers Perrin investment system', Research Report, Princeton Univ.

Mulvey, J. M., 1994b, 'Financial planning via multi-stage stochastic programs', in: *Mathematical Programming - State of the Art 1994* (Birge, J. R. and K. G. Murty, eds.), Univ. of Michigan, 151–171.

Mulvey, J. M. and H. Vladimirou, 1992, 'Stochastic network programming for financial planning problems', *Management Science* 38, 1642–1664.

Mulvey, J. M., R. J. Vanderbei and S. A. Zenios, 1995, 'Robust optimization of large scale systems', *Oper. Res.* 43, 264–281.

Mulvey, J. M. and S. A. Zenios, 1994, 'Capturing the correlations of fixed-income instruments', *Management Science* 40, 1329–1342.

Nielsen, S. S. and S. A. Zenios, 1992, 'A stochastic programming model for funding Single Premium Deferred Annuities', Report 92-08-03, Decision Sciences Department, The Wharton School, Univ. of Pennsylvania, Philadelphia; to appear in Math. Programming.

Serfling, R. J., 1980, *Approximation Theorems in Mathematical Statistics*, Wiley, New York.

Shapiro, J. F., 1988, 'Stochastic programming models for dedicated portfolio selection', in: *Math. Models for Decision Support* (Mitra, B., ed.), NATO ASI Series, Vol. F48. Springer, Berlin, 587–611.

Worzel, K. J., C. Vassiadou-Zeniou and S. A. Zenios, 1994, 'Integrated simulation and optimization models for tracking indices of fixed-income securities', *Oper. Res.* 42, 223–233.

Zenios, S. A. (ed.), 1993, *Financial Optimization*, Cambridge University Press.

Zenios, S. A. and M. S. Shtilman, 1993, 'Constructing optimal samples from a binomial lattice', *Journal of Information & Optimization Sciences* 14, 125–147.

Zipkin, P., 1992, 'The structure of structured bond portfolio models', *Oper. Res.* 40, S157–S169.

Non-Substitution Theorems
for Perfect Matching Problems [1]

Maria Elena De Giuli and Umberto Magnani

Dip.to Ricerche Aziendali, Sez. Matem. Gen. ed Appl.
University of Pavia, I 27100 Pavia, Italy

Abstract. This paper recovers and improves, in a systematic way and under less strict assumptions than the classical ones, some known results pertaining to *perfect matching problems*. It also puts forward a rule for choosing the vectors of future cash-drawings which lead to a common term structure of interest rates. These results are then framed into the theory of *non-substitution theorems* for linear economic models. In this area a special perfect matching problem dealing with *strict investment projects* is analyzed.

Keywords: perfect matching, interest rates term structure, non-substitution theorems [2]

1 Introduction

Following Hodges and Schaefer [11], the simplest version of a *matching problem* $\mathcal{P}$ can be sketched as follows [3]:

- A matrix A with m rows and k semi-positive columns $(A^j \geq [0], \forall j)$ measures the after-tax cash-flows (coupons and/or principal repayment) which are provided for future maturities 1 to m by k riskless bonds;

- the unit purchase prices of the bonds are measured by $c > [0]$, a positive row-vector;

- the j-th bond can be purchased, without any transaction cost, in any quantity x_j; as no short sale is allowed, x_j is the j-th entry of a non-negative column-vector x $(x \geq [0])$;

---

[1] Research projects *Cariplo* and *Murst 60%*.

[2] *1991 AMS Subject Classification:* primary 90A09, secondary 90C31, 90A17.

[3] The words *matching* and *perfect matching* may also be used in a broader sense, to mean the offsetting of cash-flows having common maturity and amount but opposite signs. Needless to say, these keywords have quite another meaning in other fields, for instance in graph theory.

- an investor chooses a consumption vector, i.e. a sequence of cash-flows to be withdrawn at future times 1 to m, by means of a semi-positive column-vector b; then he selects an optimal portfolio, i.e. a cheapest bond mix x among those which meet his cash constraints.

Obviously, the set of times $\{1, 2, \ldots, m\}$ is defined as the union between the grid of dates of the bonds and the one of the positive cash-flows of b. $\mathcal{P}$ embeds the search for the present values (discount factors, valuators) v_1 to v_m of each capital unit needed by the future consumption plan. All this appears clearly as soon as $\mathcal{P}$ is investigated together with its dual $\mathcal{P}'$:

$$\mathcal{P}: \begin{array}{|l} \min\limits_{x} cx \\ Ax \geq b,\ x \geq [0], \end{array} \qquad \mathcal{P}': \begin{array}{|l} \max\limits_{v} vb \\ vA \leq c,\ v \geq [0]. \end{array}$$

While $\mathcal{P}'$ is always feasible (the zero vector $v = [0]$ meets all its constraints), the feasibility of $\mathcal{P}$ depends on the *completeness* of A, i.e. on the availability of some cash-flow at each time vector b exhibits a positive entry. In this case $\mathcal{P}$ and $\mathcal{P}'$ admit optimal vectors x^* and v^*. A *perfect matching* (P.M. in the following) is achieved if the relation

$$Ax^* = b \tag{1}$$

holds for each optimum x^*, in which case $\mathcal{P}$ is called a *perfect problem*. The simplest way to set up such a problem is to complete A with $2m$ columns for the cash-flows of short term borrowing and lending opportunities. This way, a suitable chain of (one or more) banking operations of this kind allows to move any capital (of any sign) from its date to any other date, so that completeness can directly ensure both solvability and perfectness. A quicker way to get a complete problem is to assume that at least one zero-coupon bond is paid whenever a positive cash-flows is needed. But this assumption seems heavier, at least for non-short maturities. Another way to overcome the difficulties arising when the grids of dates of A and b disagree is to resort to a discounting function obtained by means of a linear combination with non-negative weights of N continuous functions ([10], [18], [20], [21]). This approach needs first the choice of number N, then the selection of the class of those functions (modified Bernstein polynomials and incomplete beta functions have been suggested) and finally the computation of the weights leading to a discounting function endowed with sensible economic properties, such as smoothness and monotonicity. Also this way works, but it introduces several *ad hoc* additional assumptions. Finally, a more naive trick in [11] treats any cash-flow falling between two dates t_1 and t_2 at which b exhibits positive entries simply by compounding it up to t_2 at a chosen interest rate.

From now on we assume that $\mathcal{P}$ is complete, hence (solvable and) perfect, simply because matrix A already incorporates the above banking opportunities. A will have $(k+2m)$ columns: the k original ones for the bonds and $2m$ extra columns for the banking operations which are available at each time 0 to $(m-1)$. Obviously, x needs new additional entries for the activation levels of these operations, and the columns of A are no more all semi-positive. Also vector c is to be completed by adding $2m$ new entries, all vanishing except those which measure the positive [negative] cash-inflow [outflow] of the borrowing [lending] operation starting at time 0. As each entry c_j of c measures a cost, the former [latter] is negative [positive], hence c has now mixed sign entries. Obviously, should some other non-short term opportunities for borrowing and lending be allowed, then some additional columns in A and entries in c will be added. In all cases, n will stand for the number of the columns of A and of the entries of x and c.

As banking opportunities have been inserted, it is quite obvious to adopt the two following additional assumptions:

- *positive interest rates apply to each banking operation,* $\qquad$ (2)

i.e. the sum of all cash-flows of each borrowing [lending] operation is negative [positive];

- no *money-pump* (*arbitrage, free-lunch*) exists.

If all banking operations last one period, we can rule out any money-pump by simply assuming a positive spread between borrowing and lending interest rates. However, should some operation with a longer life (and/or interest rates varying with time) be allowed, then the assumption that money cannot be bought cheap and sold dear is no more sufficient to get the same result. In order to cover all cases, we need to assume that each non-negative consumption program b must have a non-negative cost, just as the following implication states:

$$\{Ax \geq [0] , \; x \geq [0]\} \;\Rightarrow\; cx \geq 0. \qquad (3)$$

Many features of P.M. problems, also in their wider versions, have been analyzed in several papers (e.g., see [20], [21], [22], [5] [6], [13] and references therein). Most of them pay special attention to some relevant problems arising from the presence of *frictions* in the market (such as taxes and transaction costs) and to comparisons with conventional valuation approaches and empirical measurements. This literature also contains some empirical estimations for the markets of U.S.A. Treasury Bonds and British Government securities (*gilts*). Also see [17] for a recent application to the Italian bond market.

In many papers a sequence $\{r_i^*\}$ is computed starting from an optimum $v^* = [v_1^*, v_2^*, \ldots, v_m^*]$ for the dual problem $\mathcal{P}'$ by means of the rule

$$r_i^* = \frac{v_i^*}{v_{i+1}^*} - 1, \; i \in \{0, 1, \ldots, m-1\}, \; v_0^* = 1. \qquad (4)$$

$\{r_i^*\}$ identifies an *interest rates term structure* faced by the investor who formulates $\mathcal{P}$. As [11] states, the dual values v_i^* represent opportunity costs for transferring a unit cash-flow from the time i to the starting date, and the forward rates r_i^* may also suggest modification to the existing maturities profile b in the light of expectations of future interest rates. In this framework the interest rate r_i^* for the time period $[i; i+1]$ is not only relative to the market opportunities and to the tax bracket of the investor (as summarized by A and c), but is also conditional on the consumption vector b he chooses. In other words, vector $r^* = [r_0^*, r_1^*, \ldots, r_{m-1}^*]$ identifies a *subjective* interest rates structure, defined through a *direct approach*. This vector has been used in [16] as a starting point of an iterative procedure to get an *objective* structure of those rates by means of the well-known Cox-Ingersoll-Ross approach. In this way a P.M. problem looks like a humble minor brother of a main and more complex problem which looks for a 'true' interest rates structure.

It has been remarked ([11], [21]) that changes in vector b can produce discrete jumps in the term structure r^* and that it is not possible to make r^* independent of b. Nonetheless some empirical tests (see [17]) have shown that vector v^*, hence the underlying rates structure, exhibits a strong stability with respect to the changes in b. Therefore the following question naturally arises: how may vector b be chosen in order to get the same rates structure embedded in problem $\mathcal{P}$. Sec. 2 deals with this issue. Sec. 3 exploits some links between our problem and the theory of linear multi-sectorial economic models. Sec. 4 puts forward some suggestions for further research.

2   How to get the same rates structure

Theorems 1 and 2 below state some basic properties of a P.M. problem and show how vector b may be chosen in order to get the same rates structure. See [3] for the proofs.

Theorem 1 . *Call $\mathcal{P}$ a complete matching problem defined by the matrix A of order $(m; n)$, the row-vector $c \in R^n$ and the semi-positive column-vector $b \in R^m$:*

$$\mathcal{P}: \begin{vmatrix} \min_x cx \\ Ax \geq b, \ x \geq [0] \ . \end{vmatrix}$$

Let assumptions (2) on positive interest rates and (3) on the non-existence of any money-pump hold. Then the following propositions hold:

i) $\mathcal{P}$ is a (solvable and) perfect problem;

ii) each optimal vector v^* for its dual $\mathcal{P}'$ verifies the inequalities

$$0 < v_m^* < v_{m-1}^* < \cdots < v_2^* < v_1^* < 1; \tag{5}$$

iii) the interest rates term structure $r^* = [r_0^*, r_1^*, \ldots, r_{m-1}^*]$ defined by rule (4) is positive and verifies the inequalities

$$r_i^+ \leq r_i^* \leq r_i^-, \ \forall i, \tag{6}$$

r_i^+ [r_i^-] being the rate of interest for the time period $[i; i+1]$ in the lending [borrowing] operation starting at time i.

Theorem 2 . Let assumptions (2) and (3) hold for the complete matching problem $\mathcal{P}$ defined in theorem 1. Choose an optimum x^* for $\mathcal{P}$, an optimum v^* for its dual $\mathcal{P}'$ and a semi-positive vector $\bar{b}$. Set up the matrix E by assembling all columns A^j of A associated with the constraints of $\mathcal{P}'$ which v^* makes effective:

$$A^j \in E \Leftrightarrow v^* A^j = c_j .$$

If some z solves the system

$$\begin{cases} Ez = \bar{b} \\ z \geqq [0] , \end{cases} \tag{7}$$

then the following propositions hold:

i) The vector $\bar{x}^* \in R^n$ obtained by filling z with zeroes is optimal for the problem

$$\overline{\mathcal{P}} : \begin{vmatrix} \min_x cx \\ Ax \geqq \bar{b}, \ x \geqq [0] \ ; \end{vmatrix}$$

ii) the optimal values $c\bar{x}^*$ for $\overline{\mathcal{P}}$ and cx^* for $\mathcal{P}$ are linked by relation

$$c\bar{x}^* - cx^* = v^*(\bar{b} - b);$$

iii) each optimal vector v^* for the dual $\mathcal{P}'$ of $\mathcal{P}$ is also optimal for the dual $\overline{\mathcal{P}}'$ of $\overline{\mathcal{P}}$, therefore the rates term structure r^* defined by (4) for $\mathcal{P}'$ also fits to $\overline{\mathcal{P}}'$;

iv) if x^* is basic and non-degenerate, then both $\mathcal{P}'$ and $\overline{\mathcal{P}}'$ admit a unique and common optimum v^*, hence r^* is their unique rates term structure.

Remark 1. Theorems 1 and 2 allow to recover and to improve, in a systematic way and under less strict assumptions, some previous results. Relation (5) in theorem 1 obviously follows from (6), just as in [11] and [22], where weaker forms are preferred. Both relations emphasize a property with a plain financial meaning of every optimum for $\mathcal{P}'$. [11] deals with a complete model, as it assumes that some bond pays something at each date i with $b_i > 0$, while [22] assumes no completeness, but simply that currency can be stored at no cost.

Remark 2. Schaefer already noted ([21], p. 419) that, v^* being conditional on b, "unless it is possible for *any* b to be achieved at minimum cost with the *same set of bonds* then the choice of b will influence the resulting term structure" [4]. Theorem 2 says something more. Its main results can be translated as follows. Starting from a fixed vector b and the associated

---

[4]Italics were in original, only notation has been adapted to ours.

optimum x^*, define the portfolio P containing all non-overpriced financial activities of $\mathcal{P}$, i.e. all bonds and/or banking operations whose future cash-flows are gathered in matrix E. Note that P contains *all* exactly priced activities, not only those contained in x^* with positive weights. Should the changes in b not affect the *feasibility* of P, then they can't even affect its *optimality*, therefore its rates structure r^*. In other words, when portfolio P can meet a new b, then the changes needed to keep P optimal are simply quantitative, as no activity previously out of P must now come in; hence the same old rates structure is embedded in the new optimal portfolio $\bar{x}^*$. This means that different rates structures may arise only when some *substitution* between activities is needed in order to meet a new maturities profile $\bar{b}$. Indeed, the stability of r^* regardless of the choice of b already remarked in [17] just stems from a wide feasibility of the portfolio containing all exactly priced activities.

Remark 3. The assumption that some z solves system (7) plays a crucial role in theorem 2. It deals with quantities (the entries of z) and has a direct financial meaning, already noted in Remark 1. It has also an indirect (i.e. dual) and non-trivial financial meaning, which deals with values, as we will show now. Thanks to the Farkas-Minkowski's theorem of the alternative, that assumption is equivalent to the unsolvability of the system

$$\begin{cases} wE \geq [0] \\ w\bar{b} < 0. \end{cases} \tag{8}$$

As w is not sign-constrained, we can write it as the difference between two positive price vectors c^1 and c^2. This allows to write system (8) as

$$\begin{cases} c^1 E \geq c^2 E \\ c^1 \bar{b} < c^2 \bar{b} \\ c^1 > [0], \ c^2 > [0], \end{cases}$$

and to get the following conclusion: system (7) is solvable if and only if no positive prices vectors c^1 and c^2 exist such that c^1 prices each activity of the portfolio P associated with matrix E at least as c^2 does, but leads to a lower cost of the planned vector $\bar{b}$. This alternative way to deal with the solvability of system (7) directly recalls the optimality tests put forward by [22] for P.M. problems and by [12] and [15] for Non-Substitution Theorems in linear economic models (see sec. 3).

Remark 4. Property *(iv)* of theorem 2 is complementary to the following results, based on [19], pp. 116–117:

- if x^* and v^* are basic optima and only one of them is non-degenerate, then the same is not unique and the other is unique;

- if x^* and v^* are basic degenerate optima, then one or both are multiple optima;

- if x^* and v^* are unique optima, then both are basic and non-degenerate.

Also note that, should x^* be a basic non-degenerate optimum and the dual admit effective constraints for basic variables only, then matrix E is just the basis B associated with x^*, hence a quick alternative proof of some properties listed in theorem 2 can be given by means of Gale's lemma 9.3 in [8], [5].

3 A Non-Substitution Theorem approach

The *non-substitution* of the activities in P.M. problems directly recalls a similar phenomenon which occurs in the theory of linear multi-sectorial economic models of the Leontief type. Here we shall try to exploit this similarity. In such models the following data are assigned: an *input matrix* C and an *output matrix* D (both of order $(m; n)$, with: $n \geq m$, $C^j \geq [0]$, $D^j \geq [0]$, $\forall j$), a column-vector $b \geq [0]$ for the final demand *bill of goods* and a (*direct*) *labor requirements* row-vector $\ell > [0]$. Then, assuming constant returns to scale (i.e. that all activities are linear, short: the production model is linear), the following linear problem:

$$\mathcal{L}: \begin{vmatrix} \min_x \ell x \\ (D - C)x \geqq b, \ x \geqq [0] \end{vmatrix} \tag{9}$$

defines the search for the minimum employment program x among those which meet the final demand requirements [6]. In economic terms, the labor being the unique scarce primary good (or *factor*), every optimum x^* for problem (9) will save labor; in other words, x^* minimizes wages, hence maximizes profits. For such a problem the following well-known *Non-Substitution Theorem* is available (e.g., see [8]):

Theorem 3 (Non-Substitution Theorem) . *In the problem $\mathcal{L}$ defined by (9), let the model be* simple, *i.e. let each activity produce one output:*

$$D^j \text{ has only one positive entry, } \forall j.$$

Moreover, assume the model is productive, *i.e. the system*

$$\begin{cases} (D - C)x > [0] \\ x \geqq [0] \end{cases}$$

is solvable. Then the following propositions hold:

i) $\mathcal{L}$ is solvable, no matter how vector $b \geq [0]$ is chosen;

---

[5]On this lemma see [2].

[6]In order to avoid misunderstanding, here we use a non-standard notation $(C; D; b; \ell)$ instead of the standard one $(A; B; c + d; \ell)$, where c and d define the requirements for final consumption and growth.

ii) each optimum x^* for $\mathcal{L}$ rules out over-productions:

$$(D - C)x^* = b; \qquad (10)$$

iii) $(D - C)$ admits a basis B which is optimal for each problem $\mathcal{L}$ we can set up by choosing b in the whole set of semi-positive vectors.

Theorems 1–2 and 3 exhibit the similarity between the models underlying them. Both models are linear and require to save some scarce factor: money spent at time 0 in matching problem $\mathcal{P}$, labor in Leontief problem $\mathcal{L}$. In other words, we can see the financial activities of problem $\mathcal{P}$ as special linear technologies which transform money inputs (the negative entries of A) into money outputs (the positive ones) by means of a scarce factor (the capital to be spent at time 0); all this is done in order to get a 'net productions' vector Ax which must meet the final demand 'bill of goods' b measuring the money to be withdrawn at times 1 to m.

Moreover, a special assumption (completeness for $\mathcal{P}$, productiveness for $\mathcal{L}$) makes both problems solvable and ensures that each constraint is effective at the optimum x^*, namely that $\mathcal{P}$ is perfect in the sense (1) and that $\mathcal{L}$ avoids over-productions, just as in (10). Like vector v^* for $\mathcal{P}'$, also the optimal vector p^* which solves the dual $\mathcal{L}'$ of $\mathcal{L}$ has an economic meaning: following Gale [8], $\mathcal{L}'$ asks for a set of prices p_i^* which will maximize the value pb of the bill of goods b subject to the familiar condition that no activity shall show a positive profit.

However, beyond these similarities, some relevant differences between the two problems must be pointed out. First of all, vector ℓ in the objective function of $\mathcal{L}$ is positive, while vector c is not. Moreover, the columns of A in $\mathcal{P}$ referring to bonds describe linear technologies with one or many outputs but with no input, while the columns for the banking opportunities starting at future times have both inputs and outputs. Obviously, we can set up a problem $\mathcal{P}$ which is trivial simply because only zero-coupon bonds and one-period banking activities are allowed. In this case $\mathcal{P}$ looks like problem $\mathcal{L}$ and Non-Substitution Theorem directly applies, hence an optimal basis B (and a common rates structure r^*) exists which fits to every b. Out of this trivial case, problem $\mathcal{P}$ is to be framed into the theory of *joint productions* (i.e. non-simple) Leontief model with one scarce factor.

Unfortunately, no general Non-Substitution Theorem holds for joint productions models, hence substitution is the rule for non-trivial complete matching problems. The following theorem (see [3]) shows a way to save something from this wreckage.

Theorem 4 . *Let the linear programming problem*

$$\mathcal{P}(b) : \begin{vmatrix} \min_{x} cx \\ Ax \geq b, \ x \geq [0], \end{vmatrix}$$

be solvable and perfect, no matter how b is chosen in the set R_+^m of all non-negative vectors. Starting from any optimum x^* for $P(b)$, with $b \geq [0]$, define its active matrix, i.e. the matrix A^+ containing the columns of A associated with the positive entries of x^*. Then:

> *i) R_+^m can be split into a finite number of closed convex cones such that all problems $P(b)$ where b stays in the same cone admit a common active matrix A^+ and their duals admit a common optimum;*
>
> *ii) if some active matrix A^+ admits a semi-positive left-inverse, then R_+^m contains one cone and A^+ is optimal for each $b \geq [0]$.*

Remark 5. Theorem 4 states that substitution between activities in a linear model is a *jump-phenomenon*. The whole orthant R_+^m in the b-space can be split into a finite number, say N, of closed convex cones, according to the active matrix A^+ which turns out to be optimal for problem $P(b)$. As long as b stays in the interior of a cone, no substitution occurs, hence a common unique interest rates structure r^* appears if $P(b)$ is a P.M. problem. In this case A^+ identifies a *dominant technology over that cone* in the Johansen's sense [12]: here is a *local* result, just as the one contained in theorem 2. Substitution occurs, hence r^* may change, when b crosses the frontier of a cone and reaches the interior of another cone. A *global* result will appear when N = 1, i.e. when, following Johansen [12], there exists a *dominant technology over the whole set R_+^m*.

Remark 6. The existence of a semi-positive left-inverse of some active matrix A^+ may be viewed, in general, as a matter of chance only, unless some special assumptions are assumed. This case just occurs for theorem 3, where, in the words of theorem 4, R_+^m admits *one* convex cone which contains *all* semi-positive vectors b (for more details see the proof of theorem 5 below and [24]). Now the following question is open: how to set up a P.M. problem P which shares this nice property. An answer is in the following theorem. It refers to *projects*, i.e. to sequences of cash-flows, not necessarily to bonds and/or to banking operations only.

Theorem 5 . *Let the matrix A of order $(m; n)$ of the future cash-flows of n projects for times 1 to m, with $m \leq n$, be simple and complete, i.e. let its columns A^j and rows A_i verify the properties*

$$A^j \text{ has only one positive entry, } \forall j, \tag{11}$$

$$A_i \nleq [0], \forall i. \tag{12}$$

Then A is productive, i.e. the system

$$\begin{cases} Ax > [0] \\ x \geq [0] \end{cases} \tag{13}$$

is solvable, if and only if A is profitable, *i.e. the system*

$$\begin{cases} wA > [0] \\ w \geq [0] \end{cases} \qquad (14)$$

is solvable[7]. *Consider a plan $b \geq [0]$ of money to be withdrawn at times 1 to m and a row-vector $c > [0]$ measuring the unit present costs of projects. If A is productive or profitable, then for the problems, dual to each other,*

$$\mathcal{P}(b): \begin{vmatrix} \min_{x} cx \\ Ax \geq b, \ x \geq [0] \ , \end{vmatrix} \qquad \mathcal{P}'(b): \begin{vmatrix} \max_{v} vb \\ vA \leq c, \ v \geq [0] \ , \end{vmatrix}$$

the following propositions hold independently of the choice of $b \geq [0]$:

i) *$\mathcal{P}(b)$ is a (solvable and) perfect problem in the sense (1) and admits a basic optimal vector x^* associated with a common basis B;*

ii) *each problem $\mathcal{P}'(b)$ admits a unique (and positive) optimal vector v^*;*

iii) *$v_i^* < 1, \forall i$, when, in each project, the sum of all future cash-flows is greater than the present cost;*

iv) *if $\bar{b}$ and $\underline{b}$ are two semi-positive vectors, then the optimal values $c\bar{x}^*$ for $\mathcal{P}(\bar{b})$ and $c\underline{x}^*$ for $\mathcal{P}(\underline{b})$ are linked by relation*

$$c\bar{x}^* - c\underline{x}^* = v^*(\bar{b} - \underline{b}). \qquad (15)$$

Proof. Let A be profitable. Thanks to assumptions (11)–(12), we can extract from the n columns of A a square sub-matrix of order m with one positive entry in each column and each row. A suitable permutation of its columns generates a matrix A^* which is a Z-matrix, i.e. it has no positive off-diagonal entry. A being profitable, so is A^*, hence A^* is a K-matrix, i.e. it is a Z-matrix with semi-positive inverse. This result directly follows from standard characterizations of K-matrices (e.g., see [7]), which also ensure that both classes of Z- and K-matrices are closed under transposition, hence that A^* is productive too. Taking vanishing weights x_j for the columns of A out of A^* is enough to prove that the whole matrix A is productive.

Let A be productive and call r its rank. The existence of a vector $x^* \geq [0]$ solving (13) and with exactly r positive entries can be proved following the same proof of a standard theorem for linear systems (e.g., see [8], th. 2.11). Thanks to (11), x^* must have at least m positive entries, hence $r = m$ follows. This shows that we can extract from the n columns of A a square sub-matrix $B = A^*$ of order m, which is productive. This property, together with assumption (11), also ensures that A^* is a K-matrix. Being both classes

---

[7]Should system (13) and/or (14) be written with weaker ($\geq$) or stronger ($>$) signs for the unknowns, nothing would change in their solvability.

of Z- and K-matrices closed under transposition, A^* is profitable too. This completes the proof that A is productive if and only if it is profitable.

Now choose a vector $b > [0]$ and a vector x solving (13). Being $Ax > [0]$, some scalar $\alpha > 0$ exists which makes $A(\alpha x) > b$, hence $\mathcal{P}(b)$ is feasible. As this holds for each choice of b, $\mathcal{P}(b)$ is always feasible. Moreover, owing to the signs of c, no x solves system

$$\begin{cases} Ax \geqq [0] \\ x \geqq [0], \ cx < 0. \end{cases}$$

Thanks to a standard theorem of the alternative (e.g., see [8], th. 2.8), this fact ensures that $\mathcal{P}'(b)$ is feasible. Therefore, productivity or profitability entails feasibility of both $\mathcal{P}(b)$ and $\mathcal{P}'(b)$, hence their solvability.

A well known result for linear problems ensures that $\mathcal{P}(b)$ admits an optimal basic vector x^* associated with some basis B of A. Thanks to (11) and (12), this shows that B is a K-matrix, hence it admits a semi-positive inverse B^{-1}. Therefore the vector x^* obtained by filling $x_B = B^{-1}b$ with $(n - m)$ zeroes is feasible and shows that B is feasible for $\mathcal{P}(b)$ no matter how $b \geq [0]$ is chosen. Moreover x^* avoids any positive cash-balance, hence it makes $\mathcal{P}(b)$ perfect. Call c_B the sub-vector of c associated with the columns of B. From the equations $v^*b = cx^* = c_B x_B = c_B B^{-1}b$, relation $v^* = c_B B^{-1}$ follows, hence v^* is positive, fits to every problem $\mathcal{P}'(b)$ and verifies (15).

Start from a vector $\underline{b} \geq [0]$. Should $\mathcal{P}'(\underline{b})$ admit two optima v^* and v^{**}, then $v_t^* \neq v_t^{**}$ will hold for some t. Set up the problem $\mathcal{P}(\bar{b})$ with $\bar{b}_t > \underline{b}_t$, $\bar{b}_i = \underline{b}_i, \forall i \neq t$. As v^* also fits to its dual, its optimum $\bar{x}^*$ leads to a positive increase (15) in the minimized cost which equates both $v_t^*(\bar{b}_t - \underline{b}_t)$ and $v_t^{**}(\bar{b}_t - \underline{b}_t)$: a contradiction. This proves the uniqueness of v^*.

Finally, if $(uA - c) > [0]$ holds, u being the row-vector of m ones, then also $(uB - c_B) > [0]$ holds. As $B^{-1} \geq [0]$, this ensures $(uB - c_B)B^{-1} = (u - c_B B^{-1}) > [0]$, i.e. $u > v^*$. □

Remark 7. Theorem 5 refers to special *strict investments*, namely to projects of the P.I.P.O. or C.I.P.O. class (*point or continuous input–point output*), i.e. with one or many cash-outflows, followed by one cash-inflow at the final time. Zero-coupon bonds and saving plans are in this class, while coupon-bonds are not. Also note that relation (5) does not necessarily hold anymore, as now numbers v_i^* have quite a new meaning (see Remark 10 below).

Remark 8. Whereas the dual variables v_i^* in the P.M. problems of theorems 1 and 2 must share properties (5), the weights w_i showing the profitability of A in (14) are required neither to be strictly decreasing with time i, nor to be all positive, nor to be less than 1 (although this is a matter of normalization only). Therefore, they *don't* need to be interpreted as present values. Note, however, that, thanks to the signs of c, the usual assumption of a positive internal rate or return for each strict investment project is already sufficient for profitability.

Remark 9. The relation put forward in theorem 5 between productivity and profitability is quite similar to the one already known for linear models of productions which are simple and complete. In these models, productivity and profitability are equivalent properties and both entail *all-productivity* and *all-profitability*, in the sense that, no matter how non-negative vectors b and c are chosen, the solvability of system (13) or (14) is equivalent to the one of the respective systems

$$\begin{cases} Ax = b \\ x \geq [0], \end{cases} \qquad \begin{cases} wA = c \\ w \geq [0]. \end{cases}$$

Remark 10. Matrix B^{-1} in the proof of theorem 5 has a meaning similar to the *Leontief inverse* for linear economic models, as it measures the total (direct and indirect) requirements of present money hidden in unit consumptions planned for future times. In other words, the i-th entry of $v^* = c_B B^{-1}$ is the *shadow price* to be paid at initial time for a capital unit $(b_i = 1)$ to be withdrawn at time i; hence $v^* b = cx^* = v^* Ax^*$ is the present cost, computed at those prices, of the whole plan of future consumption.

4 Suggestions for further research

This section aims at pointing out some suggestions for further research.

The history of Non-Substitution Theorems for Leontief models starts with the pioneer works contained in the famous Cowles Commission Monograph edited in 1951 by Koopmans [14]. This history also exhibits some puzzling items (see [9]) and is still open. A lot of more recent contributions try to get those theorems in some (local or global) *restricted versions* which also fit, for instance, to joint production technologies, neoclassical production functions, many primary factors, positive rates of uniform profit and of growth. As sec. 3 has shown, P.M. problems can be usefully framed into the theory of Non-Substitution Theorems. Therefore those extensions may lead to new (local or global) results on the stability of the interest rates term structure regardless of the choice of consumption vector b.

Another promising track for getting global results is the search for financially meaningful conditions for the monotonicity of some optimal basis B, i.e. for the existence of a semi-positive left-inverse B^-. The resort to K-matrices theory, as in theorem 5, is only the easiest (and in fact almost unique) way to achieve this target, but some other ways do exist [8]. More generally, the modern theory of *qualitatively determined equilibria* in comparative statics may suggest non-trivial things on this matter. Also some useful hints may arise from sensitivity theory for optimum problems (e.g., see [4], [23]).

---

[8] For instance, an irreducible non-singular matrix M of order m, with all off-diagonal entries non-negative (i.e. $(-M) \in Z$), admits a positive inverse if and only if: *i)* M admits some principal sub-matrix or order $(m-1)$, say M_{hh}, with a negative dominant eigenvalue; *ii)* the signs of $\det(M)$ and $\det(M_{ii})$ agree, $\forall i$ (see [1]). Needless to say, the financial meaning (if any) of these conditions is still obscure to us.

Finally, as all P.M. problems we dealt with here are of the *buy and hold* kind, some further work may be done for all their *buy and sell* versions, where, owing to new data $(A; b; c)$, a bond arbitrage is needed to improve an optimal portfolio x^*.

References

[1] G. BUFFONI, A. GALATI, *Matrici essenzialmente positive con inversa positiva*, Bollettino Unione Matematica Italiana, 4^a serie, *10* (1974), 98–103.

[2] M.E. DE GIULI, *On a Theorem by Gale-Hadley-Lancaster and Its Economic and Financial Applications*, Atti 19^0 Convegno AMASES, Pugnochiuso, 25–28.9.1995, Cacucci Ed., Bari, 1995, 281–290.

[3] M.E. DE GIULI, U. MAGNANI, *On the Optimal Selection of Financial Activities*, 1995 (forthcoming).

[4] A. DEIF, Sensitivity Analysis in Linear Systems, Springer-Verlag, 1986.

[5] J.C. DERMODY, E.Z. PRISMAN, *Term Structure Multiplicity and Clientele in Markets with Transaction Costs and Taxes*, J. of Finance, *43* (1988), 893–911.

[6] J.C. DERMODY, R.T. ROCKAFELLAR, *Cash Stream Valuation in the Face of Transaction Costs and Taxes*, Mathematical Finance, *1* (1991), 31–54.

[7] M. FIEDLER, Special Matrices and Their Applications in Numerical Mathematics, Martinus Nijhoff Publishers, Dordrecht, Boston, Lancaster, 1986.

[8] D. GALE, The Theory of Linear Economic Models, McGraw-Hill, 1960.

[9] G. GIORGI, U. MAGNANI, *Equilibria Selection and Non-Substitution Theorems: Another Story of a Mare's Nest?*, Atti 7^0 Convegno AMASES, Acireale, 16–18.6.1983, Itec Ed., Milano, 1983, 247–294.

[10] S.D. HODGES, *Convex Approximation*, Univ. of Southampton, Unpubl. M. Sc. thesis, 1967.

[11] S.D. HODGES, S.M. SCHAEFER, *A Model for Bond Portfolio Improvement*, J. of Financial and Quantitative Analysis, *12* (1977), 243–260.

[12] L. JOHANSEN, *Simple and General Nonsubstitution Theorems for Input-Output Models*, J. of Economic Theory, 5 (1972), 383–394.

[13] E. KATZ, E.Z. PRISMAN, *Arbitrage, Clientele Effects, and the Term Structure of Interest Rates*, J. of Financial and Quantitative Analysis, *26* (1991), 435–443.

[14] T.C. KOOPMANS (Ed.), Activity Analysis of Production and Allocation (Cowles Commission Monograph #13), Wiley, 1951.

[15] R. MANNING, *A Nonsubstitution Theorem with Many Primary Factors*, J. of Economic Theory, *25* (1981),442–449.

[16] C. MARI, C. PACATI, *Due metodologie alternative per la stima della struttura per scadenza dei tassi di interesse: un confronto empirico sui*

dati italiani, Atti 18^0 Convegno AMASES, Modena, 5–7.9.1994, Pitagora Ed., Bologna, 1994, 409–419.

[17] P. MATRIGALI, C. PACATI, *Strutture per scadenza dei tassi di interesse come soluzioni duali di problemi di copertura*, Atti 17^0 Convegno AMASES, Ischia, 8–11.9.1993, Istituto Italiano per gli Studi Filosofici, Napoli, 1993, 625–647.

[18] J.H. McCULLOCH, *Measuring the Term Structure of Interest Rates*, J. of Business, *44* (1971), 19–31.

[19] E.D. NERING, A.W. TUCKER, Linear Programs and Related Problems, Academic Press, 1993.

[20] S.M. SCHAEFER, *Consistent Bond Prices*, Unpubl. Ph. D. Thesis, Univ. of London, 1979.

[21] S.M. SCHAEFER, *Measuring a Tax-Specific Term Structure of Interest Rates in the Market for British Government Securities*, Economic Journal, *91* (1981), 415–438.

[22] S.M. SCHAEFER, *Tax Induced Clientele Effects in the Market for British Government Securities*, J. of Financial Economics, *10* (1982), 121–159.

[23] J.E. WARD, R.E. WENDELL, *Approaches to Sensitivity Analysis in Linear Programming*, Annals of Operations Research, *27* (1990), 3–38.

[24] M. WEITZMAN, *On Choosing an Optimal Technology*, Management Science, *13* (1967), 413–428.

Commodity Futures Markets and Trading Strategies Opportunities

Paolo Falbo,* Marco Frittelli,† Silvana Stefani‡

Evidence of mean reversion in commodity prices has been recently found in the literature; however, it is still to be investigated which are the implications of this behavior in an efficient market and whether inefficiencies, if any, are really profitable. This paper analyses some possible model specifications for commodity futures prices and shows how, when mean reversion is present, one may follow trading strategies offering expected returns higher than average with lower risk. The mean reversion hypothesis is confirmed by an empirical investigation of the time series of cotton futures contracts. Moreover, empirical evidence shows that mean reversion effect systematically increases as futures contracts get closer to their maturity.

Keywords. Mean reversion, viable markets, futures markets.

1. Introduction

The existence of an equivalent martingale measure, i.e. a probability measure equivalent to the original one, such that discounted prices under it are martingales, guarantees the viability of a market. This also implies that no arbitrage is allowed: you cannot determine a strategy with a positive expected return in any state of the world (see Harrison and Pliska (1981)). However, a martingale equivalent price generating process does not forbid to some trading strategies to perform better than average with a lower risk. It will be shown that, under a mean reverting behavior, appropriate times can be easily identified for buying and selling, thereby generating dominating returns (i.e. distributed with a higher mean and lower variance than average).

As in Cochrane's (1988) analysis of GNP, Fama and French (1988) and Summers (1986) suggest a definition of the price of a stock as the sum of two components: a permanent and a temporary one. The first is a nonstationary stochastic process, a random walk, that causes a change in the price due to the arrival of new information; the second is a stationary stochastic process which represent temporary deviation about the trend. This component is of great interest as it accounts for a substantial fraction of the variation of the returns, including in this way a degree of predictability in the returns. If the deviation

* Department of Quantitative Methods, University of Brescia
† Institute of Quantitative Methods, University of Milan
‡ Department of Quantitative Methods, University of Brescia

from the trend is temporary, this means that if the price has a value below or above the mean it will revert towards it within a certain interval of time, thus the returns will show a negative autocorrelation.

Empirical evidence of mean reversion in prices has been supported by numerous studies and different tests have been implemented mainly by Poterba and Summers (1988), Fama and French (1988), Goldemberg (1988), Kim *et al.* (1991), Deaton and Laroque (1992), Bessembinder *et al.*(1995). There are different methods to test mean reversion in prices. One consists in comparing the relative variability of the returns over different horizon using variance-ratio tests. Secondly they use regression tests that also involve studying the serial correlation in multiperiod returns. Another method involves estimating parametric time -series models (ARMA) for returns or computing likelihood-ratio tests of the null hypothesis of serial independence against particular parametric alternatives, but as the returns are nearly white noise, standard ARMA techniques often fail.

In Goldemberg (1988) the author verifies that actual prices of financial futures, after elimination of drift, are better described by a mean-reverting process with reflecting barriers than by means of a standard random walk. Poterba and Summers (1988) applied some tests on variance linearity to NYSE stock returns and found a positive serial correlation over short periods and a negative correlation over longer intervals. This suggests a mean reverting behavior that, as the authors point out, can be taken into account to "judge whether financial markets are efficient in the sense of rationally valuing assets, as well as precluding the generation of excess profits". Kim *et al.* (1991) detect a mean reverting behavior in stock prices by running statistical tests based on the properties of variance linearity typical of random walk (see also Lo and MacKinlay (1988)). In Deaton and Laroque (1992), by examining the persistence measure, an indicator of series autocorrelation, it is suggested that deflated commodity prices can follow a mean reverting process. This can be explained by the role played by the existence of physical inventories on current prices distribution. Note that understanding the underlying stochastic processes is essential in a macroeconomic context to design foreign policies and risk sharing mechanisms both on demand and supply side (i.e. for developed and less developed countries). Bessembinder *et al.* (1995) use data from futures contracts to find mean reversion evidence as far as expected asset prices are concerned. They assume that the cost of carry condition holds, so the mean reversion effect they find can not be related to noise or market inefficiency.

The tendency for prices to overshoot but eventually revert to true values can be claimed as an evidence of inefficiency of the market. One theory of why stock prices deviate from fundamental values is that many traders pay attention to recent trends in returns. For example, some traders may jump on the bandwagon and buy the stocks only because past returns were high, causing the price to rise over fundamental value. Likewise, if returns have been low in the recent past, "feedback traders" (this is how they are called), will sell the asset driving the price below its fundamental value. The effect is that in the short run increases in the stock prices are followed by further increases and decreases are followed by further decreases. However prices will ultimately return to fundamental values by arbitragers and traders who pay attention to fundamental values and will discover misvalued assets. Poterba and Summers (1988) and Lo and MacKinlay (1988) find that prices move away from trend for investment horizon of two years or less, which support the feedback trader model.

This paper is organized as follows. We first show theoretically (in Paragraph 2), that a mean reverting market is martingale equivalent (i.e. it admits a martingale equivalent probability measure). Then we show that under such a hypothesis specific dominating strategies can be found, as opposed to a random walk market where no strategy can be better than others. We verify in Paragraph 3 evidence of a mean reverting behavior in the cotton futures market. We tested, through simulation techniques, some trading strategies referred to inventory holders or speculators as counterparts of typical hedgers like consumers - producers. We found a dependency of the trading strategies performances on the parameters of the process and we confirm a possible strong dominance of one strategy over another. Conclusions are contained in Paragraph 4.

2. Trading Strategies Opportunities and the Ornstein Uhlenbeck process

Consider the Ornstein-Uhlenbeck process $X = (X_t, t \geq 0)$ defined as the (unique) strong solution of the Stochastic Linear Differential Equation

$$dX_t = k(x - X_t)dt + \sigma dW_t, \quad X_0 = x, \quad t \geq 0$$

where $W = (W_t, t \geq 0)$ is a standard Brownian motion on a given filtered probability space $(\Omega, F, \mathcal{F} \equiv (F_t)_{t \geq 0}, P)$ and x, k, σ are constants with $k > 0$, $\sigma > 0$. Note that, in order to simplify the notations, we have assumed that the value x, toward which the process mean reverts, coincides with its initial value.

The solution of this equation is well known and may indeed be determined very easily by considering that

$$d(e^{kt}(X_t - x)) = e^{kt}[dX_t + k(X_t - x)dt] = \sigma e^{kt}dW_t$$

and

$$e^{kt}(X_t - x) = \int_0^t \sigma e^{ks}dW_s \quad ;$$

therefore:

$$X_t = x + \sigma e^{-kt}\int_0^t e^{ks}dW_s$$

From this explicit formula one may deduce that X is a Gaussian process with

$$E[X_t] = x \quad \text{and} \quad Var[X_t] = \frac{\sigma^2}{2k}(1 - e^{-2kt})$$

so it converges in distribution to a normal random variable with mean x and variance $\frac{\sigma^2}{2k}$ as $t \to +\infty$ ($E[\cdot]$ and $Var[\cdot]$ denote resp. the expected value and the variance w.r.to P).

Are mean reverting processes admissible for representing price processes of financial assets? If so, are there trading strategies which perform better than others?

In order to answer the first question, we apply some general results from the theory of financial assets valuation; it is well known (see Harrison and Kreps (1979)) that the *viability* of a security market model is guaranteed by the existence of an *equivalent martingale measure* i.e. a probability measure Q (also known as the *risk neutral measure)* equivalent to the original one, under which all discounted price processes of the securities in the market are martingales. Suppose now that the discounted price process of an asset is given by the mean reverting process X. In order to check for the existence of an equivalent martingale measure for X one looks at the exponential local martingale

$$Z_t = \exp\left\{\int_0^t \frac{k(X_s - x)}{\sigma}dW_s - \frac{1}{2}\int_0^t \frac{k^2(X_s - x)^2}{\sigma^2}ds\right\}$$

which is the solution of the equation $Z_t = 1 + \int_0^t Z_s \frac{k(X_s - x)}{\sigma} dW_s$. Under our assumptions Z is a martingale, so Girsanov theorem (Ch. 3, Karatsas and Shreve (1988)) assures that the process $\tilde{W}_t = W_t - \int_0^t \frac{k(X_s - x)}{\sigma} ds$ is a Brownian motion under the equivalent probability Q defined by

$$\frac{dQ}{dP} \big|_{F_t} = Z_t.$$

Rewriting the SDE, which defines X, in terms of $\tilde{W}$ one gets:

$$dX_t = k(x - X_t)dt + \sigma d\tilde{W}_t + \sigma \frac{k(X_t - x)}{\sigma} dt = \sigma d\tilde{W}_t ;$$

therefore Q is an equivalent martingale measure for X and so, a priori, it seems appropriate to consider X as a candidate for the price process of some traded asset.

Consider now a fixed time horizon $T > 0$ and a market where an asset χ, whose price is given by $(X_t, 0 \le t \le T)$, is traded. Any predictable real process $H = (H_t, 0 \le t \le T)$ such that

$$E \left[\int_0^T H_s^2 ds \right] < +\infty$$

will represent an *admissible* dynamic strategy available to agents: H_t denotes the number of the asset χ held in a portfolio at time t. The cumulative time t *gain* received from following a strategy H is given by the stochastic integral:

$$G_t = G_t(H, X) \triangleq \int_0^t H_s dX_s, \quad 0 \le t \le T$$

(note that the above condition of admissibility guarantees that this stochastic integral is well defined and preserves the martingale property).

The fundamental theorem of asset pricing tells us (see Harrison and Pliska (1981)) that the existence of a risk neutral measure is equivalent to the absence of arbitrage: the only non negative gain $G_T(H, X)$ generated by *any* predictable trading strategy H is equal to zero:

No Arbitrage $\Leftrightarrow$ $(G_T(H, X) \ge 0 \Rightarrow G_T(H, X) = 0)$ $P - a.s.$

This means that one can not expect to determine a strategy $\hat{H}$ which strictly dominates another strategy $\tilde{H}$ (in the sense that $G_T(\hat{H}, X) \geq G_T(\tilde{H}, X)$ $P-$ a.s. and $P(G_T(\hat{H}, X) > G_T(\tilde{H}, X)) > 0$). Note that we are not saying that there are no trading strategies generating positive expected returns; we negate the stronger statement that an admissible trading strategy may generate, in all states of the world, a non negative terminal gain (therefore bearing no risk) that is positive with positive probability. However, this does not necessarily imply that one can't cleverly select a strategy which performs *better* than some others; the question now is what does "better" mean. From a practical point of view (in a mean variance context) it should be evident that if $E[G_T(\hat{H})] > E[G_T(\tilde{H})]$ and $Var[G_T(\hat{H})] < Var[G_T(\tilde{H})]$ then strategy $\hat{H}$ is more appealing than $\tilde{H}$ and we say that $\hat{H}$ performs better than $\tilde{H}$.

First consider an asset having as price process the Brownian motion $B_t = x + \sigma W_t$ starting at the same value x and with the same diffusion coefficient σ as the process X. Since B is a (P)-martingale (and H is admissible), $G_t(H, B)$ is a (P)-martingale and so $E[G_T(H, B)] = 0$ for any admissible strategies H. So, as everyone would expect, there is no way to find a better strategy in the sense previously described by investing in B.

However, when one invests in assets following mean reverting processes one may easily find strategies which perform better than the buy-and-hold-till-the-end one; we show this by defining two simple strategies - $\tilde{H}$ and $\hat{H}$ - and comparing (using simulations techniques) the expected value and variance of the cumulative gains generated by investing in the asset χ having X as a price process.

$\tilde{H}$ is simply the strategy of buying the asset at time 0 and selling it at time T.

Clearly $G_T(\tilde{H}, X) = X_T - x$; so that:

$$E[G_T(\tilde{H}, X)] = 0 \text{ and } Var[G_T(\tilde{H}, X)] = \frac{\sigma^2}{2k}(1 - e^{-2kT})$$

$\hat{H}$ is defined as follows: choose two real numbers $a < b$; buy the asset at the first time the price reaches the level a and sell it at the first time the price hits the boundary b; repeat this procedure at any time before T; then at time T close the position.

We compute $E[G_T(\hat{H}, X)]$ and $Var[G_T(\hat{H}, X)]$ from the simulation of the process X (see table 1); as expected and contrary to the Brownian motion case, strategy $\hat{H}$ performs better than $\tilde{H}$ when one invests in the price process X.

Table 1

The Expected Value and the Variance of $G_T(\cdot,\cdot)$ are calculated performing 1000 simulations, each of 1000 steps, for the values $k = 0,02$, $k = 0,015$, $k = 0,01$. The values of the other parameters are: $\sigma = 1$, $x = 100$, $T = 100$; $a = x - 2\sigma = 98$, $b = x + 2\sigma = 102$.

$k = 0,020$	$\tilde{H},X$	$\hat{H},X$	$\tilde{H},B$	$\hat{H},B$
$E[G_T(\cdot,\cdot)]$	$0,06$	$3,29$	$0,16$	$0,01$
$Var[G_T(\cdot,\cdot)]$	$24,47$	$22,63$	$101,28$	$48,59$
$k = 0,015$	$\tilde{H},X$	$\hat{H},X$	$\tilde{H},B$	$\hat{H},B$
$E[G_T(\cdot,\cdot)]$	$-0,02$	$2,78$	$0,11$	$0,19$
$Var[G_T(\cdot,\cdot)]$	$30,56$	$23,84$	$94,67$	$46,26$
$k = 0,010$	$\tilde{H},X$	$\hat{H},X$	$\tilde{H},B$	$\hat{H},B$
$E[G_T(\cdot,\cdot)]$	$0,11$	$2,05$	$0,10$	$0,04$
$Var[G_T(\cdot,\cdot)]$	$44,97$	$29,84$	$104,26$	$51,49$

In order to check for the accuracy of these simulations one may compare the values resulting from the above simulations with the following theoretical values:

$$E[G_T(\tilde{H},B)] = E[G_T(\hat{H},B)] = 0,$$
$$Var[G_T(\tilde{H},B)] = \sigma^2 T = 100,$$
$$Var[G_T(\hat{H},B)] = E[\sigma^2 \int_0^T \hat{H}_s^2 ds] = 50,$$
$$Var[G_T(\tilde{H},X)] = \frac{\sigma^2}{2k}(1 - e^{-2kT}) = 25,54 \text{ for } k = 0,02,$$
$$Var[G_T(\tilde{H},X)] = 31,67 \text{ for } k = 0,015,$$
$$Var[G_T(\tilde{H},X)] = 43,23 \text{ for } k = 0,01.$$

In the next section we check the mean reverting hypothesis on commodities futures prices and show how to perform some profitable trading strategies on a commodity futures market (cotton).

3. Empirical investigation

To test the hypothesis that mean reversion models may satisfactorily represent futures prices we tried to fit real data considering a mean reverting process model and we estimated the parameters using a non-linear regression technique.

3.1 The data

Among the features of the cotton futures market, we mention the non-existence of a unique standard cotton quality continuously traded during the year. On the contrary, a wide variety of cotton qualities appears in the market in limited quantity and for relatively short periods of time. Even though a particular cotton quality has been chosen as the official underlying good for futures prices, it represents such a small portion of the global trade, that in no way operators consider its price as a representative one. In this context, the *futures nearby* is playing the role of the true *spot price* in this market (that is why we will also refer to this series as the *spot price* variable).

We recall that NYCE (the New York Cotton Exchange) offers five standard futures contracts every year. Maturities for these futures contracts are the last day of March, May, July, October and December. Typical life of every new futures is one and a half year (this fact relates to the time span of the cotton economical life cycle, starting with demand forecast and ending with delivery).

The following figure 1 plots the Futures Nearby time series for the case studied.

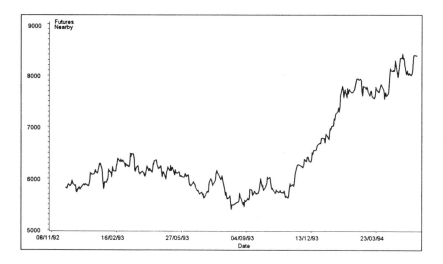

Figure 1: Futures Nearby time series

It is interesting to notice the strong rise starting right before the end of 1993.

This was due to a poor forecast of the Russian, Chinese, Indian and Pakistani production. At the harvesting period, observers realized that 10 million bales, out of 88 million, were missing with respect to expectation, causing a strong fall in supply and subsequently a price increase.

Data collected for the empirical study refer to daily time series of futures cotton market prices, from December '92 to May '94. During such a time period, 9 futures contracts time series have been selected:

n. series	Futures contract time series	n. obs.
1	May '93	58
2	July '93	91
3	October '93	135
4	December '93	200
5	March '94	240
6	May '94	299
7	July '94	314
8	October '94	271
9	December '94	229

3.2 Testing the model

The model is described by the stochastic differential equation:

$$dY_t = k \left(Y_0 e^{\delta t} - Y_t \right) dt + \sigma dW_t$$

Note that dY_t, the infinitesimal futures price movement, is proportional to the distance between the actual price level, Y_t, and a long run average price Y_0, continuously compounded at a rate δ. The estimation of the parameters will show that δ can be set equal to zero; so it can be seen as an Ornstein-Uhlenbeck process with $\delta = 0$, as discussed in the previous section.

An important role is played by the parameter k, the speed factor, or better, the force of the process reversion. For $k = 0$ the process degenerates to a standard Brownian motion without drift. For $k \in (0, 1)$ the process reacts proportionally to the distance from the historical average, the proportion being exactly k.

The discrete version of the previous SDE is :

$$Y_t - Y_{t-1} = k \left(Y_0 e^{\delta t} - Y_{t-1} \right) + \sigma \epsilon_t$$

$$Y_t = k Y_0 e^{\delta t} + (1 - k) Y_{t-1} + \sigma \epsilon_t$$

where $\epsilon_t \sim N(0, 1)$.

Under these settings the price process for a futures contract does not depend from any underlying variable. Here Y_t is a "primitive" process and is studied for its statistical properties. Therefore we do not assume any "dependence" from spot prices, like the cost of carry condition. This implies that mean reversion here can derive from noise or inefficiencies of the market (see Bessembinder *et al.*, 1995). The key purpose of this investigation is indeed to show whether actual prices of cotton futures contracts follow a mean-reverting process. As the simulation study will show, many trading strategies may be developed to take advantage of this feature.

The estimation was performed by an Ordinary Least Squares non-linear regression technique using SAS[1] (Procedure Model). For each time series the parameters in the last equation, k, δ, Y_0, were estimated using Y_t as the dependent variable and Y_{t-1}, t as explanatory variables.

The statistical significance of parameter k (k significantly different from 0) is obviously crucial for determining whether a time series is actually showing mean-reversion or not, while the (statistical) significance of δ is crucial to establish whether the "equilibrium" series is following any trend. No theoretical value is attributed to the intercept Y_0.

3.3 Results and comments

The following tables show the parameter estimates resulting from the application of the regression technique on each of the futures series. The statistical significance of these estimates are reported next to them (in the Prob|T| columns): values show the probability of type error I under the null hypothesis the the parameter value is 0 (so low values of Prob|T| mean that there are low probability of making a mistake in rejecting the null hypothesis and the parameter estimate may be considered significantly different from zero). In Table 2 the observation period was the whole life of the contracts.

[1] Statistical Application Software, SAS, New Cary

series name	R-squared	speed coeff.	Prob $|T|$	coeff. rate	prob $|T|$	Intercept	Prob $|T|$	Root MSE
may93	0.84	0.25	0.006	0.001	0.0005	5911	0.0001	64.05
jul93	0.78	0.18	0.002	0.0004	0.06	6123	0.0001	70.16
oct93	0.90	0.04	0.128	-0.0006	0.27	6396	0.0001	52.15
dec93	0.90	0.07	0.008	-0.0003	0.13	6159	0.0001	60.90
mar94	0.88	0.06	0.007	-0.0001	0.32	6189	0.0001	59.40
may94	0.98	0.0006	0.67	0.01	0.28	841	0.686	64.91
jul94	0.98	0.01	0.17	0.001	0.02	5508	0.0001	67.69
oct94	0.99	0.03	0.01	0.001	0.0001	5568	0.0001	49.47
dec94	0.99	0.04	0.01	0.001	0.0001	5816	0.0001	44.16

Table 2: Cotton futures prices (whole life)

In general we observe that the speed coefficient k is significantly different from zero in six cases out of nine (see the probability values reported in columns Prob$|T|$), with an average value of about 9-10%. Such a result suggests that mean reversion is a feature that may often characterize actual processes of cotton futures, though with a non constant speed. On the contrary there is no evidence of any significant trend in the series. The rate of growth coefficient δ oscillates from positive to negative values, which were most of the time even not statistically significantly different from zero. This evidence is confirmed by the plot of the thirty-years series of the cotton nearby (see following figure 2) and is coherent with findings of the literature (i.e. Deaton and Laroque (1992). The average fitting of the model (as measured by the R-squared) has maintained very high throughout all sets of analyses. We also report that the values of the R-squared statistic are almost entirely due to serial correlation (of order 1) of the price time series.

In tables 3 and 4 we show the results of other analyses run on different periods of the same futures contracts time series. Table 3 refers to the first 100 days of the futures, while Table 4 has considered the last 60 days, which are, as we already said, the most active.

series name	R-squared	speed coeff.	Prob $|T|$	coeff. rate	prob $|T|$	Intercept	Prob $|T|$
mar94	0.78	0.112	0.023	-0.0002	0.51	6304	0.0001
may94	0.79	0.11	0.023	-0.0002	0.47	6379	0.0001
jul94	0.94	0.14	0.0046	-0.0009	0.0001	6665	0.0001
oct94	0.78	0.16	0.01	0.0003	0.07	5944	0.0001

Table 3: Cotton futures prices (first 100 days)

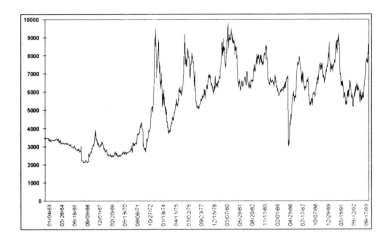

Figure 2: Cotton outlook index - 30 year weekly series

series name	R-squared	speed coeff.	Prob |T|	coeff. rate	prob |T|	Intercept	Prob |T|	Root MSE
may93	0.82	0.26	0.0001	0.0014	0.0009	5849	0.0001	67.43
jul93	0.66	0.18	0.018	0.00005	0.90	6278	0.0001	73.72
oct93	0.88	0.24	0.005	-0.001	0.0001	7063	0.0001	53.55
dec93	0.83	0.09	0.09	-0.0003	0.77	6195	0.0001	80.06
mar94	0.62	0.23	0.004	0.00007	0.81	5881	0.0001	61.65
may94	0.98	0.46	0.0002	0.004	0.0001	2258	0.0001	74.39
jul94	0.72	0.22	0.0046	0.0005	0.15	6742	0.0001	85.64

Table 4: Cotton futures prices (last 60 days)

The speed coefficient, in spite of the smaller number of observations, has always shown significant values. While the value of k for the first 100 days averaged around 12-13%, for the last 60 days period it averaged around 24%. The rate of growth coefficient δ confirms its non significance in this market.

The numerical value for k appears relatively high and it raises the question whether it is possible to devise profitable strategies to exploit such feature.

3.4 A simulation study

To show the practical relevance of our results we simulated some trajectories of futures price processes using the estimates previously found. In particular we simulated two naive trading strategies in the cotton futures market. At the end of each simulation, we recorded the gain (loss) of the strategy and the following figures show the synthetic results of all runs.

Moreover, the simulation study is a clear example of a strategy which is "better" than another one as is previously defined, even though the selected strategies are both very simple and are certainly very far from the performance of an optimal strategy. However the fact that we obtained such a clear result by means of an elementary simulation, makes the result itself even stronger. Both strategies (call them A and B) are triggered simultaneously at time t^* defined as:

$$t^* = \inf\{t < T - 15 : |Y_t - Y_0| \geq 2\sigma\}$$

that is the first time (up to 15 days before futures maturity) that the actual price Y_t differs from its long run average of twice its standard deviation. Of course the position is short when Y_{t^*} is higher than Y_0 and long in the opposite case. What makes A different from B is the closing condition. While for strategy A the position was closed after 15 days from the opening position (to "replicate" a 3 working weeks period) of the simulated process, closing day for strategy B was chosen as $\min(T, \tau)$, where T represents the maturity of the futures contract, and τ is the first time when the price process 'reverts' to its historical mean:

$$\tau = \inf\{t > t^* : Y_t = Y_0\}$$

The position was therefore closed whatever between τ and T came first. Intuitively strategy B is built to better profit of the mean reversion feature than strategy A. The comparisons were repeated 500 times for different values of the speed coefficient k. In other words, we intended to observe how the statistical distribution of the net profit of each strategy changed, ceteris paribus, as a function of the speed coefficient. In particular we examined the different distributions for each strategy corresponding to 30 values of parameter k, ranging from 0 to 0.6 with increments of 0.02 each. For the simulation we set: $T = 70$ (opening position allowed only within the first 55 days), $Y_0 = 6812$, $\sigma = 64$, δ (rate of growth coefficient) $= 0$, opening position corresponding to 200 futures standard contracts (standard contracts in the cotton futures market are of 50.000 lbs). Opening position was in average $ 681,200.

In figure 3 the plot of the average profit of strategy A and B for different values of the k parameter is shown. It is interesting to notice that the two strategies have zero average profit for $k = 0$, and that they rapidly differ even for small values of k. The net profit of the two strategies seems to assess asymptotically around $ 20,000 for strategy B and $14,000 for strategy A.

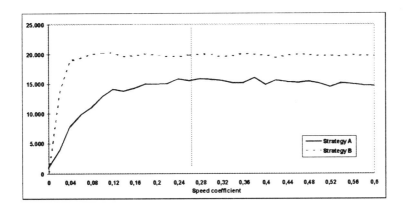

Figure 3: Average profit as a function of speed coefficients

We next considered the standard deviation series of the net profit of strategies A and B as a function of parameter k (Figure 4). Strategy B is still preferable to strategy A. Standard deviation values appear to wave around \$ 5,000 for strategy B and around \$ 11,000 for strategy A. It is also interesting to notice that for values of the speed coefficient around .25 the margins of strategy B over A are already rather 'safe', that is the difference between the two alternatives becomes evident for values of k much lower than the average value we estimated for this parameter for the last 60 days of a futures.

We considered also the average duration of strategy B, that is the time required to close the position. From figure 5 we noticed a clear tendency of the average and standard deviation strategy duration to reduce as a function of the parameter k. For a value of k equal to .25 strategy B required less than 8 days on average to close, with a standard deviation of about 6 days (recall that strategy A was on the contrary built to have fixed duration of 15 days). Note that, for comparative purposes, there is no need to adjust profits for foregone interest and transaction costs, since these should be applied to both strategies. Notice also that the difference in the two strategies perfomance is substantially unaffected by the instability of k at least for values of k greater than 0.10.

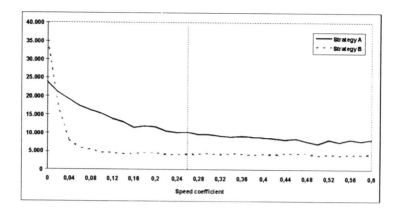

Figure 4: Standard deviation as a function of speed coefficient

4. Conclusions

A clear evidence of mean reversion has been found as far as the cotton futures market is concerned. Since a mean reverting market is still viable, as we have shown, no arbitrage opportunities are allowed. At the same time, though, we have found that mean reversion can help in performing trading strategies which are definitely dominating "random walk" strategies. Second, working on real data, through simulation of naive strategies we have proved that investors can make substantial profits taking advantage of mean reversion. This effect is apparent even when the speed coefficient k is relatively low. Thus, we believe that further investigation is needed to understand the implications of this finding on the efficient market hypothesis. In this respect it is therefore interesting to notice that mean reversion is stronger during the last period of the futures, when contracts volumes are particularly high. At the same time it would be important (from a practical point of view as well) to evaluate whether a coefficient of mean reversion as high as 24% (as we found for the last period of a futures) leaves margins for profit, net of transaction costs.

Another interesting line of research concerns the determination of "optimal" strategies, i.e. those which best capture mean reversion features (detection of the optimal stopping times).

Next one should examine whether some contract provisions, like the *on call,*

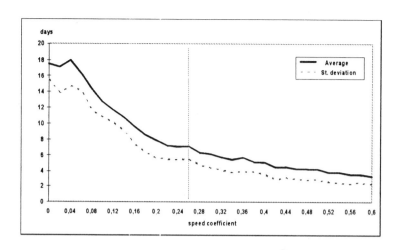

Figure 5: Time duration of strategy B as a function of speed coefficient

Falbo and Stefani (1994), freely offered along with some commodity futures contracts, are really worthless opportunities.

Acknowledgments

Special thanks are due to Romano Bonadei, president of Filati Filartex spa, who kindly offered the data used in the analysis and to Prof. Giovanni Zambruno for his helpful suggestions. For administrative purposes section 1 and 4 are attributable to Silvana Stefani, section 2 to Marco Frittelli and section 3 to Paolo Falbo.

References

Bessembinder, H., J.F. Coughenour, P.J. Seguin and M. Monroe Smoller, 1995, 'Mean Reversion in Equilibrium Asset Prices: Evidence from the Futures Term Structure', *Journal of Finance* L, 361-375

Cochrane, J.H.,1988, 'How Big is the Random Walk in GNP?' *Journal of Political Economy* 96, 893-920

Deaton, A. and G. Laroque, 1992, 'On the Behaviour of Commodity Prices', *Review of Economic Studies* 59, 1-23.

Falbo, P. and S. Stefani, 1994, 'The Cotton Futures Market: Investment Strategies and Convenience Yield Estimation', in *In Quest of the Philosopher's Stone - Nonlinearity and Volatility in Financial Markets, Proceedings from the Satellite Meeting SIS*, Imperia, 187-199.

Fama E.F. and K.R.French, 1988, 'Permanent and Temporary Components of Stock Prices', *Journal of Political Economy* 96, 247-273

Goldemberg, D.H., 1988, 'Trading Frictions and Futures Prices Movements', *Journal of Financial and Quantitative Analysis* 23, 465-481.

Harrison, J.M. and S.R. Pliska, 1981, 'Martingales and stochastic integrals in the theory of continuous trading', *Stoc. Proc. Appl.* 11, 215-260.

Harrison, J.M. and D. Kreps, 1979, 'Martingale and arbitrage in multiperiod securities markets', *Journal of Economic Theory*. 20, 381-408.

Lo, A.W. and MacKinley A.C., 1988, 'Stock prices do not follow random walks: Evidence from a simple specification test', *Review of Financial Studies* 1, 41-66

Karatzas, I. and S.E. Shreve, 1988, *Browian Motion and stochastic calculus*, Springer-Verlag.

Kim, M.J., C.R. Nelson and R. Startz, 1991, 'Mean reversion in stock prices? A reappraisal of the empirical evidence', *Review of Economic Studies* 58, 515-528.

Poterba, J.M. and L.H. Summers, 1988, 'Mean reversion in stock prices', *Journal of Financial Economics* 22, 27-59.

Summers, L.H., 1986, 'Does the Stock Market Rationally Reflect Fundamental Values?' *Journal of Finance* 41, 591-602

Financial Asset Demand in the Italian Market:an Empirical Analysis

Giorgio Calcagnini and Rita L. D'Ecclesia
Istituto di Scienze Economiche. University of Urbino 61029 Urbino,
Italy.

Abstract. The introduction of new investment instruments, i.e. long
term debt instruments and derivatives contracts, and new market organization, as well as the opening of computerized systems for transaction processing, caused different behavior among Italian investors.
In such a context an analysis of Italian asset demand may be useful
to understand investors' willingness to substitute debt securities with
equities or other instruments. This could be particularly interesting in
the view of an efficient financial instrument projecting realized by the
Italian Treasury. The empirical analysis of Italian demand for financial
instruments and the substitutability between various securities based
on a set of monthly data starting from 1987 up to 1994, is provided.
An analytical formalization of asset demand, following familiar equilibrium economic models is also provided.   .
Keywords: Asset demand, substitutability, portfolio allocation, risk
aversion.

1.Introduction

Italian financial markets have experienced relevant changes over the
last decade: mainly the introduction of new investment instruments
and financial intermediaries (i.e. Società di Intermediazione Mobiliare,
SIM) which provide a more diversified set of opportunities for portfolio
disaggregation.

The introduction in 1989 of 6-years Italian Treasury Puttable Bonds
(CTO) and in 1991 of longer term debt instruments (i.e. of 10 and

30 years Italian Treasury Bonds, BTP) in a market where the longest
maturity had always been 5 years, gave Italian investors the opportunity to modify their portfolio selection. New financial instruments
were finally launched on the Italian market together with the introduction of longer term debt instruments as well as futures and options
on government T-bonds.

Additionally, financial intermediaries began to operate in the market providing new opportunities for Italian investors to diversify their
portfolio with mutual funds, insurances and derivatives. Market practices were also modernized by the introduction of MTS, (Mercato
Telematico Secondario), in 1988 — a computerized system for transaction processing and market clearance — that generated increase in
trading volume [1] (from 30.334 securities traded in 1991 up to 105.317
securities in 1994).

The success of longer term debt securities such as the 10 years
T-Bond can be verified looking at the trading volumes on the MTS
where this security represents 54% of total trading after only three
years from its first introduction into the market.

The effects of the increasing in the trading volumes of public securities on Italian households' portfolios have been analyzed in a previous
work (see Calcagnini 1992). The nature of the relationship between
Treasury bonds and other assets within private portfolios was analyzed therein focusing on the existence of crowding out phenomena.
In this study we focus on households' asset demand features at a more
disaggregated level. We use the breakdown of Treasury securities to
asses the substitutability between various assets and to catch the main
features of Italian asset demand which may be useful for an efficient
instruments projecting[2].

The aim of this paper is twofold. First, we empirically analyze the
features of Italian demand for financial instruments and test the substitutability of debt with equity securities as well as between different
kind of debt securities, i.e. short term versus long term or floating rate
instruments versus straight bonds.

Second, based on this empirical approach, we try to describe the
behavior of Italian investors and to analytically formalize the financial
asset demand. This second step could be useful for new financial

---

[1] A description of the Italian bond market is found in Thomas J. Urich, 1993,
and A. Scalia, 1993.

[2] Holmer et al., 1993

instruments projecting where understanding the basic features which make an instrument appealing to Italian investors may be a guarantee for success.

The structure of the paper is the following: in *Section 2* a short description of the main features of financial asset returns and household portfolio dynamics in the last decade is presented; in *Section 3*, according to a first disaggregation of instruments into five main categories the substitutability between fixed income, indexed income and equity securities is analyzed; in *Sections 4* we generalize and test traditional portfolio models in order to obtain a first, more realistic formalization for the Italian market; in *Section 5* an analysis of the change occurred in the asset returns' dynamic during the last decade is presented. A summary and suggestions for further works are reported in the final *Section*.

2.Debt Instruments as Preferred Financial Assets

In financial markets, which do not provide a rich variety of financial instruments and where most of household investments have been historically directed toward fixed income instruments, the introduction of new financial instruments, as well as *puttable bonds* and *10 and 30 year T-bonds* might cause unpredictable investors reaction. We try to analyze and describe the main characteristics of investor reactions during the last eight years– starting from January 1987 up to October 1994.

A brief description of the characteristics of Italian Government Securities may be useful:

- *Buoni Ordinari del Tesoro (BOT)* are Treasury Bills sold at a discount to face value and whose return is due only to price appreciation. Bot are issued at 3, 6 and 12 months maturities. Secondary market trading for BOTs takes place on the MTS.

- *Certificati del Tesoro Zero Coupon (CTZ)* are two years Treasury Certificates sold, together with BOT, at a discount at face value. Ctz were the first discount bonds issued with a maturity longer than 12 months. The first Ctz was issued in April 1995.

- *Buoni del Tesoro Poliennali (BTP)*are fixed rate bonds issued with maturities of 3, 5, 7, 10 and 30 years. Coupon payments are made net of withholding tax and capital gains tax on bonds is withheld at maturity on the difference between the issue price and the face value of the security. The withholding tax rate is 12.5% for bonds issued after August 1987. Before that time the withholding tax rate was 6.25%. In the secondary market, BTPs are traded on the telematic market, on the over-the-counter market and on the stock exchange.

- *Certificati di Credito del Tesoro (CCT)* are floating rate Treasury bonds which make coupon payments semi-annually and are issued with a maturity of 7 years. Coupon payments are indexed off of 12 month BOT rates plus a spread which has ranged from 50 to 75 basis points over the last few years. CCTs issued before March 1991 were issued with other maturities, with the coupon payments computed differently and some being made annual coupon payments. CCTs are traded on the telematic market, on the over-the-counter market and on the stock exchange.

- *Certificati del Tesoro con Opzione (CTO)* are fixed rate bonds issued with a maturity of 6 years which make coupon payments semiannually and carry a put option that allows a bond to be redeemed at face value on the coupon date 3 years before maturity.

We try to focus on broadly defined asset categories, and so we may implicitly treat as perfect substitutes instruments that investors do not classify indifferently. We consider all financial assets available on the market, the rate of return data of which are regularly available on a monthly basis.

We suggest a first aggregation of the various forms of financial claims typically held by Italian households into five broad categories: bank deposits (*BD*), straight bonds (*SB*), floating rate notes (*FRN*), corporate bonds (*CDB*) and equities (E).

This first disaggregation is based on the main distinction between risky and non-risky securities. Bank deposits (BD) are assets that bear nominal rates of returns and also are means of payment. Straight bonds (SB) include short term and long term fixed income Treasury securities as well as T-bills and Treasury bonds. This first classification stems from the features of the Italian market. The role played by the BTPs as long term Treasury Bonds only began in 1991 with the introduction of longer maturities such as 10 years, and in 1993 with 30 year

T-Bonds. Before then, the longest term BTP traded had a 6 year maturity, so we may assume that it was basically considered by investors to be a fixed income security togher with the T-Bill. Floating rate note (FRN) instruments include all Italian Treasury certificates which pay semiannually indexed coupons and all local obligations which are issued as indexed securities. These securities are mainly medium-term maturity instruments (5-7 years). Corporate debt (CDB) includes all other debt instruments issued by private companies and international institutions that bear nominal rates of returns and are subject to substantial interest rate risks. Equity (E) includes assets that bear residual ownership risks.

Table 1: Mean Real Returns for Five Categories of Assets. 1987-94

Assets	Mean Values	Volatility
Straight Bonds (S)	5.17	1.17
Floating Rate Notes (FRN)	6.03	1.49
Corporate Debt (CDB)	5.62	0.90
Equity (E)	-0.17	26.32
Bank Deposits (BD)	1.21	0.86

Table 1 shows the average after tax real returns for these five categories of assets and their volatility (standard deviation) based on a set of monthly data starting from January 1987 up to October 1994. The net nominal returns associated with these real returns are the average rate paid by banks on deposits BD, the average between the T-Bill and the Treasury bonds rates for the straight bonds ST, the average between the rate of the Italian Treasury certificates and the rate of local obligations for FRNs and corporate bond yields for corporate debt. Finally, as a proxy for equity rates of return, we used the annualized percentage capital gains or losses on the Italian stock index-MIB for equity. The real return is derived by taking the nominal returns minus the annualized percentage change registered by the consumer price index. On average Floating Rate Notes show the highest mean real return, 6.03%, while the lowest volatility is registered by bank deposits; the lowest real returns and highest volatilities are provided by equities. Volatility in Table 1 is measured by the standard deviation of real returns. The traditional mean-variance trade off of returns is not always met. The two exceptions refer to equities and corporate debt. In the first case an explanation of this apparent contraddiction can be found in the fact that equity returns are realized returns and the confidence interval for its mean is much larger than for the other assets returns. In the second case the relatively low volatility for corporate debt returns may be due to the existence of a thin market for this kind of asset.

Table 2: Mean Real Returns for Italian Government Securities 1987-94.

Assets	Mean Values	Volatility
BOT (T-Bills 12 months)	4.97	1.31
CTO (Puttable Bonds-6 years)	5.11	1.09
CTE (Ecu T-Cert.3-5-8 years)	3.04	0.92
BTP (T-Bonds 3-30 ys)	5.50	1.06
CCT (Floating Rate Notes 3-5-7ys)	6.17	1.56

If we look at the disaggregation of Italian Treasury Securities by kind of instruments we also notice that the highest rate is found for CCTs and the lowest for the Treasury certificate denominated in ECU (CTE), which are not directly comparable with italian lire rate of returns (see Table 2).

Table 3: Correlation coefficients for 5 main categories of assets.1987-94

	r_{SB}	r_{FRN}	r_{CDB}	r_E	r_{BD}
r_{SB}	1.00				
r_{FRN}	0.947	1.00			
r_{CDB}	0.782	0.853	1.000		
r_E	-0.357	-0.311	-0.269	1.000	
r_{BD}	0.584	0.550	0.548	0.03	1.000

Table 3 shows the correlation structure of the actual returns corresponding to average real returns in Table 1. As expected high correlation is shown between floating rate note instruments and straight bonds, $\rho = 0.947$, due to the existing link between floating note rates and straight bond rates (the floating rate is equal to the T-Bill rate plus a spread).

This is outlined in Table 4 where correlations between Treasury

Table 4: Correlation coefficients for Italian Treasury Securities.1987-94

	r_{BOT}	r_{BTP}	r_{CTO}	r_{CTE}	r_{FRN}
r_{BOT}	1.00				
r_{BTP}	0.862	1.00			
r_{CTO}	0.354	0.287	1.000		
r_{CTE}	0.625	0.836	0.098	1.000	
r_{FRN}	0.930	0.893	0.324	0.683	1.000

securities instruments are shown and the highest correlation is found between T-Bill rate and FRN's rate, $\rho = 0.93$, and between the T-bill and T-Bonds' rates. High correlation is also shown between floating rate notes and corporate debt, $\rho = 0.853$, given the need to link corporate performance to the Government rates. Equity rates are negatively correlated with the other asset rates of return, with the only exception being for bank deposit rates where no correlation is shown.

Table 5: Disaggregation by Instruments of Household Sector Financial Assets.

	Oct.'94 Mean Values	'87-'94 Mean Values	'87-'94 Mean Values(%)
Short Term Debt	409.883	316.152	17.51
T-Bills	408.763	310.102	
Ecu-T-Bills	1.120	6.050	
Medium Long Term Debt	1.449.358	959.171	48.52
T-Bonds	657.237	325.213	
Floating Rate Ns	549.730	450.616	
Corporate Debt	242.391	183.343	
Equity	371.754	243.767	13.86
Bank Deposits	434.929	348.297	20.11

Table 5 shows a disaggregation of household financial assets by the five major categories, while in Table 6 a disaggregation of financial assets by investors is also provided. Most of the Italian households'

Table 6: Disaggregation of Household Sector Financial Assets

	Oct.'94 Mean Values	'87-'94 Mean Values	'87-'94 Mean Values(%)
Short Term Debt	409.883	316.152	100.00
Bank of Italy	11.026	9.071	2.87
Banks	69.173	30.935	9.78
Mutual Funds	7.868	1.811	0.57
Others	321.816	274.334	86.77
Medium Long Term Debt	1.449.358	959.171	100.00
Bank of Italy	108.837	67.144	7.00
Banks	301.708	220.031	22.94
Mutual Funds	54.720	34.316	3.58
Others	984.093	637.680	66.48
Equity	371.754	243.767	100.00
Bank of Italy	759	564	0.23
Banks	554	5.872	2.41
Mutual Funds	5.921	3.129	1.28
Others	364.520	234.202	96.08

asset demand is directed toward Treasury securities, which include all short-term debt instruments and most of the medium and long-term debt, with 48.59% of total assets; a large part of household portfolio is held in bank deposits (20.06%) and only 13.83% is held in equities. Most of the investments in Treasury securities are directed, on average, toward FRN instruments and T-Bills, as is shown in Table 7. Only starting in 1992 has there been an increased interest in BTPs which in October 1994 represented 32.75% of the total amount of Treasury Securities held by investors, against an average value of 19.7% during the period 1987-1994.

It is interesting to examine existing correlations between the assets'shares, see Table 8. High positive correlation is found between FRNs and Bank Deposits, showing a link between an increase in investor's liquidity and the choice of Indexed securities, and between FRNs and Corporate debt securities, due to the common feature of these instruments both indexed rate securities. The dynamic of house-

Table 7: Disaggregation of Household Sector Treasury Securities. Percentage by instruments. 1987-1994

	Bot	BTP	FRN	CTO	CTE	Others	Total
Mean Values	29.32	19.69	42.37	4.09	2.90	1.63	100.0
St.deviation	1.78	5.69	5.61	1.84	0.61	0.81	
Ott-94	25.52	32.75	34.20	4.21	2.94	0.38	100.0

Table 8: Correlation Coefficients Between Actual Asset Shares-1987:1994

	α_{SB}	α_{FRN}	α_{CDB}	α_E	α_{BD}
α_{SB}	1.0				
α_{FRN}	-0.966	1.00			
α_{CDB}	-0.806	0.756	1.00		
α_E	0.345	-0.329	-0.456	1.00	
α_{BD}	-0.895	0.764	0.694	-0.439	1.00

hold portfolios during te period 1987-1994 is also shown in Figure 1.

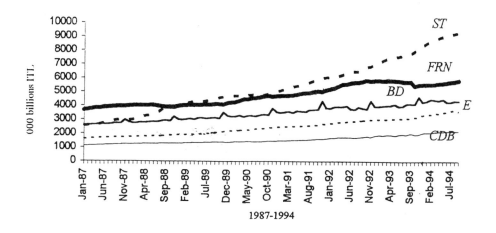

Figure 1. Portfolio Households for the Period 1987-94

On the other hand, the highest negative correlation is found between Straight Bonds and FRNs, $\rho = -0.96$, and Straight Bonds and Bank Deposits, $\rho = -0.89$. This is due to a widespread attitude to consider the Trasury Bills or the Treasury Bonds the only *fixed income investments*, so most investors transfer liquidity from their bank deposits to Treasury Bills or Bonds aiming at protecting their savings.

3.Substitutability Among Debt and Equity Securities

The substitutability for or complementarity of one asset to another is analyzed using Friedman's approach (see Friedman 1987) to describe the changes in investors' choices occurring when there are changes in expected asset returns. The model suggested is a discrete time model to analyze this aspect of portfolio behavior.

Assuming the investor's single period objective at time t is derived by the maximization of expected utility function $U(W_{t+1})$ which is a function of his/her wealth at time $t + 1$, we define:

$$\max_{\alpha_t} E[U\,(W_{t+1})]s.t. \sum_t \alpha_t = 1 \qquad (1)$$

According to standard portfolio literature for a given utility function, and assuming rates of return, r_t, normally distributed, the resulting optimal asset demand exhibits the properties of homogeneity in total wealth and linearity in the expected asset returns and is given by

$$\alpha_t^* = B\,(r_t + 1) + \pi \qquad (2)$$

where B is an appropriate transformation of the variance-covariance matrix of returns Ω:

$$B = \left\{ \frac{-U'\,[E\,(W_{t+1})]}{W \cdot U''\,[E\,(W_{t+1})]} \right\} \cdot \left[\Omega^{-1} - \left(1'\Omega^{-1}1\right)^{-1} \Omega^{-1}11'\Omega^{-1} \right] \qquad (3)$$

and

$$\pi = \left(1'\Omega^{-1}1\right)^{-1} \cdot \Omega^{-1} \cdot 1 \qquad (4)$$

This first solution is obtained assuming there is no risk free asset in the portfolio. In this case variance-covariance matrix Ω is of full rank. Alternatively, in the presence of a risk free asset bearing return r^f it is necessary to partition the asset demand system. In this second case the solution to problem 1 is given by

$$\alpha_t^* = B\left(r_t^e - r_t^f \cdot 1 + 1\right) \tag{5}$$

where

$$B = \left\{\frac{-U'\left[E\left(W_{t+1}\right)\right]}{W \cdot U''\left[E\left(W_{t+1}\right)\right]}\right\} \cdot \Omega^{-1} \tag{6}$$

and the optimum portfolio share for the risk free asset is just $1 - \alpha_t^* 1$.

The asset demands obtained using this solution are each proportional to the investor's wealth, and they depend linearly on the associated expected returns. Furthermore, the budget constraint cause the asset demands to be linearly dependent so that the matrix $B = (\beta_{i,j})$ and vector π satisfy the adding up constraints

$$\beta_j \cdot 1 = 0 \rightarrow \forall j \tag{7}$$

$$\pi' \cdot 1 = 1 \tag{8}$$

This first approach to analyze the substitutability between financial securities in the Italian market relies on very strong assumptions like 1) the normality of return rates; 2) the constant relative risk aversion and 3)independence from the intertemporal dynamics of portfolio choice. On the other hand, this simple and manageable approach provides, by a transformation of the variance-covariance matrix, an estimation of the substitutability or complementarity between two different assets.

According to the model suggested here, substitutability or complementarity among securities in investors' portfolios basically depends on the variance-covariance structure of the returns that investors associate with these assets. Since we do not have this variance-covariance matrix, we assume that observed data for rates of return during the last eight years could be used to approximate investors' preferences.

In Table 9 the transformation of Ω, computed on the basis of the variance covariance matrix of the five asset returns reported in Table 1 is shown. The main interest is focused on the off diagonal elements of Table 9 which describe the substitutability or complementarity of debt and equity securities. The element β_{ij} measures the response of the demand for security i to changes in the expected return of security j. The theoretical assumption is that all assets are gross substitutes so the empirical analysis tries to estimate the magnitude of substitutability.

Table 9: Portfolio Responses Implied by Variance Covariance structures- No risk free asset- 1987:1994

	r_{SB}	r_{FRN}	r_{CDB}	r_E	r_{BD}
SB	12.84				
FRN	-8.17	7.99			
CDB	-0.87	-2.22	5.96		
E	0.05	-0.01	0.039	0.002	
BD	-3.86	2.41	-2.87	-0.05	4.37

Table 9 shows that the five categories of financial assets considered, according to the rate of returns structure, are basically all gross substitutes. Complementarity is observed between equities and straight bonds, equities and corporate debt, and between floating rate note instruments and bank deposits. Corporate debt are largely substitutes with floating rate note instruments and with bank deposits, while straight bonds are mainly substitutes with bank deposits and floating rate note instruments. It should be pointed out how the actual investors' preferences, measured by correlations between asset shares in table 8, confirm only substitutability between Straight Bonds and Floating Rate Notes or Straight Bonds and Bank Deposits, while opposite results are found for Corporate Debt securities which according to the actual shares should be complementary.

Table 10: Portfolio Responses Implied by Variance Covariance structures for Italian Treasury Securities- 1989:1994

	r_{BOT}	r_{CCT}	r_{BTP}	r_{CTO}
Bot	8.108			
CCT	-6.438	9.056		
BTP	3.548	-10.774	28.902	
CTO	-5.218	8.156	-21.674	18.738

In Table 10, according to equation 3, the portfolio responses implied by the variance-covariance matrix of the Italian Treasury securities is reported. It is interesting to notice that all assets, Bot, BTP, CCT and CTO result as being gross substitutes with the only exception for Bot and BTP which are complementary, confirming the idea that the two assets, both bearing fixed inetrest rate, play a crucial role in Italian investors' choices and most of the times are both included in the portfolio.

Table 11: Elasticities according to the Beta coefficients of Table 9

	r_{SB}	r_{FRN}	r_{CDB}	r_E	r_{BD}
r_{SB}	2.24				
r_{FRN}	-1.53	1.75			
r_{CDB}	-0.50	-1.50	3.74		
r_E	0.02	-0.004	0.001	-0.000	
r_{BD}	-0.99	0.72	-0.80	0.001	0.26

According to the optimal marginal responses of Table 9 it is possible to derive the associated elasticities of substitution defined as

$$\epsilon_{ij} = \frac{dA_i}{dr_j^e} \cdot \frac{r_j^e}{A_i} = \beta_{ij} \cdot \frac{r_j^e}{\alpha_i} \qquad (9)$$

where r_j^e and α_i are the observed average return of asset j and portfolio share of asset i, respectively. Table 11 shows elasticities according to 9, we may notice that most of their values are all less than 1, indicating portfolio shares of all assets that display a well-known adjustment sluggishness in the short run, with the only exception for $\epsilon_{FRN,SB} = -1.53$ and $\epsilon_{CDB,FRN} = -1.50$ confirming the high substitutability of FRN with SB and with CDB. In other words, households seem to change their portfolio composition only in response to significant changes in return rates that are not very likely from month to month. From the way elasticities are calculated, we know that their values are strongly correlated with those of matrix B. Indeed, most of the elasticities have the same sign and relative magnitude of coefficients β_{ij}. Differences in the sign of β_{ij} and ϵ_{ij} emerge because r_j^e can be negative, as is the case for equities.

If we consider the presence of a risk free asset (Table 12), assuming the risk free asset is bank deposits, and apply transformation 6 to the variance-covariance matrix we see that, in this case as well, not all assets are perfectly gross substitutes. As in the case of no risk free assets, equities do not result as being gross substitutes with other financial assets[3].

---

[3]In the presence of a risk free asset, Blanchard and Plantes (1977) have shown that a necessary condition for gross substitutability of all assets is that partial correlations among asset returns not be negative. Indeed, if we look at partial correlation coefficients reported in Table 3 we notice a strong correspondence with our previously calculated β_{ij} coefficients.

Table 12: Portfolio Responses Implied by Variance Covariance structures- with Risk free asset- 1987:1994.

	r_{SB}	r_{FRN}	r_{CDB}	r_E
SB	6.811			
FRN	-5.211	5.625		
CDB	0.585	-2.714	4.539	
E	0.022	0.009	0.003	0.002

The transformation matrix B is obtained assuming the relative risk aversion for the Italian market could be well approximated by 0.5[4]. According to this matrix the optimal portfolio composition obtained using equation 2 shows very little, if any, congruence with households' actual asset allocation (see Table 13).

Table 13: Optimal Portfolio Composition according to table 9

	Optimal	Actual
ST	77.19	29.56
FRN	-87.09	27.53
CDB	97.07	8.94
E	0.26	13.86
BD	12.20	20.11

The optimal portfolio shares of the five asset aggregates indicate negative holdings of floating rate notes and the largest share of holdings in corporate securities, while straight securities have the largest positive share (29.6%) of households' observed portfolio and corporate securities the lowest (8.9%). A large discrepancy between the observed data and the optimal shares is also obtained using higher risk aversion coefficients. This result shows how the model described by equation 2 fails to represent Italian investors' behavior[5] In order to

---

[4]See Giraldi, Hamaui and Rossi, 1992.

[5]A different aggregation of assets according to a time horizon criteria is suggested. This allows us distinguish four main categories of assets: *Short-Term Debt* (S) including all open market debt instruments maturing in less than one year (basically T-Bills); *Medium and Long-Term Securities* (ML) including all other debt instruments as corporate debt, floating rate notes and straight bonds; *Bank Deposits* (BD) and *Equities* (E) as above. According to this alternative disaggregation of assets, Equities are complementary to the other three assets, while medium and long-term debt largely substitute with short-term securities having an elas-

get a better understanding of household preferences we have to take into account other factors affecting their portfolio decisions. Our idea, to be developed in a future paper, is to define a model which incorporates the existence of different risk aversion coefficients among Italian investors. At a first stage improvements may be realized collecting, where possible, data on different sectors of private investors and differencing between institutional and personal investors and studying a *segmented* relative risk aversion.

4. Understanding the Portfolio Behavior of Italian Investors

The approach used in Section 1 stems from a maximization of expected utility which is the only criterium taken into acoount by investors in the portfolio selection. A generalization of this approach is needed when means of payment, like bank deposits, are also included among the assets. A representation of asset demand which takes into account the need for means of payment is obtained by following Tobin's theory of money demand and using a linear generalization of equation 2:

$$\alpha_t^* = B(r_t^e + 1) + \delta(\frac{Y_t}{W_t}) + \lambda p_{t-1} + \pi \tag{10}$$

where $\frac{Y}{W}$, the ratio of income to financial wealth, is a proxy for the demand of means of payment, p is the inflation rate and should account for errors in the computation of real interest rates. Finally, δ and λ are two vectors of coefficients. Full Information Maximum Likelihood estimates of equation systems 10 are reported in Table 14.

We note that the model fits our observations in a satisfactorily way. R^2 vary between 0.91 in the case of straight bonds, and 0.55 in the case of equities, but uniformly low Durbin-Watson statistics indicate that residuals display significant serial correlation in all five equations. 32 out of 40 coefficients are statistically significant, however a comparison of the estimated marginal response values $\widehat{\beta_{ij}}$ with the implied optimal responses in Table 9 shows some remarkable differences. First, we observe that $\widehat{B}$ is not simmetric as we had for B; secondly, in many cases the magnitude of $\widehat{\beta_{ij}}$s is different from that of β_{ij}s. Only when

---

ticity of substitution $\epsilon_{S,ML} = -0,306$ and with bank deposits with an elasticity $\epsilon_{BD,ML} = -0,421$. However, the optimal portfolio allocation is still far from the observed allocation.

Table 14: Portfolio Responses Estimated from Model described by equation 11

	β_{ST}	β_{FRN}	β_{CDB}	β_E	β_{BD}	R^2	D.W.
ST	0.75	-0.49	1.55	-3.43	0.043	0.91	0.37
	(3.86)	(-2.35)	(5.51)	(-7.70)	(6.60)		
FRN	-0.45	0.28	-0.71	2.32	-0.03	0.89	0.43
	(-3.26)	(1.90)	(-3.53)	(7.34)	(-6.41)		
CBD	-0.05	-0.01	-0.08	0.09	-0.001	0.86	0.54
	(-1.93)	(-0.38)	(-2.01)	(1.53)	(-1.14)		
BD	-0.24	-0.006	-0.55	1.14	-0.007	0.77	1.38
	(-2.11)	(-0.05)	(-3.25)	(4.60)	(-1.97)		
E	-0.009	0.23	-0.22	-0.125	-0.004	0.55	0.47
	(-0.31)	(6.86)	(-4.59)	(-2.03)	(-4.32)		

the sign of $\widehat{\beta_{ij}}$s is taken into account, we note that it is the same of β_{ij}s in the 50% of the cases. The uniformly low Durbin Watson statistics is not surprising if we consider that the model is estimated on monthly data. As is well known in presence of transaction costs, it is very unlikely that full realignment of assets holdings to expected returns occurs within a month, especially in the presence of equities whose prices register occasional large moves which may cause a sudden shift of assets shares. A largely used model of portfolio adjustment under transaction costs is the multivariate *partial adjustment model*:

$$\alpha_t - \alpha_{t-1} = \Theta(\alpha_t^* - \alpha_{t-1}) \tag{11}$$

where α_t^* describes the equilibrium asset holdings, which in expression 10 is defined by α_t^*; and Θ is a matrix of adjustment coefficients. Using α_t^* to estimate the equilibrium asset holdings the partial adjustment model becomes:

$$\alpha_t - \alpha_{t-1} = \Phi(r_t^e + 1) + \psi(\frac{Y_t}{W_t}) + \eta p_{t-1} + \omega - \Theta\alpha \tag{12}$$

where

$$\Phi = \Theta B \tag{13}$$
$$\psi = \Theta\delta \tag{14}$$
$$\eta = \lambda\Theta \tag{15}$$

$$\omega = \Theta\pi \tag{16}$$

Here Θ is a matrix of adjustment coefficients with columns satisfying an "adding up" constraint so that the column of matrices Φ, ψ and vector η all satisfy the adding up constraint, while ω satisfies the constraint $\omega'1 = 1$.

Table 15: Immediate Marginal Responses of Asset Demands according to Model described by equation 12

	Φ_{ST}	Φ_{FRN}	Φ_{CDB}	Φ_E	Φ_{BD}	R^2	D.W.
ST	-0.05	0.11	0.13	0.04	-0.04	0.28	1.98
	(-0.81)	(1.47)	(-1.24)	(0.26)	(-1.38)		
FRN	-0.01	0.06	-0.06	0.40	0.002	0.43	1.68
	(0.24)	(0.75)	(-0.51)	(2.59)	(0.90)		
CBD	-0.04	0.03	-0.04	0.06	-0.001	0.39	2.24
	(-2.13)	(1.16)	(-0.08)	(1.06)	(-0.15)		
BD	0.09	-0.27	0.29	-0.41	0.002	0.47	2.12
	(0.84)	(-1.99)	(1.44)	(-1.67)	(0.33)		
E	0.014	0.08	-0.07	-0.08	-0.0003	0.53	2.26
	(0.92)	(4.05)	(-2.51)	(-1.83)	(-0.46)		

Table 15 reports the results of model 11 computed using Full Information Maximum Likelihood method on the set of monthly data for the five asset categories. Summary statistics for each equation, estimated coefficients and $t - statistics$ for matrix Φ of immediate marginal responses of asset demands to expected returns are shown in Table 15. The overall fit properties of all five equations do not significantly improve with the application of the partial adjustment model. Serial crrelations seem to be reduced, on the other hand we get much lower R^2s and lower statistical significance of the Φ coefficient. If we compare Table 16, where the matrix of equilibrium marginal responses B^* is reported (solved following 13, $B^* = \Phi^{-1}\Theta$), with Table 15 we can notice 10 out of 11 statistically significant coefficients have the same sign. If we compare these estimated equilibrium asset demand responses with values obtained by transformation 3, we notice very little resemblance to the implied optimal responses of Table 9. Only 12 coefficients out of 25 show the same sign while their magnitude is very different. Estimates of model 10 and 12, using the alternative asset aggregations, provide no satisfactory results either. The overall properties of fit for the four equations look very poor, low $R^2 s$ and high serial correlations are observed even applying model 12.

Table 16: Portfolio Responses Estimated from the Model described by equation 12

	β_{ST}	β_{FRN}	β_{CDB}	β_E	β_{BD}
ST	-0.005	0.103	-0.132	-0.48	-0.002
	(0.06)	(1.07)	(-1.02)	(-2.69)	(-0.98)
FRN	-0.043	-0.003	-0.06	0.799	0.0004
	(-0.45)	(-0.02)	(-0.39)	(3.59)	(0.12)
CBD	-0.043	0.139	-0.27	0.447	-0.003
	(-0.95)	(2.55)	(-3.53)	(4.14)	(-1.71)
BD	-0.123	0.452	-0.82	1.135	-0.009
	(-1.05)	(3.17)	(-4.29)	(4.05)	(-2.25)
E	-0.006	0.029	-0.051	0.077	-0.0006
	(-0.79)	(2.93)	(-3.85)	(3.98)	(-2.00)

In summary neither estimates for model 10 nor those for model 12 yield a satisfactory representation of Italian asset demand for the period 1987-94. In the next section we examine if it is plausible to assume that the stochastic structure of asset returns shown in Table 1 and Table 3 accurately reflects the perceptions of Italian investors.

Overall results seem to not support model 11 and suggest that a richer specification be tried which allows for some kind of dynamic adjustment of households' portfolios.

5.The Dynamic of Asset Returns During the Last Decade

The analysis of portfolio responses to expected return variations based on the expected utility maximization model relies on the assumption of stationary rates of return. The basic assumption is that economic agents on average accurately know the relevant properties of the world in which they live, and more importantly it assumes that these properties are stationary. The variance–covariance matrix usually reflects the stochastic structure of the real rate of returns for the observed period, but it can only be obtained ex post and may show a varying structure if computed over a different subperiod. It may be helpful to examine how stable the sample properties of asset returns summarized in Table 1 are, considering the rate of returns over subsamples of approximately three years.

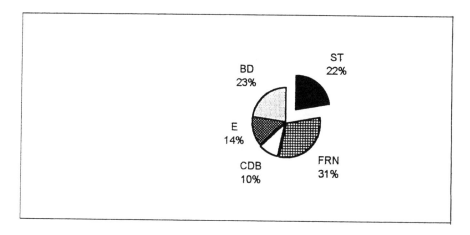

Figure 2. Assets Shares on January 1987

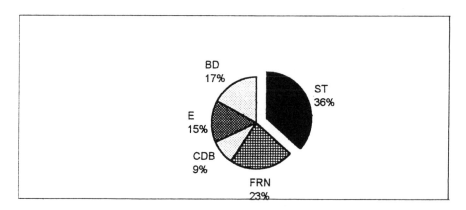

Figure 3 Assets Shares on October 1994

A first description of the change which occurred in the variance-covariance structure of returns is obtained in Figure 2 and 3. We note an investor tendency to move assets from safe bank deposits towards other safe financial assets, mainly government securities. On average bank deposits accounted for 23% of household financial assets in 1987, while 53% of wealth was held in low risk securities, mainly straight bonds and floating rate notes. In 1994 bank deposits represented 17% of households' portfolios, while low risk securities accounted for 59%. A change in household preferences also occurred between straight and floating rate instruments: in 1987 FRNs represented 31% of household holdings, while only 23% in 1994. This seems to confirm that a change occurred in the Italian rates of return structure over the observed period, partly due to the introduction of new and more sophisticated instruments (the 10-year and 30-year BTPs), and partly to a complex domestic economic and political situation.

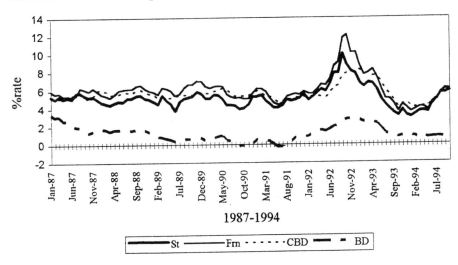

Figure 4.Assets Rates of Return. 1987-94

Table 17 reports average returns and variance covariance structures for three subsamples 1) 1987:01-1989:08, 2) 1989:09-1992:02, 3) 1992:03-1994:10. It is interesting to notice that in subsample 3 rates of return for each asset show higher mean values (with equities showing positive average return) and higher volatility, as can also be observed in Figure 4, and therefore changes in the covariances between the five asset categories are expected with respect to the other two subperi-

Table 17: Subsamples: Mean Real Returns and Variance-Covariance Structure for the Five Categories of Assets

Mean Returns	r_{FRN}	r_{ST}	r_{CDB}	r_E	r_{BD}
I Subsample:					
1987:01-89.08	5.02	5.86	5.52	-4.35	1.63
II Subsample:					
1989:09-92:02	4.93	5.74	5.44	-12.63	0.46
III Subsample:					
1992:03-94:10	5.56	6.48	5.90	16.58	1.53

Variance Covariance

I Subsample: 1987:01-89:08

	r_{FRN}	r_{SB}	r_{CDB}	r_E	r_{BD}
r_{FRN}	0.168				
r_{SB}	0.075	0.137			
r_{CDB}	0.008	0.033	0.097		
r_E	0.143	0.507	-2.238	529.393	
r_{BD}	0.145	-0.052	-0.005	0.613	0.576

II Subsample: 1989:08-92:02

	r_{FRN}	r_{SB}	r_{CDB}	r_E	r_{BD}
r_{FRN}	0.290				
r_{SB}	0.307	0.469			
r_{CDB}	0.089	0.184	0.148		
r_E	4.260	6.994	2.658	245.038	
r_{BD}	0.168	0.185	0.069	4.366	0.171

III Subsample: 1992:03-94:10

	r_{FRN}	r_{SB}	r_{CDB}	r_E	r_{BD}
r_{FRN}	3.490				
r_{SB}	4.369	5.797			
r_{CDB}	2.224	3.028	2.049		
r_E	-48.084	-56.374	-26.835	855.544	
r_{BD}	1.218	1.708	1.030	-15.525	0.612

Table 18: Subsamples: Portfolio implied responses according to the Variance-Covariance Structure for each subperiod

I Subsample: 1987:01-89:08

	r_{FRN}	r_{SB}	r_{CDB}	r_E	r_{BD}
FRN	14.09				
SB	-10.84	14.87			
CDB	1.49	-7.64	8.09		
E	0.02	-0.05	0.04	0.002	
BD	-4.76	3.66	-1.99	-0.01	3.11

II Subsample: 1989:08-92:02

	r_{FRN}	r_{SB}	r_{CDB}	r_E	r_{BD}
FRN	22.78				
SB	-15.96	17.52			
CDB	8.15	-10.14	11.85		
E	0.24	-0.27	0.20	0.01	
BD	-15.21	8.85	-10.05	-0.18	16.59

III Subsample: 1992:03-94:10

	r_{FRN}	r_{SB}	r_{CDB}	r_E	r_{BD}
FRN	5.26				
SB	-2.64	2.67			
CDB	0.29	-1.20	3.07		
E	0.07	0.01	-0.005	0.004	
BD	-2.99	1.15	-2.16	-0.087	4.09

ods. For instance, during the period 1992:02-1994-10, the standard deviation of floating rate note instruments is 1.86, while it was 0.40 during the period 1987:01-1989:08, and equities show high negative covariances while in the other two subperiods equity's returns seem to positively covariate with other instruments. Investors confronted with higher average real returns, but also with more volatile real returns. Therefore, during the period 1992-1994 changes in investor preferences might have occurred.

Table 18 shows the substitutability among the five categories of assets for the three subsamples.It is interesting to notice how for each subperiod floating rate notes result complementary with corporate debt securities while these two instruments show substitutability when considered for the overall period (Table 9). FRN and Corporate bonds show also high elasticity in the second subperiod with $\epsilon_{FRN,CBD} = 4.24$ It should also be pointed out that unlike the elasticities computed for the entire period (Table 11) elasticities for each subperiod result much higher and in some cases with opposite signs. Straight bonds result highly complementary with bank deposits for each subperiod, confirming the italian's attitude to consider Government debt securities an alternative to bank deposits and the "only" *fixed income investment*. Finally, in the third subperiod equities resul complementary with Straight Bonds agains substitutability shown in the other two subperiods. Magnitude of the coefficients $\beta_{i,j}$ largely varies among the three subperiods, lower values are found in the third subperiod confirming a change in the covariance structure.

Changes which occurred in the stochastic rates of return structure make the model suggested in equation 2 inadequate for describing Italian investors' asset demand and these changes may account for the observed discrepancies between the actual and the implied optimal portfolio allocation, among the five categories of assets.

6.Conclusions

In this paper we have studied Italians households' asset demand during the period 1987-1994 trying to empirically describe Italian investors' decisions in a period of large financial market innovations. We first adopted Friedman's approach to describe substitutability and complementarity between debt and equity securities using the powerful implications of mean variance portfolio with constant relative risk aversion. This simple, straightforward approach does not succeed in describing

Italian investors behavior: if we look at the theoretical optimal asset allocation we find very little resemblance with the actual portfolio composition observed during the analyzed period. This can be mainly due to

- the constant risk aversion assumption which does not succeed in describing different investor attitudes;

- the assumption of a Normal distribution for all rates of return, while most Treasury securities cannot be assumed to follow a Normal distribution;

- the presence of short sales in the model, while the households' assets holdings are all naturally positive.

The estimation of marginal responses of asset demand to changes in rate of returns has been exploited using some generalization of the simple portfolio approach, while trying to get a better fit of the actual data. Results were basically unsatisfactory, since the overall properties of the fit were very weak. A partial adjustment model does not provide better results either. We believe that some of the assumptions upon which theoretical models are built need to be relaxed. In particular, the assumption of constant risk aversion needs to be relaxed, especially in a context were there is a major concentration of large groups of investors which may be characterized by different risk aversion coefficients.

The aim of a future paper will be to derive a model that succeds in better describing Italian asset demands in the view of efficient financial instruments designing by the Italian Treasury. This could be realized 1) releasing the assumption of unique relative risk aversion for the entire private sector- i.e. studying agent heterogeneity; and 2)introducing various type of household debt in order to get a more appropriate disaggregation of financial net worth.

Aknowledgment: This research was partially funded by MURST 40% 1992, and CNR 95.01736.ct10

References

[1] Angelini,P.& Hendry, D.F., Rinaldi, R. (1994) An Econometric Analysis of Money Demand in Italy. *Temi di Discussione* n.219 Bank

of Italy WP.

[2] Bawa,V.S., Brown,S.J., Klein, R.W.,(1979) Estimation Risk and Optimal Portfolio Choice. North Holland. Amsterdam.

[3] Calcagnini G., (1992) Debito Pubblico e decisioni di portafoglio. Quali i riflessi sulle imprese italiane? *Moneta e Credito*, Vol. XLV n.180.

[4] Epstein,L.G., Zin S.E.,(1989) Substitution, Risk Aversion, and the Temporal Behavior of Consumption and Asset Returns: A Theoretical Framework. *Econometrica*, Vol.57,N.4

[5] Friedman, B.M.,(1985) The substitutability of Debt and Equity Securities.in Friedman ed. Corporate Capital Structure in the U.S.. NBER. Chicago.

[6] Giraldi C., Hamaui R., and N. Rossi, (1992) Vincoli istituzionali e differenziali di rendimento delle attività finanziarie in Ricerche applicate e modelli per la politica economica. Banca d'Italia.

[7] Grauer, R.R., Hakansson, N.H.,(1985) Returns on Levered, Actively Managed Long-run Portfolios of Stocks, Bonds and Bills, 1934-1983. *Financial Analyst Journal*, Sep.24-43

[8] Guiso, L. Jappeli, T., Terlizzese, D.,(1992), Earnings, Uncertanty and Precautionary Savings. *Journal of Monetary Economics* 30, 307-337. North Holland- Amsterdam.

[9] Haliassos, M. and Bertaut, C. (1995) Why do so Few Hold Stocks. *Economic Journal*. to appear.

[10] Holmer, M. Dafeng, Y. and Zenios, S. (1993) Designing Callable Bonds using Simulated Annealing. Wharton School WP 93-07-02.

[11] Scalia, A. (1993) La Microstruttura del Mercato dei Titoli di Stato. *Temi di Discussione*, 208 Bank of Italy WP.

[12] Singleton, K.J.(1990) Specification and Estimation of Intertemporal Asset Pricing Models. in Handbook of Monetary Economics (Friedman, M. and Hahn, F. editors) Elseiver Science Publisher. 584-626.

[13] Urich, T.J.,(1993) Institutional Characteristics of the Italian Government Bond Market. Money Market Center. *Banker Trust Company-WP* n.109. New York.

Italian Term Structure Movements: the Appropriateness of a Multinomial Model [1]

Adriana Gnudi[2]

[2] Istituto di Scienze Statistiche e Matematiche " M. Boldrini", University of Milano, Italy.

Abstract. In this paper we want to verify, empirically, the appropriateness of a multinomial model to describe the Italian term structure. Using the methodology suggested by Bliss and Ronn (1989), we study the empirical perturbation functions which describe the term structure evolution over the period 1990-1994. A classification of these functions is obtained using an unconstrained regression with four exogenous variables. Finally, some considerations on the significance of the chosen state variables and on the number of perturbation functions needed to describe the Italian market are presented.

Keywords. term structure, multinomial model.

1. Introduction

Extensions and criticisms to the Ho-Lee model (1986) appear in several papers, the most relevant are provided by Bliss and Ronn (1989) and Flesaker (1993). In a previous work, Abaffy et al. (1994) proposed a generalization of the Ho-Lee binomial model focusing on the suitability of a multinomial model to describe the movements of the term structure of interest rates for the Italian market.

Giacometti et al. (1994) and Bertocchi et al. (1995) tested the Ho-Lee model for the Italian market and showed how the use of fixed values of the binomial probability, π, and the short term volatility, δ, may reduce the appropriateness of the model for the italian market. On the contrary, the multinomial model allows to have different paths at each time, i.e. a changing number of perturbation functions, and non constant value of short-term volatility. In the present work we address this latter question and we look for a strategy to identify the optimal number of different perturbation functions.

[1] The work has been developed in the framework od SIGE 1994-95 and CNR n.94. 00538.CT11 and 95.00710.CT01 grants.

Section 2. recalls the multinomial model and outlines the main theorems, Section 3. illustrates the methodology used for the classification of the perturbation functions. In Section 4 the empirical results, supporting the appropriateness of a pentanomial model for the Italian market are shown. Some conclusions follow.

2. A multinomial model for pricing interest-rate derivative securities

The multinomial model proposed in Abaffy et al. (1994) is a generalization of both the well-known binomial model of Ho-Lee (1986) and the trinomial model of Bliss and Ronn (1989). It consists in the possibility not only to have k paths from each node, with $k > 2$, but also to allow k to change from time t to time $t + 1$.

The typical assumptions valid for the Ho-Lee model are still assumed:

(1) Zero-coupon bonds with maturities $T = 1, \ldots, m$ are traded at discrete points in time $t = 0, \ldots, n$.

(2) The zero-coupon bond market is frictionless.

(3) At time t, there are several possible discount functions, denoted by $P_t^i(T)$ with $t = 0, \ldots, n; i = 0, \ldots, k_t; T = 1, \ldots, m$.

(4) The transition behaviour of a discount function is characterized by perturbation functions $h_t^i(T)$ which quantify the uncertainty in the evolution of interest rates.

Moreover, it is shown that the model is consistent with the properties of:

(5) Path independence, i.e. starting from a given discount function at time $t = 0$, the same discount function is obtained whatever path is followed along a tree with the only requirement to maintain the number of movements of the same type.

(6) No arbitrage opportunities, i.e. in none of the nodes it is possible to construct a portfolio of zero-coupon bonds with a non-positive price in it and non-negative cash flows (with at least one strictly positive) in each of the $k_t + 1$ possible following states.

Following Ho-Lee notation, the term structure at time t is considered in terms of the implied prices of discount bonds, $P_t^i(T)$, where i denotes the paths that have occurred up to time t, and T is the time to maturity of the pure discount bond. Today's price is equal to the forward price in the previous period times a perturbation function. Thus, the discount functions at time t are given by

$$P_t^i(T) = \frac{P_{t-1}(T+1)}{P_{t-1}(1)} h_t^i(T) \qquad i = 0, \ldots, k_t \tag{1}$$

In Abaffy et al. (1994) k_t is assumed constant along time, thus the index t can be dropped and the following Theorems are proved.

Theorem 1. Let us suppose to be in a market where the term structure movements can be classified in $(k + 1)$ alternatives in the period following the current period $(t - 1)$. In an arbitrage-free context, the perturbation functions can be chosen so as to satisfy the following equation:

$$\sum_{i=0}^{k} h_t^i(T)\pi_t^i = 1 \tag{2}$$

for each t and T where the π_t^i satisfy:

$$\sum_{i=0}^{k} \pi_t^i = 1. \tag{3}$$

Condition of path independence holds only when some constraints on the perturbation functions hold.

Theorem 2. The multinomial model is path-independent if the following $(2k - 1)$ chains of equalities hold:

$$\frac{h_{t+1}^i(T + 1)h_{t+2}^j(T)}{h_{t+1}^i(1)} = \frac{h_{t+1}^{i+1}(T + 1)h_t^{j-1}(T)}{h_{t+1}^{i+1}(1)} = \frac{h_{t+1}^j(T + 1)h_{t+2}^i(T)}{h_{t+1}^j(1)} \tag{4}$$

where $i = 0, ..., k - 1, \quad j = 1, ..., k, \quad i + j = m, \quad m = 1, ..., 2k - 1.$

Corollary 1. For each maturity T the following equations hold

$$h_{t+2}^i(T) = [h_{t+2}^{i-1}(T)h_{t+2}^{i+1}(T)]^2, \qquad i = 1, ..., k - 1 \tag{5}$$

$$\frac{h_{t+2}^{i-1}(T)}{h_{t+2}^{i+1}(T)} = \frac{h_{t+2}^{i-2}(T)}{h_{t+2}^i(T)} = \frac{h_{t+2}^{i-3}(T)}{h_{t+2}^{i-1}(T)} = \cdots \tag{6}$$

In Abaffy et al. (1995) the following theorem is proved.

Theorem 3. The local expectations hypothesis holds if and only if $\pi^i = q^i$ for $i = 0, \ldots, k$, where q is the probability to take the corresponding path.

Note that the aforementioned Theorems can be generalized to the case where k depends on time, thus the multinomial model allows to change the number of perturbation functions from time to time. Moreover, we can allow the perturbation functions to depend on time varying state variables.

In the next section appropriateness of a multinomial model for the Italian market is provided as well as a method to classify the perturbation functions and the significance of the perturbation value on some suitable state variables.

3. A representation of the perturbation functions using Italian data

This analysis is developed according to the idea presented in Bliss and Ronn (1989). The idea is to compare, within a certain period of time, the discount functions, related to two consecutive times $(t-1)$ and t, computed at a fixed maturity T; this allows to evaluate the number of different perturbations needed to describe the behaviour of the Italian market.

From equation (1), we may consider as a reasonable representation of a perturbation function at time t and maturity T, the following function:

$$y(t,T) = \frac{P_t(T)P_{t-1}(1)}{P_{t-1}(T+1)} \qquad (7)$$

where $t = 0, \ldots, n$, $T = 1, \ldots, m$ and $P_t(T)$ is the price at time t of T-period pure discount bond.

Equation (7) describes the perturbation function as:

1. depending on t, chosen a maturity T, or
2. depending on T, given t.

Using BTP (Italian Treasury coupon bonds) weekly prices available on the wire market over the period 1990-1994, we estimate the spot rate function, and consequently the discount function, according to a function based on a modification of the one suggested by Bliss and Ronn (1989) [3].

Given the discount function, we can define $y(t,T)$ as function of t assuming fixed maturity T.

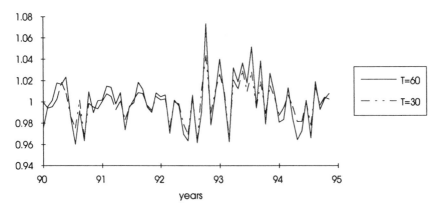

Figure 1. $y(t,30)$, $y(t,60)$ monthly value on $1/1/1990 - 31/12/1994$ period.

---

[3] The approximation function for the spot rate function is

$$r(t) = \beta_1 + \frac{\beta_2(1 - \exp(-t/r_1))}{t/r_1} + \beta_3 \exp(-t/r_2), \quad r_1, r_2 > 0.$$

94

To select a representative maturity T which describes the behaviour of the function for that value of the argument, we computed correlations for curves with different maturities. The estimated correlation between 30 and 60-months maturity is 0.95. Figure 1 shows the functions for these maturities. According to figure 2, where interest rate changes over the period 1990-1994 are reported, we may notice that a trinomial model is not always suitable to describe changes in interest rates: it may succeed in describing the interest rate dynamic only for the first 2 years, while it fails for the remaining period.

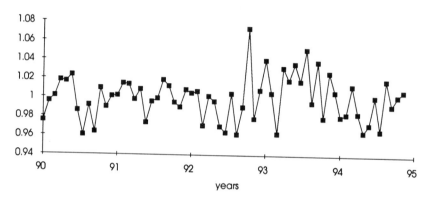

Figure 2. $y(t, 60)$ monthly values on $1/1/1990 - 31/12/1994$ period.

The same result can be shown studying function $y(t, T)$ for given values of t ($t = 37, 38, 39, 40, 42$) letting T vary (figure 3). In figure 3 the functions y are sufficiently apart to suggest the use of a pentanomial model.

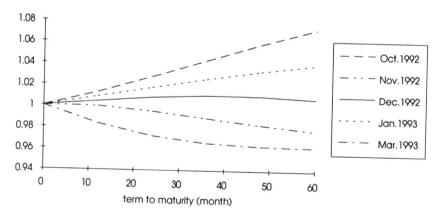

Figure 3. $y(t, T)$ monthly values with $t = 37, 38, 39, 40, 42$
on $1/1/1990 - 31/12/1994$ period.

4. A methodology to classify the perturbation functions

A further step consists in identifying suitable perturbation functions which vary over time depending on the modification of specific state variables and, at the same time, give a best fit of the previous data. Two questions arise:
1. Choose the optimal number of perturbation functions;
2. Classify the data in order to execute the fitting.
As a preliminary approach, using information provided by figures 2 and 3, we select a fixed number of perturbation functions, precisely: 3 for the trinomial model and 5 for the pentanomial model, and, at this stage, we skip the problem of the optimal number.
Concerning the second question, in order to classify each realisation, we extend to the pentanomial model the iterative approach used by Bliss and Ronn (1989) on the trinomial model. In the following we will represent the value $y(t, 60)$ as $y(t)$ and $h_t^i(60)$ as h_i.
An initial classification for the pentanomial model is carried out fixing the size of the central level and of the two intermediate levels.
Thus the classification is modified iteratively until there is no further variation in the classes. The modifications are carried out on the basis of two values:

$$\frac{h_i(t) - y(t)}{\sigma_i} \quad , \quad \frac{y(t) - h_{i+1}(t)}{\sigma_{i+1}}$$

where $i \in \{1, 2, 3, 4, 5\}$, $h_i(t)$ is the predicted value of the perturbation function on state i, σ_i is the standard deviation of the residual $y(t) - h_i(t)$. The value $h_i(t)$ is estimated using an ordinary least square regression based on four state variables: x_1,the three month zero-coupon bond rate as measure of the short-term rate[4], x_2,the term premium defined as the ten-years BTP yield less the short-term rate, x_3,a measure of the hump in the term structure [5] and x_4,the one-month change in the short term rate. We also checked that other variables, like the trading volume, do not add significance to the regression.
We verify a strong dependence of the final classification on the choice of the initial one; in order to guarantee the correctness of the classification, we identify two different methods depending on the choice of the initial levels. According to the first method, as in Bliss and Ronn (1989) for the trinomial model, the initial size of the intermediate level is evaluated using the standard deviation of the two subsets corresponding respectively to $y(t) < 1$ and

---

[4] We use as estimate of the three month zero-coupon bond rate the weighted average of rate in each issue.

[5] A measure of " hump", according with Bliss and Ronn (1989), is defined as the maximum excess, if any, of the interest rate of maturity one,two, ... ten years over the maximum between the three month zero-coupon bond rate and the ten-years BTP yield.

$y(t) > 1$. For the pentanomial model in order to fix the initial size of five levels, we extend this method iterating the first step on the values of the central level.

The second method is based on the optimization of an objective function depending on the parameter R^2 in the regression and on the numbers of observations at each level.

The two methods applied to the trinomial model give the same result, while the second method performes better on the pentanomial model (higher R^2 and " t"-student values). Therefore, to compare the trinomial and pentanomial model, we use the second method.

5. Empirical results

Results of the regression for the trinomial model are shown in Table 1. The state variable coefficients in the regression are statistically significant and similar to those shown in Bliss and Ronn (1989) and (1994).

Table 1

level	1	2	3
n.obs.	8	22	23
c	0.9917 (118.45)	1.0189 (38.20)	1.0514 (58.65)
a_1	-0.5125 (-4.35)	-0.4294 (-1.64)	-0.3936 (-2.37)
a_2	-0.9308 (-2.89)	-0.4313 (-1.25)	-0.4058 (-1.37)
a_3	5.0542 (3.14)	1.2996 (0.47)	-3.7884 (2.1462)
a_4	1.9547 (3.66)	2.4310 (3.84)	2.8206 (5.62)
R^2	0.8661	0.4889	0.7100
R^2 adj.	0.5627	0.1122	0.4259
D-W	2.7384	2.0123	1.3151

In Table 1 values of coefficients (c is the intercept value, a_1, a_2, a_3, a_4 are the coefficients for x_1, x_2, x_3, x_4 state variables) with corresponding "t"-student values are reported. Values of R^2, adjusted R^2 and Durbin-Watson statistic are also reported. In figure 4 the plot of the predicted perturbation function for the trinomial model is provided. In figure 4 we can notice that there are periods in which, there are no observations for the upper level. The values of the estimated perturbation function in this period is very irregular.

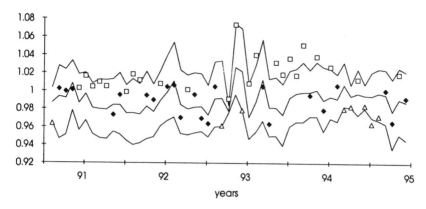

Figure 4. $y(t)$ and $h_i(t)$ monthly values
on the trinomial model on $22/8/1990 - 31/12/1994$.

In this case the trinomial model succeeds very poorly in predict the evolution of the market in the whole period. We try to split the time period and, in order to have a sufficient number of observations, we use perturbation values with two weeks as time unit. A measure of this irregular behaviour can be represented by $\gamma = \sum_{t=0}^{n}(\bar{y}_i - h_i(t))^2/n$ with $i = 1, 2, 3, \ldots$, where $\bar{y}_i$ is the average of observed values in the i-th level.

We first evaluate γ for the whole period, and, to get a better fit, we evaluate γ splitting the time period in two subperiods ($22/8/1990$-$24/6/1992$ and $24/6/1992$-$31/12/1994$).

The results for the whole period and two subperiods are shown in Table 2. Figure 5 and 6 show the plot of the perturbation functions in the second period respectively for the trinomial and pentanomial model.

Table 2

γ values (times 10^5) in trinomial model

level	$22/8/\,90 - 31/12/94$	$22/8/\,90 - 24/6/92$	$24/6/92$-$31/12/94$
1	7.98	17.003	6.208
2	3.59	3.694	3.361
3	10.791	4.391	19.385

Table 2 (cont.)

γ values (times 10^5) in pentanomial model

level	22/8/ 90 − 31/12/94	22/8/ 90 − 24/6/92	24/6/ 92-31/12/94
1	11.986	3.803	2.705
2	3.33	0.254	0.375
3	0.469	0.050	0.363
4	2.061	0.209	0.474
5	19.44	0.5	10.345

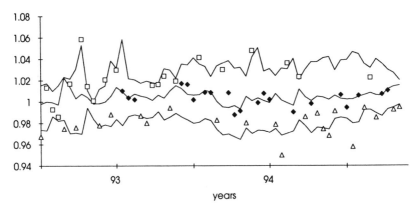

Figure 5. $y(t)$ and $h_i(t)$ values with two weeks time unit on the trinomial model on $24/6/1992 − 31/12/1994$.

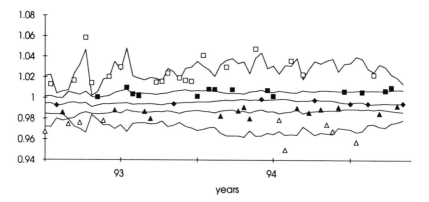

Figure 6. $y(t)$ and $h_i(t)$ values with two weeks time unit on the pentanomial model on $24/6/1992 − 31/12/1994$.

These results suggest the use of a flexible model in which the number of perturbation function can change from time to time. For instance the perturbation functions corresponding to the pentanomial model over the entire period and in the second period seem to be more regular respect to those of the trinomial model (see the results in Table 2), while in the first period the difference is negligible.

6. Conclusions

The appropriateness of a multinomial model for the Italian market looks quite attractive according to the results in table 2 and 3 and the plot of figure 5 and 6. However, further improvements may be introduced finding a strategy for the optimal choice of the number of perturbation functions over time and introducing contraints in the regression.

Acknowledgements - The author wishes to thank the anonimous referees for their careful reading and useful suggestions.

References

Abaffy,J., Bertocchi,M., Gnudi,A., Zambruno, G. (1994) 'A multinomial model for the term structure of interest rate: an optimisation approach in Stochastic Model', *Optimisation Techniques and Computer Applications, Krishna Reddy e al. eds, Wiley Eastern Limited*, 32-43.

Abaffy,J., Bertocchi, M., Gnudi, A. (1995) 'Further insights in the multinomial model', *QDMSIA* , Bergamo, to appear.

Bertocchi,M., Gnudi,A. (1995) 'Pricing puttable bonds in the Italian market', *Proc. 5th AFIR, Int. Colloq.*, CESIAF, v.2, 783-798.

Bliss,R.,Jr., Ronn,E.I. (1989) 'Arbitrage-Based Estimation of Non- stationary Shifts in the Term Structure of Interest Rates',*Journal of Finance, XLIV, n.3*, 599-610.

Bliss,R.,Jr., Ronn,E.I. (1994) 'A nonstationary trinomial model for the valutation of options on treasury bond futures contracts', *Journal of Future Markets, v.14, n.5*, 597-617.

Cox,J.C., Ingersoll,J.E.,JR., Ross,S.A. (1981) 'A Re-examination of Traditional Hypotheses about the Term Structure of Interest Rates',*Journal OF Finance, v. XXXVI, n.4*, 769-799.

Flesaker,B. (1983) 'Testing the Heath-Jarrow-Morton/Ho-Lee Model of Interest Rate Contingent Claims Pricing', *Journal of Financial and Quantitative Analysis, v.28, n.4*, 483-494.

Ho,T.S.Y.,Lee,S. (1986) 'Term Structure movements and Pricing Interest Rate Contingent Claims',*Journal of Finance, v.XLI, n.5*, 1001-1029.

Giacometti,R., Nuzzo,C. (1994) 'Embedded option pricing on interest-rate sensitive securities in the Italian market', *Operations Research Model in Quantitive Finance*,D'Ecclesia, Zenios, Phisica-Velog, Heideberg (1994) 210-234.

Replicating an Option under General Rebalancing Costs

Elisabetta Allevi*

Institute of Econometrics and Mathematical Economics, Catholic University, 20123 Milano, Italy

Abstract. Boyle and Vorst (1992) have proposed a model where option replication is discussed in a discrete time under the hypothesis of proportional transaction costs.
In this paper we introduce an extension of the Boyle-Vorst binomial option pricing model, in the sense that transaction costs are modeled as a non linear and concave function of the amount traded. We obtain an inequality which if satisfied, guarantees the existence and uniqueness of the replicating portfolio.
We add numerical examples and show that particular cases previously discussed in the literature comply with this general framework.

Keywords. Replicating portfolio, transaction costs.

1   Introduction

The analysis presented here extends the existing literature about the problem of hedging options in the presence of proportional transaction costs; this problem has been considered by Leland (1985) and Boyle and Vorst (1992) among others.

A replicating portfolio is such that the value of the portfolio at expiration is exactly equal to that of a call option in all states; the optimal hedge at time zero consists of a long position in the stock and a short position in bonds. As the number of periods increases the weights of this portfolio are rebalanced so that it replicates the payoff of the option conctract up to maturity.

In this paper we consider the model assumed by Cox, Ross and Rubinstein (1979) for the asset price, namely the multiplicative binomial lattice. For example if we consider a three-date model with two asset prices, then we have:

The author wishes to thank prof. G.M. Zambruno for his precious suggestions and comments.

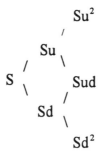

We employ a dynamic hedging strategy to replicate the payoff of a European call option.

The replicating portfolio will be determined backward from the expiration date. In other words the knowledge of Su and Sd, will enable us to determine S. Now, it is evident that it is necessary to know how much is invested in the risky asset and how much is borrowed in order to know the value of the replicant portfolio in each node.

If we indicate with Δ the number of shares held in the replicating portfolio and B the amount borrowed, then the composition of this portfolio at each node will be:

$$\Delta_3, B_3$$

$$\Delta_1, B_1$$

$$\Delta, B \qquad \Delta_4, B_4$$

$$\Delta_2, B_2$$

$$\Delta_5, B_5$$

In this replicating strategy we include transaction costs, that we suppose to incur when shares of the risky asset are traded. It is possible to introduce transaction costs also on bonds, however in this paper this further refinement will not be taken into consideration.

Boyle and Vorst (1992) have proposed a model where option replication is discussed in a discrete time under the hypothesis of transaction costs proportional to the amount traded; namely, transaction costs are of the form $k\delta$, where k is a positive constant and δ is the amount traded, to reach the new position from the old, which in turn is either $|\Delta - \Delta_1|$ or $|\Delta - \Delta_2|$.

The self-financing characteristic of the replicating portfolio is described in the following equations:

(1.1)
$$\Delta Su + Br = \Delta_1 Su + B_1 + k \, |\Delta - \Delta_1| \, Su$$

(1.2) $\Delta Sd + Br = \Delta_2 Sd + B_2 + k \, |\Delta - \Delta_2| \, Sd$.

Thus equations (1.1) and (1.2) show that the value of the portfolio in the up-state or the down-state is sufficient to cover the costs of the rebalanced portfolio, inclusive of transaction costs. In fact the strategy that satisfies both constraints (1.1) and (1.2) is said to be a replicating stategy.

The Boyle - Vorst model and the one discussed in this paper represent transaction costs as functions of absolute value of $\Delta - \Delta_1$ and $\Delta - \Delta_2$, since we don't know if there will be a sale or a purchase of the risky asset: we assume indeed that the costs are the same in both cases.

With positive transaction costs, constraints (1.1) and (1.2) are nonlinear, therefore the existence and uniqueness of a solution (Δ, B) is non trivial.

Theorem 1.1 (Boyle - Vorst 1992) In the construction of a long European call option by dynamic hedging, equations (1.1) and (1.2) have a unique solution (Δ, B), satisfying:

$$\Delta_2 \leq \Delta \leq \Delta_1.$$

Bensaid, Lesne, Pagès and Scheinkman (1992) consider a weaker version where the budget constraint is established in the following way:

$$B_{t-1}(\omega) - B_t(\omega) \geq \varphi \, (\Delta_t(\omega) - \Delta_{t-1}(\omega)) \, S_t(\omega) \qquad \forall \, t \leq T-1, \qquad \forall \, \omega \in \Omega,$$

where $\Omega = \{u, d\}^T$ is the set of paths in a binomial tree, where u stands for an up-state movement and d for a down-state movement, T is the number of periods to maturity, a path is denoted by $\omega = (\omega_1, \omega_2, ..., \omega_T)$ with $\omega_i \in \{u, d\}$. The transaction costs are incorporated in the function φ, defined as

$$\varphi(y) = \begin{cases} (1+k)y & \text{if } y \geq 0 \\ y/(1+k) & \text{if } y < 0 \end{cases}.$$

A similar version is also used in Pelsser-Vorst (1995), they have proposed

$$(\Delta_{t-1}(\omega) - \Delta_t(\omega)) \, S_t(\omega) + r \, B_{t-1}(\omega) - B_t(\omega) \geq k \, |\Delta_{t-1}(\omega) - \Delta_t(\omega)| \, S_t(\omega)$$
$$\forall \, t \leq T-1, \, \forall \, \omega \in \Omega;$$

this means that after each trade some non-negative payoff remains which can be used for immediate consumption.

2 The Model

In the description of strategies that follows a model is proposed similar to the ones previously described; the model, however, is characterized by a more general function, which allows for fixed transaction costs. More precisely we would like to define a function h that mimics transaction costs, both fixed and proportional at a decreasing rate.

There are different forms of transaction costs, that are incurred when a portfolio is rebalanced; for example there are collection costs and porfolio management fees. The portfolio management fee is meant to include the cost of adjustment and the cost of processing information.

The price of adjustment of a portfolio is variable transaction cost, one of its components is represented by fixed fees in the rebalancing of the portfolio.

Furthermore part of transaction costs can be assumed independent from the amount traded, such as the brokerage fees. On the other hand, it is likely that huge transactions are charged proportionally less than smaller ones.

We think that situation can be simulate by the following model.

Total trading costs are represented by a function $h(y)$, where $y \geq 0$ is the amount traded, and we assume that $h(y)$ is

- a non-negative continuous function,
- differentiable for $h > 0$,
- increasing,
- concave,

and $h(0) = 0$.

Now we consider the following equations with $\Delta_2 \leq \Delta \leq \Delta_1$:

(2.1) $\Delta Su + Br = \Delta_1 Su + B_1 + h(\Delta_1 - \Delta)Su$

(2.2) $\Delta Sd + Br = \Delta_2 Sd + B_2 + h(\Delta - \Delta_2)Sd;$

As in the Boyle - Vorst work, we have here a non linear system of equations (2.1)-(2.2); therefore, it is not obvious that this system has a solution.

Define the following function (obtained as the difference of 2.1 and 2.2):

(2.3) $f(\Delta) = \Delta S(u - d) - \Delta_1 Su + \Delta_2 Sd - B_1 + B_2 - h(\Delta_1 - \Delta)Su + h(\Delta - \Delta_2)Sd,$

this function is continuous in $[\Delta_2, \Delta_1]$ and differentiable in (Δ_2, Δ_1), where:

(2.4) $f'(\Delta) = S(u - d) + h'(\Delta_1 - \Delta)Su + h'(\Delta - \Delta_2)Sd.$

Since by assumption

$S(u - d) > 0$, $h'(\Delta_1 - \Delta) Su > 0$, $h'(\Delta - \Delta_2) Sd > 0$ for every $\Delta_2 < \Delta < \Delta_1$,

then $f(\Delta)$ is a function increasing for every $\Delta_2 < \Delta < \Delta_1$ and

$$f(\Delta_2) = (\Delta_2 - \Delta_1) Su - B_1 + B_2 - h(\Delta_1 - \Delta_2)Su,$$
$$f(\Delta_1) = (\Delta_2 - \Delta_1) Sd - B_1 + B_2 + h(\Delta_1 - \Delta_2)Sd.$$

Since f is increasing, the system of equations (2.1)-(2.2) has a solution if

$$f(\Delta_2) < 0 \text{ and } f(\Delta_1) > 0,$$

in other words

$$(\Delta_1 - \Delta_2) Su + h(\Delta_1 - \Delta_2)Su > B_2 - B_1$$
$$(\Delta_1 - \Delta_2) Sd - h(\Delta_1 - \Delta_2)Sd < B_2 - B_1 ;$$

and if we denote $\Delta_1 - \Delta_2 = p \ (> 0)$, and $h(\Delta_1 - \Delta_2) = q \ (> 0)$ we obtain

$$(p - q) Sd < B_2 - B_1 < (p + q) Su,$$

so that

(2.5) $$(p - q) d < \frac{B_2 - B_1}{S} < (p + q) u.$$

These conditions form the basis of an iterative procedure which can be used to obtain the composition of the replicating portfolio, and the previous remarks can be summarized in the following Theorem:

Theorem 2.1 In the construction of an European call option by dynamic hedging, if

$$(p - q) d < \frac{B_2 - B_1}{S} < (p + q) u$$

where $\Delta_1 - \Delta_2 = p \ (> 0)$, and $h(\Delta_1 - \Delta_2) = q \ (> 0)$, then equations (2.1), (2.2) have a unique solution (Δ, B) with $\Delta_2 \leq \Delta \leq \Delta_1$.

In the Boyle -Vorst version we would have

$$B_1 = \Delta Su + Br - \Delta_1 Su - k (\Delta_1 - \Delta)Su$$
$$B_2 = \Delta Sd + Br - \Delta_2 Sd - k(\Delta - \Delta_2)Sd,$$

so that

$$B_1 - B_2 = \Delta S (u - d) - k(\Delta_1 - \Delta)Su + k (\Delta - \Delta_2)Sd - \Delta_1 Su + \Delta_2 Sd.$$

Now consider the following function:

$$g(\Delta) = \Delta S (u - d) - k(\Delta_1 - \Delta)Su + k (\Delta - \Delta_2)Sd - \Delta_1 Su + \Delta_2 Sd$$

for every $\Delta_2 \leq \Delta \leq \Delta_1$, this function is differentiable and for every $\Delta_2 < \Delta < \Delta_1$

$$g'(\Delta) = S\ (u - d) + kSu + k\ Sd\ > 0$$

hence g is increasing in $(\Delta_2\ , \Delta_1)$. Moreover:

$$g(\Delta_2) = \Delta_2 S\ (u - d) - k\ (\Delta_1 - \Delta_2)Su\ -\ \Delta_1 Su + \Delta_2 Sd = (\Delta_2 - \Delta_1)Su - k\ (\Delta_1 - \Delta_2)Su,$$
$$g(\Delta_1) = \Delta_1 S\ (u - d) + k(\Delta_1 - \Delta_2)Sd\ -\ \Delta_1 Su + \Delta_2 Sd = (\Delta_2 - \Delta_1)Sd + k\ (\Delta_1 - \Delta_2)Sd.$$

Therefore, since g is increasing, the following inequality holds:

$$(\Delta_2 - \Delta_1)Su - k\ (\Delta_1 - \Delta_2)Su\ < g(\Delta) < (\Delta_2 - \Delta_1)Sd + k\ (\Delta_1 - \Delta_2)Sd,$$

namely

$$(p\ -\ q)\ d < \frac{B_2 - B_1}{S} < (p\ +\ q)\ u,\quad \text{with}\quad q\ =\ k\ (\Delta_1 - \Delta_2).$$

Therefore we can conclude that Theorem 2.1 is a generalization of Theorem 1.1.

3   Particular Case

We present now a more detailed discussion for a specific function $h(|\Delta - \Delta_i|)$ this will be useful to compare the results of the present model with Boyle-Vorst's.
Let us assume $h(|\Delta - \Delta_i|) = \alpha\ (|\Delta - \Delta_i|)^{1/2}$, where α is a positive constant and $i = 1, 2$. This case is interesting because it verifies the following property

$$\lim_{\Delta \to \Delta_i}\ h'\ (|\Delta - \Delta_i|)\ = \infty,$$

therefore this function is suitable to represent the case of a fixed share and decreasingly proportional transaction costs.
Now if we consider:

$$s_1\ :\ y = k\ |\Delta - \Delta_i|$$
$$s_2\ :\ y = k^*\ |\Delta - \Delta_i|$$

where k and k* are two positive constants, it is possible to compare this model with Boyle- Vorst's, when the proportional constant varies; it is interesting to note, that, as can be seen in the following graphs, in this model, the transaction costs are considerably higher in the case of small transactions than for large ones (cfr. Table 1).

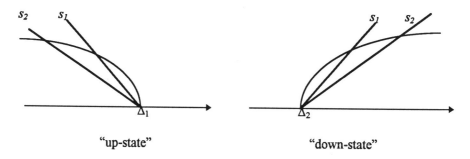

"up-state" "down-state"

In this case equations (2.1), (2.2) become

(3.1) $\Delta Su + Br = \Delta_1 Su + B_1 + \alpha (\Delta_1 - \Delta)^{1/2} Su$

(3.2) $\Delta Sd + Br = \Delta_2 Sd + B_2 + \alpha (\Delta - \Delta_2)^{1/2} Sd$,

hence we obtain

(3.3) $Br = \Delta_1 Su + B_1 + \alpha (\Delta_1 - \Delta)^{1/2} Su - \Delta Su$

(3.4) $(\Delta - \Delta_2)Sd + (\Delta_1 - \Delta)Su + \alpha (\Delta_1 - \Delta)^{1/2} Su - \alpha (\Delta - \Delta_2)^{1/2} Sd = B_2 - B_1$.

If we denote $(\Delta - \Delta_2) = x$, and $A = \dfrac{B_2 - B_1}{S}$ then we have $(\Delta_1 - \Delta) = p - x$ and equation (3.4) becomes

$$u \alpha (p - x)^{1/2} - d \alpha (x)^{1/2} = A - pu + (u - d)x;$$

so that the system (3.1)-(3.2) is equivalent to the following:

$$\begin{cases} y = u\alpha(p - x)^{1/2} - d\alpha(x)^{1/2} \\ y = A - pu + (u - d)x \end{cases}.$$

The previous system has a unique solution if and only if the straight line in the sheaf of parallel lines

$$y = (u - d)x + \beta,$$

has one intersection with the function

$$y = u \alpha (p - x)^{1/2} - d\alpha (x)^{1/2}.$$

It is easy to check, from the following graph, that the lines satisfying this condition range from r_1 to r_2. In this case we obtain again condition (2.6).

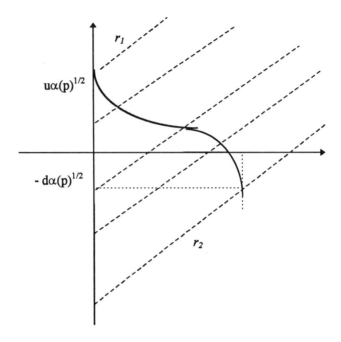

Finally if we utilize the following function

$$h(|\Delta - \Delta_i|) = \alpha \log(1 + |\Delta - \Delta_i|),$$

it is possible to describe the situation where there are no fixed transaction costs but there is again a decreasing proportional share.

4 A Numerical Example

In the following table we compare the results of the present model with those of Boyle-Vorst's. More precisely we compare $y = k (\Delta - \Delta_2)$ with $y = \alpha(\Delta - \Delta_2)^{1/2}$, when k and α take different values. From this numerical example, as well as from the previous graphs, it is evident that the difference between the two models is correlated to transactions costs. As can be seen in Table 1, up to a certain value of transactions, costs are higher in the present model than in the Boyle-Vorst model. The situation is reversed for higher numbers of transacions.

The table presented here is the result of an analysis of the down-state; an analogous table can be obtained for the up-state.

TABLE 1

Parameters : asset price = 100 , $\Delta_1 - \Delta_2 = 1/2$, d = 0.98, u = 1.05,

$\Delta - \Delta_2 \in \{1/16, 1/8, 3/16, 1/4, 5/16, 3/8, 1/2\}$,

the values of α and k have been set so that the costs are the same

for $\Delta - \Delta_2 = 1/4$.

	k = 0.125%	α = 0.0625%	k = 0.5%	α = 0.25%	k = 2%	α = 1%
1/16	0,765625%	1,53125%	3,0625%	6,125%	12,25%	24,5%
1/8	1,53125%	2,165514%	6,125%	8,662%	24,5%	34,648%
3/16	2,296875%	2,6522%	9,1875%	10,6088%	36,75%	42,435%
1/4	3,0625%	3,0625%	12,25%	12,25%	49%	49%
5/16	3,828%	3,423%	15,3125%	13,695%	61,25%	54,783%
3/8	4,59375%	3,75%	18,375%	15,003%	73,5%	60,012%
7/16	5,359375%	4,051%	21,4375%	16,205%	85,75%	64,82%
1/2	6,125%	4,331%	24,5%	17,324%	98%	69,296%

Conclusions

This paper proposes a discrete-time model for replicating an option in presence of transaction costs. In fact we think it is significant to consider the possibility that there are some fixed transaction costs and decreasing proportional.

More precisely this article develops a procedure where transaction costs are represented by a non linear function of the amount traded, but also in this case, in Section 2, we prove that there exists a solution for the "hedge ratio" of the replicating portfolio , which we have verified by the employment of a specif function in the Section 3.

References

Bensaid B., J.P. Lesne, H. Pagès and J. Scheinkman, 1992, "Derivative Asset Pricing with Transaction Costs", *Mathematical Finance*, Vol. 2, .No. 2, 63-86.

Boyle P.P. and T.Vorst, 1992, "Option Pricing in Discrete Time with Transaction Cost", *Journal of Finance*, Vol. 47, No.1,271-293

Cox J.C., S.A.Ross and M. Rubinstein, 1979, "Option Pricing: A Simplified Approach", *Journal of Finance Economics*, Vol. 7, 229-263.

Leland H.E., 1985, "Option Pricing and Replication with Transaction Cost", *Journal of Finance*, Vol.49, 222-239.

Pelsser A. and T. Vorst, 1995, "Transaction Costs and Efficiency of Portfolio Strategies", *Mimeo*.

Linear Programming and Econometric Methods for Bank Efficiency Evaluation: an Empirical Comparison Based on a Panel of Italian Banks

Andrea Resti[*]

Research and Planning Dept., Banca Commerciale Italiana, Via Verri 4, 20121 Milan, Italy

Abstract: Research on bank efficiency has developed in two separate streams: i) econometric studies, aimed at improving OLS estimates with an asymmetric structure for the residuals; ii) Data Envelopment Analysis, a linear programming model for multiple-input/multiple-output firms. These two branches of literature have developed quickly, but separately; now, the lack of correspondence between the rankings dictated by the two approaches suggests more comparative research. In this paper the two techniques have been tested on a common panel of 270 Italian banks, and this parallel application has suggested the following: i) econometric and linear programming results do not differ dramatically, when based on the same data and conceptual framework; ii) when differences arise, they can be explained by going back to the intrinsic features of the models. Moreover, some findings on Italian banks may be of interest also to the international reader: i) the efficiency scores show a high variance; ii) the banking system is split in two, between northern and southern banks; iii) there is a direct (rather than inverse) relationship between productive efficiency and asset quality; iv) the efficiency of Italian banks did not increase over the period 1988-1992.

Keywords: Efficiency, Data Envelopment Analysis, Banking, Frontiers.

1. Motivations and aims of this note

Studies on bank efficiency date back at least to the 60s[1], yet they remain an appealing and up-to-date research area, from both a micro- and a macroeconomic standpoint.

---

[*] I wish to thank Maria Luisa Di Battista,, Mario Comana, Marco Oriani, Agnese Sironi, Emmanuel Thanassolulis, Anna Torriero and an anonymous Referee for their precious comments; Marco Corbellini (AssBank, Milan) and Tim Coelli (New England University, Armidale), for providing me, respectively, with the "Bilbank" database and the Frontier 2.0 software, used for ML estimates; Gianfranco Gambarelli for his constant, warm encouragement. This said, I am the only responsible for all remaining errors.

[1] One might recall some seminal works such as (Greenbaum, 1967a and b) or (Benston, 1965).

From the point of view of the banker, the achievement of efficiency is made crucial nowadays by the squeeze experienced by bank margins in many western countries during the latest years. Credit institutions used to enjoy a wide spread between loan and deposit rates, due to the existence of market fragmentation and local oligopolies, but such advantages are shrinking, as competitive pressures increase. The growth in competition is, to some extent, the result of the deregulation process experienced during the 80s by the main advanced banking systems; removing or reducing the constraints on branch openings (as in the US and in Italy) or the ceilings on deposit rates (in the US and in Japan), making the operating framework of the different bank categories more uniform (this was the case for banks and building societies in the UK), removing constraints on the loan growth: all these are examples of regulatory changes aimed at eliminating competitive barriers among once segmented markets.

Sharper competition - which has made the banks less careful in assessing the creditworthiness of their counterparts, thereby increasing their profitability problems - has stressed the need for credit institutions to understand their productivity levels through quantitative techniques. Moreover, the reduction of regulatory constraints has increased the number of viable alternatives among which the banks can choose: therefore, the search for efficiency has become both more compelling and more complex, and the subjective appraisals of bankers need to be supported by formal schemes of efficiency analysis.

At the macroeconomic level, bank efficiency represents a socially optimal target, since it reduces the costs of financial intermediation, driving down to a physiological level the drainage of real resources due to the transfer of funds from savers to producers.

Consequently, central banks are deeply interested in the accomplishment of operating practices and market equilibria that grant the maximum productive efficiency[2], provided that this does not bring in a natural monopoly which would expropriate the consumers from the advantages due to the reduction in average costs. Of course, given some crisis situations, it may be optimal to postpone the search for efficiency, concentrating on the defence of the system's stability and preventing the dangerous "domino effects" that can arise when the less productive institutions are forced to quit the market in a traumatic way. Nevertheless, the illusory dilemma between efficiency and stability exists only in the short term: when things are put in a wider perspective, then efficiency appears as the only endogenous force which can ensure the future solidity of a banking system.

---

[2] Structure-conduct-performance, relative market power, efficient structure hypothesis, contestable markets (see Stigler, 1964; Berger and Hannan, 1993; Baumol et al., 1982) are just examples of analytic schemes used as guidelines by central bankers.

From the point of view of academic research, efficiency analysis is made an appealing theme by the fact that it developed, in the last twenty years, in two separate streams.

On the one hand, we have econometric studies, aimed at improving the standard OLS estimates with the addition of an asymmetric structure for the residuals, so to account for the distance between empirical observations and the theoretical efficient frontier. Such studies have experienced recent developments, as far as panel data and the estimation of individual inefficiencies are concerned.

On the other hand, more research on efficiency assessment has been based on the Data Envelopment Analysis algorithm for the evaluation of multiple-input/multiple-output firms. This linear programming model has been enriched, during the last fifteen years, by contributions aimed at estimating scale economies, disentangling the technical and allocative profiles of efficiency, setting limits on the economic value of each input and output.

Those two branches of literature experienced a lively development and achieved some remarkable results; yet, this did not prevent them from remaining fairly separate: as pointed out in (Berger et al., 1993), "the lack of correspondence among the efficiency levels and rankings for the different measurement approaches suggests that more research comparing these techniques is needed".

This is the goal of this paper, where the two above-mentioned techniques will be used on a common database of Italian banks. This "parallel application" will suggest some insights on the advantages and drawbacks of the different models. First, we will verify whether the econometric and the linear programming results differ so dramatically, even when built on the same data, and inside a common framework as far as the definition of inputs and outputs is concerned; second, if some notable differences should arise, we will try to trace their origins, going back to the intrinsic features of the various techniques. Finally, the empirical work will suggest some remarks on the amount of inefficiency affecting the Italian banking system, and on its distribution, that may be of some interest also to the international reader.

2. Efficiency in the banking sector: some preliminary remarks

We know that a production plan is called efficient if it is not possible to produce more using the same inputs, or to reduce these inputs leaving output unchanged[3]. This very narrow definition of efficiency can be enhanced when also allocative aspects are considered, that is, when we analyse the respondence between the production plan and the market value of inputs and outputs (see e.g. Kopp, 1981; Kopp and Diewert, 1982; Farrell, 1957). Moreover, duality theory (Diewert, 1974; Shephard, 1970) has shown that, under given conditions

---

[3] See e.g. (Varian, 1990); obviously, this is a definition of efficiency in the sense of Pareto and Koopmans.

(exogenous prices and optimal behaviour of the producer), the properties of the production function (such as subadditivity, that is, scale and scope economies) can be studied indirectly, through cost or profit functions. So, for instance, the cost function

$$C = C(\mathbf{y}, \mathbf{w})$$

gives an indirect representation of the feasible technology, since it indicates the minimum cost of producing an output vector $\mathbf{y}$, given a price vector $\mathbf{w}$ in the input market.

So far the theory. In practice, however, the observable production plans and cost levels do not follow from perfectly rational and efficient decisions; on the contrary, such factors as errors, lags between the choice of the plan and its implementation, inertiae in human behaviours, distorted communications, uncertainty, might cause the so-called x-inefficiency (see Leibenstein, 1966 and 1978) to drive real data away from the optimum. Therefore, estimation procedures must include some "filter" device to get rid of the inefficiency component and isolate the theoretical frontier. Before we take a look at the various techniques that can serve this purpose, through econometric and linear programming tools, some brief remarks must be dedicated to the problem of defining a bank's inputs and outputs[4].

The choice of inputs and outputs variables is stricly dependent on the type of efficiency one wants to assess[5]: in our analysis we shall evaluate banks with regard to their intrinsic profitability, that is, their ability to produce valuable services (including intermediation and other sellable services that make up the banks' gross income) using a limited amount of expensive resources (such as employees or capital).

Inputs and outputs are, by definition, flow variables: since data on physical quantities (such as the number of checks cashed, or loans issued) are not always available, one has to use monetary flows taken from the profit and loss account. Yet, these data have to be adjusted (see Greenbaum, 1967a, b): otherwise, banks operating in fragmented markets, and therefore enjoying higher unit prices, would appear to produce more, since they report a greater income flow.

---

[4] For a more comprehensive survey, see e.g. (Berger and Humphrey, 1990), or (Colwell and Davis, 1992).

[5] As pointed out by a Referee, "if we are looking to compare bank branches on how efficient they are in handling transactions then the inputs could be numbers of staff and expenditure on computerisation while the output variable might be the number of transactions [...]. In contrast, if we are looking to compare bank branches on their ability to attract customers then the input might be the size of the market in which they operate [...], while the output could be the numbers of financial products, such as the loans advanced."

Alternatively, one can resort to stock variables[6] such as the average amount of deposits and loans, since they continuously require (and therefore are a proxy for) the production of payment and liquidity services, and the monitoring of credit decisions. A pivotal issue, throughout the whole literature based on stock measures of banking products, is the debate on the role of deposits: on the one hand, it is argued that they are an input to the production of loans (*intermediation*, or *asset approach*); yet, other lines of reasoning (*value added approach, user cost approach*) suggest that deposits are themselves an output, involving the creation of value added, and for which the customers bear an opportunity-cost (foregoing some more profitable investment alternatives: bank deposit rates are usually lower than money market rates, and sometimes are, or used to be, zero). Putting things in this perspective, it sounds paradoxical to say that depositors incur a cost since they are the providers of an input; moreover, one could wonder why customers are willing to pay fees and charges on something which is not a bank output; finally, it does not look reasonable to exclude from the banks' typical product a market segment (retail deposits) which accounts for about 50% of the operating costs[7] - and a relevant share of the net profits - of credit institutions. For all these reasons, in our empirical analysis, we will follow the latter approach.

3. A quick glance at econometric techniques and linear programming models

The econometric approach to efficiency measurement moves from the standard OLS model, altering the structure of the residual term; this is done to account for the fact that (unless there is noise in the data) all the observed production plans must lie only on one side of the efficient frontier, that is, inside the technically feasible region.

In the first contributions of this kind, it was stated that empirical data could by no means lie above the production function or below the minimum cost line: these were the so-called "pure frontier" deterministic models (see e.g. Aigner and Chu, 1968) where the residuals - strictly *one-sided,* all positive or negative - could be directly used as a measure of productive inefficiency.

---

[6] Stock variables do not necessarily mean monetary aggregates: (Sherman and Gold, 1985) suggests an "accounting approach" based on physical quantities, such as the number of customer deposits, loans, checking accounts, and so on. The results of this criterion might be very different from those based on monetary variables, above all if the banks in the sample differ markedly in the average size of their assets and liabilities; therefore, it is somewhat surprising that (Benston et al., 1982) and (Berger et al., 1987) find out that scale economies by American banks do *not* vary considerably when one switches between the two above-mentioned approaches. Such a result, as pointed out in (Humphrey, 1990), is probably due to a high correlation between the number of accounts and the amounts in US dollars.

[7] See (Humphrey, 1992), based on Functional Cost Analysis data.

Later on, studies like (Afriat, 1972) or (Richmond, 1974) proposed to assign a well-known density function to the residuals, so to be able to make some inference on the estimated values[8]. Even so, deterministic models were very sensitive to the presence of noise in the data, since they did not include a stochastic term to control for random disturbances.

This is why stochastic frontier models (like Aigner et al., 1977; Meusen and Van Den Broek, 1977; Stevenson, 1980) were developed: here, the function to be estimated (e.g. a minimum cost frontier) is supposed to be accompanied by a composite disturbance ε, which in turn can be subdivided in two parts: beside a one-sided component (say u), representing inefficiency as in the deterministic models, we have another term (called v) accounting for noise in the data, and usually distributed as a normal. Therefore, for the i-th producer what we observe empirically is:

$$C_i = C(\mathbf{y}_i, \mathbf{w}_i) + \varepsilon_i = C(\mathbf{y}_i, \mathbf{w}_i) + u_i + v_i$$

The density function[9] for u (which is bound to be non-negative, since it represents extra costs beyond the efficient minimum) is usually a half-normal, a truncated normal, or an exponential distribution; this depends on the *a priori* beliefs of the researcher, on the respondence between such beliefs and sample data, and of course on the tractability of the log-likelihood function that follows from these assumptions.

During the latest years many extensions of the stochastic frontier models have been proposed (among others: Jondrow et al., 1982; Schmidt and Sickles, 1984; Kumbhakar and Hjalmarsson, 1993; Battese and Coelli, 1988). Special care has been paid to the construction of reliable estimators for individual inefficiencies[10]:

in fact, since in these models the sample residuals $\hat{\varepsilon}_i$ summarise both inefficiency and noise, it is necessary to disentangle these two components before one can judge the performance of the single banks in the sample. This is probably one of

---

[8] More precisely, the gamma function was preferred to simpler forms, since it guaranteed the presence of the usual asymptotic properties of maximum likelihood estimators (Schmidt, 1976). It was striking, anyway, that the structure of the residual term, instead of being chosen according to the underlying economic theory, or to its goodness-of-fit on sample data, had to be imposed *a priori* for some statistical properties to exist.

[9] Adding a stochastic term v not only makes the model more realistic, but also allows more freedom in choosing the density function for the inefficiency component u without compromising the asymptotic properties of ML estimators.

[10] Another line of research pertains to the separation of technical and allocative inefficiencies. This can be done either supposing that the two components are uncorrelated, or imposing a certain structure (based on a priori hypotheses) on the link between the two; examples of the two approaches are in (Greene, 1980), (Lovell and Schmidt, 1979 and 1980), (Kumbhakar, 1991).

the areas where panel data have turned most useful[11]: yet, in order to be able to extract information from the panel, the researcher needs to formulate a hypothesis about the evolution (or the steadiness) of individual inefficiencies over the period considered.

Among the most recent models is (Battese and Coelli, 1992), which we now describe briefly, since it will be used in our empirical test. As in [2], the cost level observed for the i-th producer at time t is supposed to "conceal" the true minimum cost frontier $C(.)$, dimmed by an inefficiency term u (positive or zero) and by a noise component v. In symbols:

$$C_{it} = C(\mathbf{y}_{it}, \mathbf{w}_{it}) + u_{it} + v_{it}$$

Moreover, the inefficiency of the banks is supposed to vary in time according to the following law:

$$u_{it} = u_i \cdot e^{-\eta(t-T)}$$

where u_i is the inefficiency level of the i-th producer at time T (the last period considered) and η is an unknown parameter (note that inefficiency decreases with t if $\eta > 0$, increases if $\eta < 0$, keeps steady if $\eta = 0$).

To complete the model, some more hypotheses are needed on the residual terms: the u_is are thought to come from a truncated normal, with unknown mode μ, while the v_{it}s are taken from a normal distribution. Based on this structure, Battese and Coelli derive the analytical form of the log-likelihood function when $C(\mathbf{y}, \mathbf{w})$ is linear in its parameters; moreover, enhancing a result due to Stevenson (1980), they build an estimator for individual inefficiencies ($\hat{u}_{it}$), which is consistent as the number of time-periods considered increases[12].

Using this model, we can proceed from general to specific, verifying (by LR tests or asymptotic t-ratios) the opportunity to switch to simpler models; for example, instead of assuming that full efficiency is the most common behaviour (as it happens when u is forced to be half-normal), it is possible to check whether the mode of the distribution of individual inefficiencies differs significantly from zero, switching to the half-normal model only if it is supported by the data. Moreover, the ML estimator should be more efficient than other consistent estimators when sample residuals agree with the distributional assumptions of the

---

[11] Panel data have also be used (see e.g. Cornwell et al., 1990) to reduce the need for distributional assumptions on the inefficiency term u, giving rise to the so-called *distribution free approach* to the econometric frontier estimation.

[12] This model, developed by its Authors for the estimation of single-output production functions, does not include auxiliary demand equations based on Shephard's lemma.

model[13]. Finally, as mentioned above, this model allows us to compute consistent estimates for the individual inefficiencies, so that we will be able to compare these values to those originated by D.E.A. models.

As an alternative to econometric techniques, linear programming models (Data Envelopment Analysis, or D.E.A.) have been used to approximate the efficient frontier - in a non-parametric way - through an envelope of hyperplanes in the input/output space. The distance between each observed production plan and this approximation of the frontier is then used as a measure of inefficiency.

The basic D.E.A. model (Charnes et al., 1978) implies an arbitrary assumption of constant returns to scale, which was relaxed by (Banker et al., 1984), where a criterion for the evaluation of scale economies was also developed; even so, however, the technically feasible region is required to be convex, a fairly non-trivial assumption.

D.E.A. was developed as a tool for analysing technical efficiency, comparing inputs and outputs without taking into account the different economic value of each of them. Cone-ratio D.E.A. (Charnes et al., 1990) makes it possible to impose a set of constraints on the weights assigned to products and production factors; when these constraints are so tight that they become a set of exact prices, we can use D.E.A. as a non-parametric framework for estimating profit or cost functions (allocative D.E.A. or A.D.E.A., see below).

In D.E.A. models, the efficiency level of a bank (producing an output vector $\mathbf{y}_0$ by means of an input vector $\mathbf{x}_0$, acquired at prices $\mathbf{w}_0$) is evaluated through a linear programming problem; this problem has to be solved once for every bank in the sample. For example, an A.D.E.A. model that we shall use in our empirical test (see Färe et a., 1985; Aly et a., 1990) is based on the solution of the following:

$$\min z_0 - \varepsilon \sum_{r=1}^{s} s_r^+$$

$$s.t. \ 1) \ [\mathbf{y}_1 \ \cdots \ \mathbf{y}_n] \lambda - \mathbf{s}^+ = \mathbf{y}_0$$

$$2) \ \mathbf{w}_0{'}[\mathbf{x}_1 \ \cdots \ \mathbf{x}_n] \lambda = z_0 \mathbf{w}_0{'} \mathbf{x}_0$$

where $\lambda \geq 0$, $\mathbf{s}^+ \geq 0$, ε is an infinitely small positive number and z_0 is unconstrained in sign; the matrices $[\mathbf{y}_1 \ ... \ \mathbf{y}_n]$, $[\mathbf{x}_1 \ ... \ \mathbf{x}_n]$ contain respectively the output and input vectors of the n banks in the sample.

Without going through the technicalities of the model[14], we note that, if it is possible to build a linear combination of banks in the sample such that it

---

[13] As far as our empirical test is concerned, a quick graphic analysis of the estimated u_is shows that they fit well with the truncated-normal distribution (for details, see Resti, 1995).

[14] A thorough and up-to-date introduction to D.E.A. can be found e.g. in (Fried et al., 1993); some recent developments are presented in (Thanassoulis and Dyson, 1992).

produces at least y_0 at a cost lower than $w_0'x_0$ (that is, the production cost faced by the bank being evaluated), then z_0 will reach values below the unity; in this case, $1-z_0$ will indicate by how much production costs can decrease without reducing the output, and will therefore serve as a measure of productive inefficiency.

Finally, we note that, if we impose that vector λ be such that $\sum_{i=1}^{n} \lambda_i = 1$, the problem becomes more realistic: in fact, in this way the technically feasible region underlying the model is no more a polyhedral cone (where returns to scale are always constant), but becomes a generic convex set.

Other extensions of D.E.A. regard the presence of "environmental" or "non-discretionary" variables, that is, variables that define the operating framework in which the production takes place, but cannot be freely modified (at least in the short term) by bank managers (Banker and Morey, 1986a and b). It is also possible (using the so-called *Free Disposal Hull* version of D.E.A., see Deprins et al., 1984) to remove the hypothesis of convexity of the feasible region[15]; both of these extensions will be used in the following.

4. An empirical comparison of the different techniques based on Italian data

In what follows, the productive efficiency of a panel of 270 Italian banks will be measured through both techniques seen above: each bank will enter the panel for $T_i=4$ or 5 years, in the period 1988-1992[16].

---

[15] Like the "pure frontier" models, D.E.A. is a deterministic methodology, therefore very sensitive to outliers and to noise in data. Hence, in the very latest years a new stream of literature has arisen on "stochastic D.E.A." (see e.g. Retzlaff-Roberts and Morey, 1993), where a noise component is added, without giving up the very flexible, non-parametric approach that makes D.E.A. peculiar. Yet, these models are still at an early stage, and lack generality, since they can be applied only to very specific situations (e.g. univariate production functions) and/or require non-trivial assumptions on the shape of the feasible region.

[16] Data for 1993 and 1994 could not be used, as the EU directives imposed a new set of accounting rules for bank statements, and the new data were not comparable; to make stock measures more reliable, we averaged the values of each year with those of the previous one. Moreover, only banks with at least four years of data were included; finally, we rejected 4 banks because they showed negative outputs for one or more years (due to trading losses) and could not be used in a translog model, and nine more banks were discarded, since their accounting data seemed "suspect" (the standardised residuals in a pooled OLS regression were bigger than 2 in absolute value).

4.1 Econometric techniques: the Battese-Coelli model

First, we are going to use econometric techniques to estimate a parametric frontier. Following a rather standard approach[17], a generic cost function will be approximated by a translog flexible form of the second order:

$$\log C_{it} = \log C(\log \mathbf{y}_{it}, \log \mathbf{w}_{it}) + u_{it} + v_{it} =$$

$$= \alpha_0 + \begin{bmatrix} \alpha'_y & \alpha'_w \end{bmatrix} \begin{bmatrix} \log \mathbf{y}_{it} \\ \log \mathbf{w}_{it} \end{bmatrix} + \begin{bmatrix} \log \mathbf{y}_{it}' & \log \mathbf{w}_{it}' \end{bmatrix} \mathbf{B} \begin{bmatrix} \log \mathbf{y}_{it} \\ \log \mathbf{w}_{it} \end{bmatrix} + u_{it} + v_{it}$$

We will consider three products (y_1: loans to customers; y_2: customer deposits; y_3: non-interest income) and the prices of two factors (w_1: fixed capital[18]; w_2: labour); all monetary aggregates are measured at 1988 prices; $\log y$ stands for a vector of logarithms, all expressed as differences from the sample mean; in other words, the j-th component of the vector will be given by : $\log y_j - \dfrac{1}{n} \sum_{i=1}^{n} \log y_{ji}$

(the same applies to $\log \mathbf{w}$).

Two standard properties of cost functions (linear homogeneity and cost-exhaustion[19]) will be used to reduce the number of parameters to be estimated: in practice, costs and prices will be re-written using w_2 as a numeraire, and the number of unknowns will drop from 25 to 19.

Table 1 shows the results of the ML estimation and requires two preliminary remarks: first, since $\mathbf{B}$ is symmetric and $b_{ij} \equiv b_{ji}$, when $i \neq j$ we have estimated the sum of the two ($\beta_{ij} \equiv 2b_{ij} \equiv 2b_{ji}$); second, the values of the parameters for w_2 are not shown, but can be computed from the restrictions reported in footnote 19. The values in the table suggest some remarks:

(1) all elasticities around the mean (vector α) have the expected sign;

---

[17] The translog is probably the most known flexible form in banking literature, and represents a second order Taylor expansion, usually around the mean, of a generic f(**x**) where all variables appear in logarithms. Although (Baumol et al., 1982) stressed its drawbacks for the study of scope economies, it is still widely used in empirical research (recent examples are Drake, 1992; Zardkohi and Kolari, 1994).

[18] Since book-value fixed capital is subject to distortions (assets may have been recorded in different years, and may have been revalued by effect of tax laws or mergers), we are going to use an adjusted version, based on the fitted value of a translog regression of book-value fixed assets on the following variables (t-stats in parentheses): a constant term (-7), the number of branches (118), and the average size (customer deposits and loans to customers) of branches (33).

[19] These properties require the following restrictions to be imposed on the parameters: $b_{y1,w1} + b_{y1,w2} = b_{y2,w1} + b_{y2,w2} = b_{y3,w1} + b_{y3,w2} = b_{w1,w1} + b_{w1,w2} = b_{w2,w1} + b_{w2,w2} = 0$; $\alpha_{w1} + \alpha_{w2} = 1$ (see e.g. Jorgenson, 1986); they seem to fit well with the data, as proved by a likelihood ratio test of 5.66 (p-value: 46.2%).

Table 1: Results of the ML estimates

Coefficient	Estimated value	Standard error	t-test (1)
α_0	10.010	0.078	128.89
α_{y1}	0.297	0.011	25.98
α_{y2}	0.636	0.013	47.20
α_{y3}	0.068	0.006	11.23
α_{w1}	0.478	0.009	55.84
$b_{y1,y1}$	0.092	0.012	7.53
$b_{y2,y2}$	0.069	0.019	3.69
$b_{y3,y3}$	0.022	0.005	4.62
$b_{w1,w1}$	0.103	0.015	7.03
$\beta_{y1,y2}$	-0.149	0.029	-5.14
$\beta_{y1,y3}$	-0.061	0.012	-4.92
$\beta_{y1,w1}$	-0.080	0.020	-4.04
$\beta_{y2,y3}$	0.024	0.013	1.86
$\beta_{y2,w1}$	0.055	0.022	2.43
$\beta_{y3,w1}$	0.040	0.017	2.37
$\sigma^2 (\equiv \sigma^2_u + \sigma^2_v)$	0.018	0.002	9.28
$\gamma (\equiv \sigma^2_u / \sigma^2)$	0.917	0.010	95.64
μ	0.367	0.078	4.72
η	0.004	0.003	1.31

(1) asymptotic t-ratios, distributed as $N(0,1)$; log-likelihood = 1827.57, corrected R^2 of the OLS model = 99,4%. Estimates based on the Davidson - Fletcher - Powell algorithm, using the Frontier 2.0 software[20]

(2) the elasticity of production costs to unit staff costs (measured around the mean, that is α_{w1}) is less marked than the elasticity to the price of capital (1-α_{w1}). This is in accordance with the fact, highlighted by recent studies on banking systems in the OECD area[21], that banks can control personnel expenses, cutting down their demand for staff when necessary, but are often unable to reduce their expense for technology, above all in the information processing field, when prices rise.

(3) among the products, customer deposits are the most cost-intensive: the result is somewhat surprising, as loans are thought to be the area in which a bank expresses its peculiar role of information provider through credit screening and monitoring. Yet, a similar finding is explained by fact that deposits, more than

---

[20] More details on Frontier 2.0 may be found in (Coelli, 1991). Note that, in order to handle large data sets (as is the case for our test), the program has to be recompiled.

[21] See (Conti and Resti, 1994).

loans, require a wide network, and therefore bring about the opening of new branches and higher operating costs;

(4) the coefficients of the second-degree terms are significantly different from zero, even if multicollinearity among variables might inflate estimated variances (as it is usual with second-order approximations);

(5) the value of η is positive, and would suggest that inefficiencies decrease in time; more exactly, it would indicate that the banks' inefficiency[22] has reduced by 4‰ ($e^{-\eta}$-1, that is, about -η itself) per year, or about 2% during 1988-1992. Yet, the t-ratio is at least doubtful: a one-sided test of H_a:η>0 leads to a fairly high p-value of 9.5%; nevertheless, we decided to retain η, since its value is anyway near zero: when it is excluded from the model (therefore imposing constant inefficiencies) no relevant differences arise[23];

(6) finally, μ is significantly different from zero, so a model with half-normal disturbances would be rejected by the data; from an economic standpoint, this means that efficiency is far from representing the most widespread behaviour in our sample, so models like (Aigner and Chu, 1968), (Aigner, Lovell and Schmidt, 1977) and (Meusen and Van den Broek, 1977), where increasing levels of inefficiency are supposed to be less and less likely, would not be appropriate for our analysis of Italian banks[24]. We note that not only μ is non-zero, but, what is more[25], its "standardised" value μ/σ_u, can be shown to be near 2.6, with an asymptotic t of 4.3.

Table 2 shows the results of some tests[26] (details on the restrictions used can be found, e.g., in Jorgenson, 1986; Berndt and Christensen, 1973): apparently, the

---

[22] Here we refer to the term u_{it} in the *translog*; for proper estimates of the individual inefficiencies, see below.

[23] When the restriction η=0 is added, the values of estimated coefficients remain quite similar to those reported in table 1 and, what is even more relevant, the distribution of the individual inefficiencies of the banks in the sample (that will be used below in the comparisons with linear programming estimates) is virtually unchanged: the correlation between estimated inefficiencies, with and without constraining η to zero, is 98.89%.

[24] To our knowledge, the only stochastic frontier analysis of Italian banks is (Cardani et al., 1991), where the model by (Stevenson, 1980) is applied to a cross-section of 94 Italian banks in 1986; the Authors find a μ near zero, but their approach differs from ours, in that they use a univariate index of output. For our data, such a choice does not seem viable in the light of the separability tests reported below.

[25] (Greene, 1993) suggests to look at the standardised value (rather than at the absolute one) of μ for a reliable test of the hypothesis that u is half-normally distributed, with μ/σ_u=0.

[26] Moreover, a test based on a grid of sample values (details are available in Resti, 1995) shows that the estimated function is almost everywhere increasing in its arguments, as a cost function must be. Some problems arise, instead, as far as the concavity postulate is concerned, as shown by the value of $b_{w1,w1}$; yet, such a result was somehow expected, since the unit price of capital was obtained from accounting data, which usually are not very precise. Note that, to circumvent similar problems, (Dermine and Roller, 1991), on

function is not homothetic, nor homogenous. Besides, it is not separable in the product vector: in other words, the three outputs of our model *cannot* be replaced by some weighted index or functional average (as it was sometimes done, in order to analyse the multiple-output banking industry by means of univariate techniques[27]): therefore, the use of a multi-product function like [5], although more complex, is justified, even required, by our data.

Table 2 Tests of some special properties of cost functions

Property	test	value	p-value
Homotheticity	$\chi^2(3)$	18.2	0.04%
Homogeneity of degree g	$\chi^2(6)$	108.4	0.00%
Separability: (y_1, y_2) from w_1	$\chi^2(4)$	75.0	0.00%
Separability: (y_2, y_3) from w_1	$\chi^2(4)$	62.1	0.00%
Separability: (y_1, y_3) from w_1	$\chi^2(4)$	90.6	0.00%

Starting from the parameters in table 1, an index of ray scale economies has been computed for each of the 1284 observations in the sample[28]. For all of them, figure 1 reports, on the vertical axis, an asymptotic t-test of the hypothesis that the index is equal to one: significantly positive (negative) values indicate scale diseconomies (economies); the size of the banks[29] is indicated on the x-axis. As one can see, the index is affected by a high variance; yet, we might cautiously say that smaller producers operate with an average cost curve that is initially increasing, and have to reach a sort of "critical mass" - below which it seems more efficient to operate as a "micro-bank"[30] - before they can enjoy any scale advantages.

On the other hand, the translog model seems to suggest that several big banks show increasing returns to scale; this is perhaps the reason why, in Italy, the larger banks have been highly interested, during the latest years, in merger and

---

French SICAVs, and (Baumol et al. 1989), on US unit trusts, treated input prices as constant, therefore deleting logw from [5]. Yet, we feel that, whenever a rough estimate is possible, it is to be preferred to a complete lack of information on prices; this is especially true for a segmented market as the Italian banking sector, where for instance unit personnel costs differ markedly between small and big banks.

[27] See. e.g. (Benston et al., 1982), (Gilligan et al., 1984).

[28] This is the reciprocal to the SE (Scale Economies) index due to (Baumol et al., 1982); values below the unity indicate scale economies.

[29] Here, as in the following graphs, the sum of customer deposits and loans to customers (divided by two) is used as a size indicator.

[30] In Italy there is a high number of very small co-operative banks (the so-called "rural banks") serving a limited local area with one or few branches; these banks usually achieve good profitability results.

acquisition projects, since they were operating on a stretch of the frontier where an increase in size would bring in some cost advantages[31].

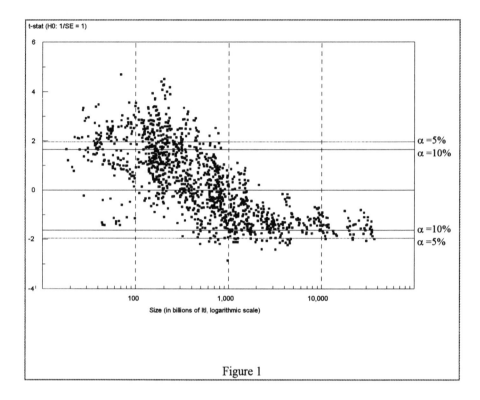

Figure 1

As said before, the model in (Battese and Coelli, 1992) allows to compute a consistent estimate of the average and individual inefficiencies. From [5]:

$$\log C_{it} = \log C(\log \mathbf{y}_{it}, \log \mathbf{w}_{it}) + u_{it} + v_{it}$$

it is evident that productive efficiency (defined as the ratio between the minimum and the actual cost) is given by:

---

[31] These findings on scale economies must be evaluated carefully, also in the light of the results obtained below through linear programming techniques. Moreover, it must be stressed that, when one approximates the banks' output through monetary stocks, one doesn't account for the different value added of loans and deposits of various sizes; smaller loans and deposits (which are probably more frequent by small banks) imply a higher value content. Anyway the results by (Benston et al., 1982) and (Berger et al., 1987) quoted above seem to temper similar worries.

$$\frac{C(\log \mathbf{y}_{it}, \log \mathbf{w}_{it})}{C_{it}} = e^{-u_{it}-v_{it}}$$

that is, netting out the stochastic disturbance, by $PE = e^{-u_{it}}$. Then it is possible to compute, by integration, the expected value of productive efficiency for every year in the sample: this amounts to 69.4% in 1988 and slowly rises to 69.8% in 1992. The quotient between actual costs and the theoretical minimum is therefore fairly high (about 1.44) and steady in time (this follows from the scarce relevance of parameter η): these values suggest that Italian credit institutions could, on average, cut their costs by 30% through a better control of x-inefficiencies, and that no generalised effort aimed at their reduction took place in the latest years.

The conditional average $E(e^{u_{it}}|\varepsilon_i)$ (where ε_i represents the vector of the T_i composite disturbances associated to the i-th bank) can be shown[32] to be a consistent estimator for the individual efficiency PE_{it}; we used it to estimate PE_{it} for all the 1284 observations in the sample, then sorted the results by geographic areas[33] and size. The first part of table 3 shows the values of efficiency indexes in four different regions, confirming a fact that belongs to the "conventional wisdom" on Italian banks: institutions located in the North (where national intermediaries have to compete with big European banks[34]) are more efficient than those operating in the southern part of the country. The PE scores of the latter are lower, in some cases by one tenth, than in the North. Anyway, this is not (or at least: not only) the consequence of a different quality in the management and other individual features of the banks: southern banks also suffer from an operating environment that is made more uncertain and costly by a deep-rooted lack of facilities and a higher credit risk. The last column in the table concerns the so-called "scattered banks", that is, those which do not belong to any specific area, since their network spreads over the whole Italian territory. Their performance looks lower than for any of the geographic areas seen before, indicating that a remarkable loss of efficiency arises when banks lack a well-defined centre of gravity (which, more than size in itself, could bring about cost subadditivities)[35].

---

[32] See (Battese and Coelli, 1992).

[33] A bank is assigned to a given region (North-West, North-East, Centre, South+Iles) if it has there its head office and at least 85% of its branches. When it does not comply with one (or both) of these requirements, then it is classified as a "scattered bank".

[34] E.g., Deutsche Bank and Credit Lyonnais have there a wide branch network

[35] This could explain why, during the latest years, some "regional" banks like Cariplo or SanPaolo Turin have reached the top positions among Italian banks, while a big "scattered bank" like Banco Roma has decided to merge with the Rome Savings and Loans to add a strong regional basis to its network.

In the second part of the table the banks were grouped by the size classes defined by the Bank of Italy's ranking criteria. X-inefficiencies seem to increase monotonically with size, offsetting, in a sense, the results found on scale economies (which arise for medium-size and bigger banks only).

Table 3 Average values of the productive efficiency indexes (percent values, econometric model)

	a) grouped by geographic areas (South includes Sicily and Sardinia)				b) grouped by size classes					Avg.
	North-west	North-east	Centre	South	Scattered	Very small	Small	Medium	Big	Very big	
1988	71.7	68.9	66.8	67.7	61.3	68.8	69.6	65.7	67.0	62.8	69.4
1989	73.5	70.4	67.0	67.5	62.4	70.2	69.4	65.7	67.1	62.9	69.5
1990	73.6	70.6	66.9	67.4	62.8	70.2	69.5	65.8	67.2	63.0	69.6
1991	73.7	70.7	67.0	67.5	62.9	70.3	69.7	65.9	67.3	63.2	69.7
1992	73.5	71.0	67.1	67.5	64.3	70.2	69.9	67.4	67.4	63.2	69.8

4.2 Linear programming techniques:
further results and comparisons with the econometric model

The same data panel will now be analysed through some D.E.A. models. In particular, we estimated individual productive efficiencies by the A.D.E.A. model described in [4], imposing both constant and variable returns to scale (henceforth: CRTS or VRTS). The results of the exercise turned out to be robust to slight changes in the sample[36], and are reported in table 4 (as before, individual values are grouped by areas and size classes; note that we reported also the number of banks in each group, since it will be relevant in the following discussion).

We see both similarities and differences between these values and those seen above.

Among the former, the most important is by no doubt the high positive correlation between individual efficiencies measured by D.E.A. and by Battese and Coelli's consistent estimator: 86.7% for the CRTS model, and 70.8% for the VRTS version (rank correlations are even slightly better: 88.5% and 72.6%).

---

[36] D.E.A. is a deterministic technique and therefore is very sensitive to outliers. Hence, it is fundamental to check that solutions are stable, and do not vary dramatically when some units are excluded from the sample. To do so, after solving the CRTS and VRTS problems using all of the 1284 observations in our sample, we deleted all those with a PE score equal to one (7 and 35 units, respectively) and re-computed the PE indexes, based on this reduced sample (this procedure is followed, among others, by Kuussaari, 1993). The correlation between PE scores before and after the elimination of efficient units is 98.5% for the CRTS problem, and 98.0% for the VRTS one; the rank correlation values are similar (98.1% and 98.4%, respectively) and seem quite reassuring to us.

Similar values look quite satisfactory, above all if one thinks that the mathematical models and the econometric one arise from quite different assumptions: for example, the former do not require any hypothesis on the distribution of the residuals (which anyway is strictly one-sided) and on the evolution in time of individual inefficiencies (the stochastic model recognises and uses the fact that the data are organised as a panel, while D.E.A. models treat all observations as a separate units, even if they belong to the same bank); on the other hand, they impose a given shape to the technologically feasible region (a convex set, or a polyhedral cone), while the parametric approach has no *a-priori* assumptions on it.

Table 4 Average values of the productive efficiency indexes (percent values, D.E.A. models)

	a) grouped by geographic areas (South includes Sicily and Sardinia)				b) grouped by size classes					Avg.
	North-West	North-East	Centre	South	Scattered	Very small	Small	Medium	Big	Very big	
1) CRTS (Constant Returns to Scale)											
1988	69.4	65.2	64.8	66.7	63.4	66.5	67.0	64.4	66.5	65.5	66.5
1989	73.4	69.2	65.4	66.5	67.3	69.0	68.6	67.6	70.2	69.2	68.8
1990	72.4	68.6	64.8	64.6	68.0	67.5	68.6	68.7	68.0	70.2	67.9
1991	73.4	70.2	67.2	65.2	68.2	68.7	70.1	69.7	69.7	71.0	69.2
1992	71.1	69.0	66.6	63.5	67.6	67.0	69.3	71.3	68.8	69.0	67.7
2) VRTS (Variable Returns to Scale)											
1988	78.1	72.0	71.1	73.4	82.9	71.6	76.9	80.3	84.6	89.0	74.3
1989	80.4	75.0	71.4	73.2	82.9	73.7	77.5	82.5	88.9	89.1	75.7
1990	78.9	73.7	70.2	70.2	82.1	71.7	76.5	83.1	83.4	87.9	73.9
1991	79.8	75.5	72.5	70.3	80.8	72.6	78.5	83.1	84.3	87.4	75.0
1992	77.4	74.4	72.0	68.0	81.7	70.8	78.1	83.5	82.5	88.0	73.4
3) Number of banks in each group											
1988	56	55	40	54	10	138	53	11	5	8	215
1989	70	72	47	69	12	186	58	13	5	8	270
1990	70	73	48	68	11	189	55	13	5	8	270
1991	70	74	48	67	11	186	58	13	5	8	270
1992	68	72	48	63	8	183	56	11	5	4	259

Two different research streams lead then to surprisingly similar results when they are implemented inside the same experimental set-up (as far as the sample selection and the definition of inputs/outputs are concerned). The result is not trivial, in the light of the previous literature: the most famous comparison of the two methodologies to banking data, that is (Ferrier and Lovell, 1990), found ranking correlations of 1-2% (statistically insignificant) between technical efficiency scores[37].

Another resemblance between tables 3 and 4 pertains to the average efficiency levels: 68.1% in the CRTS model, 74.5% in the VRTS one, and 69.5% in the composite disturbance model. This fits well with the fact - highlighted by the above-mentioned Ferrier and Lovell - that mathematical techniques treat noise as inefficiency (therefore coming to more severe evaluations) but, on the other hand, can improve the efficiency scores since their non-parametric nature enables them to envelop data more closely (this is especially true for the VRTS model).

The linear programming models also suggest that no remarkable gain of efficiency took place, in the Italian banking system, during the period 1988-92 (see the last column, where overall means are reported). More formally, when one groups the PE indexes by year and analyses the variance inside and among groups, the observation period turns out to be of little use in explaining the variations in the scores: an ANOVA F test gets a p-value of 10.1% and 17.2%, respectively, for the CRTS and VRTS models.

Moreover, the D.E.A. results suggest the presence of a marked individual component in the inefficiency levels. This was an *a-priori* of the Battese-Coelli model - where u_{it} was by assumption explained by an individual term u_i and, possibly, by time - which now appears to be validated by the linear programming results. In fact, an ANOVA test on the D.E.A. scores grouped by bank gets a substantially null p-value, meaning that the efficiency indices of each individual are relatively steady over time.

Finally, the efficiency gap between Northern and Southern regions is confirmed by the linear programming estimates; this gap does not decrease, even if the D.E.A. efficiency scores can change freely in time (while the econometric model imposed the same evolution pattern for all banks)[38].

We now turn to the differences between the results of the two approaches. The findings of the linear programming models depart from those in the previous paragraph in that the bigger banks and the "scattered" banks (two largely

---

[37] Ferrier and Lovell used a D.E.A. model with VRTS and categorical variables (see Banker and Morey, 1986a) and compared the results to those of an econometric model for the joint estimation of technical and allocative inefficiencies.

[38] D.E.A. models can also be used to separate the technical component of inefficiency (poor use of the available technology) from the allocative one (due to a bad understanding of the value of the inputs used; for more details see e.g. Farrell, 1957). For the banks in our sample, the former turns out to be prevailing (it is around 20-30%, while the latter is about 10%); moreover, the gap between Northern and Southern banks pertains to both components. Allocative inefficiency is also less variable across the banks; finally, the two components do not offset each other, since the correlation between the two can be shown to be positive.

overlapping groups[39]) get efficiency scores *above* the mean. The contrast is sharper when we shift from the CRTS to the VRTS model[40]: the latter differs

from the base D.E.A. model because the further constraint $\sum_{i=1}^{n} \lambda_i = 1$ makes it

more difficult to extend towards the smallest and the biggest producers an estimate of the efficient frontier based on the production practice of medium-size units. In other words, *it possesses less structure* than the CRTS model (where the feasible region is constrained to be a polyhedral cone spanned by the efficient production plans), which in this regard is more similar to the econometric model. The translog curve, in fact, is determined through a parametric estimate: all the observations in the sample contribute to identify the shape of the frontier, and this unique frontier is used to evaluate the efficiency of all banks, including those operating at production levels where few observations are available (this is the case of the bigger/scattered banks, see table 4). As the model structure becomes more and more flexible (shifting from the parametric model to CRTS D.E.A., and then to its VRTS extension) the estimated scores do not change much if the sample is densely populated (that is, for low and medium production levels); however, if the tails of the sample include only few banks, then dramatic differences can follow from the different ability of the three models to build that particular stretch of frontier using also the data of units located elsewhere.

Some further evidence and a visual confirmation of these remarks come from figure 2, which shows the relationship between size and the PE scores computed by: the econometric estimator (PE_B&C), the two above-mentioned D.E.A. models (PE_CRTS, PE_VRTS), and also the *Free Disposal Hull* model (PE_FDH) in which, as said before, the convexity of the feasible region is not required and the structure of the model is even less demanding than for the VRTS case. To make the curves smoother and easier to compare, every dot stands for ten adjacent observations (the dots are displayed only on the first line, since they are similar also for the remaining ones).

It is interesting to note that the CRTS model, although it is based on a quite different approach, mimics fairly well the results of the econometric estimates. The VRTS model, instead, generates a different profile, especially for the smallest and (above all) for the biggest units, which get higher scores; anyway,

---

[39] "Very large" banks constitute, in fact, 55.8% of the scattered ones, a very high incidence considered that their overall weight in the sample is only 2.8%.

[40] A further difference between econometric estimates and the VRTS model is that the latter indicates decreasing returns to scale for almost all the banks in the sample (with the exception of a group of very small banks). This seems to be due to the convexity hypothesis (typical of the VRTS model) which makes it impossible to switch back to increasing returns once that scale diseconomies are ascertained on a ray in the input/output hyperspace.

the two curves are still rather similar in the middle stretch, that is in the most thickly populated area (this explains why the correlation coefficient between PE_B&C and PE_VRTS remains fairly high). The FDH model assigns quite better scores to all the units in the sample, even if it somehow replicates, on a higher level, the profiles originated by the previous approaches; moreover, there is some evidence of an inverse correlation between the scores and the density of the sample at different production levels.

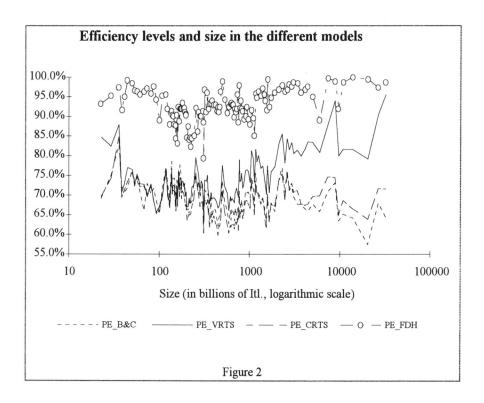

Figure 2

Summing up, the results of the linear models shift away from those of the econometric exercise when the set of hypotheses on which they are based becomes poorer and poorer. Such differences are more tangible where the sample is less thickly populated, since the units located in those regions - when there are no a priori assumptions enabling the model to trace their frontier based on the remaining observations - *are themselves used to build the minimum cost curve to which they are compared, when their efficiency is evaluated.*

4.3 Efficiency and asset quality

The analysis in the previous sections took into account the volume of issued loans, not their riskiness[41]. Yet, a lower incidence of bad loans would justify operating costs above the efficient minimum, since a good credit screening and monitoring involves higher expenses. In other words, the results above might be biased by the fact that banks with a lower ratio of bad to total loans (henceforth: BTL ratio) might have been deemed inefficient only because a more effective credit control involves higher costs.

Yet, a quick check on the data leads to exclude the existence of such a bias. As far as the econometric estimates are concerned, we note that the correlation between efficiency indexes and the BTL ratio, far from being positive, is equal to -27.7% (with a t-statistic of -10.3). With D.E.A. models, we can do something more than a mere *ex-post* correlation analysis: we can use the BTL ratio as a non-discretionary variable (Banker and Morey, 1986a), that is, a variable describing the amount or the quality of the inputs and outputs[42], that cannot be freely modified by the producer, at least in the short term. These variables are excluded from the objective function of problem [4], but appear in the constraints, to rule out "unfair" comparisons among banks of different quality.

The results of an exercise based on this kind of models agree with the above-mentioned correlations; the units labelled as most inefficient when credit quality is *not* considered (as in table 4) do *not* increase their scores more than other banks, when the BTL ratio is included in the model as a non-discretionary variable[43]. Therefore, it seems highly unlikely that their extra costs arise from a more effective monitoring of the loan portfolio.

These somewhat counterintuitive findings (higher costs with *lower* quality) might be explained by at least two reasons. First, a bad credit quality might follow from a more difficult "market environment": this could be especially true for banks in Southern Italy, where the monitoring of customers often turns out to

---

[41] Some recent literature (see e.g. McAllister and McManus, 1993) has correctly stressed the fact that, among a bank's outputs, there is also the level of protection against risk that it achieves, improving its capital endowment and asset quality. Yet, it is difficult to find a fully reliable indicator of this "output" using accounting data taken from the banks' statements. Here, we will use the "bad to total loans" ratio as a proxy of the riskiness of each bank, although we are aware of the conceptual and practical limits of such an indicator.

[42] The riskiness of the loan portfolio affects the quality of an output; the age of the building where the firm is located might be an example of a non-discretionary variable concerning inputs.

[43] More precisely, the correlation between the inefficiency levels of the banks in the "base" models and their reduction (on a percent basis) when one adds the BTL ratio as a non discretionary variable, is negative (-27.5% for the VRTS model; the results of the CRTS problem would be similar, but the use of a scale-invariant variable as the BTL ratio in this kind of models is not appropriate).

be both more costly and less effective because commercial information on potential counterparts is harder to obtain, and law enforcement is slower and more uncertain. Second, the same factors that generate x-inefficiencies (inadequate communication among decision centres inside big organisations, personal incentives to deviate from the otherwise optimal behaviour, lags in reacting to external changes...) can also lead to a poor risk management, therefore to a higher incidence of bad loans.

5. Concluding remarks

The banking industry is characterised by the presence, beside a limited number of big institutions, of a wide layer of small and very small subjects; this makes the distribution of banks in all the main advanced countries highly skewed to the right (as confirmed by the sample analysis reported in table 5 for some EU nations). Of course this is common to many other industries, but some features of financial intermediation make it especially true in the case of banks. On the liabilities side, for instance, a small bank, well-rooted in local markets, can enjoy a wide funding basis (and, more generally speaking, a broad retail banking basis) at a low price; on the other hand, a better knowledge of the productive system of their regions can make small banks more effective in collecting information on the potential borrowers, enabling them to serve some regions of the risk/return curve that would be too risky for big "outside" banks[44].

Table 5 Indicators of the frequency distribution of banks, by total assets, in six OECD countries

	Germany	France	Italy	Spain	Switzerland	Japan
# of banks	51	38	48	54	56	49
Mean	31297	28772	21401	10595	11457	74096
Median	12340	6373	9560	4253	4255	25329
90th percentile	85738	55400	63889	28658	12004	258419
Maximum	186129	244386	100174	65823	145554	398475
Skewness	2.04	3.00	1.69	2.53	3.96	2.16

Sample data based on available statements; Average figures 1990/91, in billions of US $ - Source: (Conti and Resti, 1994)

From similar reasons arises the relative lack of large institutions in the banking sector, which constitutes a problem for the estimation of efficient frontiers. Since we lack a thick grid of true observations at the highest production levels, the structure of the different models proves crucial for the computed efficiency scores. So, our empirical analysis of the biggest banks suggested quite different results according to the technique used: we found actual costs well above the

---

[44] As far as Italy is concerned, some evidence can be found in (Faini et al., 1992), (Comana, 1993).

minimum cost function, and increasing returns, in the stochastic model; but we observed production plans lying very close to the best-practice frontier estimated by VRTS D.E.A. (which shows scale diseconomies)[45].

After all, such a disagreement might be less sharp than it looks at first sight: in both cases, the models are signalling that size increases beyond a given threshold bring about an inefficient cost profile, although, as we saw, according to D.E.A. this is due to the shape of the frontier (that is, to the fact that even the best-practice banks increase their unit costs when they grow beyond a certain scale of operations), while the econometric techniques suggest that this depends on the distance between the theoretical frontier and the observed banks.

One might also note that the very distinction between scale diseconomies and x-inefficiencies (although it is clear and meaningful from a conceptual standpoint) becomes increasingly blurred when we shift to real data. Some of the theoretical reasons proposed by Leibenstein to justify the existence of x-inefficiencies (such as the lack of co-ordination in big corporations, or the lags in the process of decision-making) are the same ones that can be found in microeconomics handbooks[46], to explain the presence of decreasing returns to scale when the firm's size exceeds the optimum. The discriminating element then, between the two types of inefficiency (*along* and *away from* the frontier, so to say), is not represented by their causes (which can overlap), but by the existence of an efficient producer, who is there to show that the available technology would have allowed higher output levels.

When we evaluate large banks, the small number of observed plans makes it more difficult to find such a producer; anyway, it is still possible to "create" it, completing the model's structure with some appropriate hypotheses. For example, one might say that the cost function can be estimated through a vector of parameters that describe its shape *at any production level*; or affirm that the feasible region is *convex*, or even *a polyhedral convex cone*. Similar hypotheses can give rise to scale diseconomies or to x-inefficiencies[47]; this is why we said that they become crucial for the results of the analysis.

The knowledge of the differences in the structure of the various models must help us when reading their findings, especially for the bigger banks: so, the

---

[45] Figure 2 clearly indicates that the differences in our results are due above all to big banks; moreover, when the correlation coefficient between individual inefficiencies estimated by VRTS D.E.A and by the econometric model is re-computed, cutting off 5-10% of the banks starting from the bigger ones, it increases remarkably (from 71% to 77-80%); if more observations are excluded, no further increment in correlation arises.

[46] See e.g. (Mansfield, 1975).

[47] These impressions are confirmed by some previous studies on Italian banks based on D.E.A. models: both (Favero and Papi, 1993) and (Olivei, 1992), using VRTS D.E.A. find that x-inefficiencies decline when size increases. Yet, these findings do not survive if the model's structure is reinforced by imposing a CRTS hypothesis (again Olivei, 1992), or when a parametric estimate with composite disturbances is used (Cardani et al., 1991).

parametric frontier must be considered as a sort of ideal benchmark built through the analysis of the whole sample, not as an empirically observable alternative; conversely, one must not forget that VRTS D.E.A. and *Free Disposal Hull* can prove too magnanimous toward banks in scantily populated, extreme size classes.

Beyond these differences, all the techniques have highlighted some common elements, that we now would like to review, drawing some policy conclusions.

(1) **The efficiency scores show a high variance**: the gap between the "best" and the "worst" banks in the sample is about 40-50 percentage points. Even when the tails are removed, the difference between the third and the first quartile remains high (12-15%, depending on the model used).

(2) **The banking system is split in two**: the banks in the North of Italy are closer to the middle-European efficiency levels, while the South and the Centre of the country lag behind. What is even more striking is that, even when the techniques used do not require the gap to be constant in time, it never gets narrower (and sometimes it widens out).

The existence of efficiency gaps among banks and geographic areas should act as an incentive for adjustment processes; in other words, the "invisible hand" should induce the worst producers to leave the market, or to merge with the more efficient firms.

Yet, we feel that those adjustments will require time and will meet several hindrances. First, the extra-profits enjoyed by small producers in local markets - although decreasing - are still considerable, and form a cushion against efficiency differentials: no selection among intermediaries will take place, as long as a lower productivity will be paid for by the customers, not by the producers. Second, the lower average efficiency of the Southern banks is also due to a more difficult economic environment: consequently, an outside producer expanding into those regions will probably meet some difficulties in replicating the efficiency levels attained in the home market.

(3) **There is a direct** (rather than inverse) **relationship between productive efficiency and asset quality**: this suggests that the presence of operating expenses above the minimum, while increasing the social costs of financial intermediation, does not lead to a lower credit risk and a steadier banking system. This strong conclusion should be validated by some further research: after all, one must recall that accounting data can be biased, since safer banks often follow more prudent criteria when determining the amount of bad loans.

(4) **The productive efficiency of Italian banks did not increase over the period considered.** This lack of improvements was made sustainable by the favourable evolution of bank margins in 1988-92: the spread between loan and deposit rates, which was 6.8% in 1988, remained virtually unchanged until 1991 and increased to 7.7% in 1992, following the money market crisis and the Italian lira devaluation.

Yet the spread experienced a sharp drop in the following two years (to 5.9% in the first nine months of 1994), due to the stronger competition in the credit market caused by the opening of many new branches, and by a weak demand of loans; if this trend should continue, the consequences might be traumatic (although, in the long term, beneficial) for credit institutions. Italian banks would be forced to improve their efficiency levels without delay, and would need the help of both econometric and mathematical instruments to learn more about their own strengths and weaknesses. This seems good news for people developing and testing tools for efficiency measurement, since their research activiy might soon prove very useful.

References

Afriat S.N. (1972) 'Efficiency estimation of production functions', *International Economic Review*, 13(3), 568-598.

Aigner D.J., Chu S.F. (1968) 'On estimating the industry production function', *American Economic Review*, 58(4), 826-839.

Aigner D.J., Lovell Knox C.A., Schmidt P. (1977) 'Formulation and estimation of stochastic frontier production function models', *Journal of Econometrics*, 6, 21-37.

Aly, H. Y., Grabowski, R., Pasurka, C., Rangan N. (1990) 'Technical, Scale and Allocative Efficiencies in U.S. Banking: an Empirical Investigation', *The Review of Economics and Statistics*, LXXII, 21, 211-8.

Banker R. D., Charnes A. Cooper W. W. (1984) 'Some Models for estimating technical and scale Inefficiencies in Data Envelopment Analysis', *Management Science*, 1078-92.

Banker R. D., Morey R.C. (1986a) 'Efficiency Analysis for Exogenously Fixed Inputs and Outputs', *Operations Research*, 34(4), 513-521.

Banker R. D., Morey R.C. (1986b) 'The Use of Categorical Variables in Data Envelopment Analysis', *Management Science* 32(12), 1613-1627.

Battese G., Coelli T. (1988) 'Prediction of Firm-Level Technical Efficiencies with a Generalized Frontier Production Function and Panel Data', *Journal of Econometrics*, 38, 387-399.

Battese G., Coelli T. (1992) 'Frontier Production Functions, Technical Efficiency and Panel Data: With Application to Paddy Farmers in India', *The Journal of Productivity Analysis*, 38, 387-399.

Baumol W.J., Goldfeld S.M., Gordon L.A., Koehn M.F. (1989) *The Economics of Mutual Fund Markets: Competition versus Regulation*, Kluver Academic Publishers, Boston.

Baumol W.J., Panzar J.C., Willig R.D. (1982) Contestable Markets and the Theory of the Industry Structure, Hancourt Brace Jovanovich Inc., New York.

Benston G.J. (1965) 'Branch Banking and Economies of Scale', *The Journal of Finance*, 20(2), 312-332, .

Benston G.J., Hanweck G. Humphrey D.B. (1982) 'Scale Economies in Banking: A Restructuring and Reassessment', *Journal of Money, Credit and Banking*, 14, 435-456..

Berger A. N., Hanweck G. Humphrey D.B. (1987) 'Competitive Viability in Banking: Scale, Scope and Product Mix Economies', *Journal of Monetary Economics*, 20, 501-520.

Berger A. N., Humphrey D.B. (1990a) *Measurement and Efficiency Issues in Commercial Banking*, FED Finance and Economics Discussion Series, 151.

Berger A.N., Hannan T.H. (1993) *Using Efficiency Measures to distinguisch among alternative explanations of the Structure-Performance Relationship in Banking*, Federal Reserve Board, Finance and Economics Discussion Series, Washington.

Berger A.N., Hunter W.C., Timme S.G. (1993) 'The Efficiency of Financial Institutions: a Review and Preview of Research Past, Present and Future', *Journal of Banking and Finance*, 17/2-3, 221-249.

Berndt E.R., Christensen L.R. (1973) 'The translog Function and the Substitution of Equipment, Structures and Labour in U.S. Manufacturing, 1929-68', *Journal of Econometrics*, 1, 81-114.

Cardani A.M., Castagna M., Galeotti M. (1991) 'La misurazione dell'efficienza economica: un'applicazione al sistema bancario italiano', *Ricerche Economiche*, XLV(1), 57-77.

Charnes A., Cooper W.W., Huang Z.M., Sun D. (1990) 'Polyhedral Cone-Ratio Dea Models with an illustrative Application to large commercial Banks', *Journal of Econometrics*, 46, 73-91.

Charnes A., Cooper W.W., Rhodes E. (1978) 'Measuring the Efficiency of Decision Making Units', *European Journal of Operational Research*, 2, 429-44.

Colwell R.J., Davis E.P. (1992) 'Output and Productivity in Banking', *The Scandinavian Journal of Economics*, Special Issue on 'Productivity Concepts and Measurement Problems', S111-S130.

Coelli T. J. (1991) *Maximum-likelihood Estimation of Stochastic Frontier Production Functions with Time-Varying Technical Efficiency using the Computer Program FRONTIER Version 2.0*, Working Papers in Econometrics and Applied Statistics, University of New England, Armidale.

Comana M. (1992) 'La dimensione delle banche: tra localismo e economie di scala', *Banche e banchieri*, 2, 87-99.

Conti V., Resti A. (1994) 'What can be learned about banks' profitability from their balance-sheet?', *Proceedings of the ICCBE Meeting*, Tokio.

Cornwell C., Schmidt P., Sickles R.C. (1990) 'Production Frontiers with cross-sectional and time-series Variation in Efficiency Levels', *Journal of Econometrics*, 46, 185-200.

Déprins D., Simar L., Tulkens H. (1984) 'Measuring Labour Efficiency in Post Offices' in Marchand M., Pestieau P, Tulkens H. (eds.) *The Performance of Public Enterprises: Concepts and Measurements*, North-Holland Amsterdam.

Dermine J., Röller L.H.(1991) *Economies of Scale and Scope in the French Mutual Funds (SICAV) Industry*, Working Paper Series, S-91-28, New York University Salomon Center.

Diewert W.E. (1974) 'Applications of Duality Theory', in Intrilligator M., Kendrick D. (eds.), *Frontiers of Quantitative Economics*, vol. 2, North Holland, Amsterdam.

Drake L. (1992) 'Economies of scale and scope in UK building societies: an application of the translog multiproduct cost function', *Applied Financial Economics*, 2(4), 211-220.

Faini R., Galli G., Giannini C. (1992) 'Finance and Development: the Case of Southern Italy', *Temi di Discussione*, Banca d'Italia, Roma.

Färe R., Grosskopf S., Logan J. (1985) 'The relative Performance of publicly-owned and privately-owned electric Utilities', *Journal of Public Economics*, 26, 89-106.

Farrell M.J. (1957) 'The measurement of productive efficiency', *Journal of the Royal Statistical Society*, Series A. CXX, 253-281.

Favero C.A., Papi L. (1993) *Technical and scale efficiency in the Italian banking sector. A non-parametric approach*, Laboratorio di Analisi Monetaria, Università Cattolica del Sacro Cuore, Milano.

Ferrier G., Lovell C.A. Knox (1990) 'Measuring cost Efficiency in Banking: Econometric and Linear Programming Evidence', *Journal of Econometrics*, 46, 229-245.

Fried H.O., Lovell C.A. Knox, Schmidt S.S. (eds.) *The Measurement of Productive Efficiency*: Techniques and Applications, Oxford University Press, Oxford.

Gilligan T.W, Smirlock M.L, Marshall W. (1984) 'Scale and scope Economies in the multiproduct banking Firm', *Journal of Monetary Economics*, 13, 393-405.

Greenbaum S. I. (1967a) 'A study of bank cost', *National Banking Review*, June, 415-434.

Greenbaum S. I. (1967b) 'Competition and Efficiency in the Banking System - Empirical Research and its Policy Implications', *Journal of Political Economy*, June, 461-481.

Greene W. (1980) 'On the Estimation of a flexible Frontier Production Model', *Journal of Econometrics*, 13, 101-115.

Greene W. (1993) 'The econometric Approach to Efficiency Analysis' in Fried H.O., Lovell C.A. Knox, Schmidt S.S. (eds.) *The Measurement of Productive Efficiency: Techniques and Applications*, Oxford University Press, Oxford.

Humphrey D.B. (1990) 'Why do Estimates of Bank Scale Economies Differ?', *Economic Review*, Federal Reserve Bank of Richmond, September/October, 38-50.

Humphrey D.B. (1992) 'Flow Versus Stock Indicators of Banking Output: Effects on Productivity and Scale Economy Measurement', *Journal of Financial Services Research*, 6, 115-135.

Jondrow J., Lovell C.A. Knox, Materov I.S., Schmidt P. (1982) 'On the Estimation of Technical Inefficiency in the stochastic Frontier Production Function Model', *Journal of Econometrics*, 19, 233-238.

Jorgenson D.W. (1986) 'Econometric Methods for Modeling Producer Behavior', in Griliches Z., Intriligator M.D. (eds.), *Handbook of Econometrics*, Volume III, Elsevier Science Publishers, BV.

Kopp R.J. (1981) 'The measurement of productive efficiency: A reconsideration', *Quarterly Journal of Economics*, 96, 477-503.

Kopp R.J., Diewert W.E. (1982) 'The decomposition of frontier cost function deviations into measures of technical and allocative efficiency', *Journal of Econometrics*, 19, 319-331.

Kumbhakar S.C. (1991) 'The Measurement and Decomposition of Cost-Inefficiency: the translog Cost System', *Oxford Economic Papers*, 43, 667-683.

Kumbhakar S.C., Hjalmarsson L. (1993) 'Technical Inefficiency and Technical Progress in Sweedish Dairy Farms' in Fried H.O., Lovell C.A. Knox, Schmidt S.S. (eds.) *The Measurement of Productive Efficiency: Techniques and Applications*, Oxford University Press, Oxford.

Kuussaari H. (1993) *Productive Efficiency in Finnish Local Banking During 1985-1990*, Bank of Finland Discussion Papers, 14/93.

Leibenstein H. (1966) 'Allocative efficiency vs. X-efficiency', *American Economic Review*, 56(2), 392-415.

Leibenstein H. (1978) *General X-efficiency Theory and Economic Development*, Oxford University Press, Oxford.

Lovell C.A. Knox, Schmidt P. (1979) 'Estimating technical and allocative inefficiency relative to stochastic production and cost frontiers', *Journal of Econometrics*, 9, 343-366.

Lovell C.A. Knox, Schmidt P. (1980) 'Estimating stochastic production and cost frontiers when technical and allocative inefficiency are correlated', *Journal of Econometrics*, 13, 83-100.

Mansfield E. (1975) *Microeconomics: Theory and Applications*, W.W. Norton & C., New York.

McAllister P.H., McManus D. (1993) 'Resolving the scale efficiency puzzle in banking', *Journal of Banking and Finance*, 17/2-3, 389-406.

Meusen W., Van den Broek J. (1977) 'Efficiency estimation from Cobb-Doublas Production Functions with Composed Error', *International Economic Review*, 18/2, 435-444.

Olivei G. (1992), *Efficienza tecnica ed efficienza di scala nel settore bancario italiano: un approccio non parametrico*, Centro Paolo Baffi, Università L. Bocconi, Milano.

Resti A. (1995) *Tecniche per la misurazione dell'efficienza microeconomica nel settore bancario*, Research Doctorate Dissertation, University of Bergamo.

Retzlaff-Roberts D.L., Morey R.C. (1993) 'A goal programming method of stochastic Data Envelopment Analysis', *European Journal of Operational Research*, 71, 379-397.

Richmond J. (1974) 'Estimating the efficiency of production', *International Economic Review*, 15(2), 515-521.

Röller L.H. (1990) 'Proper quadratic cost Functions with an Application to the Bell System', *Review of Economics and Statistics*, 72, 202-210.

Schmidt P. (1976) 'On the statistical estimation of parametric frontier production functions', *Review of Economics and Statistics*, 58(2), 238-239.

Schmidt P., Sickles R.C. (1984) 'Production Frontiers and Panel Data', *Journal of Business and Economic Statistics*, 2, 367-374.

Shephard R. (1970) *Theory of Cost and Production Functions*, Princeton University Press, Princeton N.J.

Sherman H.D., Gold F. (1985) 'Bank branch operating efficiency: Evaluation with data envelopment analysis', *Journal of Banking and Finance*, 9, 297-316.

Sherman D.H., Ladino G. (1995) 'Managing bank productivity using data envelopment analysis (D.E.A.)', *Interfaces*, 25 (2), 60-73.

Stevenson R. (1980), 'Likelihood functions for generalized stochastic frontier estimation', *Journal of Econometrics*, 13, 58-66.

Stigler G.J. (1964) 'A Theory of Oligopoly', *Journal of Political Economy*.

Thanassoulis E., Dyson R.G. (1992) 'Estimating preferred target input-output levels using data envelopment analysis', *European Journal of Operational Research*, 56.

Varian H.L. (1990) *Microeconomic Analysis*, Second Edition, W.W.Norton & C., New York.

Zardkoohi A., Kolari J. (1994) 'Branch office economies of scale and scope: evidence from savings banks in Finland', *Journal of Banking and Finance*, 18, 421-432.

Measuring Managerial and Program Efficiencies in a Swedish Savings and Loan

Thomas Hartman[1] and James E. Storbeck[2]

[1] Management Department, Keele University, Keele, Staffs ST5 5BG, United Kingdom
[2] The Magellan Group, 3001 N. Lamar Blvd., Suite 107, Austin, Texas 78705, U.S.A.

Abstract. Using Data Envelopment Analysis (DEA), we measure the *managerial* and *program* efficiencies of service delivery in each of fifty branches of a Swedish savings and loan bank. The primary modeling framework used in this paper is based upon a decomposition first suggested by Charnes and Cooper [4], and later refined into its constituent components by Byrnes [3].

The service function under analysis in this study is best viewed from the traditional banking perspective of *intermediation*. That is, the bank plays the role of financial intermediary, receiving deposits from numerous customers and using these monies to generate loans and investments [5] [6]. Our concern in this paper is to measure the performance of a bank's management in achieving this transformation. Furthermore, we examine the efficiency of this service function at different levels of the organizational hierarchy.

1. Introduction

The banking industries of many countries have undergone considerable change in recent years, due to the advent of domestic deregulation policies, as well as an increase of international competition [7] [9]. Because of the rapidly changing environment for financial institutions, the flexible evaluation of performance has become an important topic to banking research and banking reality. Indeed, the rise in U.S. bank failures in recent years has underscored the importance of continuously monitoring the productivity of banks as multiproduct financial institutions [2].

In the context of the present research, organization of the banking function into a particular hierarchical form represents a "program" opportunity for the bank. In this specific example of a Swedish savings and loan, the banking function has been organized around and delivered from three types of offices or programs: the head office, the mid-sized office, and the small branch office. These organizational forms are differentiated by size of operations, the amount of "overhead" maintained, and the extent of their "service bundles." The service hierarchy thus resembles the "successively-inclusive" structure common to many retailing situations; that is, each successive service level in the hierarchy offers all services found at lower levels, plus some additional set of services unique to that level [11]. The present study, however, does not detail all service bundles and products offered throughout the organization, but focuses only on that common set of services found at all levels. In so doing, we are examining how well each organizational level performs this common banking function.

The paper is organized in the following fashion: the next section discusses the problem of assessing performance within a Swedish savings & loan, as well as the ways in which performance has been measured in such contexts. The third section explores the "inter-efficiency" framework of DEA, and explicitly links the decomposition of pure technical efficiency to concepts of managerial and program performance in this banking example. The results of our efficiency decomposition and analyses are reviewed in the fourth section, along with the implications for the improvement of branch bank performance. Concluding remarks about how these analytical techniques can be used in bank "reengineering" efforts are detailed in the final section.

2. Assessing bank performance

The problem at hand is the performance evaluation of fifty branch banks, located in twenty-six towns or villages in one region of Sweden. The data for this analysis are derived from operations during the first six months of 1994 and include a number of cost and revenue figures as well as non-monetary variables. The analysis is based on three models, named the Value-Added Model, the Productivity Model and the Simplified Productivity Model, each of them aiming to portray the relevant inputs and outputs of a bank branch. Thus, the three models differ in the choice of variables.

For the narrow purposes of constructing the intermediation model of banking performance, when constucting the Value-Added Model we use seven variables from the dataset. Inputs include Staff Costs, Computer Costs, Rent for Premises, and Other Costs; outputs are Amount of Deposits Amount of Loans and Amount of Subsidiary Loans. (All variables are stated in "current" Swedish Krona.) Clearly, the model formed with these variables suggests that the bank, functioning as a financial intermediary, uses labor, capital and other resources to transform these resources into revenue-producing assets, loans and deposits.

The choice to treat deposits as outputs can be questioned. In the banking literature we identify the 'Intermediary Model', in which deposits are regarded as inputs. The Intermediary Model is predominantly applied in studies of complete banks. When bank efficiency is studied at branch level it is, in our view, more relevant to treat deposits as outputs. We give two reasons for this. First, relative efficiency on bank branch level conveys information about the various branches' performance. This information is useful for tactical decisions, rather than strategic ones. It is assumed that the strategic decision once taken, namely to open and run a branch at a particular location, is a 'correct' decision. The market of each branch will, however, vary depending on the type of population. One branch is perhaps located in an area with predominantly younger families, another an industrial area, whereas relatively older people might make out the majority of the customers in a third branch. These differences in local markets will naturally have a significant impact on the demanded products (outputs). Thus, a bank branch which attracts large deposits may be just as vital to the profitability of the whole bank as a branch in which loans exceed deposits. Second, in modern banking bank branches enjoying surplus deposits 'sell' these retail funds to a central 'Treasury Pool'. The branch is then credited a transfer price whereby it receives a revenue. The branch will thus earn a sperad equal to to the spread it earns on loans. Therefore can both deposits and loans be regarded value creating products.

The second model, the Productivity Model, which will be used has the following inputs: i) Number of Employees, ii) Number of Terminals, iii) Premises (square meters), and iv) number of customers. The outputs are i) Amount of Deposits, ii) Amount of Loans, iii) Amount of Subsidiary Loans, and iv) Number of Transactions. The choice of variables attempts to resemble the Value Added Model using non-monetary variables. In including the amount of transactions together with deposits and loans we allow the model, however on an aggregate level, to encompass the core activities of a bank branch.

Finally, a third model is used as well, the Simplified Productivity Model, in which it is assumed the a banks output can be summarized in only one output variable: number of transactions.

3. Measuring and decomposing efficiency

The view of efficiency put forward in the present study is one of input conservation. That is, a branch is considered efficient, relative to its peers, if it is able to generate the same amount of revenue using less resources. Consequently, we develop an input-based efficiency measure within the DEA framework (see [7] for details of such models). Those bank branches that are able to minimize the ratio of outputs-to-inputs, relative to other branches, are considered perfectly efficient and are thus found on the "best practice frontier." Those branches which are less efficient are found some distance from that frontier, with their distance being the basis for measuring the extent of their inefficiency.

Comparisons of performance by "groups" or "classes" of bank branches are facilitated by application of the DEA model in an *inter*-efficiency framework [3]. In this case, bank branches are first grouped by type of office (i.e., "head," "mid-sized" or "small"). The efficiency of each branch is then assessed in relation to its own group or type. This *within*-type efficiency is depicted in Figure 1 for branch D_h, a "head office," as the ratio of distances OD''/OD_h. [NB: For purposes of graphical clarity and with no loss of generality, we limit consideration to only two frontiers in Figure 1.] This measure indicates the general relationship between head offices and the "best-practice-head-office" frontier (denoted as curve B_hC_h); it is expressed as the minimum percentage of resource usage necessary to produce a given level of output. Thus, for a given level of output, an efficiency score of 90% for a bank office indicates that, if the branch were able to produce this output using only 90% of its observed resource levels, it would be perfectly efficient and residing on the best practice frontier. Consequently, the average of this ratio over all head offices is a measure of the *managerial efficiency* of head offices. Similarly, the managerial efficiency for the group of mid-size offices is obtained by averaging these distance ratios of mid-sized offices from their own frontier, curve A_mE_m in Figure 1.

In order to derive program efficiency, we next measure the *pooled* efficiency of each bank branch against the *inter-envelope* or grand frontier, A_mC_h, which is merely a convex construction of the office-type frontiers. For branch D_h in Figure 1, this efficiency amounts to the ratio OD'/OD_h and, when computed for each branch, documents all distances from a common, fixed frontier. Taking the ratio of *pooled*-to-*within* efficiencies produces the *between*-office type efficiencies of branches, the average of which measures *program* efficiency. In Figure 1, D_h's between-type efficiency is OD'/OD''; it suggests that, even if D_h were operating at "best practice" levels (*i.e.*, point D" on the "head office frontier"), it would be

Capital

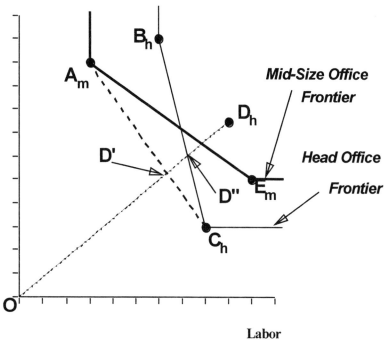

Figure 1: Efficiency Decomposition

inefficient relative to other office-type best practices. Consequently, this measure suggests that certain levels of inefficiency are associated merely with the adoption of a program, not its management.

4. Patterns of performance

The average efficiency scores associated with each of the three office types are shown in Table 1, along with averages for the group of fifty branches. The classification of office types (Small, Mid Size and Head) is the one used by the Savings Bank itself. The Head branches are in average 20% larger than the Mid Size and the Small branches. The Mid Sized and Small branches are, in average, very similar in size. The difference between these two categories lies in their product and service range rather than in size.

As the table indicates, the small branch office clearly dominates the other office types in all three efficiency dimensions. The *pooled* measure, for example, shows that small branch banks, on average, are more efficient (90.27%) than are head offices (86.24%) or mid-sized offices (86.88%). The question remains, however, as to the source of this efficiency advantage: is it managerial or programmatic?

Examination of the *within* and *between* columns in Table 1 reveals the fact that it is "some of both." That is, the average level of *managerial efficiency* for the small branch office (94.57%) is better than that for head offices (90.07%), as well as that for mid-sized offices (91.53%). However, the highest level of *program efficiency* is noted for the head-office branches, followed by that for small (95.34%) and mid-sized (94.67%) offices. Generally, however, the differences between the groups are small. We therefore turn to the second model to explore if any of the categories are found to be particularly efficient.

Table 1: Efficiency Decomposition - Value Added Model

Office Type	Pooled Mean (St. Dev.)	Within Mean (St. Dev.)	Between Mean (St. Dev.)
All (n=50)	87.29 (12.66)	91.44 (10.95)	95.29 (5.28)
Head (n=26)	86.24 (13.34)	90.07 (12.14)	95.58 (4.50)
Mid-Size (n=13)	86.88 (13.34)	91.53 (11.45)	94.67 (5.16)
Small (n=11)	90.27 (10.66)	94.57 (6.77)	95.34 (7.30)

Table 2 shows the efficiency scores for the Productivity Model. The results both confirm and deviate from the previous one. The only category to have a higher than average efficiency score is the small branch category, both the *pooled* measure (96.29%) and the *within* measure (99.53%) are higher than the respective averages (88.58% and 93.65%). When we examine the program efficiency (*between*) the mid-sized branches together with the head branches achieve the lowest average score (93.07% and 93.93% respectively). Compared with the previous model, this result indicate the superiority of the smaller branches. From a *program efficiency* perspective, both models indicate the mid-sized branches to be the inferior ones.

Table 2: Efficiency Decomposition - Productivity Model

Office Type	Pooled Mean (St. Dev.)	Within Mean (St. Dev.)	Between Mean (St. Dev.)
All	88.58	93.65	94.32
(n=50)	(13.08)	(9.73)	(7.48)
Head	86.76	92.16	93.93
(n=26)	(13.87)	(10.59)	(8.65)
Mid-Size	85.71	91.66	93.07
(n=13)	(14.27)	(10.54)	(6.76)
Small	96.29	99.53	96.72
(n=11)	(5.32)	(1.05)	(4.86)

Finally, in the Simplified Productivity Model (Table 3) it has been assumed that all output from a bank branch can be summarized in one output, namely number of transactions. These transactions are the ones that are manually performed in the branch. Transactions performed automatically are thus not included. The figures shown in table 3 confirm yet again the previous results. When focusing on the *pooled* figures the small branches appear even more superior than before with an average of 68% compared with circa 50% for the two other branch categories. However, the *within* scores tell a different story with the mid-sized branches showing a significantly higher managerial performance than the head offices and the small branches. From a program (*between*) perspective the mid-sized branches again seem to suffer under an unfavourable organizational outline (61.82%), whereas the opposite is indicated for the small branches (99.77%).

Table 3: Efficiency Decomposition - Simplified Productivity Model

Office Type	Pooled Mean (St. Dev.)	Within Mean (St. Dev.)	Between Mean (St. Dev.)
All	54.20	69.76	78.72
(n=50)	(18.63)	(19.39)	(17.73)
Head	49.65	64.01	78.27
(n=26)	(17.15)	(18.45)	(15.18)
Mid-Size	51.51	82.53	61.82
(n=13)	(15.12)	(15.16)	(9.40)
Small	68.13	68.28	99.77
(n=11)	(20.38)	(20.37)	(0.33)

Naturally the choice of variables play a decisive role in the outcomes above. A special feature of Swedish banking is that in recent years banks are strongly encouraging their customers to use telephone banking and to pay their bills using bank giro via mail. If we assume that head branches and perhaps also mid-sized branches are more active than the small branches in promoting these services or more successful in their endeavour, they will, in the short run, inevitably appear inefficient compared with the small branch category. Thus, in the short run perspective the results could indicate that the small branches are doing things right rather than the right thing, whereas in the long run the head branches could be doing the right thing, whereas the small branches might not.

This hypothesis is somewhat supported by the average scale efficiency scores presented in table 4. When we examine the scale efficiencies for the Value Added Model, and focus our attention on the head and mid-sized branch categories, they show very similar and rather high average scores. The same is true for the Productivity Model, with scale efficiency scores of circa 96-97% for all three branch categories. The small branches show a lower scale efficiency index than the other two branch categories in both the Value Added Model and, particularly, in the Simplified Productivity Model. Thus, a larger part of the small branches' inefficiencies can be explained by them being suboptimally sized than that of the

Table 4: Scale Efficiency

Office Type	Value Added Model (Pooled) Mean (St. Dev.)	Productivity Model (Pooled) Mean (St. Dev.)	Simplified Productivity Model (Pooled) Mean (Std.dev)
All	94.82	96.71	86.23
(n=50)	(5.50)	(5.54)	(15.31)
Head	97.82	96.28	91.56
(n=26)	(4.33)	(5.56)	(11.51)
Mid-Size	96.16	97.67	85.87
(n=13)	(3.78)	(3.21)	(12.05)
Small	93.43	96.59	74.07
(n=11)	(6.78)	(4.88)	(20.17)

mid-sized and head branches. This outcome *could* reflect the fact that the head branches have been relatively more successful in promoting customer 'self-service' products. The head branches will then appear scale efficient but managerially and programmatically less efficient either because the model does not include the automatic transactions or because the head branches have not reduced inputs which are no longer required.

Finally, the patterns give strong indications that the banking functions, as defined in this study, are best carried out by the small office branches of the organization. Further, we might note that the highest average level of managerial *inefficiency* is found in the head offices of the bank. Concomitantly, the highest level of program *inefficiency* is associated with the mid-sized offices. Clearly, there is a distinct disadvantage, when compared to other office types, to carrying out the bank branch function at this level of the hierarchy.

5. Conclusions: Support for reengineering

Using data from a Swedish savings and loan, this study has measured the managerial and program efficiencies of service delivery in fifty branches of the bank. Moreover, we have demonstrated how performance, with regard to the intermediation process, varies with service level. Specifically, we have shown that small branch offices, though limited in resources, tend to be the most efficient financial intermediaries in the system. Head offices, though somewhat efficient in terms of best practice, have the highest levels of managerial inefficiency, while the lowest program efficiencies are associated with mid-size branches. The paper has also pointed out the importance of choosing variables that reflect the problem at hand.

In more general contexts, it has been suggested that, due to the highly competitive nature of today's business environment, organizations need to participate in nothing short of "...the fundamental rethinking and radical redesign of business processes" [8]. The end result of such "reengineering" efforts should be a collection of activities that takes multiple inputs and creates an output consistent with "contemporary measures of performance...." In a context more directly related to the present study, Allen has suggested that the banking industry, more so than most other sectors of the economy, could benefit greatly from the reengineering movement, by attempting to disentangle the complex web of historical cost structures [1]. To that end, he has offered a typology of "levers" that drive bank costs, which he broadly classifies as *management levers* and *infrastructure levers*. The former consist of strategic and organizational management factors that are linked with customer, product, and geography. The latter factors are said to be common to all organization structures in banks: process, functions, physical plant, systems, and "pure" overhead.

It is our contention that the distinction between managerial and program efficiencies, though somewhat more narrow in its technical definition, can offer important guidance in the redesign of banking processes. After all, the focus of such analysis is not just upon determining *how well* things are managed, but also on deciding the way programs of activities can be effectively *structured*. With these twin concerns in mind, our study has endeavored to demonstrate the utility of DEA in the evaluation and continuous improvement of banking processes.

References

[1]   Allen, P., *Reengineering The Bank*, Probus Publishing, Chicago, 1994.

[2]   Barr, R., Seiford, L. and Siems, T., "An Envelopment-Analysis Approach to Measuring the Managerial Quality of Banks," mimeo, 1992.

[3]   Byrnes, P., "The Effect of Ownership on Efficiency: A Nonparametric Programming Approach," Ph.D. Dissertation, Southern Illinois University, Carbondale, Illinois, 1985.

[4]   Charnes, A. and Cooper, W.W., "Auditing and Accounting for Program Efficiency and Management Efficiency in Not-For-Profit Entities," *Accounting, Organizations and Society*, Vol. 5, No. 1, 1980, pp. 87-107.

[5]   Colwell, R. and Davis, E., "Output and Productivity in Banking," *Scandinavian Journal of Economics*, Vol. 94 (Supplement), 1992, pp. 111-129.

[6]   Drake, L. and Weyman-Jones, T., "Technical and Scale Efficiency in UK Building Societies," *Applied Financial Economics*, Vol. 2, pp. 1-9.

[7]   Hartman, T. and Storbeck, J., "Efficiency in Swedish Banking: An Analysis of Loan Operations," Paper presented at the Eighth International Seminar on Production Economics, Igls, Austria, February 21-25, 1994.

[8]   Hammer, M. and J. Champy, *Reengineering The Corporation*, Harper Business, New York, 1993.

[9]   Lewis, M. and Davis, K., *Domestic and International Banking*, Philip Allan, Oxford, 1987.

[10]   Sherman, H. and Gold, F., "Bank Branch Operating Efficiency," *Journal of Banking and Finance*, Vol. 9, 1985, pp. 297-315.

[11]   Storbeck, J., "Classical Central Places as Protected Thresholds," *Geographical Analysis* Vol. 22, 1990, pp. 4-23.

Acknowledgment. The authors wish to express their gratitude to Bankforskningsinstitutet (The Bank Research Institute) at Stockholm School of Economics for financial support and to an anonymous Savings Bank for providing data.

Bankruptcies, Indebtedness and the Credit Crunch[1]

Kari Takala[2] and Matti Virén[3]

[1] Financial support from the Swedish Economic Council, the Academy of Finland and the Yrjö Jahnsson Foundation and helpful comments from the participants of the 17th Meeting of the Euro Working Group in Financial Modelling, in Bergamo, June 1-3, 1995, in particular Giorgio Calcagnini, and two anonymous referees are gratefully acknowledged.
[2] Bank of Finland, P.O. Box 160, 00101 Helsinki, Finland.
[3] University of Turku, Department of Economics, 20500 Turku, Finland.

Abstract. This paper deals with Finnish bankruptcies. It shows that bankruptcies are strongly related to the business cycle and that they are perhaps even more strongly related to indebtedness, real interest rates and asset prices. The importance of these financial factors probably increased when the financial markets were liberalized in the early 1980s. Although there is a lot of seasonal and cyclical variation in bankruptcies the long run level (especially when adjusted to the number of firms) is almost constant representing some sort of "a natural rate of bankruptcies". What makes bankruptcies so important is the fact that they directly affect production, employment and credit expansion. The credit crunch effect in particular is scrutinized in the paper.

Keywords: bankruptcy, financial distress, credit crunch

1   Introduction

One of the prime purposes of a bankruptcy is to settle accounts with creditors and to establish a market value for the company as a whole. A major task in bankruptcy settlement is to prevent a firm from running into further debt, which is the main concern of the creditors. In most bankruptcies the amount of debt is greater than the value of the assets, which leads to financing costs to both creditors and debtors. Another difficulty crops up here, since a company is usually worth more as an operational unit than as the sum of its separate parts. It has been emphasized that a firm is a functional entity, and by far the greatest part of its value is imbedded in the cooperation between its employees.

In general, it can be argued that bankruptcies result mainly from bad management, unnecessarily risky or unlucky investment projects or, as in recent times, unexpected rapidly diminishing demand. In Finland, bankruptcies have emerged as a macroeconomic problem recently as a consequence of an unforeseen rapid decline in GDP and in total domestic demand. Several factors, like the collapse in trade with the former Soviet Union, deterioration of the terms of trade, increased foreign indebtedness because of devaluations and rising real interest rates, can be seen as primary causes of recession. However, the first hints from the growth in bankruptcies can be traced back already to the start of financial liberalization in 1983. There seems to be some evidence that the easening of bank lending and weaker ties to clients, and hence less control feedback from firms to banks, is responsible for the large losses seen during the recent recession.

The overheating of the Finnish economy occured after 1986, as interest rate regulation was abolished and the obstacles to capital movements were gradually removed. During the period of overheating, which lasted from late 1986 up to the spring of 1989, a very large number of new firms were started up. Most of the financing came in the form of bank loans. Thus, bank lending increased at a real rate of 20–30 % during this period, which obviously induced a huge increase in the prices of all financial and real assets. At the same time, indebtedness increased, of course, and when income and asset prices started to fall, indebtedness became a very serious problem.

Indebtedness, in the face of an exceptionally deep recession, was an obvious cause of the wave of bankruptcies and the credit crunch which are studied in this paper. The Finnish case is not, of course, exceptional, although the magnitude of the crisis makes it an interesting case for empirical analysis (for the shake of comparison, see e.g. Gunther, et al. 1995 and Shrieves and Dahl 1995 for the U.S. case).

In this paper we try to develop a macroeconomic model of bankruptcies. For this purpose we first look at certain stylized facts regarding Finland. We make use of data which cover a relatively long period, 1920–1994. The data are monthly, although we use mainly annual frequencies in the empirical analysis. The modelling is based on a cointegration analysis which deals with bankruptcies and certain important macroeconomic variables, both financial and non-financial. In addition to bankruptcies we model bank lending, or strictly speaking credit expansion, and total output. The purpose of this type of modelling is to see the extent to which financial variables, along with cyclical macroeconomic variables, affect bankruptcies and what kind of feedback effect exists between bankruptcies and these variables. Specifically, the credit crunch hypothesis is subjected to testing.

2   Some background on bankruptcies

2.1 Historical background

Under the law, bankruptcy petitions and proceedings are registered by the courts and related data is gathered by Statistics Finland. The number of monthly bankruptcy proceedings[1] have been available since 1922 (see Figure 2). The previous large boom in bankruptcies can be linked with the Great Depression in the early 1930s. The current high level of bankruptcies is clearly unprecedented. Even if the total number firms in existence is taken into account, the level is very high – something one could probably not forecast a decade ago (for U.S. evidence, see e.g. Meehan 1993).

Bankruptcy proceedings can also be analysed using time series components like trend, seasonal component and irregular variation. The original monthly series look quite volatile even in logs. Analysis of the structural time series model shows that the level of bankruptcies has a large variance, but the trend is fairly stable. There is clearly also seasonal variation in bankruptcies, but the pattern of seasonal variation has changed significantly over the decades. Currently, the seasonal peaks are in January and September – November, while the lowest level of proceedings are in the summer and in December. The model estimations also show that the irregular variance of bankruptcies has been a major component of the total variation of bankruptcy proceedings (see Takala and Virén 1994). It could be argued that the process of generating bankruptcies during the Second World War was quite different at least from the period of financial regulation, which lasted from after the war up to 1983.

It is useful to compare the number of bankruptcies to the total number of firms. The number of firms itself has increased faster than population (see Table 1). The structure of production could also affect the number and share of bankruptcies. Industrial companies have been relatively big in Finland, but the increased amount of small service companies may also have raised the number of bankruptcies relative to firms. This may reflect the change in the structure of production, as the number of service firms has increased with rising GDP.

---

[1] A conceptual distinction could be made between two measures of bankruptcies. We speak of bankruptcy petitions (applications) registered by the courts and bankruptcy proceedings accepted by the courts for further action. In practice there could be several bankruptcy applications made by several creditors regarding the same firm, whereas proceedings register only one case for each firm. It is also possible that the debtor himself could apply for bankruptcy. The bankrutcy resettlement procedure available from 1993 must be applied and approved by the debtor himself.

Table 1. **Bankruptcies and number of firms in Finland**

Year	Number of bankruptcies	Number of firms	Population in thousands	Bankruptcies/ population, %	Bankruptcies/ firms, %
1922	725	6763	3228	.022	1.97
1930	1945	10410	3463	.056	2.66
1940	265	15068	3696	.007	0.33
1950	406	24030	4030	.010	0.69
1960	829	32011	4446	.019	1.06
1970	1361	45352	4598	.030	1.24
1980	1057	56134	4788	.018	1.16
1985	2122	109806	4911	.043	2.57
1990	3588	133321	4998	.072	2.12
1991	6155	125121	5029	.122	4.18
1992	7348	125700	5055	.145	5.02
1993	6769	117295	5080	.133	4.93
1994	5502	118000*	5099	.108	3.77*

Starred values are forecasts. Bankruptcies/firms (i.e., the business failure rate) is computed in terms of corporate bankruptcies (i.e., individual bankruptcies are excluded).

The number of bankruptcies varies with the phase of the business cycle. When GDP grows rapidly the ratio of bankruptcies to number of firms is small. This is a result of both a smaller number of bankruptcies and a larger number of new firms start-ups. In a recession the number of bankruptcies will increase while the number of firms increases slowly or even decreases.

The number of bankruptcies depends on various factors. Firms that go into bankruptcy are mainly small companies with heavy debt with respect to cash flow or net profits. In these small companies the personal losses of entrepreneurs are also the largest. Even if we leave out those bankruptcies that have taken place without further demands on debt capital, the equity of bankrupt firms is on average only half of their total debt. In addition to the size of the firm, the industry, the phase in the business cycle and the capital structure predict the probability of bankruptcy.

In addition to these macroeconomic indicators, a few microeconomic indicators have proved to be useful in predicting bankruptcies. The number of payment failures precedes bankruptcies at the firm level as well as in the aggregate. Unfortunately, the series on payment failures covered only the period 1987 to 1994 and cannot be used in the present context.

During the 1980s the distribution of new bankcruptcies in different industries was relatively stable. Most of the bankruptcies occurred in commerce (28 %) and manufacturing (23 %), followed by construction and services, each with about a 16 per cent share (see Figure 3). The devaluation of the markka in November 1991 and the float starting in September 1992 shifted bankruptcies from the export (open) to the closed sector. One worrying feature of the recent bankruptcy boom is the fact that the share of bankruptcies applied for by debtors itself has been increasing. Whereas normal bankruptcy applications are used as means of collecting debt, this is not the case when a debtor itself applies bankruptcy.

Later we cite evidence that bankruptcies could be an indicator of an equilibrium process with supply being equated to diminishing demand. If the slowdown in demand is fast enough, there is no time to cut production and other firms try to keep up their cash flows as well. In this case firms with excess debt will get into difficulties and later on will reach the final dead end. This theory is based on the fact that total demand and supply will be cointegrated in the long-run. Despite the fact that demand and supply are integrated of order one, the bankruptcies/companies ratio will be stationary as one linear combination between these variables. Bankruptcies nevertheless have a positive mean and finite variance.

Bankruptcies are obviously related to employment and unemployment. Bankruptcies directly create unemployment. The causal relationship, however, is more complicated because unemployment can cause bankruptcies via decreased demand. In this study we cannot thoroughly analyze the bankruptcy-unemployment relationship because the historical unemployment data is somewhat deficient. Suffice it to mention that for a short sample period (1960–1993) we found that the causation goes unambiguously from bankruptcies to unemployment, not vice versa.

Money market liberalization seems to have affected the bankruptcy generation mechanism in Finland and other Nordic countries. This can be seen directly from the plot of bankruptcies. The number of bankruptcies started to rise even during 1984 (although the economy grew rather fast, at the rate of 3–5 %, until 1989). The regulation of bank lending kept the bankruptcy figures low up to the mid–1980s. After this regulation was loosened, the tight control of banks ended suddenly. For firms, financing through the stock market also became more attractive. However, debt-equity ratios began to rise slowly already in 1985. In Finland an important turning point in financing was achieved when firms involved in foreign trade started to intermediate foreign loans through their accounts. Banks demanded similar operating room and started to rapidly expand their currency loan portfolios. When the regulation of lending interest rates was abolished in autumn 1986, the supply of bank loans increased rapidly.

The increase in real bank lending rose up to as high as 30 per cent p.a. in 1986–1989. Therefore, an increase in bankruptcy was to be expected sooner or later. What was unknown at the time was that the economic slowdown would be as steep as it turned out to be. Firms' indebtedness has had the effect of a rising real interest rates very sharply for firms operating in the closed sector of the economy. These problems were not relieved with the devaluation of the markka in November 1991. Firms with foreign debt suffered from the devaluation, and those firms which operated in the domestic sector, i.e. which had only domestic returns, faced the biggest problems. They had large capital costs, wages were sticky (in fact, wage costs even increased because of the unemployment compensation system) and prices could not be in increased because of the overall excess supply in the domestic markets. Bankruptcies created further bankrutptcies because some bankrupt firms continued their activities under the bankruptcy authority. In many cases, these firms created market disturbances because they demanded much lower prices – they had no cost worries!

The increasing risk of bankruptcy in the late 1980s and early 1990s is to a large extend a consequence of the rapid growth of financing and thereof of the number of firms. Over a half of the bankrupt firms have been operating under five years. Firms 2–3 years in age have had the highest risk of ending up in bankruptcy.

2.2 The credit crunch and bankruptcies

The role of bank lending is crucial in the generation of bankruptcies, since bank debt is the major source of financing to small and medium sized Finnish firms. In every recession bank lending and credit availability decelerate. Therefore, it is useful to look at whether credit availability is now more restrictive than in similar declining phases of previous business cycles. Historically, credit crunches have started from a decline in bank deposits. The current credit crunch, however, is more or less linked to the decline in the asset prices and in collateral values and, of course, to the fall in income and the resulting failure in debt servicing. This has caused debt losses and therefore, through shrinking bank equity, forced banks to cut their lending.

In Finland, as in other Nordic countries, the state has guaranteed the BIS capital ratio requirement of 8 per cent. In this sense the credit crunch is a consequence of a capital crunch. A major reason for the debt losses has been the drop in real estate prices as well as all other asset prices. The capital crunch has especially increased bankruptcies among small and medium size firms in the closed sector. This is natural since they have relied heavily on bank credit for financing. The attendent loss in bank capital is the main difference between the current business cycle and previous ones since the Second World War.

The background for the Finnish case is such that it could come directly from a textbook. The financial markets were liberalized in a situation where the economy was experiencing one of the strongest booms since the second World War. Interest rate control was abolished, first from lending rates and, after about one year, from deposit rates. Capital controls were also abolished. Demand for credit was exceptional high because of a backlog of unsatisfied excess demand, high income growth expectations and relatively low real interest rates.

Before liberalization, there had been a very long period of excess demand and credit rationing. During that period banks had very close relationships with their customers. New customers were carefully scrutinized before they got bank loans and many of them did not get loans at all. In the case of a household, a very long history as a customer and a large downpayment were required.

With liberalization the importance of customer relationships diminished (at least temporarily). Obviously this weakened banks ability to monitor the quality of their customers. Perhaps more important, however, was the fact that banks started to compete for market shares. Banks have relatively few instruments which they can use in competition. In the Finnish case, lending was used as an instruments of competition. Thus, more advantageous lending terms were offered to new customers.[2] It comes as no surprise that those banks that competed hardest for new clients got a disproportionately large share of the bad clients with high credit risk and, in some cases, even criminal intentions (this is something one might expect on the basis of the principles of adverse selection moral hazard). In particular, savings banks adopted this kind of very aggressive growth strategy which later on led to complete disaster.

Savings banks (and to some extent cooperative banks) tried to expand their lending to the corporate sector. Because of scale considerations and customer/ownership relationships, they had to concentrate on small firms operating in the domestic market. This sectoral concentration created considerable credit risk, which was unfortunately actualized during the recent recession. As for the commercial banks, also they competed heavily for market shares. Much of their resources was used in "ownership races" in which the banks tried to gain or secure ownership in the largest firms.

Still another problem was caused by developments in the real estate market. In Finland, as in most OECD countries (see O'Brien and Browne 1992), all banks increased their lending in the real estate market relative to

---

[2] There is some evidence suggesting that banks were very poor in pricing the risks of their loan contracts. The risk premia were in some cases even negative! See e.g. Murto (1993).

the industrial and commercial sectors. It would be an exaggeration to argue that the whole housing boom originated from excessive credit expansion. In Finland the housing boom in the late 1980s was perhaps the most striking in the whole OECD area (see e.g. Loikkanen et al. 1992). When the market collapsed after 1989, banks faced a huge risk exposure. There was huge overcapacity in the construction industry and a huge stock of new unsold houses. House prices fell in real terms more than 50 per cent in the early 1990s (land prices also fell considerably although the drop in stock prices was still much more dramatic.

As a consequence Finnish banks became fragile and financially vulnerable to lower credit quality, declining profitability and deflation of collateral values. Much of this change could be seen as cyclical, but the heart of the problem seems to be structural. It has been estimated that it will take at least until the end of the decade for the increased indebtedness to melt away. The Finnish experience repeats the similar history of a bad slump in the real estate business in the US, Norway and UK (for the US case, see e.g. Syron 1991).

In Finland, the depression lasted until 1993 and an upturn started in 1994. Bankruptcies have not yet, however, decreased to the pre-recession level (nor has unemployment). Perhaps the most important change which has taken place is the decrease in indebtedness (see Figure 2). Bank lending has considerably decreased since 1990 in both nominal and real terms. It can be argued that this is caused by both demand and supply effects. The demand for credit has decreased both because of reduced investment activity and the need to restore a more healthy financial structure. Increased uncertainty may also have contributed to this course of development.

On the supply side, banks have experienced unprecedented credit losses and all banks have been in serious difficulties regarding bankruptcy or merger (or, more probably, government takeover). There are several signs that banks' behaviour has changed towards the pre-liberalization period rules. This, in turn, shows up in more stringent lending conditions, choice of customers, collateral requirements etc. Thus, non-price rationing is again used to some extent. Obviously, it is very difficult to say how much of the decrease in bank lending is caused by demand and supply considerations. In the subsequent empirical analysis we try identify both effects, but quite naturally we are more interested in the supply effects. That is because it is almost self-evident that there are demand effects. Whether there are important supply, or credit crunch, effects is already a more controversial question.

3 Empirical analysis

3.1 Outline of the analysis

In this chapter we model the behaviour of bankruptcies, credit expansion and output. The emphasis is on the analysis of bankruptcies. Thus, we try to find out to what extent bankruptcies depend on the main financial variables: indebtedness, real interest rates and stock prices. In addition, we scrutinize the importance of certain other macroeconomic variables which should matter, especially in a small open economy framework: the terms of trade, the real exchange rate, labour costs and, of course, aggregate demand.

When modelling credit expansion we pay particular attention to the reverse relationship between bankruptcies and bank credit. Thus, we try to determine whether credit expansion – when it is controlled by various determinants of the supply of and demand for bank loans – is indeed sensitive to bankruptcy risk. If a negative relationship can be asserted between bankruptcies and credit expansion, we may conclude that the credit crunch hypothesis is not completely at odds with the (Finnish) data.

Finally, we consider the link between total output and bankruptcies. The question is then whether bankruptcies help in predicting output developments. This question is analyzed with the help of a relatively simple reduced form output growth equation, which also includes stock prices together with some more conventional determinants of output.

In modelling these variables an obvious starting point would the analysis of co-integration (see Engle and Granger 1987 and Johansen 1991). We make use of this analysis although – at least at this stage – we cannot fully utilize the co-integration framework in building the empirical model for all of these variables. In some earlier analyses (see Takala and Virén 1994 for details) it turned out that bankruptcies, output and credit are co-integrated with one (and no more or no less) co-integration vector.

It is obvious, however, that the cointegration relationship is more complicated, at least in a setting in which we focus on the long-run development of an economy. Complications came especially from certain measurement problems. It is very difficult to get reliable measures of the number of firms and so to get a precise idea of the true importance of bankruptcies. Other problems concern the measurement of debt and financial assets. We have relatively good data on banks' Finnish markka loans to the public but the data on foreign loans is very deficient. Unfortunately, the latter have constituted a significant portion of firms' financing in certain periods of time. We suspect that this "missing credit" problem is also the reason why it is so difficult to establish a reliable cointegration relationship for the determination of bank loans.

Although we still intend to build a complete dynamic model for the key variables in our study, at this point we adopt a more modest approach by specifying some simple single-equation models for the above-mentioned three variables. The dynamic specifications are also quite "old-fashioned" in the sense that we apply the conventional partial adjustment approach rather than the co-integration cum error-correction model strategy. In the case of bankruptcies, however, we use both approaches in building the estimating models.

As a first step in the empirical analysis, we scrutinize the time series (unit root) properties of the data series. Most of our data are monthly although some key variables are available only on an annual basis. Hence the analysis is carried out with both frequencies. The results from these analyses are reported in Table 2.

It is not difficult to see that the data for output, financial assets and liabilities, as well as for bankruptcies, are characterized by unit roots, while interest rates, terms of trade and the real exchange rate are roughly stationary $I(0)$ variables. This distinction between the variables should obviously be kept in mind when building the estimating models – at least to avoid nonsense regression models.

As far as bankruptcies are concerned there are two quite different alternatives. Either bankruptcies are stationary or some equilibrium error between bankruptcies and, say, indebtedness and demand is stationary. The first alternative is a not a bad approximation, in particular when the number of bankruptcies is adjusted to the number of firms. Then some sort of "a natural rate of bankruptcies" emerges. Unfortunately, the second alternative does also get some support from the data. In fact, the quality of the data is not sufficiently good to allow for discriminating between these two alternative views. Thus, in the subsequent empirical analysis, both alternatives are developed.

Table 2. **Unit root tests for the time series**

	Annual data	Monthly data
Bankruptcies (b)	-1.087	-1.307
Bank lending (l)	0.038	0.308
Gross Domestic Product (y)	-0.912	..
Industrial production (ip)	-0.243	-0.507
Terms of trade (tt)	-1.904	-3.226
Real exchange rate (fx)	-2.218	-3.038
Real interest rate (rm)	-3.126	-4.639
Consumer prices	-0.500	0.371
Money supply (m1)	-0.558	-0.559
Money supply (m2)	-1.389	-1.720
Stock prices (sx-dp)	-2.847	-2.165
Real wages (w)	0.262	-0.590
Government	-2.828	-4.860
expenditure/GDP	-0.232	-1.559
Stock exchange transactions	-3.079	..
Business failure rate (b-f)	-1.629	..
Bankrupt firms' debt (db-y)	-3.380	..
Cointegration vector (û1)	-4.099	..
Cointegration vector (û2)	-4.139	..
Cointegration vector (û3)		
Critical values, 5 %	-2.902	-2.865
Critical values, 1 %	-3.524	-3.440

Results are derived for the Augmented Dickey-Fuller test. The model includes a constant term and one (with monthly data four) lagged difference terms. The estimation period is 1925–1994 (1922M5–1994M12).

3.2 The analysis of bankruptcies

The model which we use for bankruptcies in this study is quite similar to earlier bankruptcy equations (see e.g. Altman 1983 and Laitinen 1990). This comes as no surprise because if we start from a standard firm's profit condition we end up with a model which depends on aggregate demand and certain cost variables. To derive the behavioural equation for bankruptcies we may use the following expression for a firm's net wealth (in real terms) as a point of departure:

$$AN_t = (1 + r_t)AN_{t-1} + \pi_t + \tau_t, \tag{1}$$

where AN denotes the firm's net wealth. π stands for profits which are determined by $pq - C(q)$ where p denotes the output price, q output and $C(q)$ production costs. Finally, τ denotes (net) capital gains.

Clearly, AN_t can be negative (and the firm may face bankruptcy) if π and/or $\tau < 0$. More precisely, a negative value of AN_t may actualize if the previous period's debts are large, output prices low, output demand low, production costs high, and capital gains negative. The effect of interest rates r on AN_t is basically ambiguous, but assuming that they have a negative effect on profits, a negative wealth effect also arises.

In a small open economy setting, one may measure p with the real exchange rate fx (and/or with the terms of trade tt). Output demand may be proxied by the Gross Domestic Product y and capital gains by stock prices sx.[3] Firms' net wealth creates some measurement problems but the indebtedness ratio (debts/GDP) $l - y$ may serve for this purpose.

We could then postulate the following relationship between bankruptcies b and possible explanatory variables:

$$b = b(l - y, \; y, \; r, \; fx \; \& \; tt, \; sx) \tag{2}$$
$${\scriptstyle(+)} \quad {\scriptstyle(-)} \quad {\scriptstyle(+)} \quad {\scriptstyle(-)} \qquad {\scriptstyle(-)}$$

One essential ingredient should still added to this model. That is the persistence bankruptcies. Bankruptcies today cause bankruptcies tomorrow for various reasons. First, other firms suffer credit losses. Second, some bankrupt firms continue operations with much lower operating costs creating an unhealthy competitive environment. Finally, bankruptcies change the operating procedures of other firms and banks for instance in terms of trade credit, collateral and so causing additional liquidity problems. This all implies that bankruptcies (or the business failure rate) depend on the previous periods' bankruptcies.

Here, we face the difficult problem of choosing the reference variable for the number of bankruptcies. It is not at all clear whether we should relate the number of bankruptcies to the number of firms (i.e. to consider the business failure rate) or to some other scale variable. The choice is even more difficult because the number-of-firms variable is quite deficient (the

---

[3] In an open economy setting, negative capital gains may also arise because exchange rate movements. I.e., depreciation of the domestic currency may increase the amount of foreign debt expressed in domestic currency. That is by the way exactly what happened in Finland in 1991-1992. Thus, the effect (real) exchange rate on AN_t is in principal ambiguous.

definition of a "firm" has changed considerably over time). Moreover, cointegration analysis does not give a clear-cut answer to the question of whether the business failure rate is stationary or not.

For these reasons we use some alternative definitions for the dependent bankruptcy variable. The estimating equation is derived from the firm's net wealth expression (1) using in the first place a simple partial adjustment mechanism as a point of departure. The individual variables are introduced into the model so that they are (at least approximately) stationary. Thus, the equation takes the following form:

$$(b-z) = \alpha_0 + \alpha_1(b-z)_{-1} + \alpha_2(1-y) + \alpha_3\Delta y + \alpha_4 rm + \alpha_5\Delta sx + \alpha_6 fx + \alpha_7 gs + \varepsilon, \qquad (3)$$

where b denotes bankruptcies and z possible reference variables, z=n indicates population and z=f the number of firms. ϵ is the error term. The other right-hand side variables have the following definition: $(1-y)$ is the indebtedness rate, Δy is the rate of change in GDP, rm is the real interest rate (government bond yield in real terms), Δsx is the rate of change in stock prices (deflated by consumption prices), fx the real exchange rate index and gs the central-government-expenditure share of GDP. The latter variable is introduced to take the Second World War into account. During the war years, the value of gs was close to 0.5 while in normal years the value has been around 0.1.[4]

The model is estimated with annual Finnish data covering the period 1923–1994. The corresponding OLS and Instrumental Variable estimates are presented in Table 3. In addition to aggregate figures, the table also indicates some estimates for sectoral equation although the data in this respect is quite deficient. In addition, a similar specification is estimated using an error-correction model. To obtain the error-correction term we estimated some alternative long-run (co-integration) equations (see Table 4). The following set of variables was used in these co-integration equations: equation (1): {f, y, l, gs}, equation (2): {n, y, l, gs} and equation (3): {n, y, l, w, gs}.

The results from the partial adjustment specification and from the error-correction model are qualitatively almost identical. The only difference concerns the long-run properties of these models, which by definition are

---

[4] One question which naturally arises here concerns the size distribution of bankrupt firms. Does the increased number of bankruptcies necessarily imply that a disproportionally large number of small firms go bankrupt. This is a difficult question and we cannot answer it because we have not enough data. We have however data on the debt of bankrupt firms (see Figure 3). The time series of real debt db and the number of bankruptcies behave quite similarly, except for the war years. This close correspondence can be interpreted as evidence of the relative invariance of the size distribution of bankrupt firms.

different. Thus, in the case of partial adjustment specification all right-hand side variables also have a long-run effect on bankruptcies while the error correction model says that in the long run the number of bankruptcies is determined by the number of firms (or the scale of the economy), output, debt and labour costs. These variables could also be interpreted as the indebtedness ratio and the functional distribution of income. In the error-correction models the coefficient of the lagged error-correction term (co-integrating vector) is clearly significant, which suggests that the specification is indeed warranted (see Kremers et al 1992). The estimated estimated co-integrating coefficients (see Table 4) also suggest that the specification makes sense. The coefficients or error-correction terms range from -0.25 to -0.48. Thus, one could argue that a disequilibrium in terms of bankruptcies takes more than two years (but probably no more than four years) to vanish.

Clearly, increasing indebtedness increases bankruptcies. This is well in accordance with a priori theorizing and it is well in accordance with the corresponding Figure 2. In the same way, the overall economic situation, measured by GDP, affects business failures. The effect is not very strong but it appears to be quite systematic in terms of different estimating specifications and estimators. The relationship between OLS and IV estimators indicates that there is indeed some simultaneity between b and Δy. Thus, a fall in output tends to increase bankruptcies, but an increase in bankruptcies tends also to decrease output. It is interesting to note that besides GDP, the real exchange rate index also enter the equation. This variable tells that foreign export markets are very important to Finnish firms. They are always important because the domestic markets are so small. In the case of a recession, this importance may become even more crucial, and from this point of view the level of competitiveness is an essential variable.

The real interest rate effect is also positive. The corresponding coefficient is relatively large and very significant. The economic interpretation is rather straightforward: higher real interest rates make debt costs much higher and if this is not compensated by an increased cash flow, firms face financial problems. Higher real interest rates also reflect tighter money markets, and under such conditions firms may not be able to obtain additional liquidity from the banking sector.[5]

---

[5] We made an experiment to control the liquidity effect by introducing the rate of change in narrow money, $\Delta M1$, into the estimating equation. As one could expect, the coefficient of this variable turned out be negative (increased liquidity decreases bankruptcies) although the coefficient could not be estimated very precisely (the t-ratio remained at the level of one). Also the terms of trade variable tt was used as an additional regressor. Its coefficient could not, however, be estimated very precisely and, therefore, it was chopped from the final specifications.

The role real interest rates can also be explained by referring to the role of inflation. Altman (1983) has proposed that increasing inflation reduces competition between firms and shelters inefficiency. It has been said that with high inflation it is easier to raise prices and profits, which lowers the efficiency of the market in a sense by keeping bad products in the market too long.

It is also worth mentioning that the rate of change in stock prices is negatively related to bankruptcies. There is an obvious causal explanation for this finding: an increase in stock prices (as well as in other wealth prices) increases both the value of the firm and the corresponding collateral values, making it easier to handle the liquidity situation.

3.3 Modelling credit expansion

Credit expansion obviously depends on both the supply and demand determinants. Unfortunately, it is not easy to derive a meaningful reduced form equation for the amount of credit. This is generally true but especially so far Finland. The domestic bank loan market was regulated for a period of sixty years (from the mid-1930s to the mid-1980s). The basic form of regulation concerned the banks' average lending rate. Because of this regulation, the supply of and demand for loans were generally not equal. It is generally assumed that the bank loan market was characterized by excess demand. Although we cannot demonstrate that this assumption is true, we should keep it in mind in the subsequent derivation of the credit expansion estimating equation. Thus, the bank loan market is assumed to function in way which is illustrated in Figure 1.

Figure 1. **The bank loan market**

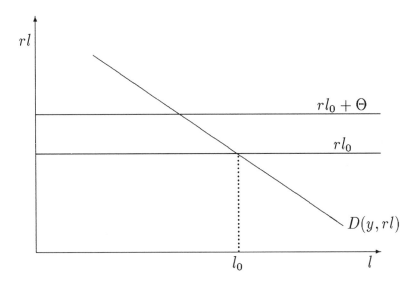

The demand for bank loans (in real terms) is assumed to depend positively on the scale variable (here, GDP) and negatively on the real interest (lending) rate (rl). Thus, $l^d = D(y, rl)$. The interest rate is exogeneously set at some level rl_o. Banks would not, however, expand their lending to l_o because that would lower their profits. Instead, they would lend less: the more the regulated interest rate deviates from the equilibrium rate the larger the rationing effect. Rationing could be thought as an exercise in which banks set a rationing premium, say Θ, on the interest rate. In practice, this premium shows up in different non-price rationing terms, as in the downpayment ratio, required length of customer relationship and the collateral requirements. The premium is not constant but depends on the determinants of the supply of bank loans. We may assume that supply depends positively on the interest rate (or, in fact, on the interest rate margin), the stock of deposits and the expected credit losses which, in turn, may be measured by bankruptcies. If the supply of loans is also written in real terms, we may end up with a specification where real loan supply depends on in addition to interest rate(s) and bankruptcies, the real amount of deposits and (negatively) the rate of inflation. The inflation effect comes via the eroding effect that it has on the real values of both bank deposits and loans.[6]

The rationing premium Θ would thus depend on the exogenous variables in the following way:

$$\Theta = \Theta(\underset{(+)}{b_{-1}}, \underset{(-)}{rl - rd}, \underset{(-)}{m_{-1}}, \underset{(+)}{\Delta p}), \tag{4}$$

where $(rl-rd)$ denotes the interest margin (for banks) and m2 the (real) money supply. The latter variable is introduced here as a proxy for bank deposits. The bankruptcy variable appears here with a time lag. Obviously, the existence of a time lag is more an empirical question and therefore we experiment with both speculations (a model with b_t or with b_{t-1}; see Table 4). As for the interest rate margin we have some data problems and hence we cannot directly apply this variable. In fact, we have only two interest rate series available: the government bond yield, which represents the market rate (rm), and the central bank's discount rate (rd). Because the lending and deposit rates have been tied to this discount rate the difference between rm and rd might reflect an opportunity cost for banks. The higher $(rm-rd)$ the higher banks' financing expenses and the less advantageous is bank lending relative to money market operations. This, in turn, would show up in higher Θ and in lower credit expansion.[7] In the empirical specification we also replace rl by either rm or rd. Here, rm is used mainly because we want to use the same variable in the bankruptcy and GDP equations.

Thus, we might derive the following linear estimating equation for credit expansion (rate of change in the real amount of bank credit):

$$\Delta l = \alpha_0 + \alpha_1 \Delta l_{-1} + \alpha_2 \Delta y + \alpha_3 \Delta b_{-1} + \alpha_4 \Delta rm + \alpha_5 \Delta \Delta p + \alpha_6 \Delta m2 + u, \tag{5}$$

---

[6] If the loan supply equation is written in terms of nominal loan supply L, which depends on the current period's nominal variables, deflation by the price level may leave the real loan supply to depend on the price level. If, however, supply also depends on the lagged values of exogenous variables, say on lagged deposits, DEP_{-1}, which are here proxied by $M2_{-1}$, then supply in real terms may also depend on the rate of change in prices.

[7] Here we ignore that fact that Θ may not be a continuous linear function with respect to the exogenous variables. Obviously, if Θ is not linear, the whole bank loan (or credit expansion) equation is not linear. If the excess demand regime changes to an excess supply regime or vice versa, we should probably try to apply genuine disequilibrium models. See, e.g., Quandt (1988). Unfortunately, the performance of such models has not been very good. All in all, there seems to be no satisfactory way of modelling credit markets which have experienced both credit rationing and deregulation (see, e.g. Basu (1994) for more detailed arguments on this problem). In fact, the existence of equilibrium credit rationing may also lead to a similar conclusion although for different reasons.

where Δ denotes the first backwards differencing operator. m2 denotes the log real money supply in terms of M2 which is used here as a proxy for bank deposits.

Estimation results for this equation are presented in Table 5. The equation performs quite well: the parameters even seem to be stable, which is somewhat surprising given the institutional and demand/supply regime shifts which have taken place in the Finnish financial markets. All the individual variables behave well according to theory. Only the bankruptcy variable is somewhat of an exception in a sense that the lagged level, but not the difference, enters the estimating equation. This might result from asymmetries in the adjustment of credit supply: extending credit and reducing credit might not behave in same way and at least the bankruptcy relationship might be different. The important thing, however, is that the coefficient of the bankruptcy variable α_3 is systematically negative and marginally significant. Thus, there is some evidence of a credit crunch. Notice also that the real interest rate variable is systematically significant (presumably merely reflecting demand behaviour): during depression periods real interest rates tend to increase and, together with increased bankruptcies, they may indeed have adverse credit supply effects.

One additional variable, i.e. the terms trade, turned out be quite an important ingredient in the credit expansion equation. This variable can be seen as a sort of leading indicator of the state of economy and, particularly, of firms' income expectations. It is no surprise that this variable has a strong positive effect on credit expansion.

3.4 Bankruptcies and output

Finally, we also an experimented with the modelling of total output (GDP). The purpose of this experiment was to see whether output growth is affected by bankruptcies (i.e. to see whether causality runs only from output growth to bankruptcies).

One can see that output growth is also almost a random walk, even unrelated with the level of per capita output (see, e.g., Table 2). Given this background it is somewhat surprising that bankruptcies can still help in predicting output growth. The same is not true in terms of other financial and non-financial variables. For instance, a univariate regression relationship between output growth and real interest rates turns out to be the following:

$$\Delta y = .052 - .362gs + .022rm - .075rm(-1) + \hat{u}1 \qquad R2 = .076, \; DW = 1.484 \qquad (6)$$
$$\;\;\;\;\;\;\;\;(5.58)\;\;\;(2.13)\;\;\;\;\;(0.33)\;\;\;\;\;\;(1.14)$$

By contrast, the corresponding model for b (or, in fact, b–f) turns out to be the following:

$$\Delta y = .072 - .431 gs - .041(b-f) + .029(b-f)(-1) + \hat{u}2 \quad R2 = .349, \; DW = 1.962$$
$$\quad\;\, (7.36) \quad (3.09) \quad\;\; (4.97) \quad\quad (3.40) \tag{7}$$

These regression relationships suggest that bankruptcies represent an essential ingredient in the transmission mechanism by which different financial and non-financial shocks affect the economy. The shocks may not show up in direct output effects (as is the case with empirical analyses using with Finnish data) but these effects may well come through bankruptcies. Thus, several VAR model studies which have shown that financial variables are rather unimportant in terms of output determination may have given misleading results just because of the omission of this.

4   Conclusions

Bankruptcies have become an important variable in many countries. The development in Finland has been particularly conspicious. Bankruptcies have been responsible for very large unemployment and output losses. More importantly, bankruptcies have caused enormous credit losses to banks, which in turn have profoundly affected the capital market and which also have placed a heavy burden on government and taxpayers.

This paper has analyzed the macroeconomic determinants of bankruptcies as well as the consequences of business failures for the financial markets. It is no surprise that bankruptcies behave cyclically. Increased demand and competitiveness reduce bankruptcies and vice versa. In the same way, one might expect that bankruptcies depend (negatively) on real interest rates and (positively) on increases in asset prices. A related factor, which we emphasize in this paper, is indebtedness. It can be argued that indebtedness itself constitutes an equilibrium error-correction term. Excessive indebtedness easily causes a wave of bankruptcies when an economy is hit by a recession with a fall in output (and asset prices) and an increase in real interest rates.

Finnish data provide strong evidence for this argument. This is true for both the stylized facts and the results of empirical analyses. Our analyses also show that bankruptcies affect the growth rate for bank loans. Thus, cyclical fluctuations may increase because bankruptcies lead to a credit squeeze, decreased liquidity, higher real rates, lower asset prices and, finally, to additional bankruptcies (as pointed out e.g. in Stiglitz 1992). Although our results are only preliminary they strongly suggest that the role of bankruptcies deserves much more attention in future analysis of the relationships between financial markets and the macroeconomy.

References

Altman, E. (1983) "Corporate Financial Distress", John Wiley & Sons, New York.

Basu, S. (1994) "Deregulation of the Australian Banking Sector: A Theoretical perspective". *Australian Economic Papers* 33, 272-285.

Bernanke, B. and M. Gertler (1989) "Agency Costs, Net Worth, and Business Fluctuations", *American Economic Review* 79, 14-31.

Engle, R.F. & C.W.J. Granger (1987) "Co-Integration and Error Correction: Representation, Estimation and Testing", *Econometrica* 55, 251-276.

Greenwald, B. and J. Stiglitz (1986) "Information, Finance Constraints and Business Fluctuations", in M. Kohn and S. Tsiang (eds.) Finance Constraints, Expectations and Macroeconomics, *Oxford University Press*, Oxford, 103-140.

Gunther, J., Lown, C. and K. Robinson (1995) "Bank Credit and Economic Activity: Evidence from the Texas Banking Decline". *Journal of Financial Services Research* 9, 31-48.

Hudson, J. & K. Cuthbertson (1993) "The Determinants of Bankruptcies in the U.K.", 1971-1988, The Manchester School 61, 65-81.

Johansen, S. (1991) "Estimation and Hypothesis Testing of Cointegration Vectors in Gaussian Vector Autoregressive Models", *Econometrica* 59, 1551-1580.

Koskela, E., Loikkanen, H. and M. Virén (1993) "House Prices, Household Saving and Financial Market Liberalization in Finland". *European Economic Review* 36, 549-558.

Kremers, J., Ericsson, N. and J. Dolado (1992) "Power of Cointegration Tests". *Oxford Bulletin of Economics and Statistics* 54, 325-348.

Laitinen, E. (1990) "Predicting Bankruptcies" (in Finnish), *Vaasan Yritysinformaatio*, Vaasa.

Meehan, J., Peek, J. and E. Rosengren (1993) "Business Failures in New England", *New England Economic Review*, Federal Reserve Bank of Boston, Nov./Dec., 33-44.

Morck, R., Shleifer, A. & R.W. Vishny (1992) "The Stock Market and Investment: Is the Market a Sideshow?", *Quarterly Journal of Economics*.

Murto, R. (1993) "Pricing Bank Credits in 1987-1992: What Went Wrong?" (in Finnish), *Bank of Finland Discussion Papers* 4/93.

O'Brian, P. & F. Browne (1992) "A Credit Crunch?, The Recent Slowdown in Bank Lending and its Implications for Monetary Policy", *OECD Working Paper* No. 107.

Quandt, R.E. (1988) "The Econometrics of Disequilibrium". *Blackwell*, London.

Shrievers, R. and D. Dahl (1995) "Regulation, Recession, and Bank Lending Behavior: 1990 Credit Crunch". *Journal of Financial Services Research* 9, 5-30.

Starck, C. ja M. Virén (1991) "Forecasting the Behaviour of Bankruptcies", in R. Flavell (ed.) Modelling Reality and Personal Modelling, *Physica Verlag*, Heidelberg.

Stiglitz, J.E. (1992) "Capital Markets and Economic Fluctuations in Capitalist Economies", *European Economic Review* 36, 269-306.

Syron, R.F. (1991) "Are We Experiencing a Credit Crunch?", Federal Reserve Bank of Boston *New England Economic Review*, July/August, 3-10.

Takala, K. and M. Virén (1994) "Macroeconomic Effects of Bankruptcies". University of Turku, *Discussion Paper* No. 44.

Williamson, S. (1987) "Financial Intermediation, Business Failures, and Real Business Cycles", *Journal of Political Economy* 95, 1196-1216.

Table 3.   Estimates for the bankruptcy equation

	(1)	(2)	(3)	(4)	(5)	(6)	(7)	(8)	(9)	(10)	(11)	(12)
const.	2.966	.985	-1.071	-1.126	-.140	-.297	-1.271	-1.808	.131	.338	.527	.929
	(5.74)	(2.88)	(2.37)	(2.44)	(0.23)	(0.47)	(1.31)	(1.76)	(0.31)	(3.14)	(0.88)	(2.26)
b(-1)	.796	.797	.741	.741	.779	.781	.544	.544	.753	.913	.718	.817
	(17.88)	(17.84)	(14.52)	(14.50)	(12.39)	(12.36)	(7.01)	(6.88)	(9.31)	(21.28)	(11.74)	(15.60)
l-y	.410	.430	.491	.506	.501	.540	1.058	1.199	.867	2.821	.622	.272
	(3.22)	(3.32)	(3.77)	(3.82)	(2.28)	(2.41)	(3.22)	(3.50)	(1.80)	(1.82)	(2.62)	(3.03)
Δy	-1.196	-.723	-1.143	-.828	-5.417	-4.540	-2.810	.055	-.282	-.868	-2.007	-.784
	(1.72)	(0.82)	(1.72)	(1.00)	(4.67)	(3.14)	(1.54)	(0.02)	(1.64)	(2.70)	(1.60)	(0.93)
rm	.856	.819	1.004	.977	.739	.674	3.057	2.837	.921	.495	2.547	.630
	(2.29)	(2.16)	(2.74)	(2.64)	(1.18)	(1.06)	(3.03)	(2.74)	(1.03)	(0.20)	(3.72)	(1.40)
Δsx	-.166	-1.675	-.150	-1.510	-.333	-.335	-.231	-.233	-.246	-.117	-.253	-1.448
	(1.56)	(1.57)	(1.46)	(1.47)	(1.79)	(1.80)	(0.84)	(0.83)	(0.98)	(1.56)	(1.34)	(1.15)
fx	-.850	-.867	-.814	-.826	-1.005	-1.039	-1.259	-1.377	-.261	-3.222	-.919	-.562
	(5.11)	(5.16)	(5.21)	(5.24)	(3.63)	(3.71)	(3.10)	(3.30)	(0.66)	(2.77)	(3.30)	(2.91)
gs	-.057	-.056	-.059	-.058	-.037	-.033	-.175	-.168	-1.088	-6.698	-.066	-.044
	(5.30)	(5.11)	(5.63)	(5.54)	(2.10)	(1.95)	(5.40)	(5.07)	(0.47)	(1.03)	(3.64)	(3.50)
R2	0.963	0.963	0.960	0.960	0.908	0.907	0.909	0.905	0.793	0.940	0.934	0.920
SEE	0.199	0.199	0.192	0.192	0.333	0.334	0.523	0.533	0.487	0.134	0.360	0.240
DW	2.063	2.016	2.049	2.016	1.556	1.484	1.780	1.700	1.190	1.241	2.096	1.962
LM1	0.392		0.358		2.206		1.055		4.393	3.148	0.513	0.069
JB	4.477	4.618	2.328	2.308	2.414	4.057	0.424	0.455	629	472	253	0.269
Chow	4.074		3.345		1.657		3.645		9.033	5.483	1.910	3.799
dep.var.	b	b	b-η	b-η	b-f	b-f	db-y	db-y	BA	BI	bc	br
estimator	ols	iv	ols	iv	ols	iv	ols	iv	ols	ols	ols	ols

dep. var. denotes the definition of the dependent variable. b denotes bankruptcies. l banks' total credit supply. y real GDP. rm real yield on government bonds. sx the Unitas stock index deflated by consumption prices. fx the real exchange rate. gs the share of central government expenditure of GDP. w the real wage rate and M1 the nominal money stock. (b−η) indicates that the number of bankruptcies is divided by population (η). (b−f) that it is divided by the number of firms (f) and (bd−y) that the dependent variable is the debt of bankrupt firms in relation to GDP. In the case of (b−η) specification, also all other relevant variables are divided by population. ba, bi, bc and br denote sectoral bankruptcy variables for agriculture, industry, commerce and other branches, respectively. Due to zero observations, the first two sectoral equations are expressed in levels (not in logs). All variables, except rm and fx are expressed in logs. (−1) indicates that the variable is lagged by one year. (½), in turn, indicates a half-year lag. Numbers in parentheses are unadjusted t-ratios (heteroscedasticity/autocorrelation adjusted t-ratios are so close to these unadjusted ratios that they are not reported). LM is the Godfrey autocorrelation test statistic in the presence of a lagged dependent variable. JB is the Jarque-Bera test for residual normality and Chow is the Chow stability test statistic for the period 1945. Under the null hypothesis, the distribution of LM1 is standard normal, the distribution of JB is chi square with two degrees of freedom while the distribution of Chow is (approx.) F(9,54). OLS denotes the ordinary least squares estimator and iv the instrumental variable estimator. With this estimator, the list of instruments includes lagged Δy, the discount rate (rd), the terms of trade tt, fx, the growth rate of industrial production (ip) and money supply (m1).

Table 4. **Error-correction model estimates for bankruptcies**

(1) $b = 1.556 + .546f - 1.564y + 1.698l - .131gs + û1$
        (2.03)   (1.84)   (4.77)   (14.76)   (7.78)

$R2 = 0.862, SEE = 0.370, DW = 0.576, ADF1 = 3.31.$

$\Delta b = -.027 - 2.115\Delta y + 2.451\Delta l - .047\Delta gs - .245û1(-1)$
        (0.86)   (3.29)   (7.96)   (3.48)   (3.85)

$R2 = 0.553, SEE = 0.191, DW = 1.628, JB = 2.048, Chow = 0.900.$

(2) $b = -89.643 + .143\eta - 4.098y + 2.327l - .119gs + û2$
        (8.43)   (8.52)   (10.97)   (20.84)   (9.52)

$R2 = 0.930, SEE = 0.264, DW = 0.864, ADF1 = 4.10.$

$\Delta b = -.069 + .172\Delta\eta - 2.645\Delta y + 2.372\Delta l - .042\Delta gs - .348û2(-1)$
        (1.12)   (2.86)   (4.15)   (7.32)   (3.10)   (4.12)

$R2 = 0.621, SEE = 0.177, DW = 1.642, JB = 1.615, Chow = 0.676.$

(3) $b = -127.167 + .175\eta - 4.809y + 1.411l - .089gs + 3.103w + û3$
        (10.78)   (11.10)   (13.72)   (6.86)   (7.94)   (5.02)

$R2 = 0.949, SEE = 0.229, DW = 1.267, ADF1 = 4.23.$

$\Delta b = -.080 + .203\Delta\eta - 3.219\Delta y + 2.050\Delta l - .037gs + 1.775\Delta w - .479û3(-1)$
        (1.87)   (3.63)   (5.61)   (7.74)   (2.80)   (3.32)   (5.05)

$R2 = 0.677, SEE = 0.164, DW = 1.695, JB = 0.407, Chow = 0.734.$

$\Delta b = -.067 + .190\Delta\eta - 3.068\Delta y + 1.941\Delta l - .039\Delta gs + 1.446\Delta w + .487\Delta rm$
        (1.57)   (3.37)   (5.31)   (7.17)   (3.01)   (2.56)   (1.59)
        $- .072\Delta sx - .427û3(-1)$
        (0.83)   (3.98)

$R2 = 0.693, SEE = 0.163, DW = 1.708, JB = 0.714, Chow = 0.497.$

The first equation is the cointegration equation and the latter equation(s) the respective error corrections model(s). ADF1 denotes the Augmented Dickey-Fuller test statistic for unit root (the 5 per cent critical value is 2.90). Otherwise, notation is the same as in Table 1.

Table 5. Estimates for the credit expansion equation

	(1)	(2)	(3)	(4)	(5)	(6)	(7)	(8)
const.	−.015	−.097	−.173	−.094	−.145	−.147	−.149	−.145
	(0.24)	(2.08)	(3.87)	(2.01)	(3.66)	(3.68)	(3.66)	(3.59)
$\Delta l(-1)$	.176	.404	.406	.377	.380	.364	.403	.398
	(1.94)	(4.53)	(4.52)	(4.08)	(4.28)	(3.94)	(4.49)	(4.45)
Δy	.399	.395	.403	.259	.373	.296	.425	.329
	(2.46)	(2.76)	(2.81)	(1.41)	(2.62)	(1.61)	(3.00)	(2.11)
$b(-1)$	−.036	−.011	−.011	−.012	−1.011	−1.165	−.518	−.952
	(3.92)	(1.82)	(1.87)	(1.98)	(2.21)	(2.29)	(1.57)	(1.78)
rm	.420	–	–	–	–	–	–	–
	(2.70)							
Δrm	–	−.192	−.192	−.205	−.188	−.192	−.195	−.189
		(2.24)	(2.22)	(2.30)	(2.17)	(2.20)	(2.19)	(2.15)
Δp	−.813	–	–	–	–	–	–	–
	(6.05)							
$\Delta\Delta p$	–	−.698	−.699	−.702	−.692	−.694	−.697	−.719
		(7.96)	(7.98)	(7.94)	(7.97)	(7.97)	(7.89)	(8.16)
tt	.274	.136	.128	.144	.130	.135	.123	.129
	(7.06)	(3.65)	(3.55)	(3.78)	(3.69)	(3.74)	(3.45)	(3.57)
$\Delta m2(-\frac{1}{2})$	.444	.474	.478	.507	.465	.483	.477	.457
	(3.23)	(4.72)	(4.74)	(4.84)	(4.76)	(4.76)	(4.64)	(4.62)
rm−rd	–	–	–	–	–	–	–	–
R2	.758	.812	.812	.809	0.816	0.815	0.809	0.811
SEE	.046	.040	.040	.041	0.040	0.040	0.040	0.040
DW	1.406	1.821	1.844	1.757	1.838	1.803	1.825	1.840
LM1	2.753	0.421	0.289	..	0.424	..	0.322	0.290
JB	0.215	0.089	0.056	0.224	0.330	0.647	0.033	0.055
Chow	0.418	1.848	2.000	..	1.794	..	2.076	1.915
dep.var.	Δl	Δl	$\Delta(l-\eta)$	Δl	Δl	Δl	Δl	Δl
b.var	b	b	b−η	b	b−f	b−f	db−y	b
estimator	ols	ols	ols	iv	ols	iv	ols	iv

b.var denotes the definition of the bankruptcy variable. In column (8), it is not lagged (as it is in other equations). Notation is the same as in Table 1.

Figure 2.

Bankruptcies and indebtedness

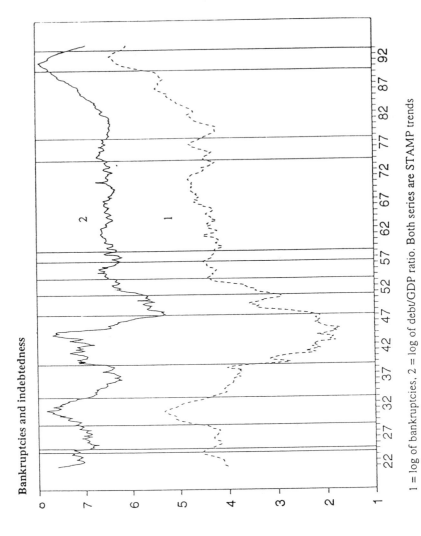

1 = log of bankruptcies, 2 = log of debt/GDP ratio. Both series are STAMP trends

Figure 3

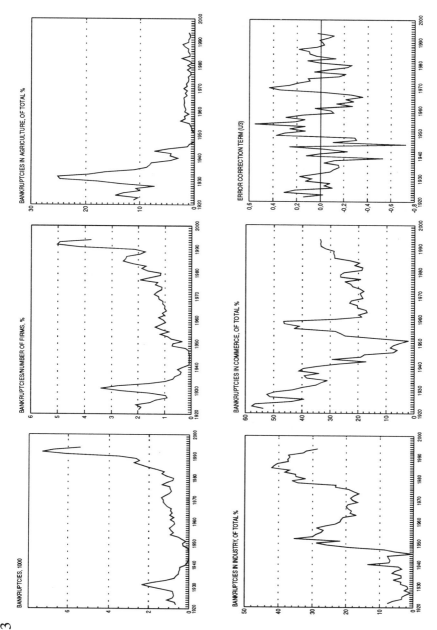

Bankruptcy Prediction:
Discriminant Analysis versus Neural Networks

Damiano Carrara[1] and Enrico Cavalli[2]

1 RadiciFin spa, Via S.Giovanni Bosco 7, 24100 Bergamo, Italy

2 Dipartimento di Matematica, Statistica, Informatica e Applicazioni, Università di Bergamo, P.zza Rosate 2, 24129 Bergamo, Italy

Abstract. The paper presents a comparison between two different approaches to the problem of bankruptcy prediction: the traditional discriminant analysis method and possible solutions based on neural networks. The performance of a simple mathematical model applied to economic and financial ratios obtained from a small sample of manufacturing companies balance-sheets is compared with the performance of some BPN family neural networks trained with the same set of information. The results obtained from the neural networks suggest some interesting improvements and practical applications which are the object of the second and third section of the experiment programme in progress.

Keywords: Bankruptcy Prediction, Discriminant Analysis, Neural Networks

1. Bankruptcy prediction

One of the most important issues that managers are facing today in almost every field of business is the evaluation of their clients' solvency conditions. This is due to the fact that extending credit to customers is a very effective way of stimulating sales. Yet the costs associated with granting credit are not trivial. First of all the customer might not pay. Secondly the firm has to bear the costs of carrying the receivables. Thus the credit-policy decision involves a trade-off between the benefits of increased sales versus the costs of granting credit. This regards credit to other firms (*trade credit*) and credit granted to consumers (*consumer credit*). We focus on trade credit and observe that receivables represent a major investment of financial resources by Italian firms.

Then it is worth to spend some effort to develop techniques and tools useful to reduce the chance that a customer will not pay. Bankruptcy prediction is the evaluation of a company's behaviour based on the analysis of its economic and financial indicators to quickly diagnose the economic and financial imbalances leading to bankruptcy. It helps prevent from getting involved with unsound clients thus minimising investment and losses.

The importance of this subject for the most part of the Italian businesses is out of question and also in the small and medium sized companies the credit management function is growing beyond the limits of credit collection. The following table shows the trend over the years 1970-1991 of trade receivables over total assets in twenty years in Italy on a sample by Mediobanca:

	1970	1975	1980	1983	1985	1987	1989	1991
Total sample	17.2	20.9	26.9	26.7	26.4	24.4	24.1	21.6
Food	14.5	14.8	29.6	26.2	27.4	30.1	31.1	27.8
Chemicals	**11.4**	**19.5**	**22.1**	**25.4**	**26.9**	**21.3**	**16.6**	**14.6**
Consumer electronics	25.5	25.8	38.9	39.6	40.4	39.2	37.6	34.7
Mechanics	33.1	33.7	37.5	33.6	32.1	30.7	34.3	34.5
Textile fabrics	**21.4**	**28.2**	**30.7**	**34.4**	**34.1**	**37.0**	**34.3**	**34.5**
Ship building	25.7	24.1	16.3	23.8	25.0	20.8	21.1	14.3
Retailing	1.6	4.9	10.8	5.3	5.6	6.5	7.3	6.6

The same information can be retrieved by examining a table on the average collection period referred to trade receivables:

	1970	1975	1980	1983	1985	1987	1989	1991
Total sample	83	101	100	110	104	112	112	114
Food	38	42	85	86	89	98	94	87
Chemicals	**89**	**95**	**94**	**98**	**93**	**99**	**89**	**97**
Consumer electronics	124	77	121	129	128	121	126	115
Mechanics	160	176	197	201	196	190	199	193
Textile fabrics	**81**	**84**	**80**	**112**	**100**	**124**	**127**	**134**
Ship building	381	218	221	298	386	267	329	201
Retailing	3	9	14	9	10	13	15	14

Over the last three years (1992-1994) they worsened on account of the world and Italian recession which has caused a slowing down of the demand increasing rate, a high interest rate and difficulties in financial sourcing, liquidity shortage and delayed payments, and inflation. These factors are the most important events responsible for the growth of a firm's investment in trade receivables.

The basic assumption is that economic and financial imbalances appear in balance sheets at least one year before the company goes bankrupt. More specifically a situation of financial distress is revealed by a number of financial and economic indicators that usually get worse when the firm is having significant problems in meeting its debt obligations. However only some financially distressed firms ultimately file for legal bankruptcy; most do not, because they are able to recover or otherwise survive. Nonetheless these firms will spend resources to avoid going bankrupt and their business will increasingly suffer.

2. Linear discriminant analysis

Since Altman's work in the sixties, linear discriminant analysis has become one of the most widely employed techniques for bankruptcy prediction. As there is wide literature on this subject, we will only briefly provide the basic assumptions of this technique as a starting point for the comparison between the statistical approach and the connectionist approach to bankruptcy prediction.

Linear discriminant analysis is based on the assumption that it is possible to distinguish businesses into two categories that are discrete and defined, mutually exclusive and whose sum represents the whole population: healthy firms and unsound firms. The function is obtained on the basis of two samples of businesses representing both healthy and unsound companies. A numerical score is obtained from the discriminant function, that expresses business profile risk which is defined by an average of selected and weighted economic and financial indicators.

Here we refer to the work done by C. Rossi referenced in bibliography, that will be the term of comparison for the first phase of our work. As a matter of fact, we compared the results given by the three models built by C. Rossi with those given by three simple neural networks. Here are C. Rossi's steps:

- definition of a sample of both of healthy and unsound companies (the sample of unsound companies was obtained by considering the textile companies gone bankrupt in Bergamo over the years 1987 and 1988);
- calculation of the most widely used economic and financial ratios for each company;
- selection by a univariate analysis of those indicators that show the greatest difference in the two subsets of companies;
- building up of a discriminant function (ALPHA model) with two financial indicators (current ratio and financial independence)
- building up of a discriminant function (BETA model) with the same two financial indicators and one economic indicator (return on investment);
- building up of a discriminant function (GAMMA model) with three financial indicators (current ratio, financial independence and liabilities flexibility);
- statistical verification of the selected indicators by the Student T test and the Fisher F test;
- statistical verification of the discriminant functions by multivariate Fisher test.

The sample is made by the two subsets of the companies still healthy at the end of year 1988

Ref.	Company	Current Ratio	Solvency Ratio	R.O.I.	Current Debt Ratio
1	CINQUINI INCAB spa	2.17178	0.26106	0.07837	0.404671
2	SABER srl	1.40289	0.34429	0.01077	0.636271
3	PERTOR srl	1.28042	0.35776	0.04521	0.629091
4	CONFEZ.IBER srl	1.29662	0.30385	0.43205	0.688091

5	CAMIC.SASCA srl	1.15453	0.49209	0.08937	0.349371
6	SADRICAM srl	2.02236	0.44196	0.15131	0.387031
7	CONFEZ.SIMMY srl	0.76113	0.21267	0.15789	0.686951
8	AFION srl	2.92165	0.66548	0.08585	0.332991
9	CAMIC.BERGAM. srl	1.77468	0.26441	0.06493	0.478121
10	ELGA TRICOT srl	1.42915	0.27554	0.16118	0.688591

and of the companies which went bankrupt before the end of year 1988

Ref.	Company	Current Ratio	Solvency Ratio	R.O.I.	Current Debt Ratio
A	MEC SPORT spa	0.67083	-0.44284	-0.29639	1.304450
B	SOFT J.CONF. srl	1.16617	0.12120	0.03743	0.797800
C	TREVITEX srl	1.16145	0.22151	0.18905	0.773000
D	CONFEZ.C.A. srl	0.98325	0.04975	0.14911	0.917950
E	EMPORIO srl	1.01213	0.08100	-0.09918	0.918870
F	L.B.M. srl	0.56555	-0.05586	-0.07729	0.771750

ALPHA model

The function obtained is $Z = 0,37760 X_1 + 5,62259 X_2$ and when applied to the indicators of our table it classifies the companies by increasing Z as follows:

A	F	D	E	B	7	C	10	9
-2.253	-0.123	0.612	0.791	1.075	1.453	1.637	2.032	2.086

4	1	2	3	5	6	8
2.146	2.201	2.409	2.444	3.156	3.168	4.728

The function is able to well classify only outside the boundaries set by $Z = 1.075$ and $Z = 2.032$. If we use as discriminant value of Z the average of the interval (1.553) the function fails to classify the 7th health company and the unsound company A.

A graphical evidence of this fact is given by the discriminant line $X_2 = 0.27629 - 0.06004 X_1$ (fig. 1a)[1].

BETA model

The function obtained is $Z = 0,93090 X_1 - 11.58628 X_2 - 2.11212 X_3$ and applied to the indicators of our table it classifies the companies by increasing Z as follows:

8	6	5	4	3	2	1	10	9
-10.61	-7.323	-6.965	-5.640	-5.432	-5.318	-5.212	-4.863	-4.853

C	7	B	D	E	F	A
-4.047	-3.506	-2.569	-1.807	-1.671	-0.284	-5.132

[1] In all the figures, that are hard-copies of the screen, "fallimento" stands for "bankruptcy" and "solvibilità" stands for "solvency". In this figure "Indice di disponibilità" stands for "Current ratio" and "Indice di indipendenza finanziaria" stands for "Current debt ratio".

The result of this model is the same as the result of the ALPHA model.

GAMMA model

The function obtained is $Z = -0.06790 \, X_1 - 5.18007 \, X_2 + 11.60125 \, X_3$ and applied to the indicators of our table it classifies the companies by increasing Z as follows:

8	5	6	1	9	3	2	4	10
0.217	1.426	2.063	3.195	4.057	5.358	5.503	6.321	6.464

7	C	B	F	E	D	A
6.816	7.741	8.548	9.204	10.17	10.32	17.38

GAMMA model is the only one that can provide a value for Z (7.27881) for which it is possible to classify all the companies in the sample correctly. But even the GAMMA model, applied to the ratios of the same companies calculated five years later, fails to classify one healthy and one unsound company and C. Rossi's work confirms once again what is already definite in literature.

The evaluation of a company's risk of going bankrupt is a good example of a field where the economic theory does not have a complete model of the situation. We know many things about how companies fall into economic distress and financial bankruptcy, about crisis processes and company decline, but we do not have a complete theory. Even when evaluating the situation of a firm, we consider qualitative information and we draw from our personal expertise to make heuristic considerations. Yet the symbolic approach can deal only with quantitative data and requires the pre-specification of a functional form and restrictive assumptions about the statistical distributions of the variables and errors of the model. That's why an algorithm has not been found that is unique, able to always give a good response and stable over time.

3. Neural Networks

To solve a problem like bankruptcy prediction we regard as useful the application of neural network technology. With regard to the major limits of the symbolic approach, we observe that neural networks have some advantages. Basically, they do not require the pre-specification of a functional form to describe the problem nor do they require restrictive assumptions about the characteristics of the statistical distributions of the variables and errors of the model. The experiments developed in various fields by a number of authors also show that neural networks can deal with imprecise and noisy variables, the lack of an element effects very slightly if at all their performance and they are able to adapt gradually to model changes over time.

The considerable number of aspects of neural networks theory and the reasons inspiring them that have contributed to the connectionist approach are not being examined here. We recall only the most prominent ones. Given that many processes of unconscious intelligence, like image and sound recognition, cannot be the result of long deductive chains or derive from complex algorithms, the connectionist paradigm assumes that a natural or artificial system can behave in an "intelligent" way if it exhibits the following features:

- it possesses a large number of elementary units (neurons);
- each unit is interconnected with the other units and is able to perform relatively simple calculations, like weighted sums and threshold decisions;
- the links are not rigid and can be modified through learning processes generated by the interaction between the network and the environment or an appropriate "tutor" (some connections are created or reinforced while others are weakened or deleted);

The network result derives from the collective behaviour of all units and depends on how those units interact with each other according to links with different strengths. That is why neural networks are said to be fault (lack of elements) tolerant. Each i_{th} neuron has:

- an activation threshold
- a state $S_i(t)$ at time t;
- a weight w_{ij} representing the link with each other neuron j.

The dynamic of the system is given by three rules:

- an activation rule adjusting the state of the neurons;
- a learning rule modifying the weights of the links;
- an iteration rule sequencing the activation of the neurons.

The network evolves through the learning process towards a stable situation, by modifying the weights according to the learning rule to minimise the differences between the results obtained and the results desired. Should the learning be good, the weights are set at their final state and the network runs only with the activation rule. The weights configuration represents the knowledge of the problem incorporated in the network and implicitly defines the functional form of the model.

The different types of each of the three rules above define different network families. The network we are using, which is allegedly very suitable for classification problems, belongs to the family of the "back-propagation" networks with "supervised learning". The neurons lie on a certain number of slabs (input, output and 0 to 3 hidden slabs). Each neuron receives impulse from all the neurons of the preceding slab; the weighted sum of the impulses is the input of the activation function, whose output is compared with the activation threshold and gives the state of the neuron. An input vector, representing the state of the input neurons (information on the problem to solve) passes through the hidden slabs being modified until it reaches the output slab where the state of the neurons represents the network response. This response is compared with the desired one given in the training slab and the network computes the error done and tries to minimise it by backwards modifying the weights. After a sufficiently large number of iterations, if the error gets under the established threshold, we can say that the network learnt and could be able to classify new situations.

Neural networks allow to concentrate the effort on the problem, as no "traditional" programming is usually required. Instead it is necessary to:

- define a learning (weighting-correction) procedure and an iteration for the adjustment;
- prepare a set of examples (training-set) that is representative of the problem to be solved;
- define the threshold of acceptability for the network response;
- define a sequence for the submission of the examples and for the weights adjustment;
- prepare a test set to check the generalising capacity of the network, i.e. its ability to give correct responses for new situations;

There are no precise rules for the assignment of the initial weights and for the choice of the other learning and running parameters within a given network paradigm. Empirically the procedure followed is trying different configurations and observe the network learning behaviour.

4. Experiment programme

The use of neural networks in the analysis of company bankruptcy is recent, but the results obtained seem to be positive. As we are now concerned with the application of neural networks to economic problems rather than with the development of neural networks technology, we selected an existing tool running on PCs and Workstations in Windows environment: Explore-Net. We also chose that paradigm, the multi-layer-back-propagation (MBPN), reported in the literature as the most commonly used for the type of problems to which bankruptcy prediction belongs: classification. The complete definition of the problem addressed is the prediction of bankruptcy for small and medium-sized manufacturing companies of the chemical-textile sector.

The experiment programme is subdivided into three sections:

a) Section one: the aim of the first section is to check the capacity of a neural network to reproduce the results of the linear discriminant models presented in the 2nd paragraph of this paper by using the same indicators and the same sample. A second goal is to get familiar with all the possibilities offered by the tool and by the network paradigm which has been chosen. This section has already been completed and in the next paragraph we will discuss the problems encountered and the results obtained.

b) Section two: the aim of this section is to check the capacity of a neural network to classify companies subject to bankruptcy risk, distinguishing among "healthy", "vulnerable" and "unsound" businesses. We decided to limit the work to the chemical-textile sector for two reasons: from the economical point of view, it is interesting to develop a research on a major national product sector; from the informatics point of view, the required sample for the network training should be small enough to be handled with an acceptable time and the similarity of the financial and economic structures of the companies in the sample should allow the building of a network with better performance. The neural networks lack of precision is often stressed in literature and we have been in contact with developers that faced the same problem. We think that limiting the variety of the situations to be addressed should improve the network precision. We are already working on a sample of about 400 companies whose balance-sheets we obtained thanks to the C.C.I.A.A. of Bergamo. The selection of the relevant indicators is based on the same procedure adopted by C. Rossi. A neural network for this selection is also being developed, but we expect to encounter unacceptable time requirements for learning due to the great number of neurons.

c) section three: in this section we will try to enable the network to refine its output by considering the development of a company's situation over time. We will train the network with the indicators over the years 1990-1992 (or with their trends). The final result may be a system made by at least two networks specialised in specific tasks. Another point still debated is the opportunity of introducing in the networks input data information about the macroeconomic environment. We will also check the ability of the network to have a stable behaviour over time, by considering the 1991-1993 time interval for balance sheet indicators and the state of the companies in 1994-1995.

5. Discussion of the results

At first we used a BPN paradigm for all the models, changing only the number of neurons on the input slab (2 for ALPHA, 3 for BETA and 3 for GAMMA). All networks had one single hidden layer with the same number of neurons of the input layer, one output neuron whose value was ranging between 0 (unsound) and 1 (healthy), the input slab connected to the output slab, the normal learning rule, the logistic activation function and the initial weights set to 0.5. After training 1000 epochs, that means submitting to the network 1000 times the sample, all the three networks learnt to give an output in the interval 0.9-1 for the unsound companies and in the interval 0-0.1 for the healthy ones; the whole sample has been classified correctly. Yet the three networks had a very different learning performance as shown in the table below. After further learning the networks improved their precision but the result was not significant with respect to the time required. Even the change of the number of hidden layers, of the learning rule, of the initial weights and of the other parameters did not lead to significant improvements of performance. Yet in some cases the network could not learn (fig. 3)[2].

# of learning epochs required by the network	ALPHA	BETA	GAMMA
begin to discriminate	690	420	70
discriminant value 0.5	770	510	180
discriminant intervals 0-0.25 and 0.75-1	900	690	640
discriminant intervals 0-0.1 and 0.9-1	1200	980	1100

A graphical presentation of the learning process for the three networks is given in fig. 2a, 2b, 2c[3]. It provides a clear evidence of how a network, by means of its adaptive characteristics, learns to correct its responses to give the right ones. The shape of the lines is determined by the modifications of the weights at each learning cycle. Learning could be stopped as soon as the desired behaviour is achieved or if the impossibility to achieve it becomes evident. Let us suggest some comparisons with the statistical model:

- The networks learning performance has been low for those companies (7 and C) that ALPHA and BETA model did not classify correctly;

- The improved performance of ALPHA network after a few epochs associated with the fact that ALPHA model have not been able to discriminate correctly all the companies suggests that a statistical model behaves like a "rough" (less trained) network: after 300 epochs the networks performed like the statistical models;

- After 360 epochs GAMMA network gave the same ranking of businesses by the output value as GAMMA model does.

The linear discriminant function can be seen as a network with feed-forward connections, with no hidden layers, with 2 or 3 input neurons (X_1,X_2,X_3), 1 output neuron (Z), activation function $f(x)=x$, weights equal to the X coefficients and activation threshold = 0. The discriminant function is a straight line (fig.1a) and the two half-spaces delimited by this line cannot have that such a simple shape that discriminates the two groups of companies.

Even the simplest network (ALPHA network with one hidden layer) after a 1500 epochs training drew a line performing the discrimination (fig.1b)[4]. And from the literature we know that while networks with one (hidden) layer can perform linear separation on the plane space, two-layer networks can generate convex geometrical shapes, while networks with at least three layers can separate the input space into shapes of any configuration. Indeed, working with neural networks we cannot get responses exactly equal to 0 or 1, but we have two

---

[2] In this figure "aziende sane" stands for "healthy companies" and "aziende fallite" stands for "bankrupt companies".

[3] See note 2.

[4] In the figure referenced "Indice di disponibilità" stands for "Current ratio" and "Indice di indipendenza finanziaria" stands for "Current debt ratio".

intervals whose limits are 0-0.5 and 0.5-1 and whose width can be defined arbitrarily. This leads to the fact that a network will not draw a discriminating line, but a discriminant region whose width depends on the intervals size.

The complexity of the regions depends on the number of neurons. Yet even in the simplest case neural networks seem to have another advantage on linear discriminant analysis. With ALPHA and GAMMA networks we carried on the same validation test developed by C. Rossi with her discriminant models using the same indicators calculated for year 1990 on the 10 healthy companies of the original sample. The results are summarised in the following table (underlined figures represent the classification errors).

Ref	Current Ratio	Solvency Ratio	Current Debt Ratio	Situation in 1991	ALPHA model	ALPHA network	GAMMA model	GAMMA network
1	3.481	0.397	0.275	healthy	3.547	1	0.897	1
2	1.439	0.277	0.687	healthy	2.098	0.960	6.440	0.955
3	0.992	0.054	0.644	bankrupt	0.680	0	_7.126_	0.008
4	1.485	0.402	0.563	healthy	2.819	0.999	4.353	1
5	1.212	0.109	0.544	bankrupt	1.070	0.001	_5.662_	_0.804_
6	1.187	0.450	0.375	healthy	2.978	1	1.935	1
7	0.935	0.244	0.497	healthy	1.723	0.946	4.442	1
8	1.070	0.280	0.714	healthy	1.978	0.960	6.761	0.957
9	1.318	0.083	0.574	healthy	_0.967_	_0.001_	6.134	_0.230_
10	0.287	-1.975	2.220	bankrupt	-10.995	0	35.978	0

Both ALPHA model and ALPHA network failed to classify a healthy company: the financial independence ratio of that company is close to the values typical of the unsound companies in the sample. Nonetheless with further training the network "learnt" the new patterns and became able to classify correctly the 9th firm as well. Its new discriminant region is shown in fig. 1c[5]. The same considerations apply to the classification failure made by GAMMA network for the 9th company.

A different interesting situation determined the failure of GAMMA network for the 5th company. This company's ratios were "normal"; despite this it went bankrupt: a deeper view of the company's situation showed that it had a unique important customer that went bankrupt! This is an information that cannot be retrieved from the balance-sheet analysis. Indeed, after further learning with this validation set, the network "learnt" even if slowly and with some difficulty, but from the theoretical point of view maybe this is not correct: it should be better to add a new piece of information that justifies the situation or the case should be dropped. Otherwise in a non-trivial situation the network could learn wrong patterns.

---

[5] See note 4.

6. Conclusions

The main conclusions, drawn from the experiment performed, towards the application of neural networks to bankruptcy prediction can be summarised as follows:
- Neural networks have shown that they are able to perform a classification task with results that are very close to or even better than those of the discriminant analysis;
- Neural networks give the opportunity to classify businesses in more than two categories; in particular, it is possible to define a "grey area" that contains all the businesses that the human expert as well as the network cannot classify as "healthy" or "unsound" through the ratio analysis only;
- Neural networks can perform an everlasting learning, by subsequent training stages every time a new set of data, covering different situations, is available.

On the other hand, we expect a number of difficulties and problems developing the 2nd and 3rd phase of the experiment:
- the processing time required for completing the training due to the large number of neurons and the width of the sample;
- the need to carry out a large number of tests to identify the combination of parameters for the best training; in the experiment developed in section one, the network has been used in its simplest form, but it can be implemented with up to 3 hidden layers, any number of neurons, different activation and learning rules and other parameters;
- the trap of overfitting (this problem did not rise in this first phase of the work due to the very small sample and the lack of a appropriate validation set to test the generalization ability of the networks);
- the criticality of the sample identified, since the networks learning heavily depends on the quality of the training input data;
- the possibility of unacceptable network behaviour from the financial point of view that need to be analysed checking both the network architecture and the training sample: it is usually difficult to distinguish between problems driven by the network and problems due to the data.

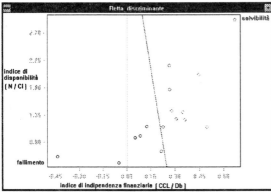

fig. 1a - ALPHA model discriminant line

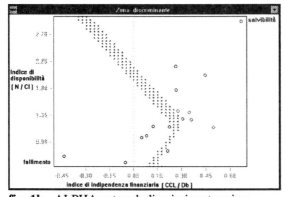

fig. 1b - ALPHA network discriminant region

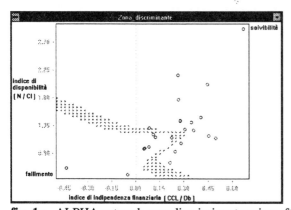

fig. 1c - ALPHA network new discriminant region after further training

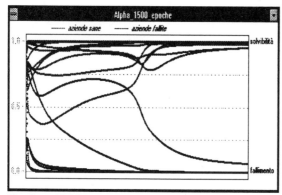

fig. 2a - ALPHA network learning process

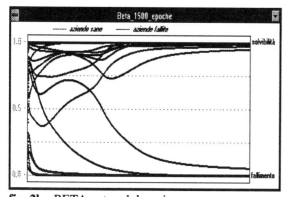

fig. 2b - BETA network learning process

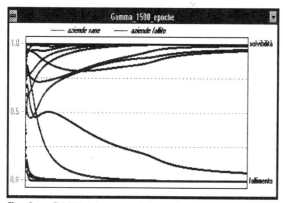

fig. 2c - GAMMA network learning process

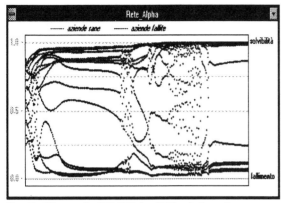

fig. 3 - Network APLHA in difficult learning

References

Altman E.I., "Financial Ratios, Discriminant Analysis and the Prediction of Corporate Bankruptcy", in "Journal of Finance", September 1968.

Altman E.I., "Corporate Financial Distress", Wiley & Sons, New York 1983.

Altman E.I., "Bankruptcy and Reorganisation", John Wiley, New York 1981.

Altman E.I., "Application of Classification Techniques in Business, Banking and Finance", JAI Press, Greenwich 1981.

Appetiti S., "L'utilizzo dell'analisi discriminatoria per la previsione delle insolvenze: ipotesi e test per un'analisi dinamica", Servizio Studi della Banca d'Italia 1984.

Appetiti S., "Identifying Unsound Firms in Italy. An attempt to use trend variables", in "Journal of Banking and Finance" n.2, June 1994.

Alberici A., "Analisi dei bilanci e previsione delle insolvenze", ISEDI 1975

Dallocchio M., "Credit management: economia e finanza delle politiche commerciali", ETAS, Milano 1993.

HNC Incorporated, "Neurosoftware manual", San Diego 1991.

Ross-Westerfield-Jordan, "Fundamentals of Corporate Finance", Irwin, USA 1993.

Rossi C., "Indicatori di bilancio, modelli di classificazione e previsione delle insolvenze aziendali", Giuffrè, Milano 1988.

Rossi C., "La valutazione delle condizioni di solvibilità delle imprese: un modello basato sull'analisi discriminatoria", Cacucci, Bari 1993.

Varetto F.-Marco G., "Bankruptcy diagnosis and neural networks", International Seminar on European Financial Statement Data Bases: Methods and Perspectives, Bressanone 1993.

Rough Set Approach to Stock Selection: an Application to the Italian Market[1]

Salvatore Greco[2], Silvestro Lo Cascio[3] and Benedetto Matarazzo[2]

[2] Università di Catania - Facoltà di Economia
Corso Italia, 55 - 95129 Catania - Italy

[3] Department of Finance - Erasmus University of Rotterdam
P.O. Box 1738 - 3000DR Rotterdam - The Netherlands

Abstract. The rough set theory is a useful tool for decision analysis. It allows a well structured procedure to organize quantitative and qualitative information. Most applications have been directed to problems characterized by "granularity" of the representation. Stock selection typically deals with large quantitative data sets. Finance theory describes assets in terms of their relative position within the stock market. Availability of long time series and computation technology have been powerful factors towards a full formalization of portfolio selection procedures. Recent empirical studies, meaningfully called "behavioural finance", support an alternative description of the financial world. In this view, unexplainable anomalies for financial economics become effects of some psychological bias. Our rough set approach to stock selection is linked with the last mentioned researches. Our purpose is to show the practical relevance of organized information in this field. Results confirm the efficiency of rough set analysis as learning tool for the investor, although it cannot replace traditional methodology.

Keywords. Rough set, stock selection, behavioural finance.

1 Introduction

Our purpose is to employ the rough set approach to support stock evaluation procedures. In this field, quantitative data are recorded and processed, providing the usual information described by financial economics. The development of finance theory has been strictly connected with quantitative empirical results. However, investors' knowledge is composed also of some qualitative information which may support quantitative evidence or add new insights. The relevance of qualitative information, market segmentation and psychological biases has been analyzed in the so called "behavioural finance". See e.g. De Bondt and Thaler (1985). Rough set approach can be a suitable instrument in building an integrated framework of quantitative and qualitative information. Rough set analysis was implemented to cope with the organisation of qualitative data. Quantitative data, when used, were transformed into qualitative data by means of a specific codification. This codification carries a certain loss of the informative content of

---

[1] Partial financial support from Italian University and Scientific Research Ministry (M.U.R.S.T.) is acknowledged.

data. Our aim is to reduce this loss, preserving some of ordinal properties of quantitative data. The codification procedure we adopt is based on the Pairwise Comparison Table (PCT) (Greco et al., 1995). It allows comparisons on pairs of objects characterized by different data values. In section 2, the concept of knowledge is introduced and the fundamental ideas behind rough set approach are presented. Section 3 deals with the formalization of rough set approach and the specific codification adopted for stock market data. Section 4 presents some basic concepts about risk management in portfolio selection. Section 5 compares multi-factor model and rough set approaches with an empirical analysis on the Italian stock market. The final section concerns the evaluation of the results and some reflections for future researches.

2 Knowledge and Rough Set Analysis

Knowledge is usually defined as *something people have in their mind and they can express through natural language* (Dubois and Prade in Pawlak,1991). Knowledge is acquired from data, both qualitative and quantitative. But translating data into knowledge is not a straightforward task. A set of data is generally disorganized and incomplete, but, at the same time, it contains useless details. On the contrary, knowledge is organized, useful and expressed in a rather synthetic way. We may say that knowledge is *summarized* and *organized* data. On knowledge definition see e.g. Pawlak (1991).

A formal framework for the transformation of data into knowledge has been developed by Pawlak (1982) and called rough set theory. It successfully deals with problems raised by *granularity* of data, defined as a quality of the specific representation of the reality; it expresses the imprecision deriving from the limited number of components effectively contained in the representation, as compared with the potentially infinite complexity of the real phenomena. Objects represented by the same limited information are then *indiscernible* one from another.

The basic idea of rough set theory consists of replacing each imprecise concept by a well defined reference framework. This framework stems from two elements called, respectively, lower and upper approximation. The lower approximation is the set of all objects surely matching the concept to be explained, whereas, the upper approximation consists of all objects which may possibly match it.

Rough sets have often been compared to fuzzy sets. However, basic hypotheses of the two approaches are clearly discernible. *Granularity*, which affects the sharpness of representation, characterizes rough sets, while *vagueness*, which is linked to graduality of evaluations, is the basic concept of fuzzy sets. Borrowing the concept from sharpness of pictures, Dubois and Prade in Pawlak (1991) pag. X explain the difference between rough and fuzzy sets by means of the following metaphor: rough set theory is about the size of the pixels forming an image, while fuzzy set theory deals with the existence of more than two levels of grey.

3 Basic Concepts of the Rough Set Theory

3.1 Introductory Remarks

The rough set concept proposed by Pawlak (1982) is founded on the assumption that every object of the universe of discourse is associated with some information (data, knowledge). For example, if objects are assets listed on a market, their price behaviour and economic characteristics form information about the assets. Objects characterized by the same information are indiscernible (similar) in view of available information about them. The indiscernibility relation generated in this way is the mathematical basis of the rough set theory.

Any set of indiscernible objects is called elementary set and forms a basic granule (atom) of knowledge about the universe. Any subset Y of the *universe* U can either be expressed precisely in terms of the granules or roughly only. In the latter case, subset Y can be characterized by two ordinary sets called lower and upper approximation. The two approximations define the *rough set*. The lower approximation of Y consists of all elementary sets included in Y, whereas the upper approximation of Y consists of all elementary sets having a non-empty intersection with Y. Obviously, the difference between the upper and the lower approximation constitutes the boundary region, including objects which cannot be properly classified as belonging or not to Y, using the available data. Cardinality of the boundary region says, moreover, how exactly we can describe Y in terms of available data.

3.2 Information Table and Indiscernibility Relation

For algorithmic reasons, data about objects will be represented in the form of an information table. The rows of the table are labelled by *objects*, whereas columns are labelled by *attributes* and entries of the table are *attribute values*. Formally, by an *information table* we understand the 4-tuple $S=<U,Q,V,f>$, where U is a finite set of objects, Q is a finite set of *attributes*, $V = \bigcup_{q \in Q} V_q$ and V_q is a domain of the attribute q, and $f:U \times Q \rightarrow V$ is a total function such that $f(x,q) \in V_q$ for every $q \in Q$, $x \in U$, called an *information function* (cf. Pawlak , 1991).

Let $S=<U,Q,V,f>$ be an information table and let $P \subseteq Q$ and $x,y \in U$. We say that x and y are indiscernible by the set of attributes P in S iff $f(x,q)=f(y,q)$ for every $q \in P$. Thus every $P \subseteq Q$ generates a binary relation on U which will be called a *P-indiscernibility relation*, denoted by I_P. Obviously, I_P is an equivalence relation for any P. Equivalence classes of the relation I_P are called *P-elementary sets* in S and $I_P(x)$ denotes the P-elementary set containing object $x \in U$.

$Des_P(x)$ denotes a *description* of object $x \in U$ in terms of values of attributes from P, i.e.

$$Des_P(x) = \{(q,v_q): f(x,q)=v_q, \ \forall q \in P\}.$$

Since all objects being in the same equivalence class are indiscernible, they must have the same description, then $\forall y \in I_P(x)$

$$Des_P(y) = Des_P(x).$$

3.3 Approximation of Sets

Let $P \subseteq Q$ and $Y \subseteq U$. The *P-lower approximation* of Y, denoted by $\underline{P}Y$, and the *P-upper approximation* of Y, denoted by $\overline{P}Y$, are defined as:

$$\underline{P}Y = \{x \in U : I_P(x) \subseteq Y\},$$
$$\overline{P}Y = \{x \in U : I_P(x) \cap Y \neq \varnothing\}.$$

The *P-boundary* (doubtful region) of set Y is defined as

$$Bn(Y) = \overline{P}Y - \underline{P}Y.$$

Set $\underline{P}Y$ is the set of all elements of U which can be certainly classified as elements of Y, employing the set of attributes P. Set $\overline{P}Y$ is the set of elements of U which can be possibly classified as elements of Y, using the set of attributes P. The set Bn (Y) is the set of elements which cannot be certainly classified to Y using the set of attributes P.

With every set $Y \subseteq U$, we can associate an *accuracy of approximation* of set Y by P in S, or in short, accuracy of Y, defined as:

$$\alpha_P(Y) = \frac{card(\underline{P}Y)}{card(\overline{P}Y)}.$$

Let S be an information table, $P \subseteq Q$, and let $\mathcal{Y} = \{Y_1, Y_2, ..., Y_n\}$ be a partition of U. The origin of this partition is independent on attributes from P. Subsets Y_i, i=1,...,n, are classes of partition $\mathcal{Y}$. By P-lower (P-upper) approximation of $\mathcal{Y}$ in S we mean sets $\underline{P}\mathcal{Y} = \{\underline{P}Y_1, \underline{P}Y_2, ..., \underline{P}Y_n\}$ and $\overline{P}\mathcal{Y} = \{\overline{P}Y_1, \overline{P}Y_2, ..., \overline{P}Y_n\}$, respectively. The coefficient

$$\gamma_P(\mathcal{Y}) = \frac{\sum_{i=1}^{n} card(\underline{P}Y_i)}{card(U)}$$

is called the *quality of approximation of partition* $\mathcal{Y}$ by set of attributes P, or in short, *quality of classification*. It expresses the ratio of all P-correctly classified objects to all objects in the system.

3.4 Reduction and Dependency of Attributes

We say that the set of attributes $R \subseteq Q$ *depends* on the set of attributes $P \subseteq Q$ in S (denotation $P \rightarrow R$) iff $I_P \subseteq I_R$. Discovering dependencies between attributes is of primary importance in the rough set approach to information table analysis.

Another important issue is that of attribute reduction, in such a way that the reduced set of attributes provides the same quality of classification as the original set of attributes. The minimal subset $R \subseteq P \subseteq Q$ such that $\gamma_R(\mathcal{Y}) = \gamma_P(\mathcal{Y})$ is called $\mathcal{Y}$-*reduct* of P (or, simply, *reduct* if there is no ambiguity in the understanding of $\mathcal{Y}$) and denoted by $RED_{\mathcal{Y}}(P)$. Let us notice that an information table may have more than one $\mathcal{Y}$-reduct. Intersection of all $\mathcal{Y}$-reducts is called the $\mathcal{Y}$-*core* of P, i.e. $CORE_{\mathcal{Y}}(P) = \cap RED_{\mathcal{Y}}(P)$. The core is a collection of the most relevant attributes in the table.

3.5 Decision Rules

An information table can be seen as *decision table* assuming that $Q=C \cup D$ and $C \cap D=\varnothing$, where set C contains so called *condition attributes*, and D, *decision attributes*.

From the decision table $S=<U,C \cup D,V,f>$ a set of *decision rules* can be derived. Let C and D generate indiscernibility relations I_C and I_D, respectively, on U. The resulting C-elementary sets in S are denoted by X_i (i=1,...,k) and called *condition classes*. Similarly, D-elementary sets in S are denoted by Y_j (j=1,...,n) and called *decision classes*.

$Des_C (X_i) \Rightarrow Des_D (Y_j)$ is called (C,D)-decision rule. The rules can be also expressed as logical statements "if ... then ..." relating descriptions of condition and decision classes. The set of decision rules for each decision class Y_j (j=1,...,n) is denoted by $\{r_{ij}\}$. Precisely,

$$\{r_{ij}\} = \{Des_C (X_i) \Rightarrow Des_D (Y_j): X_i \cap Y_j \neq \varnothing, i=1,...,k\}.$$

Rule r_{ij} is *exact* iff $X_i \subseteq Y_j$, and r_{ij} is *approximate* otherwise. Approximate rules are consequences of an approximate description of decision classes in terms of condition classes (blocks of objects - granules - indiscernible by condition attributes). It means that using the available data, one is unable to decide whether some objects (from the boundary region) belong to a given decision class or not.

Procedures for derivation of decision rules from decision tables were presented by Slowinski and Stefanowski (1992), Grzymala-Busse (1992), Skowron (1993), Stefanowski and Vanderpooten (1994) and by Ziarko et al. (1993).

Decision rules derived from a decision table can be used for classifying *new objects*. Specifically, the *classification* of a new object can be supported by matching its description to one of the decision rules. The matching may lead to one of four situations (cf. Slowinski and Stefanowski, 1994):

    a) the new object matches one exact rule,

    b) the new object matches more than one exact rule indicating the same decision class,

    c) the new object matches one approximate rule or several rules indicating different decision classes,

    d) the new object does not match any of the rules.

3.6 An Example

Table 1 represents a decision table S where $U=\{x_1, x_2, x_3, x_4, x_5, x_6, x_7, x_8, x_9, x_{10}\}$ is the universe, $C=\{c_1, c_2, c_3\}$ is the set of condition attributes and d is the decision attribute (van den Bergh et al., 1995).

Table 1. The decision table S

U	c_1	c_2	c_3	d
x_1	0	M	L	0
x_2	0	M	L	0
x_3	0	M	L	0
x_4	0	H	M	1
x_5	0	H	M	1
x_6	1	L	L	0
x_7	1	M	M	0
x_8	1	M	M	0
x_9	1	M	H	1
x_{10}	1	H	L	1

We observe that $\{c_1, c_2, c_3\}$-elementary sets $=\{c_1, c_2\}$-elementary sets=atoms, that is:

$$\{x_1, x_2, x_3\}, \{x_4, x_5\}, \{x_6\}, \{x_7, x_8\}, \{x_9\}, \{x_{10}\}.$$

Thus we have:

set $\{c_1, c_2, c_3\}$ is dependent in S (IND$\{c_2, c_3\}$=IND$\{c_1, c_2, c_3\}$); $\{c_1, c_2, c_3\}\rightarrow\{d\}$; $\{c_2, c_3\}\rightarrow\{c_1, c_2, c_3\}$; $\{c_2, c_3\}\rightarrow\{d\}$.

Let $\mathcal{Y}=\{Y_0, Y_1\}$ be the partitition induced by the the decision attribute d on S, i.e., $Y_0=\{x_1, x_2, x_3, x_6, x_7, x_8\}$ and $Y_1=\{x_4, x_5, x_9, x_{10}\}$ are the $\{d\}$-elementary sets. In this case we have $\alpha_C(Y_0)=\alpha_C(Y_1)=\gamma_C(\mathcal{Y})=1$, RED$_\mathcal{Y}(C)$=CORE$(C)$=$\{c_2, c_3\}$.

Then the considered classification could be obtained taking into account only the two attributes c_2 and c_3. So these attributes (the core) cannot be eliminaed without reducing the quality of the classification.

From the decision table S the exact decision rules presented in Table 2 can be extracted.

Table 2. Decision rules

Rule #	c_1	c_2	c_3	d	(+)
1	0	M		0	x_1, x_2, x_3
2		L		0	x_6
3	1		M	0	x_7, x_8
4		H		1	x_4, x_5, x_{10}
5			H	1	x_9

(+) Objects supporting the rules

E. g. rule 1 means "if c_1=0 and c_2=M then d=0" and it is derived from the objects x_1, x_2, x_3 of the decision table S.

3.7 Pairwise Comparison Table

Let A be a finite set of objects and C the set of (condition) attributes. The attributes can mean quantitative variables but they are not limited to.

For any $q \in C$ let T_q be a set of binary relations such that $\forall$ v'_q, $v''_q \in V_q$ exactly one binary relation $t \in T_q$ is verified. For interesting applications it should be card $(T_q) \geq 2$.

Furthermore, let T_d be another set of binary relations defined on set A such that at most one binary relation $t \in T_d$ is verified $\forall$ x,y $\in$ A.

The *pairwise comparison table* (PCT) (Greco et al., 1995) is defined as information table $S_{PCT} = \langle B, C \cup \{d\}, T_q \cup T_d, g \rangle$ where $B \subseteq A \times A$ is a non-empty *sample of comparisons*, d is a decision attribute corresponding to the comprehensive pairwise comparison and $g:B \times (C \cup \{d\}) \rightarrow T_q \cup T_d$ is a total function such that $g[(x,y),q] \in T_q$ $\forall(x,y) \in A \times A$, and $\forall q \in C$, and $g[(x,y),d] \in T_d$ $\forall(x,y) \in B$. It follows that for any pair of actions $(x,y) \in B$ there is verified one and only one binary relation $t \in T_d$. Thus, T_d induces a partition of B. In fact, information table S_{PCT} can be seen as decision table since the set of condition attributes C and decision attribute d are distinguished.

Since in this paper we consider S_{PCT} related to statistical problems, the attribute of C can be considered independent variable while d is a dependent variable. Furthermore the increases and decreases with respect to pairwise comparisons of data can be represented in terms of binary relations defined as follows

$$T_p = \{\Delta_p^h, h \in [-l_p, r_p]\}$$

where h is a relative integer and l_p, r_p are positive integers $\forall p \in C \cup \{d\}$; then $\forall(x,y) \in B$

- $x\Delta_p^h y$, h>0, means that the increase from x to y has degree h with respect to attribute p,

- $x\Delta_p^h y$, h<0, means that the decrease from x to y has degree h with respect to attribute p,

- $x\Delta_p^0 y$ means that x is similar (asymmetrically equivalent) to y.

Therefore, $\forall(x,y)$, $(w,z) \in B$ and $\forall p \in C \cup \{d\}$:
- if $x\Delta_p^h y$ and $w\Delta_p^k z$, $k \geq h \geq 0$, then the increase from w to z is not smaller than the increase from x to y with respect to attribute p,
- if $x\Delta_p^h y$ and $w\Delta_p^k z$, $k \leq h \leq 0$, then the decrease from w to z is not smaller than the decrease from x to y, with respect to attribute p.

Let $c_p: A \rightarrow \Re$ be a function which gives quantitative evaluations of attribute p. Then, in order to measure the increases (when $c_p(x) > c_p(y)$) or decreases (when $c_p(x) < c_p(y)$) according to investors' perceptions one can use a function $k_p: \Re^2 \rightarrow \Re$ satisfying the following properties $\forall$ x, y, z $\in$ A:

$$c_p(x) > c_p(y) \Leftrightarrow k_p[c_p(x), c_p(z)] > k_p[c_p(y), c_p(z)],$$

$$c_p(x) > c_p(y) \Leftrightarrow k_p[c_p(z), c_p(x)] < k_p[c_p(z), c_p(y)],$$

$$c_p(x) = c_p(y) \Leftrightarrow k_p[c_p(x), c_p(y)] = 0.$$

Typical representatives of k_p are

$$k_p[c_p(x), c_p(y)] = c_p(x) - c_p(y)$$

and, if $c_p(z) > 0 \ \forall z \in A$,

$$k_p[c_p(x), c_p(y)] = \frac{c_p(x)}{c_p(y)} - 1.$$

The increases and the decreases measured by k_p are then transformed into a set of specific binary relations Δ_p^h using a set of thresholds $\{\delta_p^h, h \in [-l_p, r_p]: \delta_p^0 = 0, \delta_p^{h-1} < \delta_p^h\}$, in the following way:

$$k_p[c_p(x), c_p(y)] \in]\delta_p^{h-1}, \delta_p^h] \Leftrightarrow x\Delta_p^h y \text{ for } h \in [-l_p, 0],$$

$$k_p[c_p(x), c_p(y)] \in [\delta_p^h, \delta_p^{h+1}[\Leftrightarrow x\Delta_p^h y \text{ for } h \in [0, r_p]$$

where $\delta_p^{-l_p-1} = -\infty$ and $\delta_p^{r_p+1} = +\infty$.

Table 3 (adapted from Stefanowski (1992)) shows a synthetic comparison between rough set approach and the traditional statistical approach.

3.8 Rough Set Analysis of PCT

Since PCT is an information table, we can adapt all the concepts of the rough set analysis to it.

Let $S_{PCT} = \langle B, C \cup \{d\}, T_q \cup T_d, g \rangle$ be an information table associated with a given information about a phenomenon under observation. Two pairs of objects $(x,y), (w,z) \in B$ will be considered *indiscernible* by the set of attributes $P \subseteq C \cup \{d\}$ in S_{PCT} iff $g[(x,y),q] = g[(w,z),q] \ \forall q \in P$. Thus, every $P \subseteq C \cup \{d\}$ generates a binary relation on B, which will be called *PCT-P-indiscernibility relation*, denoted by I_p^{PCT}. It has the same properties as I_p. Equivalence classes of I_p^{PCT} are called P-elementary sets in S_{PCT} and $I_p^{PCT}(x,y)$ denotes the P-elementary set containing $(x,y) \in B$.

A crucial problem related with PCT is approximation of the set of binary relations T_d by attributes from set C. Let $\mathcal{B} = \{B_1, B_2, ..., B_n\}$ be the partition of B induced by T_d. Each class B_j $(j=1,2,...,n)$ corresponds univocally to binary relation $t_j \in T_d$.

Let $P \subseteq C$ and $B_j \in \mathcal{B}$ $(j=1,...,n)$. The *P-lower* and the *P-upper approximations* of B_j are respectively defined as

$$\underline{P}B_j = \{(x,y) \in B: I_p^{PCT}(x,y) \subseteq B_j\},$$

$$\overline{P}B_j = \{(x,y) \in B: I_p^{PCT}(x,y) \cap B_j \neq \varnothing\}.$$

The definition of the *P-boundary* of set B_j is the same as in 3.3:

$$Bn\,(B_j) = \overline{P}\,B_j \underline{-P}B_j\,.$$

Table 3. Rough set approach and Statistics

Problem	Statistical methods	Rough set approach
Goals	Identification and estimation of parameters in structural equations	Reducing redundant attributes and objects, generating decision algorithm
Representation of data	Two entry table which represents a sample	Information table
Type of attributes	Quantitative attributes in a classical case	Qualitative attributes; quantitative attributes are transformed to qualitative ones upon application of some thresholds
Requirements of data	The sample is to be statistically representative; multivariate normal distribution	No requirements; possibility of analysing small information tables
Operators of data aggregation	Mean value, covariance matrix, test statistics	No operator; original form of data during the analysis
Reduction of data	Selection of attributes with the most discriminative power; exemplary tools: test statistics	Minimal subsets of attributes ensuring the same quality of classification as the whole set
Final result	Functional representation	Decision rules which are logical statements

P-lower and P-upper approximation of $B_j \in \mathcal{B}$ (j=1,...,n) can be seen as a rough approximation of relation $t_j \in T_d$, called, in short, *rough binary relation*. This definition of the rough binary relation generalizes that of Pawlak (1994) because the indiscernibility relation I_P^{PCT} is defined directly on $B \subseteq A \times A$ and is not derived from indiscernibility defined on set A.

Using I_P^{PCT} and rough approximations based on it, one is able to maintain all basic concepts and properties of the rough set theory: approximation measures, reduction and dependency of attributes, reducts and the core, and decision rules.

Let us pass to exploitation of the rough set concepts in statistical problems.

The rough set analysis of the PCT leads to a *set of decision rules* (exact and approximate) which can be considered as a suitable description and/or explanation of the analyzed phenomenon.

This model can then be used to establish sets of binary relations between the elements of a set of new objects $\mathcal{A}$ and the elements of a set of reference objects $\mathcal{C}$.

In general, with respect to the peculiar features of the considered problem, we can have $C \subseteq A$ or $C \subseteq \mathcal{A}$ or also $C \subseteq A \cup \mathcal{A}$. However from a theoretical point of view no constraint is imposed on C and for particular problems also "ideal" objects which do not belong to $A \cup \mathcal{A}$ can be considered.

The results so obtained can be considered as a basis for discussing the classification of new objects belonging to $\mathcal{A}$.

Let us remark that, from the set of decision rules applied on $(\mathcal{A} \times C) \cup (C \times \mathcal{A})$, we can derive:

1) the set of lower approximations of relations $t_j \in T_d$ (j=1,...,n) on $(\mathcal{A} \times C) \cup (C \times \mathcal{A})$,

2) the set of upper approximations of relations $t_j \in T_d$ (j=1,...,n) on $(\mathcal{A} \times C) \cup (C \times \mathcal{A})$.

For a given j, the lower approximation of t_j is composed of all pairs $(x,y) \in (\mathcal{A} \times C) \cup (C \times \mathcal{A})$ matching exact rules indicating univocally decision class j, according to situation a) or b) described in 3.5.

Similarly, for a given j, the upper approximation of t_j is composed of all pairs $(x,y) \in (\mathcal{A} \times C) \cup (C \times \mathcal{A})$ matching exact or approximate rules indicating decision class j, possibly not univocally, according to situation a), b) or c) described in 3.5.

The lower approximations represent only certain relations t_j, whereas the upper approximations represent all possible relations t_j among pairs of actions from $(\mathcal{A} \times C) \cup (C \times \mathcal{A})$.

The boundary is composed of all doubtful relations t_j.

4 Return Sensitivities for Financial and Real Factors

4.1 A Risk Model for Portfolio Management

The orientation towards supporting the investment decision demands theoretical and practical insights into the risks concerned. A multi-factor representation of portfolio returns provides such kind of insight.

The relevant *attributes* of an investor's portfolio may be divided into *direct return* related attributes and *indirect return* related attributes. The first category is based on the description of securities by means of their joint probability distribution. The second category stems from all the specific tastes, goals and constraints of the investor or of the problem to be faced, which are not directly connected with returns. Decision aid has to deal with both categories, making a convenient integration of available information. This distinction of attributes is introduced by Hallerbach (1994).

Risk to be faced concerns all expected outcomes, which may be expressed in terms of the value of relevant attributes. Multi-factor models supply information about exposures for direct return related attributes in terms of sensitivities of returns for changes perceived in the environment. The latter class of attributes can be evaluated, either transforming the analytical expression of those data in a way they may be embedded in the multi-factor model, or looking for some specific procedures. The qualitative nature of some attributes, especially for the indirect return related class, allows for a fruitful use of the rough set approach.

In 4.2 and 4.3, we will briefly introduce the structure and the information provided by a multi-factor model.

4.2 Multi-Factor Return Generating Process

The return of a security i for the period $t=(a,b)$, may be modelled as a function $\phi_{it} = (.)$ of a set of stochastic variables $\left\{\delta_{jt}\right\}_{j=1,...,k;}$, so that:

$$r_{it} = \phi_{it}(\delta_{1t},...,\delta_{kt}) + \varepsilon_{it},$$

where the random error term ε_{it} stands for the unmodelled part of the return.

Most literature about financial markets developed models describing all or some features of the joint probability distribution of returns. Models may be grouped in different classes. *Market Models* (MM) specify a linear relationship between the return on individual securities and the return of a portfolio of all securities which are traded in the market. The *Capital Assets Pricing Model* (CAPM) of Sharpe (1964), Lintner (1965) and Mossin (1966) is an equilibrium model based on a perfect and competitive capital market. Investors are assumed to choose (E, σ^2) efficient portfolios of securities. Next to the above mentioned models, *Single Index Models* (SIM) and *Single Factor Models* (SFM), were developed to simplify the Markowitz (1952 and 1959) portfolio problem.

The SFM is directly related to the *Arbitrage Pricing Theory* (APT), when security returns are generated by a one-factor model. The APT approach was first introduced by Ross (1977) and has been considered a valid alternative to CAPM assumptions for a pricing procedure. Traders hunt for "free lunches" in the market and market equilibrium relies on their arbitrage activity. Price co-movements of securities should be connected by traders' arbitrage. APT return generation function links prices to a (set of) factor(s), able to explain a specific market covariance structure. Ex-post testing is performed by means of factor analysis on price time series. APT may also be derived as a special case of SFM with the equilibrium perspective.

The step from SIM and SFM to *Multi Index Models* (MIM) and *Multi-Factor Models* (MFM) is straightforward: the model remains the same, except for the number of factors or indices which may be more than one and should be uncorrelated. A MIM or MFM can be specified as:

$$r_{it} = a_i + \sum_{j=1}^{k} b_{ij}\Delta_{jt} + e_{it}, i \in N \tag{4.1}$$

with:

$$E(e_{it}) = 0, \tag{4.2}$$

$$Cov(\Delta_{jt}, e_{it}) = 0, \forall j, \tag{4.3}$$

$$Cov(\Delta_{jt}, \Delta_{st}) = 0, \forall j \neq s, \tag{4.4}$$

$$Cov(e_{ht}, e_{it}) = 0, \forall h \neq i, \tag{4.5}$$

where: Δ_{jt} = random changes on index or factor j ,

a_i = constant intercept,

b_{ij} = sensitivity coefficient for index or factor j,

e_i = random zero-mean disturbance term.

Indices and factors are proxies for the true common factors conditioning securities' returns. There is a restriction of diagonality on residuals (4.5), implying the exhaustivity of factors influence. The assumption about factor's uncorrelatedness (4.4) is not restrictive. Any set of correlated indices or factors can be easily transformed into a set of orthogonal indices or factors and uncorrelated residuals of the other indices or factors.

For the purpose of describing risk exposures, return conditioning need not to be exhaustive. Thus, the diagonality assumption of the "exact" MIM and MFM does not play a leading role. A reasonable requirement is a sufficient approximation, tuned on the goals of the framework supporting the investment decision.

4.3 Factors and Indices: Risk Exposures as Sensitivities

A crucial element of MIM and MFM is the number and identification of the indices or factors entering in the model. Adding more indices will generally reduce the residual covariance. Any covariance model will be positioned in between of the extremes of the SIM or SFM at one hand and the "full covariance model", with a factor for each security, on the other. Factors or indices should provide meaningful information with respect to direct return related attributes, while explaining a substantial amount of price covariance.

In MFMs practical implementation, the investor has to identify a convenient set of factors, providing both a significant explanation of the return generating process and a suitable description of risk exposures.

One may distinguish between *statistically extracted* factors and *pre-specified* factors. Factor analysis is the most important procedure which allows for the first category. Main components of the variance-covariance price structure describe some "artificial" factors. These factors should be compared with contemporaneous signals from the environment and, eventually, recognized as a combination of economic and/or financial influences. While providing the best statistical fit for a return generating function on a given set of data, the approach is not designed to give information about the risk exposures on direct return related attributes. There are little chances that the interpretation of artificial factors may yield significant risk information.

Pre-specified factors are better suited for a decision support framework. Portfolio attributes are qualified to describe investor's aptitude towards his position. Direct return related attributes are associated with the features of the joint probability distribution of returns. MFMs describe returns as a linear function of a set of factors and factor *sensitivities* provide a link between the *joint probability distribution of factors* and returns. Thus, pre-specified factors to be used for the evaluation of risk exposures should represent or be connected with the chosen attributes.

In this way, the risk of not achieving the "expected return" is decomposed in more components with an intuitively appealing content. Each factor plays the role of conditioning variable on portfolio returns, describing a contemporaneous relationship between returns and economic innovation (changing expectations). Forecasting activity will be focused on factor distributions. Sensitivities, characterizing each security, will be the instrumental variables for portfolio composition.

In Fig.1, we show the connections between direct return related attributes, factors, MFMs sensitivities and security returns.

Fig. 1 Multi-Factor Model for direct return risk exposures.

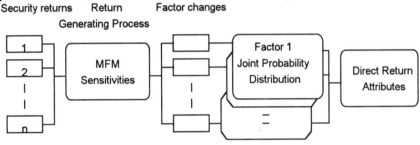

MFMs using economic variables can be distinguished in *predictive* models, *pricing* models and *risk* models. Predictive models are intended to identify the relationship between the levels of economic variables known in advance and the level of expected returns or expected risk premia. This approach is followed by Fama and French (1989), Chen (1991) and Ferson and Harvey (1991). In pricing models, returns are related to contemporaneous unexpected changes in economic variables. The APT is the best example of such a pricing model. Risk models look also to the relation between returns and economic innovation, but without the restriction that risks should be priced. As a result, pricing models are a subset of risk models. It is interesting to notice that, in general, there will be a ``*discrepancy between variables performing well in a pricing context and variables which are able to explain significant proportion of return variability*``. On this subject, see Hallerbach (1994).

In a MFM context, the risk exposures of a portfolio or a security, is expressed in terms of sensitivities. The estimated values of these parameters are the fundamental variables for practical risk management. Expectations with respect to factors' behaviour are translated by means of sensitivities into expected returns and expected volatility of returns.

Each factor may even deserve a specific expectation model. This may be useful in improving the quality of the estimated sensitivity. It also guarantees a convenient "normalization" of the distribution of employed data.

Linearity of the model depends on the normality of returns and factors' innovations distributions. Thus, data should be treated in a two stages process. First, from data towards normalized changes. Then, confronting these changes one can get a linear combination of sensitivities to be used for portfolio composition.

5 Rough Set Approach on MFM Inputs

5.1 Introductory Remarks

Because of the nature of investors' knowledge, MFMs may not be able to use all the available information. Moreover, changing sensitivities and other inconsistencies observed on quantitative analysis may become explainable in a more flexible qualitative context. Investment risk also depends on market behaviour and psychological biases, which are qualitative in nature. The usual approach to cope with these problems is to transform the involved variables or use proxies for behavioural processes. Rough sets can provide an alternative approach for the problems and, in general, for the use of qualitative information in investment risk management.

Our empirical analysis has the aim of showing the possibility to structure qualitative information about financial markets, in line with investor perceptions of market behaviour. At this "pioneristic" stage, we employed monthly data selected as inputs of a MFM, transforming their changes into qualitative perceptions. These data have been processed by means of a rough set algorithm.

5.2 Description of the Data Set

The MFM inputs adopted as starting data set are intended for the analysis of an investment in Italian stocks. All the variables are transformed into monthly logarithmic changes, referred to the first day of the stock exchange settlement month for daily data or to the calendar month for monthly data. Thus:
$$x_t = \ln(a_t) - \ln(a_{t-1}),$$
where a_t is the level at time t.

The portfolio considered as dependent variable is an equally weighted portfolio of 22 Italian "blue chips" listed for a long period also on the London SEAQ market. The stocks under consideration are: Alleanza, Banca di Roma, Benetton, Comit, Credit, Eridania, Ferfin, Fiat ord, Fiat priv, Fiat rnc, Gemina, Generali, Ifi priv, Italgas, Mediobanca, Montedison, Pirelli Spa, Olivetti ord, Sip ord, Sip rnc, Stet, Stet rnc. Their capitalization represents about 75% of total market capitalization. This portfolio has been selected in order to get a representation of the Italian market, oriented to the international investor.

Recorded price changes have been corrected for dividend reinvestments, new stocks and stock splits. Price data were provided by the financial magazine "Milano Finanza" as well the dividend and other adjustments information.

Seven factors have been selected as proxies of risk exposures. We considered five factors with daily observations and two factors displaying monthly records.

The first five factors come from financial markets. We have:
- (1) ITSHOR: Italian overnight rate, observed in London.
- (2) ITGO15Y: The average rate on Italian government bonds with maturity between 1 to 5 years, observed and computed in London.
- (3) USLONG: United States long term government bonds rate, observed in London.
- (4) USCORP: United States corporate bonds rate for bonds with BAA Moodys' rating.

- (5) US$LIT: US$-Italian Lira exchange rate.

These data are referred to the first day of the settlement month as the portfolio data. They were provided by "Datastream".

The other factors under consideration are:

- (6) CPI: Consumer price index, observed by OECD.
- (7) BUSINESS: Business confidence index, observed by OECD.

These data have monthly observations and were provided by "Datastream".

5.3 MFM Results

We present two estimations of return sensitivities for changes in the selected factors.

The first is referred to a period of 6 years from 1987 to 1992. A stepwise regression has been performed, leading to the inclusion of only 5 variables at a 5% limit. Both R^2 and F display very significant values. Signs and magnitudes of estimated sensitivities are in line with economic intuitions.

The second estimation employs 1991-'92 data in a multivariate regression where all factors were entered at the same time. R^2 and F maintain significant values. Given the small size of the sample and market conditions during the specific period, only ITGO15Y and US$LIT sensitivities had significant coefficients.

Experiences on the Italian and Dutch markets show that MFM applications generally require time series with some 50-60 observations, in order to provide reliable insights about risk exposures as expressed by market behaviour (Lo Cascio, 1995 and Hallerbach, 1994). Because of its statistical nature, MFM information takes into consideration only relatively stable market habits, performing poorly on sporadic behaviours.

MFM ESTIMATIONS

6 years period (1987-'92)			2 years period (1991-'92)		
$R^2 = 0.51$;			$R^2 = 0.54$;		
F = 8.3213; DW= 2.2;			F = 4.799; DW= 2.5;		
Variable	Sensitivity	t	Variable	Sensitivity	t
(2) ITGO15Y	4.93	3.95	(1) ITGO15Y	3.67	2.70
(4) USCORP	-13.04	-2.30	(4) USCORP	0.34	0.03
(1) ITSHORT	-2.80	-2.93	(1) ITSHORT	-1.76	-1.66
(7) BUSINESS	0.14	2.41	(7) BUSINESS	0.14	1.78
(5) US$LIT	-0.53	-2.03	(5) US$LIT	-0.63	-2.10
Constant	0.37	0.71	(3) USLONG	0.06	0.26
			(6) CPI	5.22	1.54
			Constant	1.16	1.90

5.4 Rough Set Analysis Results

We employed 1991 data, comparing each month with all the others. Each comparison yields an 8 elements vector: its first 7 elements are the differences between the values of each factors, considered as condition attributes, and the last is the difference between the values of monthly return, considered as decision attribute. Pairwise comparisons are oriented considering only non-negative differences between returns. This simplification is possible because of the simmetry of thresholds for both condition and decision attributes, i.e. $\delta_p^h = \delta_p^{-h}$, $\forall\, h \in [-l_p, r_p]$ and $p \in C \cup \{d\}$. From pairwise comparisons we obtained 66 vectors, corresponding to the $C_{12,2}$. Vector values have been coded according to the set of thresholds shown in Table 4.

The rough set analysis gives the following results:
- there is one dependent attribute in the set $C = \{c_1, ..., c_7\}$: c_4 (USCORP). This means that c_4 is not relevant in the further analysis;
- there is only one reduct, which is also the core: $C - \{c_4\}$;
- there are 65 elementary sets and the quality of approximation is equal to 1;
- the set of decision rules is composed of 34 rules presented in Table 5.

Table 4. The set of thresholds

attributes\degrees	-2	-1	1	2
Itshort	-0.26	-0.09	0.09	0.26
Itgo15y	-0.71	-0.24	0.24	0.71
USlong	-2	-0.67	0.67	2
UScorp	-0.49	-0.16	0.16	0.49
US$Lit	-5	-1.67	1.67	5
CPI	-0.27	-0.09	0.09	0.27
Business	-15	-5	5	15
Portfolio	-5	-1	1	5

Rules may be used to compare investor's expectations with some reference monthly data. Expectations will be represented by means of a 7 elements vector of forecasted values on condition attributes. Differences between expected and reference data are coded. Then, decision rules, obtained with rough set analysis, will be applied as proposed in 3.8. The results may be considered a starting point for a discussion about possible market behaviour.

Decision rule application can be supported by the knowledge of the data from which each decision rule has been derived. For instance, rule 1 is generated by the following pairs of monthly data: March-April, March-November, May-June, May-July, May-September, July-February, September-February, October-April and October-November.

In Table 6 we show the results of decision rules application on January 1992 data (considered as investor's expectations) taking as reference all 1991 monthly data. Each row has the following meaning: between January 1992 and the reference month in the first column there is the binary relation Δ_d^h where h has the value in the second column; this inference is supported by the rule indicated in the third column. E.g. for the first row between January 1992 and January 1991 there is the binary relation Δ_d^{-1} and this is derived from the application of rule number 14.

The rules with * provided a correct return prediction.

Table 5. The set of decision rules

n. rule\att.	IT SHORT	IT GO15Y	US LONG	US CORP	US$LIT	CPI	BUSI NESS	PORT FOLIO
1			0				-1	0
2	0		0		1			0
3			1			-2	0	0
4			0			0	1	0
5		1	-1		1		0	0
6						-2	-1	0
7		-1	1				0	0
8			0			0	0	0
9		-1	-1				1	0
10		0	1				0	0
11				0	0	0	0	1
12	0		1				2	1
13	0	2	-1					1
14			2					1
15	0		1				1	1
16			0			-1		1
17			-1				-1	1
18			-1			-2		1
19		2			0			1
20		1					1	1
21		0				-2		1
22	2						0	1
23						-1	-1	1
24			1		1	-1		1
25	0	1				1		1
26		0	-1				0	1
27	2		1					2
28		-1	-1			-1		2
29		2				1		2
30				1				2
31			-1				2	2
32	2		0			1		2
33			-2				1	2
34		0	0			1		2

Table 6. Decision rules application

Reference month	Binary relation on decision attribute	Rule
January 1991	-1	14
January 1991	1	21
February 1991	0	6
February 1991	1	17
February 1991	1	18
February 1991	-1	20*
February 1991	-2	27
March 1991	0	1
March 1991	0	2
May 1991	1	18*
May 1991	1	21*
June 1991	0	7
June 1991	1	18
July 1991	0	10
July 1991	1	26*
August 1991	-1	14
September 1991	0	10
September 1991	1	26*
October 1991	0	1
November 1991	0	2
December 1991	0	6*
December 1991	1	17
December 1991	1	18
December 1991	-1	15
December 1991	-1	20

6 Conclusions

Comparing the two approaches of MFM and rough set on the same risk management problem, we may draw the following considerations:

a) MFM is suitable in estimating rather stable phenomena, but may loose its descriptive power with small samples and during turbulent periods. Rough set analysis performs well also with few cases and reacts to all signals. While MFM requires the usual statistical properties for the considered variables, rough set approach takes all the available information in its original form. This may explain the satisfactory results obtained with rough set analysis on a small set of data.

b) In a risk management perspective sensitivities and rough set decision rules give alternative representations of risk exposures. The first are in line with economic forecasting, market and firm analysis; the last capture all the simplest structures of market behaviour. Rough set results should be considered a learning tool, providing a specific integration of classical market description for the investment process.

c) The introduction of strictly qualitative variables in portfolio risk management is an attractive field for future researches. Rough set approach appears at this moment the most promising tool to face this problem. This is especially relevant in behavioural finance, which has been studying market reactions and investors aptitudes by means of traditional methodologies. The application of rough set may provide a useful tool for testing the effects of psychological variables and introducing a different perspective of data analysis.

References

van den Bergh, J.C.J.M., Matarazzo, B., Munda, G., 1995, *Measurement and Uncertainty Issues in Environmental Management*, Discussion Paper 81, Tinbergen Institute, 1995.

Chen, N. F., 1991, "Financial investments opportunities and the Macroeconomy", *Journal of Finance,* 46(2), 529-554.

De Bondt, W., Thaler, R., 1985, "Does the stock market overreact?", *Journal of Finance*, 40(3), 793-805.

Fama, E., K. French, 1989, "Business conditions and Expected returns on Stocks and Bonds", *Journal of Financial Economics*, 25(1), 23-50.

Ferson, W., Harvey, C., 1991, "Sources of predictability in portfolio returns", *Financial Analysts Journal*, 47(3), 49-56.

Greco, S., Matarazzo, B., Slowinski, R., 1995, *Rough Set Approach to Multi-Attribute Choice and Ranking Problems*, Warsaw University of Technology, Institute of Computer Science, Technical Report, 38.

Grzymala-Busse, J.W, 1992, "LERS - a system for learning from examples based on rough sets", in Slowinski, R., (ed.), *Intelligent Decision Support. Handbook of Applications and Advances of the Rough Sets Theory*, Kluwer Academic Publishers, Dordrecht, 3-18.

Hallerbach, W., 1994, *Multi Attribute Portfolio Selection*, Ph. D. Thesis, Erasmus University Rotterdam.

Lintner, J., 1965, "Security prices, Risk, and Maximal gains from diversification", *Journal of Finance*, 20(4), 587-615.

Lo Cascio, S., 1995, *An Explanation of Calendar Effects in the Italian Stock Market*, Università di Catania.

Mossin, J., 1966, "Equilibrium in a Capital Asset Market", *Econometrica*, 34, 768-783.

Markowitz, H., 1952, "Portfolio Selection", *Journal of Finance*, 7(1), 77-91.

Markowitz, H., 1959, *Portfolio selection: Efficient diversification and Investments*, John Wiley, New York.

Pawlak, Z., 1982, "Rough sets", *International Journal of Information & Computer Sciences*, 11, 341-356.

Pawlak, Z., 1991, *Rough Sets. Theoretical Aspects of Reasoning about Data*, Kluwer Academic Publishers, Dordrecht.

Pawlak, Z., 1994, *Rough sets, Rough Relations and Rough Functions*, Warsaw University of Technology, Institute of Computer Science, Technical Report, 24.

Ross, S. A., 1976, "The Arbitrage Theory of Capital Asset Pricing", *Journal of Economic Theory*, 13/3, 341-360.

Sharpe, W. F., 1964, "Capital Asset Prices: A Theory of Market Equilibrium under Conditions of Risk", *Journal of Finance*, 19(3), 425-442.

Skowron, A., 1993, "Boolean reasoning for decision rules generation", in Komorowski, J., Ras, Z. W., (eds.), *Methodologies for Intelligent Systems*, (Lecture Notes in Artificial Intelligence, Vol. 689), Springer -Verlag, Berlin, 295-305.

Slowinski, R., Stefanowski, J., 1992, "RoughDAS and RoughClass software implementations of the rough sets approach", in Slowinski, R. (ed.), *Intelligent Decision Support. Handbook of Application and Advances of the rough Sets Theory*, Kluwer Academic Publishers, Dordrecht, 445-456.

Slowinski, R., Stefanowski, J., 1994, "Rough classification with valued closeness relation", in Diday, E. et al., (eds.), *New Approaches in Classification and Data Analysis*, Springer-Verlag, Berlin, 482-488.

Stefanowski, J., 1992, "Rough sets theory and discriminant methods as tools for analysis of information systems. A comparative study", *Foundations of Computing and Decision Sciences*, 17(2), 81-98.

Stefanowski, J., Vanderpooten, D., 1994, "A general two-stage approach to inducing rules from examples", in Ziarko, W., (ed.), *Rough Sets, Fuzzy Sets and Knowledge Discovery*, Springer-Verlag, Berlin, 317-325.

Ziarko, W., Golan, D., Edwards, D., 1993, "An application of DATALOGIC/R knowledge discovery tool to identify strong predictive rules in stock market data", in *Proc. AAAI Workshop on Knowledge Discovery in Databases*, Washington D.C., 89-101.

Takeover Algorithms [1]

Gianfranco Gambarelli

Dept. of Mathematics, Statistics, Informatics and Applications
University of Bergamo, Piazza Rosate n. 2, 24129 Bergamo, Italy

Abstract. A power index provides a reliable forecast of the expected division of power in a committee, where the "weights" of the participants are known. Among the numerous indices, the most well known and applied are those of Shapley-Shubik and Banzhaf-Coleman. Interesting applications of power indices are found when it is necessary to study what variations in the index of a certain player would be produced by changes in his weight. For example, in finance, a shareholder can evaluate the outcome of a potential take-over bid, by knowing a priori how the configuration of a major shareholding would change. He could also estimate how his controlling position would change, if he were to buy a block of shares from another major shareholder.
This paper extends an existing algorithm for the computation of the variations of the Shapley-Shubik index in the above quoted cases, to the Banzhaf-Coleman index, and consequently provides a rapid method for the calculation of the latter.

Keywords: Power index, Banzhaf-Coleman, Shapley-Shubik, takeover, OPA, shares, seats, government.

1. Introduction

A power index provides a reliable forecast of the expected division of power in a committee, where the weights (shares, seats, votes, etc.) of the participants are known. The most well known and applied indices are those of Shapley-Shubik (1954) and Banzhaf-Coleman (1965 and 1964).
Interesting applications of power indices are found when it is necessary to study what variations in the index of a player would be produced by changes in his weight. For example, in the world of finance, a shareholder can evaluate the outcome of a take-over bid by knowing a priori how the configuration of a major

[1] This paper has been jointly financed by MURST (40 and 60 percent) and Committee 10 of C.N.R. The author would like to thank Barbara Botti, Stefania Mercanti and Sonia Mora for their contributions.

shareholding would change. He can also estimate how his controlling position would change, were he to purchase a block of shares from another major shareholder. (These calculations are more or less impossible to carry out manually if there are more than four or five shareholders involved.)

In the same way a political party can evaluate the effect that the introduction of a new electoral law would have if it extended the vote to a new category of voters (e.g. immigrants, emigrants, the disabled, prison inmates, young people) who would presumably share similar political ideals.

For all these cases which modify the game, it has been proved by Gambarelli (1983) that the power index of the players involved (no matter how the index is defined, as long as it respects suitable criteria of monotonicity) is a monotonic step function of the number of shares exchanged. The discontinuity points of such a function are common to various indices and are defined by two generating formulae illustrated in the above-mentioned paper.

A subsequent algorithm by Arcaini and Gambarelli (1986), based on a paper by Mann and Shapley (1962), provides for the automatic calculation of variations to the Shapley-Shubik index taking into consideration all discontinuity points reached (without having to completely recalculate the index each time, but by keeping the values previously calculated).

This paper applies the technique used in Arcaini and Gambarelli (1986) to the Banzhaf-Coleman index and results in a rapid method for the calculation of this index. This provides a global algorithm which generates the "power" function of a player both for the Shapley-Shubik index and the Banzhaf-Coleman index, in the case of an exchange of shares between two players and between a major player and an ocean of small players.

2. Power indices

Let us take a shareholders' meeting made up of n members ("players"), each with a given weight (in terms of seats, votes, shareholdings, etc.) where the majority needed to come to a decision is simple majority (later it will be illustrated that the same criteria can be applied to more complex majorities).

Let us suppose that in the formation of various coalitions no hostility or affinity between the various members exists. In examples of this type there are more sophisticated models developed in Owen (1977, 1981) (here we will consider each group of firmly united members as a single player).

Each player might ask what his expectations of control at this assembly would be, depending on the various coalitions that could be formed.

If for example there are three players (A, B, and C) and their weights are respectively 40, 30 and 30, it is easy to verify that a coalition between two players is necessary to exceed the majority of 50. It is, therefore, reasonable to assign to each member the same power of control, i.e. a coalition power value of 1/3.

The same is true if the weight distribution is (49,49,2) where player C, although having a nominal power value of 2 percent, has in reality a coalition power value of 33.3 percent. If the distribution of weights is (51,48,1), player A by himself has a majority and therefore has complete control. The coalition power values are expressed as (1,0,0). If the distribution of weights were (50,30,20), then player A would have to form a coalition with one of the other two players to obtain a majority, whereas a coalition between the other two would obtain nothing. Obviously player A is more powerful than the other two who have equal power values each. What would be a reasonable expectation of power sharing ?

For a solution to this problem it is necessary to introduce the concept of "crucial player". A player is crucial to a coalition only if he is needed to form a majority. In the previous example player B is crucial for the coalition (A,B) but not for (A,C), neither for the coalition of all three (as a majority is formed without B). Similarly, player C is only crucial for one coalition (A,B). However, player A is crucial for three coalitions (A,B),(A,C),(A,B,C).

The Banzhaf-Coleman index is calculated by assigning to each player a power factor which is proportional to the number of coalitions in which he is crucial. In this case (3/5,1/5,1/5).

Another way of calculating the player's power was established by Shapley and Shubik. They assigned each player an expected gain based on the probability of him being crucial, by joining an already existing coalition. If for example player B joins player A, then player B is crucial to the coalition (A,B). If player C joins player A, then player C is crucial to the coalition (A,C). In the other four cases, player A is the crucial player in the coalition being formed. The totals show that the Shapley-Shubik index is 4/6 for A and 1/6 for B and C, i.e. (2/3, 1/6, 1/6). The difference, therefore, between the Banzhaf-Coleman index and the Shapley-Shubik index is found in the bargaining model. The first doesn't take into account the order of formation of the winning coalition, while the second one does (the first uses combinations and the second permutations). This is why the Shapley-Shubik index is more suitable for forecasting share trading situations, where coalitions that can change voting power are already established. The latter index is more suitable for regulations governing electoral systems. In conclusion, the two general formulae for the two indices are given.

Let N be the set of n players. The Banzhaf-Coleman index assigns to the n-th player a power β_i proportional to the number of coalitions for which he is crucial.

As illustrated in the example: A is crucial for (A,B), (A,C) and (A,B,C); B is crucial for (A,B); C is crucial for (A,C) and therefore $\beta_A = 3/5$, $\beta_B = \beta_C = 1/5$.

The Shapley-Shubik index assigns the n-th player the power of :

$$\Phi_i = \frac{1}{n!} \Sigma \ (s-1)! \ (n-s)!$$

where the summation is extended to all coalitions of s members for which the i-th player is crucial (varying s from 1 to n). In our example:

$$\Phi_A = \frac{1}{3!} \; ((2-1)!*(3-2)! * 2 + (3-1)!*(3-3)! * 1) = 2/3$$

$$\qquad\qquad\qquad\qquad \uparrow \qquad\qquad\qquad\qquad \uparrow$$
$$\qquad\qquad\qquad (AB)+(AC) \qquad\qquad (A,B,C)$$

$$\Phi_B = \Phi_C = \frac{1}{3!} \; ((2-1)!*(3-2)!*1) = 1/6$$

For other less well-known and applied indices see (Gambarelli, 1994a).

3. Share trading between two players

Let us suppose the initial distribution of shares between three players A, B, and C is (51, 40, 9). Obviously any share trading between B and C would not change the situation as A will always have a majority. So, we will consider what will happen in a trading of shares between A and C. Were C to purchase one share from A, the share distribution would become (50, 40, 10) and the power distribution (according to the Shapley-Shubik index) would become (2/3, 1/6, 1/6).

If, however, C purchased two shares from A, the distribution of shares would be (49, 40, 11) and the power distribution would be (1/3, 1/3, 1/3).

The power distribution would be the same even if C were to purchase 40 shares from A as in this case the share distribution would be (11, 40, 49) and each player would be in the same position as the others regarding possible coalitions. The situation would only change if C bought 41 shares from A: in this case the distribution would be (10, 40, 50) and the power factor of C would rise to 2/3.

With one more share, C would acquire the majority alone and his power factor would rise to 100 percent. The power of C is therefore a monotonic function of the number of shares acquired from A. The crucial shares that change the position of C from one of a majority to a minority are 10, 11, 50, 51 (see figure 1).

If instead of using the Shapley-Shubik index the Banzhaf-Coleman index is used, the power factor changes, but the crucial share-holdings remain the same (see figure 2).

In Gambarelli (1983) it was proved that no matter how a power index is defined (as long as it has monotonic properties) the sequence of crucial shareholdings corresponding to the share trading between two players, i and j, is always the same. The formulas which generate the sequence of these crucial stocks d_s in a coalition of n shareholders are the following:

$$d_s = q - \sum_{h=1}^{n} b_h w_h \quad \text{and} \quad d_s = t - q - \sum_{h=1}^{n} b_h w_h \tag{1}$$

where q is the majority quota, w_h are the weights (intended as shareholdings or the percentage of company capital held) of the shareholders, t is the total weight, and b is a binary vector (assuming the values 0 or 1) meeting the conditions $b_i = b_j = 0$. The two summations are also subject to the following conditions:

$$-H < \sum_{h=1}^{n} b_h w_h < H$$

where H is the minimum between q and $(t-q)$.
In the example, $t=100$, $q=51$, $t-q=50$ (rounded up), $i=1$ and $j=3$. The binary vectors considered are $(0,0,0)$ and $(0,1,0)$. From these formulas the crucial shareholdings 10, 11, 50, 51 are generated.
It should be noted that this example could be applied to forecast the changes in a parliamentary majority following a shift of the electorate from one party to another.

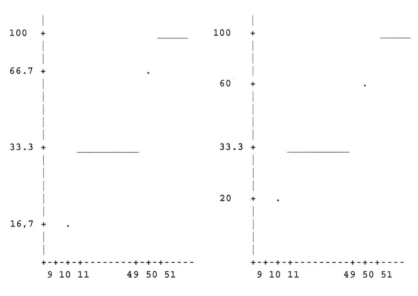

Figure 1   Figure 2

4. Share trading between one player and an ocean of players

Suppose a company has three major shareholders A, B and C and an ocean of minor shareholders which are not interested in control. Let the initial breakdown of shares between the major shareholders be (20,15,4). What would happen if the third shareholder started to buy shares on the market from minor shareholders (the ocean) to increase his power factor in the company?

If C purchased one share from the ocean, the share distribution would become (20, 15, 5) and the power factors (according to Shapley-Shubik) would be (2/3, 1/6, 1/6), as the majority shareholding would go from 19.5 to 20.

If C purchased two shares from the ocean, the share distribution would become (20, 15, 6) and the power factors would be (1/3, 1/3, 1/3). This power distribution would remain the same even if C were to purchase 30 shares; the situation would only change if C bought 31 shares. In this case, the share distribution would become (20, 15, 35) and the power factors (1/6, 1/6, 2/3). With the purchase of one more share C would acquire the absolute majority and his power factor would be 100 percent.

Applying the Banzhaf-Coleman index, although there are different power factors (0, 1/5, 1/3, 3/5, 1), the critical stocks are the same as those above. This is shown more clearly in fig. 3 and 4.

In Gambarelli (1986) it was proved that also in these cases, however the power index is defined (as long as it is monotonic), the power of the raider (i-th player) to form coalitions is a monotonic step function of the number of shares purchased from minor shareholders. The critical stocks d_s are generated using the following formula:

$$d_s = -\frac{M}{t\,b_i - q} - w_i \quad , \text{ where } q, t, b \text{ and } w_h \text{ are defined as in (1)}$$

$$\text{and} \quad M = \sum_{h=1, h \neq i}^{n} (t b_h - q) * w_h \quad \text{under the conditions: } M \geq 0 \text{ for } b_i=0; M \leq 0 \text{ for } b_i=1.$$

In this example, the third player is involved (i=3). Initially t=39, q=19.5, w=(20,15,4) and these change as w_3 increases. The formula, with the necessary roundings, generates the critical points 5, 6, 35 and 36.

Note that the model proposed here differs from classical oceanic games (see for example (Milnor and Shapley, 1961)) as it supposes that all power is held by major shareholders. It is, therefore, more suitable for incomplete information imperfect markets, where the minor shareholders are obviously excluded from the board of directors and where the means and the information owned by the raider renders the power of the ocean, which is not able to form a coalition, completely ineffective. (Our model describes this type of situation as well, because the i-th player could be a syndacate of shareholders.)

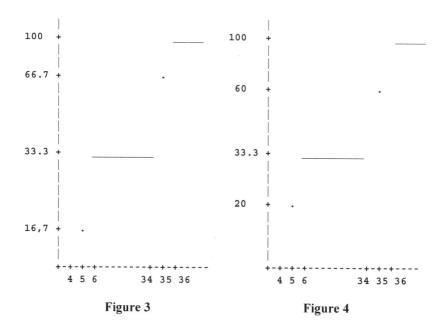

Figure 3   Figure 4

This model could also be applied to political-electoral problems, as it can describe variations in the index following the introduction of electoral legislation which extends the vote to new categories of voters (eg. immigrants, emigrants, disabled persons, prison inmates, young people, etc.) presumably favouring the same political party.

5. The Algorithms Generation of the indices

To generate the Shapley-Shubik index, we can refer to the algorithm of Arcaini and Gambarelli (1986) mentioned in the introduction. This algorithm is suitable only for weighted majority games (defined exclusivelyby weights and a majority quota), while other techniques are preferable for general games (see for example Gambarelli (1980 and 1990)).

We suggest a new method to compute the Banzhaf-Coleman index, using the idea of Mann and Shapley (1962). The Mann and Shapley method is based on the assumption that the Shapley-Shubik index can be expressed in the following form:

$$\Phi_i = \sum_{k=0}^{n-1} H_{k,n}\, c_k$$

where $H_{k,n} = k!(n-k-1)!/n!$, $c_k = \sum_{j=q-w_i}^{q-1} c^i_{jk}$ and c^i_{jk} is the number of ways in which k players, different from i, have a sum of weights equal to j $(0 \le j \le t-w_i)$.

In fact, each player is crucial to a coalition only if the others have insufficient total weight without him $(j < q)$ and sufficient weight with him $(j + w_i \ge q)$.

The Banzhaf-Coleman index can be calculated using the same method, omitting the $H_{k,n}$ coefficient and applying a final normalization. If we thus define:

$$B_i = \sum_{k=0}^{n-1} c_k \quad \text{and} \quad B = \sum_{i=1}^{n} B_i,$$

the Banzhaf-Coleman index for the i-th player becomes:

$$\beta_i = B_i/B.$$

Observe that the quantity B can only be obtained at the end of processing.
The calculation of c^i_{jk} necessary for the evaluation of c_k can be made as follows:

$$c^i_{jk} = c^i_{jk}{}^{-1} + c^i_{j-}{}^{-1}{}_{w_i,k-1}$$

where the last term is considered null if one of its indices is negative. The parameter c^i_{jk} is positive only when:

$$j = \sum_{h=1}^{k} w_{r_h}$$

where r_h is the weight of the r_h-th player $(r_h \ne i)$.

As it is not necessary to calculate subsequent increases of the coefficients H_{kn}, this means a significant reduction in computation time.

The algorithms described above can be implemented in such away to have a suitable framework for the user to play with.

The program input consists of:
- the chosen scenario:
  a) exchange of weights between two players
  b) exchange of weights between one player and the ocean of players

- the chosen index:
  a) Shapley-Shubik
  b) Banzhaf-Coleman

- the initial conditions:
  w $= (w_1, \ldots, w_n)$ players' weights (in descending order)
  q $=$ majority percentage
  h,k $=$ players involved in the exchange between two players, or
  i $=$ the player involved in an exchange with the ocean.

The program supplies the discontinuity points, i.e. the critical stocks, and the variations of power indices of the involved players in each of these points. The results can be illustrated by tables or figures similar to those of Section 3.

6. Further developments

The outlook for extending this paper includes: other power index applications with different coalition probabilities (see Owen 1977, 1981 and 1995), power indices for indirect control (see Gambarelli and Owen, 1994a), further developments on take-over theory (see Gambarelli and Szego, 1982), (Gambarelli, 1991, 1993, 1994c, Gambarelli and Owen, 1994b) and portfolio theory (see Szego, 1980 and Gambarelli, 1982).

There are also studies on political application problems (see Brams, 1975 and Holler, 1981), (Brams and Fishburn, 1983), (Owen and Shapley, 1989), (Gambarelli and Holubiec, 1990), (Gambarelli, 1991, 1994b and 1994c)).

References

Arcaini, G. and Gambarelli, G. (1986) "Algorithm for Automatic Computation of the Power Variations in Share Tradings" Calcolo, 23,1,13-9.

Banzhaf, J. F. (1965) "Weighted Voting doesn't Work: a Mathematical Analysis " Rutgers Law Review, 19, 317-43.

Brams, S. J.(1975) Game Theory and Politics. Free Press, N.Y.

Brams, S. J. and Fishburn, P. C.(1983) Approval Voting. Birkhauser, Boston.

Coleman, J. S. (1964) Introduction to Mathematical Sociology. Free Press of Glencoe, New York.

Gambarelli, G. (1980) "Algorithm for the numerical computation of the Shapley value of a game" Rivista di Statistica Applicata, 13, 1, 35-41.

---- (1982) "Portfolio Selection and Firms' Control" Finance, 3, 1, 69-83.

---- (1983) "Common Behaviour of Power Indices" Internat. Journal of Game Theory, 12, 4, 237-44.

---- (1990) "A new approach for evaluating the Shapley value" Optimization, 21, 3, 445-52.

---- (1991) "Political and Financial Applications of the Power Indices" In G. Ricci ed., Decision Processes in Economics. Springer-Verlag, Berlin-Heidelberg, 84-106.

---- (1993) "An index of stability for controlling shareholders" Modelling Reality and Personal Modelling. Proc. of the EURO Working Group of Financial Modelling Meeting, Curacao (R. Flavell ed.). Physica-Verlag, Heidelberg, 116-27.

---- (1994a) "A Quick Introduction to the Theory of Games" In G. Ricci ed. Proc. of the NATO International Summer School on Dynamic Games, Villasimius, Springer-Verlag (forthcoming).

---- (1994b) "Electoral Systems and Data Processing" Congreso Iberoamericano de Informatica y Derecho organizado por el Ministerio de Justicia de la Nacion Argentina, Bariloche.

---- (1994c) "Power Indices for Political and Financial Decision Making" Annals of Operations Research, 51, 165-173.

Gambarelli, G. and Holubiec, J. (1990) "Power indices and democratic apportionment" Proc. of the 8-th Italian-Polish Symposium on Systems Analysis and Decision Support in Economics and Technology (M. Fedrizzi and J. Kacprzyk eds.). Onnitech Press, Warsaw, 240-55.

Gambarelli, G. and Owen, G. (1994a) "Indirect Control of Corporations" International Journal of Game Theory 23, 4, 287-302.

---- (1994b) "50 Years of Game Theory" Journal of European Business Education, 4, 1, 30-45.

Gambarelli, G. and Szegö, G.P. (1982) "Discontinuous solutions in n-person games" In G.P. Szegö ed., New Quantitative Techniques for Economic Analysis, Academic Press, New York, 229-44.

Mann, I. and Shapley, L.S. (1962) "Values of Large Games, VI: Evaluating the Electoral College Exactly" Rand Corp., RM 3158, Santa Monica, CA.

Milnor, J.W. and Shapley, L.S. (1961) "Values of Games, II: Oceanic Games" Rand Corp., RM 2646, Santa Monica, CA.

222

Holler, M.J., ed. (1981) Power, Voting and Voting Power. Physica-Verlag, Wurzburg.

Owen, G. (1977) "Values of Games with a Priori Unions" Lecture Notes in Econ. and Mathem. Systems, 141, 76-88.

---- (1981) "Modification of the Banzhaf-Coleman Index for Games with a Priori Unions" in M.J. Holler ed., 232-8.

---- (1995) (III ed.) Game Theory. Academic Press, New York.

Owen, G. and Shapley, L.S. (1989) "Optimal Location of Candidates in Ideological Space" Internat. Jour. of Game Theory, 18,3, 339-356.

Shapley, L. S. and Shubik, M. (1954) "A Method for Evaluating the Distributions of Power in a Committee System" American Political Science Review, 48, 787-92.

Szegö, G. P. (1980) Portfolio Theory. Academic Press, N.Y.

The Number of Arbitrage Pricing Theory Factors: An Assessment of the Power of Multivariate Tests Used

Michael J. Page

Graduate School of Business, University of Cape Town, Rondebosch, 7700, RSA

Abstract. In spite of Shanken's (1982) rejection of its testability, a vast body of literature has developed over the last two decades involving empirical tests of the Arbitrage Pricing Theory. The majority of the earlier studies focused on the determination of the number and pricing of the APT factors. The core methodology employed has involved the use of factor analysis and cross-sectional generalised least squares procedures with conclusions being reached of anywhere between one and nine independently priced factors.

This paper investigates the extent to which prior research conclusions may be influenced by the power of the multivariate tests used. An extensive simulation analysis of a variety of pre-defined priced factor economies is employed. The conclusions are threefold. Firstly, the diversity of past results can to a large extent be explained by the low power of the procedures employed. Secondly, thin trading, with its impact on covariance estimation, biases the results towards a multi factor conclusion being reached. Finally, the existence of moderate levels of non-normalities in the returns distribution does not significantly impact on the results.

Keywords. Arbitrage Pricing Theory, factor analysis, market micro-structure

1. Introduction

This paper examines the effect of market microstructure, thin trading and non-normality on the methodologies currently used in empirical research into the number and pricing of the Arbitrage Pricing Theory (APT) factors. Over the last two decades there has been considerable investigation and debate into this aspect of the theory, and the lack of consensus is evidenced by the fact that the number of priced factors "found" commonly range from one (Trzinka, 1986) to five (Roll and Ross, 1980; Cho, Eun and Senbet, 1986). Much of the debate as to the reason for these inconsistent findings has focused on the small sample properties of the factor analytic techniques used, and on such issues as the convergence or otherwise of the Ross strict factor structure and the more general approximate factor structure of Chamberlain and Rothschild (Ross, 1976; Roll and Ross, 1980; Chamberlain and Rothschild, 1983; Brown, 1989).

The implications of thin trading and non-normality examined in this paper, while alluded to by many researchers, have only been expressly addressed by Shanken (1987). As discussed further below, a principal components methodology is used in preference to the maximum likelihood procedure of Roll and Ross (1980). This approach is consistent with the approximate factor structure approach and can be tested using an approximate χ^2 procedure under the standard assumptions of multivariate normality (Bartlett, 1950:77)[1].

The paper is divided into six sections. Section 2 presents a brief overview of the Arbitrage Pricing Theory as developed by Ross (1976), while relevant empirical research into the theory is discussed in Section 3. Reference is made to both the methodologies employed and the consequent findings. Section 4 describes the methodologies employed for simulating the data and investigating the robustness of the traditional test procedures empoyed in APT research. The results of the analysis are presented in Section 5 where the implications of market microstructure effects, thin trading and non-normalities on the test procedures are assessed by comparing simulation results against what would theoretically be expected in the absence of such effects, and against benchmark simulations conducted in their absence. The final section gives summary conclusions and assesses the potential implications for empirical research of using robust covariance estimates.

2. Overview of the Arbitrage Pricing Theory

Ross (1976) initially presented an heuristic argument for his theory. Beginning with *the neoclassical assumptions of perfectly competitive and frictionless markets*, he assumed that the random returns of a set of assets could be described by a simple factor generating model of the form (Roll and Ross, 1980:1076);

$$\tilde{r}_i = E(\tilde{r}_i) + \beta_{i1}\tilde{\delta}_1 + \ldots\ldots + \beta_{ik}\tilde{\delta}_k + \tilde{\varepsilon}_i, \quad i = 1,\ldots,n \tag{1}$$

where; $E(\tilde{r}_i)$ is the expected return on the ith asset; δ_j is the mean zero j^{th} factor common to the returns of all assets; β_{ij} represents the sensitivity of the ith asset to the jth factor; and, $\tilde{\varepsilon}_i$ is the idiocyncratic risk of the ith asset and is sufficiently independent to permit the law of large numbers to apply. As suggested by Roll and Ross, *(t)oo strong a dependence in the $\tilde{\varepsilon}_i$'s would be like saying that there are*

---

[1]Given the conceptual difference between components analysis and factor analysis, comparative analyses are also conducted using principal factor procedures where the squared multiple covariances (correlations) are used as (initial) communality estimates.

more than simply the k hypothesised factors (1980:1076).

Given equation (1) and the assumption of a large asset market, Ross then showed that a well diversified arbitrage portfolio involving no net investment could be constructed in such a way as to have zero sensitivity to each of the k factors. Additionally, given the well diversified nature of the portfolio, Ross suggested the influence of the idiocyncratic risk components would be negligible and the total portfolio risk would therefore approximate zero. In an efficient market, the absence of arbitrage possibilities implies such a portfolio must have a zero expected return and it therefore follows that the expected return for the ith security is given by;

$$E(\tilde{r}_i) = \rho + \beta_{i1}\lambda_1 + \beta_{i2}\lambda_2 + \dots + \beta_{ik}\lambda_k \tag{2}$$

where; ρ is the rate of return on any riskless asset or on all zero-beta portfolios (Ross, 1976:343); and, λ_j represents the excess return, or market premium, on a portfolio with only j[th] factor systematic risk. This interpretation arises because any portfolio constructed such that $\beta_{Pj} = 1$ and $\beta_{Pi} = 0$, $\forall i \neq j$ will provide an expected return $E(\tilde{r}_P) = \rho + \lambda_j$, giving $\lambda_j = E(\tilde{r}_P) - \rho$.

Unfortunately the heuristic argument presented above presumes that economic agents do not become increasingly risk averse[2] as the number of assets increases and the law of large numbers acts to ensure that the idiocyncratic risk component becomes negligible. If such agents do exist, the presence of some idiocyncratic risk can continue to influence the pricing relationship. In order to rule out this possibility Ross suggested five additional assumptions needed to be made relating to the preferences of economic agents (1976:347-351). At least one asset must exist with limited liability so that there is some bound to the losses for which an agent is liable; at least one risk averse agent believing that returns are generated by equation (1) must exist who is not asymptotically negligible and for whom the coefficient of relative risk aversion is uniformly bounded; all agents must be risk averse and have homogeneous expectations; the aggregate demand for all assets must be a positive function of total wealth implying the economy as a whole wishes to hold some of each asset; and finally, the expected returns of the sequence of assets must be uniformly bounded.

While equation (2) can be interpreted as a multifactor generalisation of the CAPM, the approach used in its development is quite different. The argument provided by Ross suggests that it holds in all but the most profound cases of disequilibria. As such the theory provides an ex-ante pricing equation that does not rely on market equilibrium. Contrary to the CAPM, no central role exists for the

---

[2]As the number of assets increases aggregate wealth will, in general, also increase. Additionally, with increasing wealth it is conceiveable that some economic agents may become more risk averse.

market portfolio and its identification would therefore appear to be unnecessary when undertaking empirical research. Additionally, while a necessary assumption is that all economic agents have equal ex-ante expectations, the theory does not require that all agents believe that returns are generated in a fashion described by equation (1). Unlike the CAPM, the Arbitrage Pricing Theory *does not require the stringent homogeneity of anticipations of mean-variance theory* (Ross, 1976:355).

The random return for the ith asset can now be described by combining equations (1) and (2) to produce;

$$\tilde{r}_i = \rho + \beta_{i1}\left(\lambda_1 + \tilde{\delta}_1\right) + \beta_{i2}\left(\lambda_2 + \tilde{\delta}_2\right) + \dots + \beta_{ik}\left(\lambda_k + \tilde{\delta}_k\right) + \tilde{\varepsilon}_i. \tag{3}$$

In spite of the simple heuristic employed by Ross, several assumptions are necessary to rigorously derive the Arbitrage Pricing Theory from the return generating equation described by equation (1) and, since Ross's original development, several researchers have provided additional derivations and approximations to account for such issues as the fact that the diversification of the type described by Ross can only apply approximately in an economy containing a finite number of assets. Some of these subsequent derivations have relied on arbitrage alone and others have sought to provide more robust derivations under equilibrium conditions[3].

3. Prior empirical research

Empirical research into the validity of the Arbitrage Pricing Theory can be broadly classified into four areas. The first relates to the empirical testability of the theory itself, the second focuses on the estimation of the number and pricing of the factors, the third deals with the identification of the economic factors determining returns, and the fourth examines the ability of the model to explain certain CAPM anomalies. The review presented below is restricted to the first two areas which relate explicitly to empirical tests of the number of priced APT factors.

3.1 Testability of the theory

In support of his view that Roll's critique remains relevant for empirical tests of the Arbitrage Pricing Theory, Shanken has, on two occasions, raised questions as to whether the theory is more amenable to empirical verification than the Capital Asset Pricing Model. He initially suggested that the methodology whereby one seeks to test whether the expected returns vector is a linear combination of the unit vector and the factor loadings matrix *rules out the very expected return*

---

[3]See Chamberlain (1983); Chamberlain and Rothschild (1983); Dybvig (1983); Stambaugh (1983); Ingersoll (1984); Grinblatt and Titman (1985).

differentials which the theory seeks to explain (1982:1134). When Dybvig and Ross (1985) developed an approach that they contended established equilibrium restrictions to factor models that led to testable implications for the theory, Shanken again reiterated his concerns by stating that the restrictions involved testing *joint hypotheses that cannot be verified without observing the entire universe of assets* (1985:1189). Dybvig and Ross reject this conclusion and argue that testing the theory on a subset is valid and that any bias when using subsets of data is towards rejection of the theory and, contrary to the assertion of Shanken, that the chance of spurious acceptance is small (1985:1184).

Chamberlain and Rothschild defined an approximate factor structure as an *(a)ppropriate concept for investigating the relationship between factor loadings and asset prices* (1983:1282). Although less restrictive than the strict factor structure employed by Ross (1976) in his development of the Arbitrage Pricing Theory, Chamberlain and Rothschild suggest the approximate structure is still sufficient as a condition for reaching Ross's conclusions. Based on their analysis they also suggest that if security returns can be explained by an approximate k-factor structure then only k eigenvalues are unbounded and principal components analysis can be applied to test the relationship since *factor analysis and principal components analysis are asymptotically equivalent* (1983:1296-1301).

While not rejecting the testability of the theory outright, Kryzanowski & To (1983) suggest several assumptions need to be tested before unambiguous testing of the Arbitrage Pricing Theory can be carried out. The assumptions, which they stress are not prerequisites for the theory, are; the mean return vector and variance-covariance matrix must be intertemporally stationary; security returns must be characterized by an explicit underlying factor structure with one or more general factors impacting on all securities; the underlying factor structure is congruent (across time and across subsets of assets); and, the loading coefficients are also intertemporally stationary (1983:32-33). In tests using both Rao and Alpha factor analysis across samples of NYSE Toronto Stock Exchange securities, Kryzanowski and To concluded that the first factor *has perfect generalizability* and that the second of their stated assumptions is therefore met (1983:42).

In an extensive critique of the methodologies employed in early empirical tests of the Arbitrage Pricing Theory, Dhrymes, Friend and Gultekin (1984) suggested that they suffer from several basic limitations. Firstly, they contended that it is impermissible to carry out independent tests on whether a single risk-factor is priced using the two stage procedure of factor analysis followed by cross-sectional generalized least squares regressions. Only *unambiguous "F-tests" or asymptotic chi-square tests on the significance of the vector of risk premia* should be carried out (1984:345). Secondly, they suggested that the three-to-five factors of Roll and Ross (1980) are not robust and depend on the size of the group analyzed. In reply, Roll and Ross, disputed these conclusions and stated that not only can t-tests be appropriately employed but that, *if there actually are fewer than thirty "pervasive"* *factors generating returns, then factor analyzing groups of size thirty or more is* *equivalent in every way except statistical power and computational cost* (1984:349). They further suggested that the increasing number of common factors is expected but that these will tend to be non-priced industry specific factors and have no associated risk premium.

3.2 Number and pricing of APT factors

In spite of Shanken's position, a vast body of literature has developed over the last two decade involving empirical tests of the Arbitrage Pricing Theory. In the first major empirical research published in the literature, Roll and Ross (1980) developed a test procedure that they believed was designed to be definitive. Using maximum likelihood factor analysis and generalized least squares regression procedures on daily security returns data, Roll and Ross reached the conclusion that three factors, and possibly a fourth, are definitely priced for New York and American Stock Exchange securities. Although recognizing that their comparisons across groups of securities result in some positive dependence and lead to an overstatement of the significance of the relationship *between explanatory variables* *and expected returns*, they none-the-less maintained that their Hotelling T^2 test procedure showed no evidence that adjacent group intercept estimates differed (1980:1099-1100). In contrast to the approach of Roll and Ross, Brown and Weinstein used a bilinear paradigm introduced by Kruskal to test for the equivalence of the factor prices across groups of securities. Using the same data as Roll and Ross, they concluded in favour of the three factor model since, *while the* *adequacy of the given factor model (measured by the Chi-square statistics)* *increases with the number of factors, the proportion of securities for which the* *factors are the same across groups decreases with the number of factors* (1983:728).

   In order to resolve the factor comparability problem across groups, Cho (1984) used the technique of inter-battery factor analysis. Using daily data for approximately twelve hundred securities spanning the period used by Roll and Ross, Cho concluded, firstly that the number of factors ranges from two to nine and is dependent upon industry groups selected, and secondly that there is no tendency for the number of common factors to increase with sample size. When testing at a ten percent level rather than the fifty percent level employed by Roll and Ross, Cho found that *there are five or six inter-group common factors that* *generate daily returns for two groups and that these inter-group common factors do* *not depend on the size of groups* (1984:1499). Finally, Cho could not reject the hypothesis that risk-free rate and risk premia were common across groups and different from zero.

With respect to the two stage testing procedure generally followed in empirical research, Chen has suggested the number of factors assumed in the generalized least squares regression test impacts on the result. She suggested that too few results in the underestimation of the Type I error while too many adversely impact on the power of the test because of the high probability of a Type II error (1983:1400). Using larger groups of securities of up to one hundred and eighty, and by following a multi-step procedure designed to estimate *portfolio loading, so as to "balance estimation errors with other desirable properties"*, she did however reject the null hypothesis that the selected five factor loading coefficients were equal to zero (1983:1397).

In contrast to much of the prior debate, Pari and Chen (1984) have suggested that significant residual correlations violate the Arbitrage Pricing Theory development and that tests using the maximum likelihood estimation procedures implicitly recognize this. They also suggest that the use of daily data is inappropriate because of the resultant departure from multivariate normality. Using monthly returns data for equally weighted industry portfolios over the six year period 1975 to 1980, Pari and Chen reached the conclusion that a three factor return-generating process resulted in no statistically significant cross-sectional dependence among the residuals and that all three factors were priced over the period studied while the residual risk was not. This result, they suggest, supports the APT in preference to the CAPM.

In one of the early simulation studies of the robustness of the Arbitrage Pricing Theory, Cho, Elton and Gruber generated returns consistent with the zero beta CAPM as well as with actual historical returns. When running tests of comparison against Roll and Ross's results they found that seven factors were required to obtain results consistent with those of Roll and Ross. Finally, based on the simulated data Cho, Elton and Gruber concluded that the commonly employed two stage procedure had *a slight tendency to overstate the number of factors at work in the market* (1984:8).

Dhrymes, Friend, Gultekin and Gultekin (1985) were amongst the first researchers to examine the instability of the number of factors determined empirically. They found that the number of factors increases as both the number of observations and number of securities increase. Additionally, a joint χ^2 test of the risk premia pricing proved to be exceedingly variable across groups and *provides very little support for the key implication of the APT model.*[4]. Dhrymes et. al. do however acknowledge the influence of the number of factors specified from the factor loading estimation when running the generalized least squares procedure, and that the number of priced factors is much smaller than the number

---

[4]Dhrymes et. al. (1984) used a joint χ^2 test of the entire vector because of their criticism of independent t-statistics of the pricing condition.

determined in the first stage factor analysis. Subsequent work by Trzcinka (1986) supported the finding that the number of factors identified is a function of the size of group analyzed. He computed the eigenvalues for successively larger groups of securities and tested the (un)boundedness of the eigenvalues by running a series of regressions of eigenvalues against the number of securities in the group (1986:352). As results showed all eigenvalues grew larger with number of securities and the χ^2 statistic resulted in the rejection of the hypothesis that a constant k principal components could adequately capture the variation in asset returns (1986:367). Additionally, Trzcinka stated that *(o)ne should not conclude from this study that only one factor is important for security pricing. We have found evidence that there is one large factor and no obvious way to choose more than one* (1986:367).

Burmeister and McElroy (1988) carried out empirical research into Arbitrage Pricing Theory by testing of the *nesting* process[5] using three different regression procedures[6] and concluded that while the CAPM restrictions on the APT are rejected, the APT restrictions on the linear factor model are not. This result is contrary to the findings of Gultekin and Gultekin (1987) and Cho and Taylor (1987) but, as stated by Brown, *the research provides new measures and interpretations of the factors of the Arbitrage Pricing Theory* and has *developed new and innovative methods of jointly estimating factor sensitivities and risk premia* (1988:734).

Much of the inconsistency of the findings might be attributed to the low power of the statistical procedures and additional small sample problems with the techniques employed. Shanken (1987) investigated the impact of poor covariance estimates resulting from non-synchronous trading on the factor structure of returns by estimating the covariances and factor structure using both the standard covariance estimator and the Cohen, Hawawini, Maier, Schwartz and Whitcomb (1983a, 1983b) covariance adjustment with three lags. He found that the estimates were significantly downwardly biased when using the standard estimator and that the first five factors explained almost double the covariance when using the adjusted estimators. As an extension of this area of research, Brown employed an extensive simulation study to show that, in an exact k-factor economy, principal components and eigenvalue analysis of the covariance matrix will *lead an investigator to the false inference that the one important "factor" is the return on an equally weighted market index* (1989:1247).

---

[5] In a universe where returns are generated by a linear factor model, Burmeister and McElroy suggest that the CAPM is *nested* inside the APT which is in turn *nested* in the linear factor model.

[6] The multivariate regression procedures employed were iterated nonlinear weighted least squares regression, iterated nonlinear seemingly unrelated regression, and iterated nonlinear three stage least squares regression.

4. Methodology

The conflicting views of researchers undertaking empirical analysis into the Arbitrage Pricing Theory are reflected in their conclusions which range from the very favourable to such comment as that by Dhrymes, Friend, Gultekin and Gultekin who, when commenting on the initial findings of Roll and Ross (1980), suggested *(i)t is difficult to imagine a more complete rejection of the crucial implications of such APT models, using the flawed methodology of splitting the universe of assets into 30 security groups* (1985:674). This research seeks to add further insight to the debate through the use of an extensive simulation combined with several of the techniques used in prior empirical work. By simulating data with known returns characteristics clearer conclusions can be reached relating to the inherent empirical validity of the theory versus the power of the techniques currently employed.

The analysis is based on returns data for securities drawn from six different k-factor simulated economics. In order to directly assess the impact of the number of factors on the statistical techniques employed, two sets of single, three and five factor economics are simulated. The choice of a single factor economy is based on the continuing prominence of the single factor market model developed by Sharpe et. al., while the three and five factor economies are representative of the number of priced factors generally found in empirical research into the Arbitrage Pricing Theory.

For each of the economies, equation (3) was used to simulate weekly underlying and observed returns[7]. The choice of weekly data in preference to daily or monthly data is based on the work of numerous researchers including Roll and Ross (1980), Trzcinka (1986) and Perry (1982) who have found weekly data preferable because the problems of non-synchronous trading, non-normalities, unstable variance and autocorrelations induced by bid-ask spread have been shown to have a more profound impact when using daily data. Additionally, most empirical research in South Africa needs to be undertaken using weekly or monthly returns series because of the paucity of data[8]. Carrying out the simulation based on similar interval data therefore provides a point of reference for subsequent empirical research.

4.1 Simulation design

The first step in the simulation design involved generating one thousand three hundred daily returns for the k priced factors under the assumption that they are

---

[7] The term "underlying" is used to represent the return that would occur if prices adjusted continuously in the absence of microstructure effects and were measured as such.

[8] The Johannesburg Stock Exchange only maintains three years of daily data on their computer system as opposed to approximately twenty years of weekly data.

orthogonal, normally distributed, and contribute equally to the variance of returns for the economy as a whole[9]. Since it is possible to rotate any set of m correlated factors into an equivalent set of k orthogonal factors ($k \leq m$) the orthogonality assumption imposes no constraints on the generalizability of the results. The assumption of equal contribution to average variance is the same as the approach used by Brown and, as he has shown, is not inconsistent with the empirical evidence suggesting one dominant market index having the major impact on security returns (1989:1247).

For each of the simulated economies, the factors were simulated as equivalent normally distributed independent random variables having the parameters presented in table 1. The mean and variance of the factors were selected so that, once the idiosyncratic risk components had been added, the individual securities would have daily returns distributions similar to those of Johannesburg Stock Exchange listed securities.

Table 1. Parameters used for the six simulated economies

Simulated economy	Number of factors (k)	μ_k	σ_k^2	σ_ε^2	Average proportion of variance explained
1 and 4	1	0.0010000	0.0001080	0.0003760	22.3%
2 and 5	3	0.0003333	0.0000360	0.0003760	22.3%
3 and 6	5	0.0002000	0.0000216	0.0003760	22.3%

For each of the simulated economies μ_k is the mean and σ_k^2 the variance of each of the independent factors while σ_ε^2 is the variance of the simulated idiosyncratic component.

As a second step in the simulation design, the factor loadings (the $b_{i,j}$'s) and the idiosyncratic risk components were then simulated for each of the m securities. The $m \times k$ factor loadings were obtained as random drawings from a normal distribution with unit mean and a variance of 0.04, while the idiosyncratic risk components were simulated from both normal and non-normal distributions[10]. The generation of non-normal idiosyncratic risk components enables the implications of non-normalities in underlying returns to be directly investigated as opposed to merely relying on the non-normalities induced through thin trading. For all

---

[9]Trading is assumed to occur once per day at the close.

[10]The pairs of simulated economies presented in the table, namely 1/4, 2/5 and 3/6, differ only to the extent that the securities for first of each pair of economies were simulated to have normal idiosyncratic risk components while the securities for the second were simulated to have fourth moments of 7.5 (kurtosis of 4.5).

securities the idiosyncratic risk components were assumed to be identically distributed with zero mean and skewness, and with variance given in table 1. Daily underlying returns for each security were produced as;

$$r_{i,t} = \sum_{j=1}^{k} b_{i,j} f_{j,t} + \varepsilon_{i,t}$$

where; for each of the k factors $f_{j,t} \sim N(\mu_k; \sigma_k) \: \forall \: j, t$ and $\varepsilon_{i,t} \sim N(0; \sigma_\varepsilon)$ or $D(0; \sigma_\varepsilon; 0; 4.5)$.

Abstracting from the bias induced by the randomly distributed factor loadings, the orthogonal nature of the factors as well as their zero correlation with the idiosyncratic risk components implies that, on average, the daily security returns will be distributed with a mean of 0.001 and variance of 0.000484[11]. These numbers are consistent with prior empirical findings on the Johannesburg Stock Exchange (Page, 1993). In addition, the proportion of variance explained by the factor(s) will average 22.3%[12].

The final stage of the data simulation procedure, the daily underlying data were transformed into observed weekly data series. This stage allows for delays in the price adjustment process resulting from transaction price adjustments lagging behind quotation price adjustments (the Fisher effect) and for the additional frictions resulting from inventory positions and transaction costs (Cohen, Hawawini, Maier, Schwartz and Whitcomb, 1983:264). This step involved converting the simulated underlying daily returns into observed weekly returns for each security by first inducing autocorrelation into the returns series for up to three lags and then by allowing for delayed price adjustment due to infrequent trading. The parameters used to induce an autocorrelation structure were estimated from a sample of well-traded Johannesburg Stock Exchange listed securities and the observed returns computed as;

$$r_{i,t}^o = \gamma_{i,t,0} r_{i,t} + \gamma_{i,t,1} r_{i,t-1} + \gamma_{i,t,2} r_{i,t-2} + \gamma_{i,t,3} r_{i,t-3};$$

where; $r_{i,t}^o$ and $r_{i,t}$ are the observed and underlying returns for security i on day t; and $\gamma_{i,t,0}, \gamma_{i,t,1}$ and $\gamma_{i,t,2}$ are drawings from independently distributed normal distributions with $\gamma_{i,t,0} \sim N(0.8; 0.1^2)$, $\gamma_{i,t,1} \sim N(0.1; 0.1^2)$, $\gamma_{i,t,2} \sim N(0.1; 0.1^2)$, and $\gamma_{i,t,3} = 1 - \gamma_{i,t,0} - \gamma_{i,t,1} - \gamma_{i,t,2}$.

The final observed returns were then estimated by converting the above adjusted returns into daily price series and by assuming the m simulated securities were

---

[11] $m_s = k m_k = 0.001$ and $s_s^2 = k s_k^2 + s_e^2 = 0.000484$

[12] The simulations were also carried out using data for which the proportion of variance explained by the factor(s) averaged 50.2%. These results are available from the author on request.

equally likely to have daily trading probabilities of 10%, 50% or 90%. For any day when the security did not trade, the previous day's price was taken as the closing price (Dimson, 1979) and every fifth observed price used to compute the weekly observed returns series.

4.2 Test procedure

For each of the simulated economies, and for each iteration, portfolios of securities varying in size from twenty through to sixty were analyzed to investigate the number and pricing of the factors[13]. The analyses were carried out on both the underlying and observed weekly data. As an initial step principal components analysis of the variance-covariance matrix was carried out. This approach is conceptually simpler than factor analysis in that the resultant approximate factor structure based on the first k eigenvalues is unique and does not suffer from the rotational problems commonly associated with factor analysis (Brown, 1989:1248). In addition, while conventional factor analysis remains the dominant approach in tests of the APT its appropriateness has been called into question (Raveh, 1985). The approximate factor structure also allows for weak correlation between the residuals and does not make the implicit assumption that residual returns unexplained by the priced factors be uncorrelated across securities. Relaxing this assumption explicitly allows for the existence of non-priced factors which have been mentioned by numerous researchers including Roll and Ross (1980:1075). It is the existence of such common factors that has led to conclusions being reached which suggest that, while increasing the number of securities analyzed may result in more factors being found, the number of priced factors should not increase[14]. Lee and Comrey do point out however that component analysis does not make the assumption that each variable (security) consists of a common and unique part and that the factor dimensions using component analysis mix common, specific and random error variance together (1979:302). Finally, through an analysis of twenty years of data, Shukla and Trzcinka (1990) concluded that the one-vector principal components approach resulted in an empirical pricing error smaller than or equal to the five factor maximum likelihood approach. They do however suggest that the *superiority of any technique must be decided on a case-by-case basis* even though principal components and eigenvectors should not be *ruled out a priori* (1990:1563).

---

[13]The approach adopted in this paper is based on the procedure adopted originally by Roll and Ross (1980). It has subsequently been employed by the majority of researchers into the APT and can be contrasted with the multivariate linear regression test developed by Jobson (1982).

[14]Brown and Weinstein make explicit mention of the impact of non-priced factors on mean zero stochastic error terms even though they assume the matrix is diagonal in their testing of the APT using the bilinear paradigm (1983:717).

The significance of the principal component eigenvalues were tested using an approximate χ^2 likelihood statistic developed by Bartlett (1950:77-82). For a variance-covariance matrix of order m, the statistic for testing the equivalence of the remaining eigenvalues after the first k have been removed is given by:

$$\chi^2 = -\left\{n - \frac{1}{6}(2m + 11) - \frac{2}{3}k\right\} \ln\left(V_{m-k}\right)$$

where; n is the length of the series of data used in the estimation of the matrix; V is the estimated variance-covariance matrix; $\frac{1}{2}(m - k - 1)(m - k + 2)$ is the number of degrees of freedom; and, V_{m-k} is given by;

$$V_{m-k} = |V| \bigg/ \left\{\lambda_1 \lambda_2 \ldots \lambda_k \left[\frac{m - \lambda_1 - \lambda_2 \ldots - \lambda_k}{m - k}\right]^{m-k}\right\}$$

Given the dominance of factor analytic procedure in the literature, comparative principal factor analyses were also carried out for selected portfolio sizes and for a subset of the simulated economies. As opposed to principal components analysis, principal factor analysis uses an adjusted covariance matrix, with the main diagonal replaced with communality estimates, as input. While several approaches can be adopted for estimating the communality, the squared multiple covariance (SMC) has the advantage of providing a lower bound estimate of the communality and, (l)argely because of this property, Guttman (1956) recommends the SMC as the "best possible" estimate (Harman, 1976:87)[15]. For each security the squared multiple covariance is computed as[16];

$$SMC_i = \sigma_i^2 - \frac{1}{v^{ii}}$$

where, v^{ii} is the diagonal element of V^{-1} corresponding to the ith security.

In addition to replacing the diagonals with communality estimates the decision must be made as to whether one should iterate to an optimal solution through continuous re-estimation and substitution of the communality estimates. Analyses were carried out using both procedures to assess the implications of using poorer communality estimates. Statistical testing for the number of factors when using a principal factor procedure relies on a χ^2 procedure developed by Ripp (1953) which is independent of the type of factor solution (Harman, 1976:184). The

---

[15]Thurston (1947) has suggested that the final factor loadings depend directly on the sizes of the diagonals (communalities) that are placed in the correlation (covariance) matrix.

[16]It must be noted that the SMC's in this research are computed from the variance-covariance matrix and are analogous to, but not equal to, the squared multiple correlations given in Harman (1976:87). The approach used here reflects the fact that the analyses are undertaken using the variance-covariance matrix directly rather than the correlation matrix.

specific statistic to test for the significance of k factors is given by;

$$U_k = \left(n - \tfrac{1}{6}(2m + 11 - 4k)\right)\left\{\ln\left|\mathbf{BB'} - \mathbf{U}^2\right| - \ln|\mathbf{V}| + tr\left[\mathbf{V}\left(\mathbf{BB'} - \mathbf{U}^2\right)^{-1}\right] - m\right\}$$

where; **B** is the $m \times k$ loading array; $\mathbf{U}^2$ is the corresponding diagonal array of security communalities; and, U_k is asymptotically distributed as χ^2 with $\tfrac{1}{2}\left[(m-k)^2 + m - k\right]$ degrees of freedom[17].

Finally, it must be noted that the above formulae relate to statistical significance and;

> it does not follow that all the factors which reach statistical significance in a large sample necessarily remove a very large fraction of variance; and hence some of them may be comparatively unimportant in practice. Again, even if they are numerically important, this has no necessary implications of psychological or other reality of the factors (Bartlett, 1950:82).

Just as not all statistically significant common factors remove a large fraction of the (co)variance, not all can be presumed to be priced. Roll and Ross (1980) therefore proposed a method of cross-sectional generalized least squares regressions to identify the number of priced factors. The power of cross-sectional regression procedures to identify pricing is assessed in the simulation by using the methodology outlined by Roll and Ross (1980:1090-1091) and Cho, Elton and Gruber (1984:6-7), together with the reverse Helmet rotation proposed by Brown (1989:1253). The importance of using generalized least squares procedures in preference to ordinary least squares is well documented (Brown, 1989:1252; Pindyck and Rubinfeld, 1981:164-168; Roll and Ross, 1980:1090). It is normally used in a time series context to correct for bias and inefficiency in ordinary least squares caused by autocorrelation and heteroscedasticity in the residuals. While the cross-sectional pricing regressions do not use time series data, heteroscedasticity is present in the general factor model because the common factors do not necessarily explain the requisite proportion of each security's variance to ensure equal residual (idiosyncratic) variance across all securities. The equivalent of autocorrelation also exists because of the possible existence of numerous non-priced factors.

The generalized least squares procedure used in this study differs from that employed by Roll and Ross (1980) and Cho, Elton and Gruber (1984) in that it is appropriately adjusted to allow for loadings based on the variance-covariance

---

[17]The use of the variance-covariance matrix in preference to the correlation matrix changes the number of degrees of freedom. When using the correlation matrix an additional m degrees of freedom are lost and the resultant number of degrees of freedom becomes $\tfrac{1}{2}\left[(m-k)^2 - m - k\right]$ (Harman, 1976:205).

matrix in the case of the principal components analysis rather than the correlation matrix used in the traditional principal factor procedure. While recognizing that some econometric problems do exist, Roll and Ross suggest that a *natural generalised least squares cross-sectional regression for each day t is*;

$$\hat{\lambda}_t = \left(\hat{B}'\hat{V}^{-1}B\right)^{-1}\hat{B}'\hat{V}^{-1}r_t = \Gamma\,r_t$$

where, $\hat{B}$ is the estimated factor loading matrix; $\hat{V} = \hat{B}\hat{B}' + D$ is the estimated covariance matrix; r_t the vector of returns at time period t; and $\hat{\lambda}_t$ is the vector of estimated premia for time period t.

Using the above, together with the fact that the principal component and principal factor procedures constrain the covariance matrix of $\hat{\lambda}_t$ to be diagonal, allows one to conduct mutually independent t-tests for the significance of the risk premia. The approach is based on the arithmetic mean sample returns with the premia estimates being given by;

$$\bar{\lambda} = \Gamma\,\bar{r},$$

and having a diagonal covariance matrix of[18],[19];

$$\tfrac{1}{T}\left(\hat{B}'\hat{V}\hat{B}\right)^{-1}$$

As the simulation procedure did not involve the addition of a zero-beta or risk-free coefficient, it is assumed equal to zero for the generalized least squares procedure and the difficulties associated with using an augmented matrix of loadings, namely $\left[1 : \hat{B}\right]$, is thereby avoided.

It has been suggested by Brown that the procedure outlined above is biased towards finding a single priced factor and several non-priced factors since;

> ....*suppose that a generalised least squares regression of mean returns against the underlying factor loading revealed that each of the original k factors were priced (with t-values equally significant and greater than two). Then it is possible to show that the first principal factor, the equally weighted market index, will appear to be a priced factor (t-value greater than $2\sqrt{k}$) and that the remaining factors implied by the principal factor solution will not be priced (t-value equal to zero) ......* (Brown, 1989:1252).

As a solution to the problem, he suggests that one consider a rotation which,

---

[18] As pointed out by Roll and Ross (1980), the estimation errors in $\hat{B}$ result in the significance tests for $\hat{\lambda}$ being only asymptotically correct.

[19] The factor loadings and uniquenesses are re-adjusted where appropriate so that the t-statistics are not under-estimated (Cho, Elton and Gruber, 1984:6).

although not affecting the Arbitrage Pricing Theory relationship, will *retrieve the k "equally important" factors*. The rotation proposed is the inverse of the Helmet matrix, and according to Brown it lends to more powerful tests of the asset pricing relationships to the extent that each of the factor prices is measured with equal statistical precision (1989:1253)[20,21]. The Helmet matrix is given as;

$$
\mathbf{T} = \begin{pmatrix}
\frac{1}{\sqrt{k}} & \frac{1}{\sqrt{2}} & \frac{1}{\sqrt{2\times3}} & \cdot & \cdot & \frac{1}{\sqrt{(k-1)k}} \\
\frac{1}{\sqrt{k}} & \frac{1}{\sqrt{2}} & \frac{1}{\sqrt{2\times3}} & \cdot & \cdot & \frac{1}{\sqrt{(k-1)k}} \\
\cdot & 0 & \frac{-2}{\sqrt{2\times3}} & \cdot & \cdot & \frac{1}{\sqrt{(k-1)k}} \\
\cdot & 0 & 0 & \cdot & \cdot & \cdot \\
\cdot & \cdot & \cdot & \cdot & \cdot & \cdot \\
\frac{1}{\sqrt{k}} & 0 & 0 & 0 & 0 & \frac{-(k-1)}{\sqrt{(k-1)k}}
\end{pmatrix}
$$

The rotation approach was utilized in a second generalized least squares analysis and compared to the pricing relationship found based on the unrotated loading matrix[22].

For each of the six economics examined one hundred and fifty iterations were carried out and summary statistics computed for the eigenvalues, χ^2 significances, and the cross-sectional generalized least squares rotated and unrotated pricing regressions.

5. Results and discussion

The results of the simulation are presented in two sections. In the first the results of the principal component analyses for each of the economies are discussed. In the second section the evidence of the generalized least squares pricing regression is presented.

Figures 1 to 3 plot the first five eigenvalues as a function of portfolio size for the one, three and five factor normally distributed security idiosyncratic risk component economies[23]. Each of the figures presents two graphs with differently scaled vertical axes so as to more clearly display the dispersion over the second through fifth eigenvalue curves.

---

[20]Of course the problems highlighted by Chen (1983:1400) still remain. If too few factors are extracted the Type I error is underestimated (even after rotation) while if too many are extracted the power of the test is weak and the chance of a Type II error large.

[21]This approach is different to the varimax rotation procedure often chosen as the default option in many factor analysis procedures. The problems of using varimax rotation over too many factors and causing excessive dispersion of variance is also not applicable here (Lee and Comrey, 1979:320).

[22]For k=2 the rotation procedure produces, as expected, a matrix $\mathbf{T}^{-1} = \mathbf{T}'$ that rotates the factor loading matrix through $\pi/4$ radians.

[23]The graphs for the non-normally distributed idiosyncratic risk condition were found to be almost identical and are therefore not presented.

Figure 1. Eigenvalues as a function of portfolio size: Single factor economy

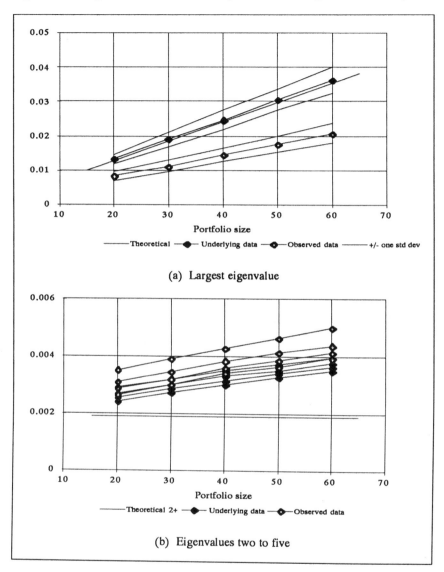

(a) Largest eigenvalue

(b) Eigenvalues two to five

Figure 2. Eigenvalues as a function of portfolio size: Three factor economy

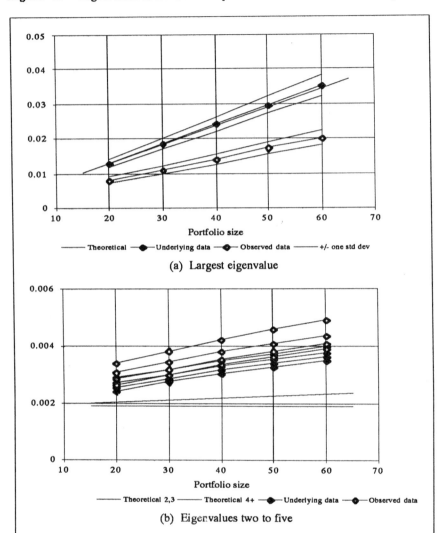

(a) Largest eigenvalue

(b) Eigenvalues two to five

Numerous aspects of the figures merit discussion, particularly given the high degree of similarity between the average eigenvalue curves. Theoretical eigenvalue curves are also presented in each figure using formulae derived by Brown (1989:1250) for a k-factor economy. The formulae are based on *large* portfolios analyzed using principal components analysis and give[24];

---

[24]*Large* in this context refers to the number of securities in the portfolio and not the number of observations used in the computation of the variance-covariance matrix.

$$\lambda_1 = \sigma_\varepsilon^2 \left[\frac{R^2}{(1-R^2)k} \left[(m-1)\sigma_b^2 + km \right] + 1 \right]$$

$$\lambda_{2,3,....,k} = \sigma_\varepsilon^2 \left[\frac{R^2}{(1-R^2)k} (m-1)\sigma_b^2 + 1 \right] \tag{4}$$

$$\lambda_{k+1,...,m} = \sigma_\varepsilon^2$$

where; m equals the number of securities being analyzed; σ_f^2 is the variance of the k independently and identically distributed factors; σ_b^2 is the variance of the k independently and identically distributed factor loadings; σ_ε^2 is the variance of the idiosyncratic risk component for each security; and, $R^2 = k\sigma_f^2 / (k\sigma_f^2 + \sigma_\varepsilon^2)$

The weekly simulation parameters of $\sigma_\varepsilon^2 = 0.00188$, $\sigma_b^2 = 0.04$ and $k\sigma_f^2 = 0.00054$ result in identical R^2 values and the difference between the eigenvalues across the one, three and five factor economies represented in the figures is therefore determined exclusively by k[25]. Table 2 gives the theoretical eigenvalues for the three simulated economies containing securities with normally distributed idiosyncratic risk components for portfolios ranging in size from twenty through to sixty.

Table 2. Theoretical eigenvalues against the number of securities in the portfolio analyzed for the three simulated economies

Economy	k	m	λ_1	$\lambda_{2,...,k}$	$\lambda_{k+1,...}$	$\partial\lambda_1/\partial m$	$\partial\lambda_{2,...,k}/\partial m$
Economies simulated to have (a) normal idiosyncratic risk & (b) average communality of 22.3%							
1	1	20	0.013090		0.001880	0.000562	
		40	0.024322		0.001880	0.000562	
		60	0.035554		0.001880	0.000562	
2	3	20	0.012817	0.002017	0.001880	0.000547	0.000007
		40	0.023761	0.002161	0.001880	0.000547	0.000007
		60	0.034705	0.002305	0.001880	0.000547	0.000007
3	5	20	0.012762	0.001962	0.001880	0.000544	0.000004
		40	0.023648	0.002048	0.001880	0.000544	0.000004
		60	0.034535	0.002135	0.001880	0.000544	0.000004
R^2=0.223140 for each of the economies, and $\partial\lambda_{k+1,...}/\partial m = 0.000$.							

From the table it can be seen that for the second simulated economy a principal components analysis of a portfolio of size forty should theoretically yield the

---

[25]Under the assumption of independence of successive returns, the weekly variances are equal to five times the daily parameters.

following results: A first eigenvalue of 0.023761, second and third eigenvalues of 0.002161, and all subsequent eigenvalues of 0.001880. In addition the first eigenvalue should increase (decrease) by 0.000547 as the portfolio size analyzed increases (decreases) by one, the second and third should increase (decrease) by 0.000007, while all subsequent eigenvalues should remain unchanged.

Figure 3. Eigenvalues as a function of portfolio size: Five factor economy

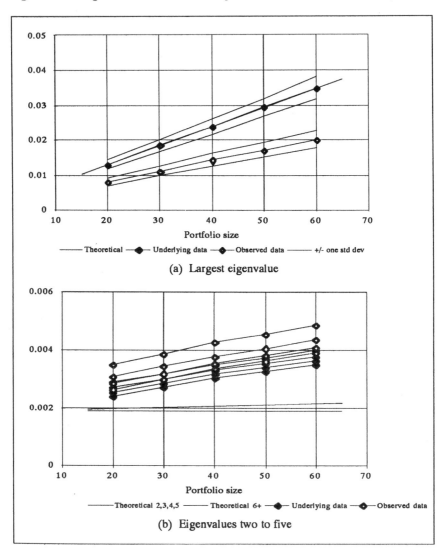

(a) Largest eigenvalue

(b) Eigenvalues two to five

For all economies and for the underlying return data, the average of the simulated first eigenvalues for the different portfolio sizes are consistent with the theory. The level of thin trading and the microstructure effects simulated into the data results in an almost fifty percent reduction in the first eigenvalue across all portfolio sizes. This decrease is consistent across all the simulation iterations as reflected in the fact that the standard deviation does not increase.

The curves of the second through fifth eigenvalue averages are almost identical for the one, three and five factor economies and also similar to those for the second through tenth presented by Brown for his four factor simulated economy (1989:1256). In all cases the plots for the second through to k^{th} eigenvalues highlight that the values are greater than theory would suggest and also that the rate of change in eigenvalue as a function of portfolio size is greater than given by the partial derivative of equation 4(b), namely;

$$\frac{\partial \lambda_{2,3,\ldots,k}}{\partial m} = \frac{\partial}{\partial m} \left(\sigma_e^2 \left[\frac{R^2}{\left(1 - R^2\right)k}(m - 1)\sigma_b^2 + 1 \right] \right)$$

$$= \sigma_e^2 \frac{R^2}{\left(1 - R^2\right)k} \sigma_b^2$$

In addition, the $k+1^{th}$ and higher eigenvalues exhibit patterns similar to the 2nd through to k^{th} eigenvalues and their slopes clearly deviate from the expected value of zero[26]. This result is supported by Trzcinka's analysis (1986:358).

Contrary to what was found to be the case with the first eigenvalue, the impact of thin trading and market microstructure on the subsequent eigenvalues is to increase them. The combination of these two effects is to significantly alter the eigenvalue plot and its use as a criteria for selecting the appropriate number of factors is of questionable value when principal components analysis is used in the presence of thin trading[27,28]. Given the similarity between the eigenvalue plots across the one, three and five factor economies, together with the simulated eigenvalue patterns for the second through to k^{th}, and $k+1^{th}$ and higher eigenvalue groups, the technique is also unlikely to provide a reliable cut-off even for well traded portfolios. This finding has profound implications for international empirical research into the APT, particularly given the relatively thin trading position of many international stock markets.

---

[26]The results of taking the partial derivatives with respect to portfolio size for all eigenvalues are presented in table 2.

[27]Cattel (1966) has suggested that the trend in a plot of all eigenvalues will exhibit a "scree" pattern and that the scree invariably begins at the kth eigenvalue when k is the true number of factors (Harman, 1976:163).

[28]Kryzanowski and To (1983:49) produce scree diagrams for samples of Canadian securities.

In common with the findings of Brown (1989:1258), the simulations conducted in this study suggest that the small sample properties of eigenvalues may lead to the conclusion of one dominant factor and a *multiplicity of smaller pervasive factors responsible for security returns*[29]. The χ^2 tests conducted using principal components analysis for portfolios of size twenty and sixty securities are reported in tables 3 and 4 for each of the economies[30]. The interpretation of the tables is best described by an example. Consider the 4.7 in the third row of table 3 under the column headed 0.5. This number implies that 4.7% of the one hundred and fifty simulations of portfolios of size twenty (for the first economy) resulted in p-values of between 0.5 and 0.6 that, after the extraction of the first three, the remaining eigenvalues were not significantly different. Additionally, 91.3% of the simulations had p-values greater than 0.5 that, after the extraction of the first three, the remaining eigenvalues were not significantly different[31].

The results presented in the top half of table 3 show a remarkable degree of similarity between the single, three and five factors simulated economies when the underlying returns data are used and the idiosyncratic risk components are normal. For all three economies represented there is no consistent evidence to suggest that the results are influenced by portfolio size. For all three economies approximately half of the simulated portfolio groups had at least an even chance that the eigenvalues after the first were equal, about eighty-five percent had at least an even chance that the eigenvalues after the third were equal, and about ninety-five percent had at least an even chance that the eigenvalues after the fifth were equal[32].

The impact of non-normalities in the idiosyncratic risk component is highlighted in the lower half of the table and shows some consistency with the views of Kryzanowski and To that the χ^2 *test statistic is quite sensitive to departures from normality* (1983:42). A lower percentage of the portfolios simulated have at least an even chance that the remaining eigenvalues are equal after the removal of the first k, for all values of k. The percentages that had at least an even chance that the eigenvalues after the first, third and fifth were equal averaged thirty-five, seventy-five and ninety-two respectively across the three economies.

---

[29]It must be noted however that Brown (1989) used an inappropriate number of degrees of freedom in computing the theoretical χ^2 distribution as he failed to distinguish between principal component analyses based on the full covariance matrix versus the correlation matrix.

[30]The format used in the tables and appendices is the same as that employed by Roll and Ross (1980) and as displayed in their table II.

[31]The 91.3% is obtained by adding the 49.3%, 15.3%, 12.7%, 9.3% and 4.7%.

[32]These values are computed by summing the contents of columns 0.5 to 0.9 for each row of the tables.

Table 3. Cross-sectional distribution of the χ^2 statistic when using principal components analysis : <u>Underlying returns data</u>

Economy	m	n	Probability that the remaining eigenvalues are not significantly different after the removal of the first "n"									
			0.9	0.8	0.7	0.6	0.5	0.4	0.3	0.2	0.1	0.0
Securities simulated to have normally distributed idiosyncratic risk components												
1	20	1	8.0	9.3	9.3	17.3	10.0	11.3	12.0	7.3	7.3	8.0
	60		8.0	8.0	11.3	6.7	8.0	12.7	8.7	11.3	14.7	10.7
	20	3	49.3	15.3	12.7	9.3	4.7	2.7	2.7	2.0	0.7	0.7
	60		36.0	16.7	11.3	9.3	8.7	9.3	4.7	2.0	2.0	0.0
	20	5	73.3	10.7	9.3	4.0	0.0	1.3	0.7	0.7	0.0	0.0
	60		66.0	16.0	9.3	5.3	2.7	0.7	0.0	0.0	0.0	0.0
2	20	1	10.7	8.7	14.0	9.3	6.0	6.7	7.3	12.7	14.0	10.7
	60		10.7	9.3	6.7	8.0	10.0	13.3	8.0	14.7	7.3	12.0
	20	3	43.3	12.7	10.0	8.7	10.0	4.7	2.7	4.7	2.0	1.3
	60		38.0	19.3	15.3	7.3	6.0	2.7	2.7	3.3	3.3	2.0
	20	5	62.7	15.3	10.7	2.0	2.0	2.7	2.7	1.3	0.7	0.0
	60		72.7	12.7	3.3	3.3	3.3	0.7	1.3	2.0	0.7	0.0
3	20	1	8.7	11.3	11.3	7.3	16.0	8.0	8.0	13.3	8.7	7.3
	60		8.0	8.0	8.7	8.7	8.0	12.7	9.3	10.7	12.0	14.0
	20	3	40.0	21.3	13.3	9.3	4.0	4.0	4.7	0.0	2.0	1.3
	60		33.3	20.0	12.7	12.0	4.0	6.7	1.3	6.0	4.0	0.0
	20	5	66.7	14.0	7.3	4.7	3.3	2.0	0.7	0.7	0.0	0.7
	60		68.0	14.7	6.7	2.7	3.3	3.3	1.3	0.0	0.0	0.0
Securities simulated to have non-normally distributed idiosyncratic risk components												
4	20	1	5.3	5.3	7.3	6.7	10.0	10.0	12.0	10.0	11.3	22.0
	60		4.0	4.7	5.3	6.7	10.7	10.7	7.3	14.0	14.7	22.0
	20	3	25.3	19.3	14.0	10.7	6.0	5.3	4.7	6.7	6.7	1.3
	60		24.7	17.3	12.7	6.0	14.0	6.0	6.7	3.3	5.3	4.0
	20	5	49.3	18.7	9.3	6.0	5.3	3.3	2.7	4.0	1.3	0.0
	60		56.7	14.0	10.7	6.7	2.7	3.3	2.7	1.3	1.3	0.7
5	20	1	2.7	8.7	6.7	5.3	8.7	11.3	10.7	12.0	14.7	19.3
	60		2.7	7.3	4.0	5.3	8.7	10.7	11.3	13.3	13.3	23.3
	20	3	28.0	18.0	10.7	8.7	11.3	6.7	7.3	2.0	4.7	2.7
	60		26.7	12.7	18.0	9.3	7.3	8.0	7.3	3.3	3.3	4.0
	20	5	49.3	19.3	8.0	9.3	5.3	2.0	4.0	1.3	0.7	0.7
	60		62.7	14.7	6.7	6.7	3.3	0.0	3.3	2.0	0.0	0.7
6	20	1	8.7	6.7	6.0	8.0	8.7	13.3	12.0	12.0	10.0	14.7
	60		4.7	4.0	6.7	6.0	10.7	9.3	13.3	13.3	8.0	24.0
	20	3	29.3	25.3	13.3	10.0	6.0	6.0	3.3	4.0	2.7	0.0
	60		27.3	12.7	17.3	10.0	5.3	7.3	5.3	8.7	4.0	2.0
	20	5	60.7	17.3	9.3	6.0	2.0	2.0	2.0	0.7	0.0	0.0
	60		56.7	16.7	8.7	7.3	4.7	3.3	1.3	0.0	1.3	0.0

The impact of market microstructure and thin trading on factor structure estimation, highlighted by the comparative eigenvalue curves shown the figures is clearly evident when tables 3 and 4 are compared. The existence of market microstructure, and thin trading in particular, results in more common factors being required before the remaining show statistical evidence of being equivalent. In the case of the single factor economy, when analyzing the size twenty portfolios, less than five percent of the simulated portfolio groups had at least an even chance that the eigenvalues after the first were equal, less than thirty percent had at least an even chance that the eigenvalues after the third were equal, and less than seventy percent had at least an even chance that the eigenvalues after the fifth were equal. A similar pattern of results is evident for the three and five factor (normal and non-normal idiosyncratic risk) economies. This trend is consistent with Shanken's finding that the first five factors account for double the covariation in daily returns when using an adjusted covariance matrix in preference to the standard estimator of Pearson. In contrast to the underlying returns results, there appears to be little difference between the results for normal and non-normal idiosyncratic risk economies when based on the observed returns data. This is consistent with the findings of Brown and Weinstein who, while noting that the bilinear testing procedure they adopted requires that the idiosyncratic risk components of returns be normal, also found their results were not materially affected by the non-normal probability distribution of daily returns (1983:721). The contrast with the results presented in table 4 occurs because the thin trading and other microstructure induced biases dominate the moderate levels of non-normality simulated into the underlying returns for economies four to six.

In addition to the substantial increase in the number of factors required when using principal components analysis and χ^2 test statistics in the presence of thin trading, the trend of an increasing number of factors being necessary as portfolio size increases is also apparent. For all three economies the percentage of portfolios that had at least an even chance that the eigenvalues after the k were equivalent declines markedly as portfolio size increases. When analyzing the size sixty portfolios for the single factor economy, less than one percent of the simulated portfolio groups had at least an even chance that the eigenvalues after the first were equal, less than ten percent had at least an even chance that the eigenvalues after the third were equal, and approximately thirty-five percent had at least an even chance that the eigenvalues after the fifth were equal. This result contrasts sharply with the evidence of table 3 but is consistent with much of the empirical evidence[33].

---

[33]See for example Dhrymes, Friend and Gultekin (1983,1984); Upton (1985); Trzcinka (1986).

Table 4. Cross-sectional distribution of the χ^2 statistic when using principal components analysis : <u>Observed returns data</u>

Economy	m	n	Probability that the remaining eigenvalues are not significantly different after the removal of the first "n"									
			0.9	0.8	0.7	0.6	0.5	0.4	0.3	0.2	0.1	0.0
Securities simulated to have normally distributed idiosyncratic risk components												
1	20	1	0.7	0.0	0.0	1.3	0.0	1.3	1.3	2.0	6.7	86.7
	60		0.0	0.0	0.0	0.0	0.7	0.0	0.0	1.3	2.0	96.0
	20	3	6.0	4.7	2.7	8.0	7.3	7.3	7.3	9.3	15.3	32.0
	60		0.7	0.7	2.0	1.3	2.7	6.0	3.3	6.0	14.0	63.3
	20	5	20.7	15.3	11.3	10.7	10.7	8.0	7.3	5.3	6.0	4.7
	60		5.3	10.0	5.3	8.0	6.7	9.3	6.0	12.0	17.3	20.0
2	20	1	0.0	1.3	0.7	0.7	0.7	1.3	4.7	4.7	6.7	79.3
	60		0.0	0.0	0.0	0.0	0.0	0.0	0.7	0.0	4.0	95.3
	20	3	7.3	6.0	3.3	4.7	8.7	5.3	10.7	14.7	10.7	28.7
	60		0.0	0.0	2.7	4.0	2.0	4.0	4.7	14.0	13.3	55.3
	20	5	22.0	13.3	18.7	7.3	8.0	12.7	6.0	4.7	4.7	2.7
	60		6.7	8.7	6.7	8.7	7.3	6.7	12.0	12.0	14.7	16.7
3	20	1	0.0	0.7	0.7	1.3	2.0	0.7	3.3	4.7	4.7	82.0
	60		0.0	0.0	0.0	0.0	0.7	0.0	0.0	1.3	7.3	90.7
	20	3	9.3	6.7	8.7	6.0	6.0	6.7	4.0	12.0	17.3	23.3
	60		1.3	2.0	4.7	5.3	1.3	6.0	6.7	11.3	11.3	50.0
	20	5	31.3	10.0	10.0	10.7	10.7	8.0	6.7	6.7	2.7	3.3
	60		13.3	6.7	8.7	13.3	6.0	6.7	7.3	10.7	12.7	14.7
Securities simulated to have non-normally distributed idiosyncratic risk components												
4	20	1	0.0	0.0	0.0	0.0	1.3	0.7	1.3	1.3	2.0	93.3
	60		0.0	0.0	0.0	0.0	0.7	0.0	0.7	0.0	0.7	98.0
	20	3	4.0	3.3	4.7	4.7	5.3	8.7	8.0	12.0	17.3	32.0
	60		0.7	0.7	0.7	0.0	1.3	2.7	4.7	5.3	10.0	74.0
	20	5	18.0	12.0	12.0	8.7	11.3	9.3	8.0	8.7	4.7	7.3
	60		3.3	4.7	4.7	5.3	6.7	8.0	9.3	10.7	12.7	34.7
5	20	1	0.0	0.7	1.3	0.7	1.3	0.7	3.3	4.0	8.0	80.0
	60		0.0	0.0	0.0	0.0	0.0	0.0	0.0	0.0	2.0	98.0
	20	3	5.3	6.0	6.7	6.0	5.3	9.3	11.3	9.3	8.0	32.7
	60		0.0	1.3	1.3	2.7	4.0	2.7	5.3	3.3	13.3	66.0
	20	5	25.3	10.7	11.3	8.7	4.7	10.7	5.3	6.0	7.3	10.0
	60		7.3	5.3	7.3	3.3	6.7	9.3	8.7	14.0	11.3	26.7
6	20	1	0.0	0.0	0.0	0.7	0.7	2.0	1.3	4.7	6.0	84.7
	60		0.0	0.0	0.0	0.0	0.0	0.7	0.0	0.7	3.3	95.3
	20	3	4.7	5.3	7.3	4.7	7.3	7.3	7.3	10.0	16.7	29.3
	60		0.7	1.3	2.0	2.7	0.7	2.7	6.7	7.3	13.3	62.7
	20	5	22.7	15.3	8.7	12.7	9.3	6.0	5.3	6.0	6.0	8.0
	60		6.0	6.0	6.7	8.0	5.3	10.7	6.0	15.3	11.3	24.7

The overall results of the principal components analysis highlight two issues. Firstly, the technique has low power. There is little to distinguish between the simulation results when the data were generated by a single factor economy from those when the data were generated by three or five factor economies. This result applies both when using the less formal scree diagram approach and when using the χ^2 likelihood ratio statistic suggested by Bartlett (1950). Secondly, the significant bias introduced into the variance-covariance matrix as a result of thin trading and market microstructure leads to empirical conclusions that there is a higher number of significant common factors and that the number increases as the size of the portfolio analyzed increases[34]. This finding is consistent with that of both Kryzanowski and To (1983), who found for United States data that as sample size increases from ten to fifty Rao and Alpha factor analyses produce minimum numbers of factors (at the one percent level of significance) ranging from two to eight, and Trzcinka (1986), who showed that for k greater than one there is no obvious way to choose the number of factors and that the number *found* tends to increase as the group size increases[35]. However, as suggested by Roll and Ross (1980) when they first conducted empirical research into the Arbitrage Pricing Theory, this aspect is not necessarily critical in tests of the theory. As long as more factors are suggested by the factor analytic technique employed than are truly pervasive, the cross-sectional pricing regression procedure should result in a stable number of priced factors as the size of the portfolio being analyzed increases.

Although the simulation analysis has highlighted some deficiencies in the principal components approach suggested by Brown (1989), it cannot be automatically inferred that these apply when the factor approaches used by other researchers are employed[36]. Tables 5 and 6 present the simulation results when principal factor analyses (with and without iteration to the optimal solution) are used in preference to components analyses.

---

[34]This bias was shown in Page (1993).

[35]Dhrymes, Friend and Gultekin tentatively suggest that the methodology employed in empirical research "discovers" factors equal to ten percent of the sample/group analyzed (1984:346). In reply, Roll and Ross (1983) contend however that the increased factors relate to non-priced industry specific factors. Upton (1985) suggests that the effects of group size and length of time period analyzed on the number of significant factors using factor analysis is influenced by the differing effect these two parameters have on the χ^2 statistic and its corresponding degrees of freedom. He suggests that for large time series the number of significant factors will most certainly be overstated while the positive relationship between number of factors and group size observed empirically is strengthened in that an opposite effect is suggested based on the partial derivatives of the χ^2 statistic and its degrees of freedom as group size increases.

[36]See for example Roll and Ross (1980); Reinganum (1981); Kryzanowski and To (1983); Cho, Elton and Gruber (1984); Cho (1984); Shanken (1987).

Table 5. Cross-sectional distribution of the χ^2 statistic when using principal factor analysis : <u>Underlying returns data</u>

Economy	m	n	Probability that "n" factors are sufficient to explain the communality									
			0.9	0.8	0.7	0.6	0.5	0.4	0.3	0.2	0.1	0.0
SMCs as communality estimates and no iteration												
1	20	1	40.0	22.7	9.3	6.7	8.0	2.7	2.7	4.0	2.7	1.3
	60		34.7	14.7	13.3	10.7	8.0	5.3	5.3	4.0	2.7	1.3
	20	3	86.7	4.0	6.7	1.3	0.0	1.3	0.0	0.0	0.0	0.0
	60		74.7	12.0	8.0	4.0	0.0	1.3	0.0	0.0	0.0	0.0
	20	5	93.3	5.3	0.0	1.3	0.0	0.0	0.0	0.0	0.0	0.0
	60		94.7	5.3	0.0	0.0	0.0	0.0	0.0	0.0	0.0	0.0
2	20	1	37.3	25.3	9.3	6.7	6.7	4.0	2.7	1.3	5.3	1.3
	60		34.7	14.7	13.3	9.3	10.7	2.7	4.0	5.3	1.3	4.0
	20	3	81.3	8.0	4.0	2.7	1.3	2.7	0.0	0.0	0.0	0.0
	60		76.0	9.3	6.7	2.7	1.3	1.3	1.3	1.3	0.0	0.0
	20	5	92.0	2.7	2.7	2.7	0.0	0.0	0.0	0.0	0.0	0.0
	60		92.0	4.0	1.3	2.7	0.0	0.0	0.0	0.0	0.0	0.0
3	20	1	37.3	20.0	10.7	8.0	9.3	8.0	2.7	1.3	1.3	1.3
	60		26.7	18.7	9.3	6.7	6.7	12.0	2.7	6.7	8.0	2.7
	20	3	84.0	9.3	4.0	0.0	0.0	1.3	0.0	0.0	0.0	1.3
	60		66.7	13.3	4.0	6.7	5.3	2.7	1.3	0.0	0.0	0.0
	20	5	92.0	6.7	0.0	0.0	0.0	0.0	0.0	1.3	0.0	0.0
	60		86.7	10.7	1.3	1.3	0.0	0.0	0.0	0.0	0.0	0.0
SMCs as initial communality estimates with iteration to final solution												
1	20	1	44.0	17.3	6.7	8.0	13.3	2.7	5.3	1.3	0.0	1.3
	60		34.7	14.7	14.7	5.3	9.3	8.0	2.7	6.7	1.3	2.7
	20	3	84.0	8.0	4.0	1.3	2.7	0.0	0.0	0.0	0.0	0.0
	60		78.7	6.7	6.7	4.0	2.7	0.0	1.3	0.0	0.0	0.0
	20	5	94.7	5.3	0.0	0.0	0.0	0.0	0.0	0.0	0.0	0.0
	60		96.0	2.7	1.3	0.0	0.0	0.0	0.0	0.0	0.0	0.0
2	20	1	29.3	25.3	8.0	12.0	8.0	5.3	2.7	4.0	2.7	2.7
	60		18.7	20.0	5.3	13.3	10.7	8.0	4.0	12.0	5.3	2.7
	20	3	81.3	9.3	2.7	2.7	1.3	2.7	0.0	0.0	0.0	0.0
	60		65.3	10.7	12.0	1.3	6.7	1.3	1.3	1.3	0.0	0.0
	20	5	93.3	5.3	0.0	1.3	0.0	0.0	0.0	0.0	0.0	0.0
	60		86.7	8.0	2.7	1.3	1.3	0.0	0.0	0.0	0.0	0.0
3	20	1	37.3	20.0	10.7	8.0	9.3	8.0	2.7	1.3	1.3	1.3
	60		26.7	18.7	10.7	6.7	6.7	12.0	1.3	6.7	8.0	2.7
	20	3	86.7	6.7	4.0	0.0	1.3	0.0	0.0	0.0	0.0	1.3
	60		66.7	14.7	4.0	5.3	6.7	1.3	1.3	0.0	0.0	0.0
	20	5	96.0	2.7	0.0	0.0	0.0	0.0	1.3	0.0	0.0	0.0
	60		86.7	12.0	0.0	1.3	0.0	0.0	0.0	0.0	0.0	0.0

Table 6. Cross-sectional distribution of the χ^2 statistic when using principal factor analysis : <u>Observed returns data</u>

Economy	m	n	Probability that "n" factors are sufficient to explain the communality									
			0.9	0.8	0.7	0.6	0.5	0.4	0.3	0.2	0.1	0.0
SMCs as communality estimates and no iteration												
1	20	1	30.7	17.3	8.0	6.7	8.0	9.3	5.3	6.7	6.7	1.3
	60		10.7	12.0	9.3	8.0	9.3	14.7	9.3	9.3	8.0	9.3
	20	3	77.3	6.7	6.7	4.0	2.7	1.3	1.3	0.0	0.0	0.0
	60		53.3	17.3	9.3	8.0	6.7	1.3	2.7	0.0	1.3	0.0
	20	5	89.3	4.0	2.7	1.3	2.7	0.0	0.0	0.0	0.0	0.0
	60		85.3	9.3	2.7	1.3	0.0	1.3	0.0	0.0	0.0	0.0
2	20	1	32.0	12.0	10.7	13.3	5.3	5.3	6.7	8.0	4.0	2.7
	60		14.7	20.0	4.0	12.0	6.7	10.7	10.7	4.0	8.0	9.3
	20	3	73.3	12.0	4.0	5.3	2.7	1.3	1.3	0.0	0.0	0.0
	60		56.0	24.0	8.0	1.3	4.0	2.7	2.7	0.0	0.0	1.3
	20	5	88.0	8.0	4.0	0.0	0.0	0.0	0.0	0.0	0.0	0.0
	60		89.3	4.0	4.0	0.0	0.0	2.7	0.0	0.0	0.0	0.0
3	20	1	17.3	20.0	16.0	8.0	13.3	2.7	9.3	2.7	6.7	4.0
	60		10.7	13.3	12.0	8.0	8.0	12.0	6.7	10.7	10.7	8.0
	20	3	77.3	13.3	2.7	4.0	2.7	0.0	0.0	0.0	0.0	0.0
	60		54.7	17.3	9.3	10.7	1.3	1.3	2.7	2.7	0.0	0.0
	20	5	92.0	4.0	1.3	2.7	0.0	0.0	0.0	0.0	0.0	0.0
	60		89.3	5.3	1.3	1.3	2.7	0.0	0.0	0.0	0.0	0.0
SMCs as initial communality estimates with iteration to final solution												
1	20	1	18.7	12.0	17.3	14.7	8.0	6.7	6.7	4.0	6.7	5.3
	60		9.3	12.0	9.3	10.7	5.3	6.7	8.0	10.7	8.0	20.0
	20	3	72.0	12.0	10.7	4.0	0.0	0.0	0.0	0.0	1.3	0.0
	60		46.7	16.0	9.3	6.7	4.0	4.0	5.3	2.7	2.7	2.7
	20	5	89.3	9.3	0.0	0.0	1.3	0.0	0.0	0.0	0.0	0.0
	60		74.7	8.0	8.0	4.0	2.7	0.0	1.3	1.3	0.0	0.0
2	20	1	30.7	17.3	9.3	8.0	6.7	6.7	6.7	4.0	2.7	8.0
	60		6.7	8.0	9.3	16.0	8.0	10.7	10.7	9.3	8.0	13.3
	20	3	70.7	14.7	5.3	2.7	2.7	1.3	2.7	0.0	0.0	0.0
	60		48.0	20.0	10.7	6.7	4.0	1.3	6.7	0.0	2.7	0.0
	20	5	88.0	8.0	2.7	0.0	1.3	0.0	0.0	0.0	0.0	0.0
	60		84.0	4.0	6.7	2.7	1.3	1.3	0.0	0.0	0.0	0.0
3	20	1	17.3	20.0	16.0	8.0	13.3	4.0	8.0	2.7	6.7	4.0
	60		10.7	13.3	12.0	8.0	8.0	12.0	6.7	10.7	10.7	8.0
	20	3	80.0	12.0	2.7	4.0	1.3	0.0	0.0	0.0	0.0	0.0
	60		56.0	17.3	13.3	6.7	0.0	1.3	2.7	2.7	0.0	0.0
	20	5	96.0	1.3	2.7	0.0	0.0	0.0	0.0	0.0	0.0	0.0
	60		89.3	5.3	1.3	2.7	1.3	0.0	0.0	0.0	0.0	0.0

Given the extensive computer processing time involved, only the three economies containing securities having normal idiosyncratic risk were simulated. In addition, only seventy-five iterations were undertaken.

A comparison of tables 5 and 6 suggests that the use of squared multiple covariances (SMCs) as communality estimates is sufficiently robust in that there appears to be no marked and consistent change in the distribution of the χ^2 statistic when iterations are carried out to obtain improved communality estimates. The use of principal factor analysis over principal components analysis does however result in an increased likelihood that fewer factors are necessary. As the table highlights, there was a greater than even chance of concluding that one factor is sufficient in over eighty percent of the groups, across all three economies. Additionally, the technique provides a substantial improvement in the consistency of the results for the observed data relative to the underlying data. This finding suggests that factor analytic techniques may be preferable to the approach suggested by Brown (1989) in spite of his comments concerning the uniqueness of the solution when employing principal components and its consequent advantage over factor analysis.

The improved results found for the principal factor technique in the presence of this trading can be explained directly by the impact of thin trading on the variance-covariance matrix[37]. Thin trading has a significant effect on pairwise covariance estimation by both biasing it downwards and by reducing the efficiency of the estimate. A uniform level of thin trading across a portfolio of securities results in the off-diagonal elements being downwardly biased relative to the main diagonal (the variance estimates are less affected by thin trading). For principal factor analysis (as well as other factor analysis techniques) the main diagonal is replaced with estimates of the communalities. The squared multiple correlations are just a lower bound of the estimates (Harman, 1976:87). As alternative estimates include the highest off-diagonal *covariance*, the adjusted matrix when employing factor analysis merely becomes a less efficient estimate of the variance-covariance matrix (multiplied by a scalar) when there is a uniform level of thin trading. In contrast to this, the principal components approach, which does not involve replacement of the main diagonal with communality estimates, uses a variance-covariance matrix that has reduced efficiency and a higher level of bias.

In common with the preceding analysis, the results of the second stage testing of the Arbitrage Pricing Theory highlight the low power of the methodology. The generalized least squares regressions used to investigate the *effect of factors on equilibrium returns* (Cho, Elton and Gruber, 1984:6) do not produce clearly discernible differences for the one, three and five factor simulated economies. As stated in the methodology the zero beta coefficient λ_0 needs to be estimated and,

---

[37]Page (1993) has shown that the thin trading effect dominates the other market microstructure effects in its impact on covariance estimation.

for the current analysis, an external estimate of $\lambda_0 = 0$ was used in preference to augmenting the factor loading matrix. As the study utilizes simulated returns the *true* λ_0 is known[38]. Additionally, Roll and Ross have suggested that by not augmenting the loading matrix the estimates of the factor premia remain statistically independent and testing for the number of priced factors is thereby reduced to a simple t-test (1980:1091).

Table 7. Cross-sectional generalized least squares regressions of mean returns on component loadings: Percentages of groups with at least k factors significant at the five percent level: <u>Unrotated loading matrix</u>

Economy	m	k 1	2	3	4	5
\multicolumn{7}{c}{Underlying data : Average security communality of 22.3%}
1	20	87.3	2.7	0.0	0.0	0.0
	40	87.3	1.3	0.0	0.0	0.0
	60	88.7	0.0	0.0	0.0	0.0
2	20	84.7	5.3	0.0	0.0	0.0
	40	88.7	2.7	0.0	0.0	0.0
	60	89.3	2.0	0.0	0.0	0.0
3	20	88.0	1.3	0.0	0.0	0.0
	40	91.3	0.7	0.0	0.0	0.0
	60	90.7	0.0	0.0	0.0	0.0
\multicolumn{7}{c}{Observed data : Average security communality of 22.3%}
1	20	91.3	30.7	8.0	0.7	0.0
	40	94.7	42.0	3.3	0.7	0.0
	60	94.0	45.3	4.0	0.7	0.0
2	20	90.0	26.7	6.0	0.0	0.0
	40	94.0	27.3	2.0	0.7	0.0
	60	94.7	36.7	2.7	0.7	0.0
3	20	91.3	20.7	2.7	0.0	0.0
	40	94.0	32.7	4.7	0.0	0.0
	60	94.7	42.0	2.7	0.0	0.0

Table 7 presents the percentage of portfolios with at least a specified number of risk premia being significant when testing at the five percent level of significance. The results are presented for portfolios of size twenty, forty and sixty. Additionally, the table is based on generalized least square regressions used the first five unrotated component loadings[39]. The low power of the procedure is clearly evident from the table. Little difference is evident between the results for the one, three and five factor simulated data. For the underlying returns data only a

---

[38]This approach is consistent with that used by Cho, Elton and Gruber (1984).
[39]Only the results for the three economies consisting of securities having normally distributed idiosyncratic risk components are presented. The results for the non-normal condition exhibited an almost identical pattern.

single factor appears to be priced. When testing at the five percent level one would expect to find two or more factors significant five percent of the time if only one priced factor described the returns generating process. When the observed data is analyzed however, the results for all three simulated economies suggest two, or possible three, priced factors are necessary. As was found to be the case with the χ^2 test of the principal component analysis itself, the impact of thin trading leads to the conclusion that more priced factors are necessary than is suggested when analyzing the underlying data. Additionally, there is some evidence to suggest that the number of priced factors found using the generalized least squares procedure may be influenced by the size of the portfolio analyzed. The results for the underlying data exhibit a tendency for the percentage of groups having at least two factors significant to decrease as the size of the portfolio increases. A similar pattern occurs at the third factor in the case of the observed data.

Finally, it is clear from table 7 that the percentage of groups having at least k factors significant decreases as the average communality increases. This result is somewhat surprising and can possibly be explained by that fact that the generalized least squares regressions were constrained to have a λ_0 equal to zero.

Table 8. Cross-sectional generalized least squares regressions of mean returns on component loadings: Percentages of groups with at least k factors significant at the five percent level: Rotated loading matrix

Economy	m	1	2	k 3	4	5
Underlying data : Average security communality of 22.3%						
1	20	51.3	22.0	6.0	1.3	0.0
	40	56.7	15.3	5.3	2.7	0.7
	60	48.7	18.7	4.0	2.0	0.0
2	20	53.3	18.7	4.7	0.0	0.0
	40	52.0	16.0	1.3	0.0	0.0
	60	53.3	20.0	4.7	0.7	0.0
3	20	62.0	17.3	4.7	0.7	0.0
	40	60.0	22.0	4.7	1.3	0.0
	60	54.0	24.7	6.7	2.7	0.7
Observed data : Average security communality of 22.3%						
1	20	86.7	52.0	16.0	6.7	1.3
	40	85.3	56.0	22.0	6.7	0.0
	60	86.7	59.3	26.7	7.3	0.0
2	20	80.7	46.0	18.7	0.7	0.0
	40	80.0	55.3	22.7	2.0	0.0
	60	84.0	53.3	23.3	2.7	0.0
3	20	86.7	56.7	21.3	2.7	0.7
	40	88.0	57.3	25.3	3.3	0.0
	60	89.3	56.0	25.3	4.0	0.0

The reverse Helmert rotation suggested by Brown as a means of measuring the factor pricing with *equal statistical precision* (1989:1253) results in an increased number of factors being found to be significant. These results are presented in table 8. The lower power of the generalized least squares procedure remains however in that the results for the one, three and five factor economics remain remarkable similar. Using the rotation procedure results in an over-estimation of the number of priced factors for the single factor economies and an under-estimation for the five factor economies. This problem is also exacerbated in the presence of thin trading.

5. Conclusion

Dybvig and Ross have argued that tests of the Arbitrage Pricing Theory on subsets of data are *typically valid* and that, in cases for which the testability becomes biased, any bias is towards rejection. They consequently suggest *there is little danger of spurious acceptance of the APT* (Dybvig and Ross, 1985:1195).

The simulations conducted in this paper provide evidence that contradicts the statement of Dybvig and Ross. Under conditions of thin trading, the low power of the empirical procedures commonly employed is likely to lead to the conclusion that security returns are more consistent with the Arbitrage Pricing Theory than the Capital Asset Pricing Model. The finding results because of the significant biases induced in the variance-covariance matrix by thin trading and is consistent with the results provided by Kryzanowski and To who found, in a comparative analysis of NYSE and Toronto Stock Exchange securities, that the Canadian factor structures produced a first factor of lower relative importance and generalizability and a larger number of relevant factors (1983:50)[40].

Eigenvalue plots are shown to be remarkably similar for both one, three and five factor simulated economies with the presence of significant levels of thin trading resulting in the first eigenvalue being biased upwards. Additionally, for both the well traded and thinly traded conditions, the eigenvalues did not conform to what one would theoretically expect. The $k+1^{th}$ and higher eigenvalues appear to increase as the size of the portfolio analyzed increased rather than remaining constant. Principal components analysis is also shown to be a poor substitute for factor analysis when thin trading is present. The χ^2 test procedure is more biased towards a multiplicity of factors when based on the full variance-covariance matrix than when squared multiple covariances are used as communality estimates.

Although the above suggests that empirical evidence supporting the Arbitrage Pricing Theory may be spurious, rejection of the theory based on the evidence that the number of factors increases as the size of the portfolio being analyzed increases

---

[40]In their context generalizability referred to the factor being common across all securities.

is inappropriate. This study has shown that this *evidence* can result from biases in covariance estimation due to market microstructure and thin trading effects. When data are generated by a k-factor economy downward bias in covariance estimation results in more factors being found as sample size increases. This trend does not however occur when the underlying variance- covariance matrix is used in the analysis.

As with the χ^2 analysis, the generalized least squares regression procedure was shown to lack power. The results of the pricing regressions for the one, three and five factor economies show no discernible differences and in both cases the underlying data using the unrotated loading matrix lead to the conclusion of one priced factor with slight evidence that there may be two. This result is consistent with Brown's contention that regression based on the unrotated matrix will be biased towards finding a single priced factor. For the thin-traded observed data two priced factors were found. The reverse Helmet rotation results in more factors being priced but the pattern remains as for the unrotated generalized least squares regression analysis. The power of the procedure remains low in its ability to differentiate between the one, three and five factor economies. More priced factors are also found when the loading matrix is estimated using a thin trading induced biased variance-covariance matrix.

The impact of non-normalities in the idiosyncratic risk component of security returns was found to be negligible. While this aspect of the research was limited to the consideration of a moderate amount of kurtosis with no simulations conducted using skewed data, the finding is none-the-less relevant given the characteristics of the empirical distributions presented in chapter three. The evidence of the Johannesburg Stock Exchange is that while daily returns (logarithm price relatives) exhibit leptokurtic characteristics there is no evidence of consistent skewness.

The overall conclusion of the simulation study is therefore three-fold. Firstly, the diversity in the results of the vast body of empirical research into Arbitrate Pricing Theory as an alternative to the Capital Asset Pricing Model can to a large extent be explained by the low power of the procedures currently employed. Both the principal components/principal factor analysis and the subsequent generalized least squares regressions are unable to clearly distinguish between the one, three and five factor economies. A researcher's predilection to one or the other is therefore likely to influence the conclusions drawn. Secondly, thin trading, with its impact on covariance estimation, biases the results towards a multifactor conclusion being reached. It does not bias towards rejection of the APT as suggested by Dybvig and Ross. Finally, the existence of moderate non-normalities in the returns distribution does not significantly impact on the results. The simulation study therefore supports the findings of Brown who has stated:

> *... mechanical application of purely statistical approaches to determining the number of pervasive factors in equity returns may lead to false inferences. Unfortunately, it seems that economic analysis and intuition are essential ingredients to the process* (1989:1261).

The power problem highlighted by this research has also been alluded to by Brown and Weinstein and they have suggested the adoption of a Bayesian approach which allows *degrees of belief in respective models to be modified by the data* since with very many observations it is possible to *reject any hypothesis at one's favourite level of statistical significance* (1983:733-735).

Robust estimation of the variance-covariance matrix is a necessary step in any testing of the Arbitrage Pricing Theory. While bivariate approaches exists for covariance estimation in the presence of thin trading problems result when using the approach in a multivariate context. Covariance matrices estimated using a full dataset are, by construction, positive semi-definite and as such have eigenvalues greater than or equal to zero. Recognizing the rank/matrix inversion necessity of having a gramian or positive definite matrix, these matrices can nonetheless be factor analyzed. Pairwise estimation of covariance using Dimson (1979) and Cohen, Hawawini, Maier, Schwartz and Whitcomb (1980, 1983a, 1983b) procedures on the other hand, can result in an estimated variance-covariance matrix that is not positive semi-definite. As a consequence the eigenvalues can be negative and the factor loading matrix is undefined[41]. Additionally χ^2 test procedures cannot be used. While re-estimation of the covariance matrix based on the positive eigenvalue eigenvectors might be considered, this technique is inherently biased towards fewer factors[42]. It also does not recognize the relative efficiency of the pairwise covariance estimates - increasing the leads and lags for higher levels of thin trading reduces the estimation bias but produces less efficient estimates.

References

Bartlett, M.S, 1950, "Tests of significance in Factor Analysis", Journal of the Royal Statistical Society, 3, 77-85.

Brown, S.J, 1989, "The number of factors in security returns", *Journal of Finance*, 44, 1247-1262.

---

[41]This condition is equivalent to the Heywood case whereby the estimated residual variance for a security is found to be negative. The condition has been referred to by prior researchers who have tended to deal with the problem by exclusion (Shanken, 1987:225).

[42]The rank of the matrix becomes equal to the number of positive eigenvalues.

Brown, S.J., and M.I. Weinstein, 1983, "A New Approach to Testing Asset Pricing Models: The Bilinear Paradigm",*Journal of Finance*, 38, 711-743.

Chamberlain, G., and M. Rothschild, 1983, "Arbitrage, factor structure, and mean-variance analysis on large asset markets", *Econometrica*, 51, 1281-1304.

Chen, Nai-Fu, 1983, "Some Empirical Tests of the Theory of Arbitrage Pricing", *Journal of Finance*, 38, 1393-1414.

Cho, D.C., 1984, "On Testing the Arbitrage Pricing Theory: Inter-battery Factor Analysis", *Journal of Finance*, 39, 1485-1502.

Cho, D.C., E.J. Elton, and M.J. Gruber, 1984, "On the Robustness of the Roll and Ross Arbitrage Pricing Theory", *Journal of Financial and Quantitative Analysis*, 19, 1-10.

Cho, D.C., and W.M. Taylor, 1987, "The Seasonal Stability of the Factor Structure of Stock Returns", *Journal of Finance*, 42, 1195-1211.

Cohen, K.J., G.A. Hawawini, S.F. Maier, R.A. Schwartz and D.K. Whitcomb, 1980, "Implications of Microstructure Theory for Empirical Research on Stock Price Behaviour", *Journal of Finance*, 35, 249-257.

Cohen, K.J., G.A. Hawawini, S.F. Maier, R.A. Schwartz and D.K. Whitcomb, 1983a, "Estimating and Adjusting for the intervalling-effect bias in Beta", *Management Science*, 29, 135-148.

Cohen, K.J., G.A. Hawawini, S.F. Maier, R.A. Schwartz and D.K. Whitcomb, 1983b, "Friction in the trading process and the estimation of systematic risk", *Journal of Financial Economics*, 12, 263-278.

Dhrymes, P.J., I. Friend and N.B. Gultekin, 1984, "A Critical Reexamination of the Empirical Evidence on the Arbitrage Pricing Theory", *Journal of Finance*, 39, 323-346.

Dhrymes, P.J., I. Friend, N.B. Gultekin and M.N. Gultekin, 1985, "New Tests of the APT and Their Implications", *Journal of Finance*, 40, 659-674.

Dimson, E., 1979, "Risk measurement when shares are subject to infrequent trading", *Journal of Financial Economics*, 7, 197-226.

Dybvig, P.H., 1983, "An explicit bound on individual assets' deviations from APT pricing in a finite economy", *Journal of Financial Econ*, 12, 483-496.

Dybvig, P.H., and S.A. Ross, 1985, "Yes, the APT is testable", *Journal of Finance*, 40, 1173-1188.

Grinblatt, M., and S. Titman, 1985, "Factor pricing in a finite economy", *Journal of Financial Economics*, 12, 497-507.

Gultekin, M.N., and N.B. Gultekin, 1987, "Stock Return Anomalies and the Tests of the APT", *Journal of Finance*, 42, 1213-1224.

Harman, H.H., 1976, *Modern Factor Analysis*. 3rd ed. Chicago: University of Chicago Press.

Ingersoll Jr., J.E., 1984, "Some Results in the Theory of Arbitrage Pricing", *Journal of Finance*, 39, 1021-1039.

Kryzanowski, L., and M.C. To, 1983, "General Factor Models and the Structure of Security Returns", *Journal of Financial and Quantitative Analysis*, 18, 31-52.

Lee, H.B., and A.L. Comrey, 1979, "Distortions in a Commonly used Factor Analytic Procedure", *Multivariate Behavioral Research*, 14, 301-321.

Page, M.J., 1993, The Arbitrage Pricing Theory: An assessment of the robustness of empirical techniques employed under conditions of thin trading and in the presence of non-normalities, University of Cape Town, unpublished PhD thesis.

Pari, R.A., and S. Chen, 1984, "An Empirical Test of the Arbitrage Pricing Theory", *Journal of Financial Research*, 7, 121-130.

Perry, P.R., 1983, "More Evidence on the Nature of the Distribution of Security Returns", *Journal of Financial and Quantitative Analysis*, 18, 211-221.

Reinganum, M.R., 1981, "The Arbitrage Pricing Theory: Some Empirical Results", *Journal of Finance*, 36, 313-321.

Roll, R., and S.A. Ross, 1980, "An Empirical Investigation into the Arbitrage Pricing Theory", *Journal of Finance*, 35, 1073-1103.

Roll, R. and S.A. Ross, 1984, "A Critical Reexamination of the Empirical Evidence on the Arbitrage Pricing Theory: A Reply", *Journal of Finance*, 39, 347-350.

Ross, S.A., 1976, "The Arbitrage Theory of Capital Asset Pricing", *Journal of Economic Theory*, 13, 341-369.

Shanken, J., 1982, "The Arbitrage Pricing Theory: Is it Testable?", *Journal of Finance*, 37, 1129-1140.

Shanken ., 1985, "Multi-Beta CAPM or Equilibrium-APT?: A Reply", *Journal of Finance*, 40, 1189-1196.

Shanken, J., 1987, "Nonsynchronous Data and the Covariance-Factor Structure of Returns", *Journal of Finance*, 42, 221-231.

Shukla, R., and C. Trzcinka, 1990, "Sequential Tests of the Arbitrage Pricing Theory: A Comparison of Principal Components and Maximum Likelihood Factors", *Journal of Finance*, 45, 1541-1564.

Stambaugh, R.F., 1983, "Arbitrage Pricing with Information", *Journal of Financial Economics*, 12, 357-369.

Trzcinka, C., 1986, "On the Number of Factors in the Arbitrage Pricing Model", *Journal of Finance*, 41, 347-368.

Upton, D.E., 1985, "Sample Size, Chi-Square Bias, and the Number of Factors", Texas Tech University Working Paper.

Tests for Randomness in Multiple Financial Time Series[1]

József Varga

Janus Pannonius University, Faculty of Business & Economics,
Pécs, Rákóczi u. 80., Hungary

Abstract. There exist tests for randomness in multiple time series but the exact distributions of these test statistics are unknown. The asymptotic distributions do not provide adequate approximation to the exact ones in small samples. In this paper there are suggested modified test statistics asymptotically equivalent to their original counterparts. The adequacy of the approximations is examined by simulation experimens. The modified statistics are obtained using the asymptotic means and covariances. These moments involve nuisance parameters which are replaced by their sample counterparts giving consistent estimates of the parameters. It is suggested to use these statistics for testing the hypotheses based on randomness of multiple time series e.g. the weak form of financial market efficiency at small and new financial markets. Results of such a test are reported using the stock prices data of Budapest Exchange.

Keywords. Market efficiency, LM test, random walk.

1   Introduction

There are several economic hypotheses implying randomness of time series; such as market efficiency, (Fama 1970), the life-cycle-permanent income hypothesis (Hall 1978), rational expectations (Friedman 1979) among others. The implication is the joint randomness of multiple time series but the tests are usually performed on one time series at a time.

Recently in their paper Malliaris and Urrutia (1990) investigated a very recent methodology to estimate the magnitude of the random walk component of certain macroeconomic time series. They applied the Lo and MacKinlay (1988) and Cochrane (1988) variance-ratio test to the data sample used by Nelson and Plosser (1982) who studied the stationarity properties of macroeconomic variables. McQueen and Thorley (1991) used Markov chain model to test the random walk

---

[1] Partial financial support from MKM 751/1995 is acknowledged.

hypothesis of stock prices. Numerous studies explored the time-series properties of economic data using the Dickey and Fuller (1981) methodology.

The tests based on sample lag autocorrelation coefficients can be adapted in multiple case, considering also the cross-correlation of time series involved. It is important because the nature of the economic time series is such that several time series may have lag and lead relationships, and therefore the univariate tests are not able to cover these relationships. If the time series is a sample from a normal distribution, the tests can be derived from the likelihood ratio principle. The distributions of these tests are unknown but the asymptotic distributions can be obtained. Dufour and Roy (1985) observed that for relatively small sample, the null distribution of sample autocorrelations can be approximated by a normal distribution matching the first two moments. It can be shown that such approximations are adequate for the sample lag cross-correlations. These test statistics are standardized by their estimated exact means and variances. The exact moments are obtained using the assumption that the time series is Gaussian. The unknown population covariances of these moments are replaced by their sample counterparts. There is a joint test for randomness in the literature which can be modified. Dufour and Roy (1986) observed that the asymptotic distribution of a modified test in the univariate case approximated the exact distribution well. The approximation in the multiple case can be implemented knowing only the first two moments of the sample lag autocovariances, autocorrelations and cross-covariances, cross-correlations. Experimentation suggests that the approximation is adequate in small samples and could be suitable even when the samples are from nonnormal distributions. The small sample properties could make possible to use these test statistics to test the weak form of the random walk hypothesis at new financial markets, where only the data of a short period may be relevant.

2   Tests for randomness in multiple time series

The most simple joint test could be to investigate the sample lag autocorrelation coefficients and also the lag cross-correlations of two time series. As an example it is shown for the daily closing stock price series of The Boeing Company (BOEING) and Bethlehem Steel Corporation (BETHLEHEM) in the period of 02.01.1991–17.12.1991. Analysing the results shown in the *Table 1, 2 and 3*, the randomness of the two-dimensional vector time series can be accepted, because the autocorrelation structure of the unique series shows this feature and it is also supported by the cross-correlations. The largest cross-correlation between the returns x_{it} and x_{jt^*} will be contemporaneous if markets are efficient. Lead and lag relationships must be considered although any correlations are likely to be small. The cross-correlations between absolute returns should help to summarize the interdependence of price volatilities for different assets. Accurate models will probably be multivariate generalizations of the univariate models already known in the literature.

Table 1 Autocorrelation Function of the BOEING Stock Price Series
(Standard errors are white-noise estimates)

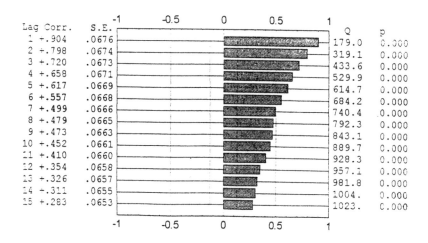

Lag	Corr.	S.E.	Q	p
1	+.904	.0676	179.0	0.000
2	+.798	.0674	319.1	0.000
3	+.720	.0673	433.6	0.000
4	+.658	.0671	529.9	0.000
5	+.617	.0669	614.7	0.000
6	+.557	.0668	684.2	0.000
7	+.499	.0666	740.4	0.000
8	+.479	.0665	792.3	0.000
9	+.473	.0663	843.1	0.000
10	+.452	.0661	889.7	0.000
11	+.410	.0660	928.3	0.000
12	+.354	.0658	957.1	0.000
13	+.326	.0657	981.8	0.000
14	-.311	.0655	1004.	0.000
15	+.283	.0653	1023.	0.000

Table 2 Partial Autocorrelation Function
(Standard errors assume AR order of $k-1$)

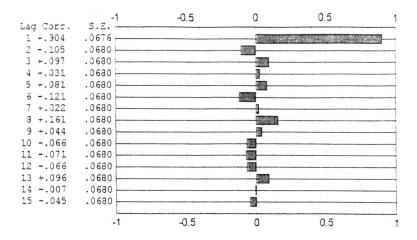

Lag	Corr.	S.E.
1	+.904	.0676
2	-.105	.0680
3	+.097	.0680
4	-.031	.0680
5	+.081	.0680
6	-.121	.0680
7	+.022	.0680
8	+.161	.0680
9	+.044	.0680
10	-.066	.0680
11	-.071	.0680
12	-.066	.0680
13	+.096	.0680
14	-.007	.0680
15	-.045	.0680

Table 3. Cross-correlation Coefficients (BOEING with BETHLEHEM)

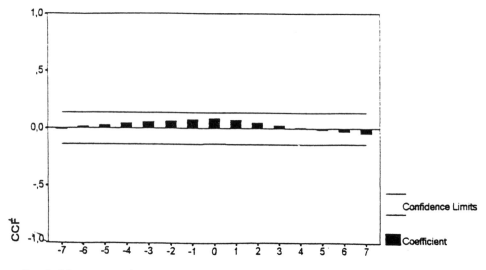

Let $\{x_t\}$ be an m-variate stationary stochastic process with

$$E(x_t) = \mu$$

and

$$cov(x_t, x_{t+k}) = E((x_t - \mu)(x_{t+k} - \mu)') = \Gamma_k = (\gamma_k(ij)),$$

$$\rho_k = \rho_k(ij) = \gamma_k(ij) / \{\gamma_o(ii)\gamma_o(jj)\}^{1/2}, \quad k=0,1,2,\ldots$$

Let $\{x_t\}$ $t=1,2,\ldots,n$ be a sampled time series of size n and let us define for $k=0,1,\ldots,n-1$

$$C_k = \frac{1}{n}\sum_{t=1}^{n-k}(x_t - \bar{x})(x_{t+k} - \bar{x})' = (c_k(ij)), \qquad \bar{x} = \frac{1}{n}\sum_{t=1}^{n}x_t,$$

$$R_k = (r_k(ij)) \quad \text{and} \quad r_k(ij) = c_k(ij) / \{c_0(ii)c_0(jj)\}^{1/2}, \qquad k=0,1,2,\ldots$$

Let $x_t = (x_{t1}\ldots x_{tm})'$ $t=1,2,\ldots,n$ be the sampled time series, $\bar{x} = (\bar{x}_1\ldots\bar{x}_m)'$,

$\bar{x}_i = \frac{1}{n}\sum_{t=1}^{n}x_{it}$ $(i=1,2,\ldots,m)$ and $e_{it} = x_{it} - \bar{x}_i$ $(i=1,2,\ldots,m; t=1,2,\ldots,n)$.

Then

$$c_k(ij) = \frac{1}{n}\sum_{t=1}^{n} e_{it} e_{jt+k} \ .$$

Tests for lag k (k=1,2,...) autocorrelation and cross-correlation, $\rho_k(ij)$, can be based on the statistic $r_k(ij)$. The nullhypothesis in these tests is that $\{x_t\}$ t=1,2,...,n is a random sample and the alternative hypothesis is that $\rho_k(ij) \neq 0$. Such a test can be derived from the likelihood ratio principle. A suggested portmanteau statistic to test this statistic is $Q_k = \Sigma_{ij} r_k^2(ij)$. Cleroux and Roy (1987) suggested an analogous test based on

$$QC_k = \sum_{ij} c_k^2(ij) / \sum_{ij} c_o^2(ij) \ .$$

An asymptotically equivalent Lagrange multiplier test can be based on the ststistic

$$QS_k = n(\text{vec}\, R_k)' \left(R_o^{-1} \otimes R_o^{-1}\right)(\text{vec}\, R_k),$$

where $\otimes$ denotes the standard direct product of matrices and vec A is the vector obtained by stacking the columns of the matrix A. This statistic can be derived from the proposals of Hosking (1980) and Li and McLeod (1981) and alternatively can be written as

$$QS_k = n(\text{vec}\, C_k)' \left(C_o^{-1} \otimes C_o^{-1}\right)(\text{vec}\, C_k).$$

Under the null hypothesis of randomness, $r_k(ij)$ are asymptotically normal and both Q_k and QS_k are distributed as the chi-squared variable with m^2 degrees of freedom. In small samples however the distribution of these statistics are unknown. Except for some partial successes, there has been no practical solution to the distribution of the sample lag autocorrelation $r_k(ij)$. Only recently, Ali (1984) and Dufour and Roy (1985) observed that for relatively small samples, the null distribution of $r_k(ij)$ can be well approximated by a normal distribution matching the first two exact moments. It is suggested to approximate the null distribution of $r_k(ij)$, $i \neq j$ by a normal distribution matching the first two moments and alternatively the statistic $r_k(ij)$ can be modified to

$$\bar{r}_k(ij) = \left(r_k(ij) - E(r_k(ij))\right) / \left\{\text{var}(r_k(ij))\right\}^{1/2}$$

and the distribution of of this modified statistic is approximated by normal distribution. The nuisance parameters $\rho_0(ij)$ of $E(r_k(ij))$ and $\text{var}(r_k(ij))$ are replaced by their consistent estimates $r_0(ij)$.

The statistic QS_k can alternatively written as

$$QS_k = (\text{vec}\, C_k - E_k)' A_k^{-1} (\text{vec}\, C_k - E_k),$$

where E_k is the asymptotic mean vector which is a zero vector under the null hypothesis of randomness, and $A_k = (C_o \otimes C_o)$ is the estimated asymptotic covariance matrix for vec C_k. Using the exact moments of $r_k(ij)$ and the experience with approximations of its distribution, it is suggested that the statistic QS_k be modified to

$$QA_k = \left(\text{vec}\,C_k - \tilde{E}(\text{vec}\,C_k)\right)' \tilde{B}_k^{-1}\left(\text{vec}\,C_k - \tilde{E}(\text{vec}\,C_k)\right),$$

where $\tilde{B}_k$ is the estimated exact covariance matrix for vec C_k, B_k and $\tilde{E}(\text{vec}\,C_k)$ is the estimated first moment of vec C_k, E(vec C_k). Both B_k and E(vec C_k) involve nuisance parameter $\rho_o(ij)$, which are replaced by their consistent estimates.

QA_k can be shown asymptotically equivalent to QS_k and can be seen as the mean and covariance corrected QS_k. The null distribution of QA_k can also be approximated by chi-squared distribution with m^2 degrees of freedom. One could also modify QS_k by correcting only the covariance matrix of vec C_k or by correcting only the mean of vec C_k. These modified statistics are respectively,

$$QAV_k = \left(\text{vec}\,C_k\right)' \tilde{B}_k^{-1}\left(\text{vec}\,C_k\right)$$

and

$$QAM_k = \left(\text{vec}\,C_k - \tilde{E}(\text{vec}\,C_k)\right)' \tilde{A}_k^{-1}\left(\text{vec}\,C_k - \tilde{E}(\text{vec}\,C_k)\right).$$

Following Hosking (1980), QS_k may be modified to $Qh_k = \{n/(n-k)\}QS_k$ and following Li and McLeod (1981) to $QM_k = QS_k + m^2/n$. The statistics Q_k, QC_k, and QS_k also can be modified following these lines of modifications. These modifications are not considered here. The null distribution of $r_k(ij)$ is approximated by standard normal distribution and the null distribution of each of the rest of the statistics referred to as Q statistics is approximated by a chi-squared distribution with m^2 degrees of freedom.

3   Simulating the exact distributions

Previous section contains a proposal to approximate the null distribution of the statistics $\bar{r}_k(ij)$, $i \neq j$ by the normal distribution and the Q statistics by the chi-squared distribution with m^2 degrees of freedom. The adequacy of these approximations is investigated here by simulating the exact distributions.

Assume that x_t $(t=1,2,\dots,n)$ are identically and independently distributed normal variables with

$$E(x_t)=\mu, \qquad \text{cov}(x_t)= \Sigma=(\sigma_{ij}),$$

where $\mu=(\mu_1,...,\mu_m)'$ is an $m\times 1$ vector of means and Σ is an $m\times m$ matrix of the covariances. The statistics $r_k(ij)$ and the Q statistics defined before are independent of scaling for x_t. It means that without loss of generality, we may assume, that $\sigma_{ii}=1$ ($i=1,2,...,m$); $var(x_t)=1$ so that the correlation between x_{it} and x_{jt} ($i\neq j$) is σ_{ij}.

For the simulation we need to select the sample size n, the number of components of the vector time series m, the lag k and the parameters μ and $\Sigma=(\sigma_{ij})$. Since the statistics $\bar{r}_k(ij)$ as well as the Q statistics are independent of the choice of the location parameter μ, it is set to 0.

We have to pay attention to the degree of contemporaneous collinearity among the components of the vector time series. If $\Sigma=I$, the components are uncorrelated; in the other extreme a perfect linear relationship exists among the components when Σ is singular.

Let $\Sigma=C\Lambda C'$, where C is an orthogonal matrix and $\Lambda=\mathrm{diag}(\lambda_1,...,\lambda_m)$ a diagonal matrix, $\lambda_i>0$ $i=1,2,...,m$ and $\lambda_1 \geq \lambda_2 \geq ... \geq \lambda_m$. The degree of collinearity may be controlled by choosing the ratio λ_1/λ_m. If $\lambda_1=...=\lambda_m$, then the components are uncorrelated and if the ratio λ_1/λ_m increases, the collinearity increases. Setting

$$\lambda_i = \frac{1-(i-1)(1-\beta)}{m-1}, \qquad m\geq 2, \quad 0<\beta\leq 1,$$

it is assumed that $\lambda_1=1$, $\lambda_m=\beta$ and λ_i for $1<i<m$ are equispaced between λ_1 and λ_m. If $\beta=1$, the components are uncorrelated and the degree of collinearity increases as β approaches 0.

The $(ij)th$ element of the orthogonal matrix C can be chosen arbitrarily to $\{2/(m+1)\}^{1/2}\sin(\pi ij/(m+1))$. For this choice, C is necessarily an orthogonal matrix. For a given parameter β, number of components m, sample size n, a random sample of $x_1,...,x_n$ is generated from the normal distribution with mean vector 0 and covariance matrix $\Sigma=C\Lambda C'$.

We use the result that for the $m\times 1$ vector Y which is normal with mean vector 0 and covariance matrix I, $X=C\Lambda^{1/2}Y$ is normal with mean vector 0 and covariance matrix Σ. From the sample $x_1,...,x_n$ the statistics $\bar{r}_k(ij)$ and the Q statistics are computed. This procedure is replicated 1 500 times. The sampling distributions of $\bar{r}_k(ij)$ and the Q statistics are estimated from these replications. They are compared with the corresponding approximate distributions reported in *Table 4*. (To save space the results are reported at only the nominal probability levels of .05, .10, .90, .95, .975 and sample size 50, $m=2$, $\beta=1$ and lag 1 and 3.

As can be observed from Table 4, the null distribution of $\bar{r}_k(ij)$ is well approximated by the standard normal distribution. As it was shown by the experiment, accuracy improves as sample size increases and deteriorates as the lag k increases.

The accuracy of the approximations to the distributions of the Q statistics is unaffected by the collinearity except the Q_k statistic. For the parameter value $\beta=1$, the approximation to the distribution of Q_k is adequate for a sample size of as little as 20, but it was wholly inadequate even for a sample size of 40 when $\beta=0.1$.

In the *Table 5*, the accuracy of the approximation improves with an increase in sample size and declines with increasing lag. With the exception of QA_k and QAV_k, none of the approximations is adequate for a sample size of 30 and a lag of 1. Of the statistics Q_k and two of its modifications, QH_k and QM_k, the approximation to the distribution of QH_k seems to be the most adequate. Thus QH_k is recommended, if one must choice among these three statistics. In the case of QA_k and QAV_k, the approximations are adequate at the right tails (these are right-tailed tests) and both of them are inadequate at the left tails of the distributions. They are also adequate for $n \geq 20$ at lag 1 and $n \geq 30$ at lag 3. There is a very little difference between these two statistics, the QA_k is recommended for practical applications, since QAV_k is an approximation to QA_k in that $E(c_k(ij))$ is approximated as 0 in QAV_k.

It follows therefore, that the most adequate approximations are the approximations to the distributions of $\bar{r}_k(ij)$ and QA_k by their asymptotic distributions.

Table 4. Null Distribution of $\bar{r}_k(ij)$: $m=2$ and $\beta=1$.

Lag k	Sample size n	Component i	j	Simulated distribution at nominal probability level of				
				.05	.10	.90	.95	.975
1	20	1	1	.042	.098	.882*	.942	.974
		1	2	.048	.098	.896	.947	.976
		2	1	.047	.097	.898	.956	.982
		2	2	.052	.105	.897	.946	.972
1	50	1	1	.054	.106	.897	.949	.978
		1	2	.044	.096	.903	.954	.974
		2	1	.049	.097	.905	.947	.972
		2	2	.045	.098	.896	.943	.968*
3	50	1	1	.051	.097	.905	.953	.971
		1	2	.045	.086	.897	.949	.974
		2	1	.052	.099	.901	.950	.978
		2	2	.048	.098	.904	.948	.977

* Deviates from the nominal probability by more than two times its standard error

In these statistics, consistent estimates of the exact means and covariances of sample cross-correlations and covariances were used. These moments were computed on the assumption that the time series x_t is Gaussian. To investigate the robustness of the accuracy of these approximations, four nonnormal distributions for x_t were considered. These distributions are:

(1) a U-shaped distribution with density function $f(x)=5.5\,x^{10}$ for $|x|<1$,
(2) the centered chi-squared distribution with one degree of freedom,
(3) the Cauchy distribution,
(4) the stable distribution with characteristic exponent 1.1 and skewness parameter 1.

(For a description of stable distributions see Fama (1963).)

Distributions (1) and (2) are included to determine the sensitivity to other departures from normality. Distributions (3) and (4) are included to determine the sensitivity of the accuracy to thick-tailed distributions. In general, the chosen distributions represent reasonably extreme departures from normality to present a worst-scenario assesment of the accuracy.

Table 5. Null Distribution of Q_k, QS_k, QA_k, QAM_k, QAV_k, QH_k and QM_k; $m=2$ and $\beta=1$.

Lag k	Sample size n	Statistic	Simulated distribution at nominal probability level of				
			.05	.10	.90	.95	.975
1	20	Q_k	.049	.100	.916*	.968	.987
		QS_k	.046	.093	.948*	.983*	.995*
		QA_k	.037	.079*	.899	.954	.984*
		QAM_k	.051	.103	.954*	.986*	.995*
		QAV_k	.031*	.068*	.888	.953	.984*
		QH_k	.043	.085	.924*	.976*	.994*
		QM_k	.018*	.055*	.936*	.980*	.996*
1	20	Q_k	.052	.100	.903	.950	.983*
		QS_k	.048	.100	.923*	.966*	.991*
		QA_k	.046	.091	.897	.950	.984*
		QAM_k	.053	.098	.924*	.973*	.982
		QAV_k	.046	.089	.894	.953	.980
		QH_k	.048	.098	.913*	.961*	.987*
		QM_k	.035*	.081*	.919*	.965*	.992*
1	20	Q_k	.039	.089	.898	.951	.977
		QS_k	.049	.105	.936	.973	.993
		QA_k	.035	.079	.889	.948	.975
		QAM_k	.051	.104	.943	.978	.992
		QAV_k	.032	.074	.884	.946	.977
		QH_k	.037	.081	.902	.953	.984
		QM_k	.031	.080	.935	.974	.991

* Deviates from the nominal probability by more than two times its standard error

The procedure used to generate a sample from these distributions is the following. Let x_t be the t th sample, which is an $m \times 1$ vector. $x_t = C\Lambda^{1/2}y_t$, where C and Λ are defined as before and the m components of y_t are generated as a random sample of size m from one of the chosen four distributions.

The simulated distributions of $\bar{r}_k(ij)$ and QA_k are reported in *Table 6*, when samples are from the four nonnormal distributions.

Table 6. Empirical Null Distribution of $\bar{r}_k(ij)$ and QA_k;
$k=1$, $n=40$, $m=2$ and $\beta=1$.

Statistic	Nominal probabilty level	Simulated distribution			
		1	2	3	4
$\bar{r}_k(1,1)$	.05	.042	.028*	.054	.039*
	.95	.926	.975*	.947	.948
	.975	.961*	.987*	.976	.975
$\bar{r}_k(1,1)$	.05	.047	.033*	.046	.038*
	.95	.965*	.949	.949	.946
	.975	.984*	.963*	.977	.971
$\bar{r}_k(1,1)$	.05	.048	.046	.054	.044
	.95	.956	.956	.948	.949
	.975	.978	.972	.974	.980
$\bar{r}_k(1,1)$	.05	.056	.027*	.052	.047
	.95	.958*	.944	.949	.950
	.975	.964*	.987*	.971	.972
QA_k	.05	.049	.258*	.037*	.038*
	.95	.948	.923*	.943	.957
	.975	.973	.940*	.978	.911*

* Deviates from the nominal probability by more than two times its standard error

The accuracy of the approximations is robust enough with respect to different assumption of the distribution for X_t, except the case of the centered chi-squared distribution with one degree of freedom. The actual probability of QA_k exceeds the corresponding nominal probability at the probability level of .05 and is below those probability at the levels of .95 and .975. In the case of $r_k(ij)$ the actual probability tends to be below the nominal probability at the left tail of the distribution and higher at the right tail.

4 Testing the weak form of market efficiency at a new and small financial market

The nature of the economic time series is such that several time series may have lag and lead relationships, but the tests used to investigate the randomness of economic time series can be performed for one time series at a time. Most of these univariate tests are based on sample lag autocorrelation and cross-correlations and such tests may not cover these relationships. A joint test is needed which can be the Lagrange multiplier (LM) test. The null distribution of the test statistic is unknown, its asymptotic distribution is known to be a chi-squared distribution. Modifications to the LM test are suggested, some of them were already suggested. These modifications can be approximated by their asymptotic distributions, which is a chi-squared distribution. It is found that the asymptotic distribution of these statistics provides adequate approximation to the null distribution for relatively small samples.

The joint randomness of multiple time series can be performed using the LM test to analyze several economic hypotheses. Such a hypothesis can be the weak form of financial market efficiency which can be tested using the proposed LM test at new financial markets.

The Dickey-Fuller test was used to investigate the random walk hypothesis (that is the weak form of market efficiency) for two stocks of the NYSE and for twelve of the BSE stocks. Results are shown in *Table 7*.

Table 7. Dickey-Fuller test values of two stocks at the New York Stock Exchange (NYSE) and the same test values of twelve stocks at the Budapest Stock Exchange (BSE) in the period of 03.01.1993 – 15.12.1993.

	Stocks	DF test values
NYSE	BETHLEHEM	0.491*
	BOEING	0.324*
BSE	BONBON	0.194*
	DH	0.586*
	FOTEX	0.408*
	HUNGAG	2.587*
	KONTRAX	1.549*
	KONZUM	0.088*
	GARAG	1.083*
	IBUSZ	2.314*
	SKALA	0.141*
	NOVOTR	0.523*
	PICK	1.689*
	STYL	1.316*

* The random walk hypothesis is true at the 10 per cent significance level.

To compare the proposed multivariate tests with this univariate one, the QA_k values were computed for the two US stocks and for all pairs of the twelve Hungarian stocks. For all pairs of stocks the statistic QA_k shows the random behavior of the time series. The results using the statistic QA_k are also in accordance with results of other statistics, such as the augmented Dickey-Fuller test and the restricted vector autoregressive test. These test results are not reported here.

References

Ali, M. M., 1984, 'Distributions of the Sample Autocorrelations When Observations are from a Stationary Autoregressive-Moving Average Process', *Journal of Business and Economic Statistic*, 2, 271-278.

Ali, M. M.,1987, 'Durbin-Watson and Generalized Durbin-Watson Tests for Autocorrelations and Randomness' *Journal of Business and Economic Statistic* 5, 195-203.

Cleroux, R. and R. Roy, 1987, 'On Vector Autocorrelation in Time Series' in *Proceedings of the Business and Economics Section,* American Statistical Association, 654-658.

Cochrane, J. H., 1988, 'How big is the random walk in GDP?', *Journal of Political Economy* 96, 833-920.

Dickey, D. A. and W. A. Fuller, 1981, 'Likelihood ratio statistics for auto-regressive time series with a root', *Econometrica* 49, 1057-1072.

Dickey, D. A. and R. J. Rossana, 1994, 'Cointegrated Time Series: A Guide to Estimation and Hypothesis Testing' *Oxford Bulletin of Economics and Statistics,* 1994, 3, 325-365.

Dufour, J. M., and R. Roy, 1985, 'Some Robust Exact Results in Sample Autocorrelations and Tests of Randomness' , *Journal of Economics* 29, 257-273.

Engle, R. F. and C. W. Granger, 1987, 'Co-integration and Error Correction: Representation, Estimation and Testing', *Econometrica* 1987, 2, 251-276.

Fama, E.F., 1963, 'Mandelbrot and the Stable Paretian Hypothesis', *Journal of Business* 36, 420-429.

Fama, E. F., 1970, 'Efficient Capital Markets: A Review of Theory and Empirical Work', *Journal of Finance* 25, 383-417.

Friedman, B. M., 1979, 'Optimal Expectations and the Extreme Information Assumptions of Rational Expectations' Macromodels', *Journal of Monetary Economics* 5, 23-41.

Hall, R. E., 1978, 'Stochastic Implications of the Life Cycle-Permanent Income Hypothesis: Theory and Evidence', *Journal of Political Economy* 86, 971-987.

Hosking, J. R. M., 1980, 'The Multivariate Portmanteau Statistic', *Journal of the American Statistical Association,* 75, 602-608.

Lo, A., and A. C. MacKinlay, 1988, 'Stock market prices do not follow random walks : Evidence from a simple specification test', *Review of Financial Studies* 1, 41-66.

Malliaris, A. G., and J. L. Urruta, 1990, 'How big is the random walks in macro-economic time series. Variance ratio tests', *Economics Letters* 34, 113-116.

McQueen, G., and S. Thorley, 1991, 'Are stock returns predictable ? A test using Markov chains', *The Journal of Finance,* Vol. XLVI. 1, 239-263.

Nelson, C., and C. Plosser, 1982, 'Trends and random walks in macroeconomic time series: Some evidence and implications', *Journal of Monetary Economics* 10, 139-162.

Stock, J. H., 1987, 'Asymptotic Properties of Least Squares Estimators of Cointegrating Vectors' *Econometrica,* 1987, 5, 1035-1056.

On SSB Utility Theory[1]

Margherita Cigola[2] and Paola Modesti[3]

[2] Istituto di Metodi Quantitativi, Bocconi University, Milano, Italy
[3] Faculty of Economics, University of Genova, Genova, Italy.

Abstract. The SSB functional is interpreted as the difference between two probabilities. This interpretation allows one to represent preference relationships with no use of a utility function and agrees with a recent interpretation of expected utility advanced by Castagnoli and Li Calzi.

Keywords. SSB utility theory, conditional probability, random benchmark.

1 Introduction

In 1982 Fishburn introduced a new theory for modelling decision making under uncertainty. His theory was based on a functional which assigns a real number to every pair of random alternatives in the choice set. Very few requests are made for this functional: skew-symmetry and bilinearity, hence he named Skew-Symmetric Bilinearity (for short SSB) his representation of the choice theory. This model is more general than the expected utility one, which is included as a special case; moreover the preference relation represented by an SSB functional is not necessarily transitive. The generality of Fishburn model makes it suitable for describing a very large class of preference relationships but it may be also a limiting factor for its immediate interpretation.

In a different context, Castagnoli and Li Calzi have provided a new interpretation for the expected utility. More precisely they showed that the expected utility of a random quantity X can always be read as the probability that X *does better* than another independent random quantity V used as a subjective benchmark.

In this paper we give an interpretation for the SSB utility of a pair of random quantities X, Y following an approach analogous to the one followed by Castagnoli and Li Calzi. The second section will describe the SSB model and the third one will summarize the above mentioned expected utility interpretation. In the fourth section some necessary technical details will be examined. The fifth section contains the announced interpretation of SSB utility and finally some conclusions and remarks will be drawn in the last sections.

[1] Partial financial support from C.N.R. and M.U.R.S.T. is aknowledged.

2   SSB utility theory

As is well known, the von Neumann – Morgenstern (VNM) expected utility theory cannot provide a model for some common preference structures like non-transitive preferences. Thus several generalizations were introduced. We are interested in the *Skew-Symmetric Bilinear (SSB)* utility proposed by Fishburn (1982) which, for instance, accomodates the systematic failure of the independence axiom and allows preference cycles (see also Fishburn (1984a), (1984b) and (1984c)).

Let the choice alternatives be represented by random variables (r.v.'s) taking values in a set $A \subseteq \mathbf{R}$; we denote with $X, Y \in \mathbf{X}$ any pair of r.v.'s and with F and G the respective probability distribution functions. If transitivity is dropped, it is impossible to represent preferences in the form:

$$X \succeq Y \Longleftrightarrow u(X) \geq u(Y)$$

where u is a *utility* function.

In the SSB model a functional $\varphi : \mathbf{X} \times \mathbf{X} \to \mathbf{R}$ is introduced which is linear with respect to the distribution functions (hence bilinear: see Fishburn (1988), 67–68) and skew-symmetric, that is:

$$\varphi(X, Y) = -\varphi(Y, X) \qquad \forall X, Y \in \mathbf{X}$$

φ is called *SSB functional*. If $\succeq$ is a preference relation on $\mathbf{X}$, we say that $(\mathbf{X}, \succeq)$ has an SSB representation if there exists an SSB functional on $\mathbf{X} \times \mathbf{X}$ such that:

$$X \succeq Y \Longleftrightarrow \varphi(X, Y) \geq 0 \qquad \forall X, Y \in \mathbf{X}$$

φ is unique up to an increasing linear transformation (i.e. a similarity transformation).

$(\mathbf{X}, \succeq)$ has an SSB representation if and only if some suitable axioms are assumed.

Moreover, it is possible to define φ directly on the set $A \times A$ and to obtain the integral form:

$$\varphi(X, Y) = \int_{-\infty}^{+\infty} \int_{-\infty}^{+\infty} \varphi(x, y) \mathrm{d}F(x) \mathrm{d}G(y) \qquad \forall X, Y \in \mathbf{X}$$

if φ satisfies some conditions of measurability[2]. When φ happens to be separable, that is $\varphi(x, y) = u(x) - u(y)$, we obtain the VNM utility model.

The SSB utility theory offers also a suggestive interpretation for the function φ defined on $A \times A$: one might view $\varphi(x, y)$ as a measure of the intensity of preference for x compared to y or the *regret* of getting y instead of x when x is preferred to y (see Loomes and Sugden (1982)).

---

[2] Following the notation used by Fishburn, we denote with φ both the functional defined on $X \times X$ and the function defined on $A \times A$.

3 Expected utility without utility

Castagnoli (1990) and later Castagnoli and Li Calzi (1993a, 1993b and 1994), advanced an interesting interpretation of the classical expected utility model. Their main steps are here shortly described.

Let us define a lottery over monetary outcomes to be any real-valued r.v. X with cumulative distribution function F. If the preferences $\succeq$ of an agent satisfy the VNM's axioms, there exists a cardinal real valued VNM utility function u over money such that, given any two lotteries X and Y with distribution functions F and G respectively, one has:

$$X \succeq Y \Longleftrightarrow \int_{-\infty}^{+\infty} u(x)\mathrm{d}F(x) \geq \int_{-\infty}^{+\infty} u(x)\mathrm{d}G(x) \tag{1}$$

It seems natural to assume the function u to be non-constant and increasing. If u is also bounded and (right-)continuous, it is always possible to normalize its range by a convenient positive affine transformation in order to obtain an increasing function U such that:

$$\lim_{x \to -\infty} U(x) = 0 \quad \text{and} \quad \lim_{x \to +\infty} U(x) = 1$$

Thus U can be looked at as a cumulative distribution function. It is well known that there exists a r.v. V with distribution U on some opportune probability space. Moreover this r.v. V can always be assumed to be independent of any lottery to compare. Thus we may write:

$$\int_{-\infty}^{+\infty} U(x)\mathrm{d}F(x) = \Pr\{X \geq V\}$$

and (1) may be restated as:

$$X \succeq Y \Longleftrightarrow \Pr\{X \geq V\} \geq \Pr\{Y \geq V\}$$

so that two gambles X and Y are compared with respect to their likelihood of yelding outcomes which are not worse than those associated with some independent reference lottery V. Thus the agent, when making a choice, is averaging probabilities instead of utilities, i.e. he is ranking lotteries on the basis of their *expected probability* of outperforming V rather than of their expected utility. In such a context V can be interpreted as a random benchmark, more precisely a VNM–benchmark.

4 Preliminary results

In this section we introduce some basic notions and the symbology which we need in the ensuing sections.

Let X, Y and V be real r.v.'s on a measurable space $(\Omega, \mathcal{A})$ with distribution functions F, G and H respectively. Let us consider their joint distribution function:

$$Q(x, y, v) = \Pr\{X \leq x, Y \leq y, V \leq v\}$$

Q is absolutely continuous with respect to its marginal distribution functions F and G, in fact:

$$F(x) = 0 \Longrightarrow Q(x, y, v) = 0$$

and

$$G(y) = 0 \Longrightarrow Q(x, y, v) = 0$$

Hence we also have:

$$F(x)G(y) = 0 \Longrightarrow Q(x, y, v) = 0$$

i.e., Q is absolutely continuous with respect the product measure $F \times G$.

Let us now consider the Radon–Nikodým derivative of Q with respect to the product measure $F \times G$:

$$\lim_{h,k \to 0} \frac{Q(x+h, y+k, v) - Q(x, y+k, v) - Q(x+h, y, v) + Q(x, y, v)}{[F(x+h) - F(x)][G(y+k) - G(y)]} =$$

$$= Q'_{FG}(x, y, v)$$

Because of the absolute continuity of Q with respect to $F \times G$, the existence of the above limit is ensured by the Radon–Nikodým theorem and Q'_{FG} is unique up to sets of null $F \times G$–measure.

Moreover, we observe that Q'_{FG} may be interpreted as the "conditional probability":

$$\Pr\{V \leq v \mid X = x, Y = y\}$$

We note that when the r.v.'s X and Y are stochastically dependent, the above conditional probability has to be intended with respect to the product measure and not with respect to the joint probability measure (see Rényi (1970)):

$$\Pr\{X \leq x, Y \leq y\}$$

Of course, if X and Y are stochastically independent, the above mentioned difference vanishes.

In such a way Q admits the integral representation (see, for instance, Billingsley (1986) or Feller (1966)):

$$Q(x, y, v) = \int\limits_{-\infty}^{x} \int\limits_{-\infty}^{y} Q'_{FG}(s, t, v) \mathrm{d}F(s) \mathrm{d}G(t)$$

and it also holds:

$$\int\limits_{-\infty}^{y} Q'_{FG}(s,t,v)\mathrm{d}G(t) = \int\limits_{-\infty}^{y} \Pr\left\{V \le v \mid X = x, Y = y\right\}\mathrm{d}G(t) =$$

$$\Pr\left\{Y \le y, V \le v \mid X = s\right\} = Q'_F(s,y,v)$$

i.e. Q'_{FG} turns out to be also the Radon–Nikodým derivative of the conditional measure Q'_F with respect to G. In such a way, the integral:

$$\int\limits_{-\infty}^{+\infty} \left[\int\limits_{-\infty}^{y} Q'_{FG}(x,t,v)\mathrm{d}G(t)\right]\mathrm{d}F(x) = \int\limits_{-\infty}^{+\infty} Q'_F(x,y,v)\mathrm{d}F(x) =$$

$$= \int\limits_{-\infty}^{+\infty} \Pr\left\{Y \le y, V \le v \mid X = x\right\}\mathrm{d}F(x)$$

represents a mixture of the bivariate distributions family Q'_F weighted with F. In particular, putting $x = y = v$ we have:

$$\int\limits_{-\infty}^{+\infty} \left[\int\limits_{-\infty}^{x} Q'_{FG}(x,t,x)\mathrm{d}G(t)\right]\mathrm{d}F(x) = \int\limits_{-\infty}^{+\infty} Q'_F(x,x,x)\mathrm{d}F(x) =$$

$$= \int\limits_{-\infty}^{+\infty} \Pr\left\{Y \le x, V \le x \mid X = x\right\}\mathrm{d}F(x) = \tag{2}$$

$$= \Pr\left\{Y \le X, V \le X\right\} = \Pr\left\{X \ge Y \vee V\right\}$$

where with $\vee$ we have denoted the supremum[3] of the r.v.'s.

We are now ready to discuss the announced SSB interpretation.

5 SSB utility without utility

We recall that the preference relationship beetween a pair of random quantities X and Y, with distribution functions F and G respectively, is represented by the skew-symmetric bilinear functional

$$\varphi(X,Y) = \int\limits_{-\infty}^{+\infty}\int\limits_{-\infty}^{+\infty} \varphi(x,y)\mathrm{d}F(x)\mathrm{d}G(y)$$

in the sense that

$$X \ge_{SSB} Y \Longleftrightarrow \varphi(X,Y) \ge 0$$

and the above representation holds if and only if the SSB axioms are assumed.

---

[3] For *supremum* of the pair of r.v.'s (X,Y), we mean the r.v.:

$$(X \vee Y)(\omega) = X(\omega) \vee Y(\omega) \quad \forall \omega \in \Omega$$

The following property holds:

$$\varphi(x,y) = -\varphi(y,x) \quad \forall x,y \in \mathbf{R}$$

Moreover, it seems reasonable (remember the meaning of regret function we have attributed to φ) to assume φ increasing with respect to x (and hence decreasing with respect to y): this implies that $\varphi(x,y) > 0$ if and only if $x > y$.

Thus the function φ may be seen as a signed measure (charge) on $\mathbf{R}^2$. We can consider the two subsets of $\mathbf{R}^2$, $\Delta^+ = \left\{(x,y) \in \mathbf{R}^2 : x \geq y\right\}$ and $\Delta^- = \left\{(x,y) \in \mathbf{R}^2 : x \leq y\right\}$ and the consequent decomposition of φ :

$$\varphi = \varphi^+ - \varphi^-$$

where

$$\varphi^+(x,y) = \varphi(x,y)\mathbf{I}_{\Delta^+}(x,y)$$
$$\varphi^-(x,y) = -\varphi(x,y)\mathbf{I}_{\Delta^-}(x,y)$$

that is φ^+ and φ^- are the positive and the negative part of φ and $\mathbf{I}_B(x,y)$ is the characteristic function of the subset $B \subseteq \mathbf{R}^2$.

We can write:

$$
\begin{aligned}
\varphi(X,Y) &= \int_{-\infty}^{+\infty}\int_{-\infty}^{+\infty} \varphi^+(x,y)\mathrm{d}F(x)\mathrm{d}G(y) - \int_{-\infty}^{+\infty}\int_{-\infty}^{+\infty} \varphi^-(x,y)\mathrm{d}F(x)\mathrm{d}G(y) = \\
&= \int_{-\infty}^{+\infty}\int_{-\infty}^{+\infty} \varphi(x,y)\mathbf{I}_{\Delta^+}(x,y)\mathrm{d}F(x)\mathrm{d}G(y) - \int_{-\infty}^{+\infty}\int_{-\infty}^{+\infty} \varphi(x,y)\mathbf{I}_{\Delta^-}(x,y)\mathrm{d}F(x)\mathrm{d}G(y) = \\
&= \int_{-\infty}^{+\infty}\left[\int_{-\infty}^{x} \varphi(x,y)\mathrm{d}G(y)\right]\mathrm{d}F(x) - \int_{-\infty}^{+\infty}\left[\int_{-\infty}^{y} \varphi(x,y)\mathrm{d}F(x)\right]\mathrm{d}G(y)
\end{aligned}
$$

$$(3)$$

Let us now suppose that both φ^+ and φ^- are bounded and that φ^+ is right–continuous with respect to x for every y, which implies that φ^- is right–continuous with respect to y for every x because of the shew–simmetry assumption. As φ is unique up to increasing linear transformations, we can normalize φ by reducing its image set to the interval $[-1,1] \subset \mathbf{R}$: thus its positive and negative parts assume values in $[0,1]$, are Borel measurable and increasing functions of x and y respectively, i.e. they are two distribution functions.

Under the above assumptions we can consider φ^+ and φ^- as *stochastic kernels* that is we can say that for every pair X,Y there exists a r.v. $V(X,Y) = V$ such that:

$$\Pr\left\{V \leq x \mid X = x, Y = y\right\} = \varphi^+(x,y)$$
$$\Pr\left\{V \leq y \mid X = x, Y = y\right\} = \varphi^-(x,y)$$

where the conditional probability is measured by the product measure $F \times G$. In other words, recalling the previous section, there always exists a multivariate distribution function Q for X, Y and $V(X, Y)$ such that:

$$Q'_{FG}(x, y, x) = \varphi^+(x, y)$$

and

$$Q'_{FG}(x, y, y) = \varphi^-(x, y)$$

We note that the skew-simmetry of φ implies that:

$$\varphi^+(x, y) = \varphi^-(y, x)$$

thus it is:

$$\Pr\{V \le x \mid X = x, Y = y\} = \Pr\{V \le x \mid X = y, Y = x\}$$

i.e. we have constructed a r.v. V for which a sort of *conditional exchangeability* between X and Y holds.

By (2) and (3) with some computation we get:

$$\varphi(X, Y) = \Pr\{X \ge Y, X \ge V\} - \Pr\{Y \ge X, Y \ge V\} =$$
$$= \Pr\{X \ge Y \vee V\} - \Pr\{Y \ge X \vee V\}$$

so that

$$X \ge_{SSB} Y \Longleftrightarrow \varphi(X, Y) \ge 0 \Longleftrightarrow \Pr\{X \ge Y \vee V\} \ge \Pr\{Y \ge X \vee V\} \quad (4)$$

We have so obtained, introducing a third random variable V, an interpretation of the SSB model which involves only probabilities making no use of utility functions.

6 The nontransitive convex representation

We shall mention briefly another interesting model proposed by Fishburn (1982) and named *nontransitive convex representation*. In this work the preferences $\succeq$ are again described by a functional ϕ defined on $\mathbf{X} \times \mathbf{X}$ in the usual sense:

$$X \succeq Y \Longleftrightarrow \phi(X, Y) \ge 0$$

where ϕ is not necessarily skew-symmetric but it has only to satisfy:

$$\phi(X, Y) \ge 0 \Longleftrightarrow \phi(Y, X) \le 0$$

and the property of bilinearity is substitued by the linearity with respect to its first argument.

It is possible to translate also this model in a probabilistic language under assumptions analogous to the previous ones[4]. Nevertheless, the loss of skew-symmetry makes ϕ^+ and ϕ^- two really *different* functions. Thus, we can

---

[4] In this context, in order to normalize ϕ multiplying it by a positive constant number, it is necessary that:

$$\sup \phi = -\inf \phi$$

state that for every pair of r.v.'s X, Y there exist *two* r.v.'s $V(X, Y) = V$ and $V'(X, Y) = V'$ such that:

$$\Pr\{V \leq x \mid X = x, Y = y\} = \phi^+(x, y)$$
$$\Pr\{V' \leq y \mid X = x, Y = y\} = \phi^-(x, y)$$

that is, we find two random benchmarks which allow us to write:

$$\phi(X, Y) = \Pr\{X \geq Y \vee V\} - \Pr\{Y \geq X \vee V'\}$$

finding an expression quite similar to the previous one.

7 The meaning of V

In the previous sections we have revisited the SSB functional as the difference of two probabilities.

The startpoint is the function $\varphi(x, y)$ which, for us, represents a sort of stochastic kernel in order to obtain, for every pair $X, Y \in \mathbf{X}$, a third r.v. $V = V(X, Y)$. Since in the SSB model there exists a unique functional φ representing the decision maker's preferences, in the probabilistic framework we have a unique "conditional distribution function" which provides a rule for constructing $V(X, Y)$. This choice process generates a set $\mathbf{V}$ of random benchmarks fully determined by φ (e.g.: if we consider n alternatives then $\mathbf{V}$ contains n^2 r.v.'s).

For the meaning that the difference:

$$\Pr\{X \geq Y \vee V\} - \Pr\{Y \geq X \vee V\}$$

assumes, we may state that the first term gives a measure of the *preferability* of X with respect to Y while the second term provides the measure of the counterpart.

According to this, we may now discuss the meaning of the benchmark V.

Consider a decision maker who has to choose between X and Y. Suppose that he wants to use a decision criterion involving (as synthesis index) only probability measures. The simplest way to measure the *preferability* of X with respect to Y, only using a probability measure, may be to consider:

$$\Pr\{X \geq Y\}$$

i.e. the probability that X outperforms Y.

Nevertheless, in this hypothetical approach, we may note that something is missing: if we measure the "distance" between X and Y only in a probabilistic sense, we don't take into account the "distance" between the effective values assumed by X and Y.

Consider the following example:

	$Pr(\omega_s)$	$X(\omega_s)$	$Y(\omega_s)$
ω_1	0.6	1,000	999
ω_2	0.4	5,000	1 million

where $\{\omega_1, \omega_2\}$ represents a partition of the events space Ω.

Since:
$$\Pr\{X \geq Y\} = \Pr\{\omega_1\} = 0.6$$

and
$$\Pr\{Y \geq X\} = \Pr\{\omega_2\} = 0.4$$

according to the above criterion, the choice would be X, but this may be in contrast with many realistic preference relationships. The problem can be solved by considering a *level parameter* which allows to take into account, in some way, the different values assumed by X and Y. Thus the above choice process may be modified by introducing a sort of performance threshold value, for example the certain quantity $v = 20,000$, and by requiring that X outperforms both v and Y; thus the resulting measures are:
$$\Pr\{X \geq Y \vee v\} = 0$$

and
$$\Pr\{Y \geq X \vee v\} = 0.4$$

We have so obtained a more realistic decision criterion simply introducing a minimum level of acceptance.

The r.v. V works exactly in this way: it plays the role of a random threshold which allows to *rescale* the values of X with respect to the values of Y and viceversa. In this sense the dependence of X and Y is justified: the minimum level assumes a standardization role and, in general, it must be chosen according to the scale of values to rearrange. Hence, we obtain a set $\mathbf{V}$ of r.v.'s V and we can confirm the meaning of *random benchmark* for every V in $\mathbf{V}$. Of course, in this context, they will be SSB-random benchmarks.

Finally, the property of V:
$$\Pr\{V \leq x \mid X = x, Y = y\} = \Pr\{V \leq x \mid X = y, Y = x\}$$

is now explained by the meaning of V. Since V is a sort of standardization factor, it seems natural that it presents a symmetric behaviour when measured with respect to X and Y.

The context changes when we consider the model of nontransitive convex utility: in this case we find two different random benchmarks. The decision maker is requiring two different levels of acceptance: he evaluates in a different way the involved probabilities. If, for instance, V is greater than V', the term $\Pr\{X \geq Y \vee V\}$ will "count" less than $\Pr\{Y \geq X \vee V'\}$: for Y it will be easier to outperform $X \vee V'$ than for X to do better than $Y \vee V$. In this case, the decision maker is, in some sense, more pessimistic as he underestimates the positive part of the probabilities difference.

In order to show how our interpretation works, we now provide some relevant examples:

1. Let $V(X,Y)$ be the infimum[5] $X \wedge Y$ of (X,Y), we obtain:

$$\varphi(X,Y) = \Pr\{X \geq Y\} - \Pr\{Y \geq X\} = $$
$$= 2 \cdot \Pr\{X \geq Y\} - \Pr\{X = Y\} - 1$$

In this case the function φ turns out to be:

$$\varphi(x,y) = \begin{cases} 1 & \text{if } x > y \\ 0 & \text{if } x = y \\ -1 & \text{if } x < y \end{cases}$$

for every pair (X,Y) considered.

Moreover if $\Pr\{X = Y\} = 0$, we get that $X \geq_{SSB} Y$ if and only if $\text{Prob}\{X \geq Y\} \geq 1/2$ and we can observe that this order relationship coincides with the β-dominance, for $\beta = 1/2$, proposed by Wrather and Yu (1982), according to which X dominates Y with probability $\beta \geq 1/2$ if $\Pr\{X \geq Y\} \geq \beta$.

2. Let be $V(X,Y) = X \vee Y$. Then the SSB utility can be interpreted as:

$$\varphi(X,Y) = \Pr\{X \geq X \vee Y\} - \Pr\{Y \geq X \vee Y\} = $$
$$= \Pr\{X \geq Y\} - \Pr\{Y \geq X\}$$

In other words, we have the same result obtained with $V = X \wedge Y$.

3. Let V be a portfolio containing X and Y that is $V(X,Y) = \alpha X + (1-\alpha)Y$, $\alpha \in [0,1]$, then we have:

$$\Pr\{V \leq x \mid X = x, Y = y\} = $$
$$= \Pr\{\alpha X + (1-\alpha)Y \leq x \mid X = x, Y = y\} = $$
$$\Pr\{(1-\alpha)Y \leq (1-\alpha)x \mid Y = y\} = $$

$$= \begin{cases} 1 & \text{if } x \geq y \\ 0 & \text{otherwise} \end{cases}$$

and similarly:

$$\Pr\{V \leq y \mid X = x, Y = y\} = $$
$$= \begin{cases} 1 & \text{if } y \geq x \\ 0 & \text{otherwise} \end{cases}$$

hence we obtain again the same expression, provided in the previous examples, for the SSB function φ.

---

[5] For *infimum* of the pair of r.v.'s (X,Y), we mean the quantity:

$$(X \wedge Y)(\omega) = X(\omega) \wedge Y(\omega) \quad \forall \omega \in \Omega$$

4. Consider the degenerate r.v.'s:

$$X \rightsquigarrow F(t) = \begin{cases} 0 \text{ if } t < x \\ 1 \text{ if } t \geq x \end{cases}$$

and

$$Y \rightsquigarrow G(t) = \begin{cases} 0 \text{ if } t < y \\ 1 \text{ if } t \geq y \end{cases}$$

thus:

$$\varphi(X, Y) = \varphi(x, y) = \Pr\{x \geq V \vee y\} - \Pr\{y \geq V \vee x\}$$

Let H be the probability distribution function of the random benchmark V, then one has[6]:

$$V \vee x \rightsquigarrow \widetilde{H}(t) = \begin{cases} 0 & \text{if } t < x \\ H(t) & \text{if } t \geq x \end{cases}$$

and

$$V \vee y \rightsquigarrow \widehat{H}(t) = \begin{cases} 0 & \text{if } t < y \\ H(t) & \text{if } t \geq y \end{cases}$$

hence:

$$\Pr\{y \geq V \vee x\} = \widetilde{H}(y)$$

and

$$\Pr\{x \geq V \vee y\} = \widehat{H}(x)$$

So φ turns out to be:

$$\varphi(x, y) = \begin{cases} H(x) & \text{if } x > y \\ 0 & \text{if } x = y \\ -H(y) & \text{if } x < y \end{cases}$$

and it is immediately verified that $\varphi(x, y) = -\varphi(y, x)$. Moreover, it also holds that:

$$x \geq y \Longleftrightarrow \varphi(x, y) \geq 0$$

This simple example points out that the probabilistic description of the choice is perfectly consistent with the features of the SSB model.

The first examples show that, even if we consider different benchmarks, it may be we are dealing with the same function φ. This can occur since the choice of a specific function φ individuates a conditional probability Q'_{FG} only on a restriction of $\mathbf{R}^3$.

---

[6] Note that in this case the r.v. $X \vee Y$ coincides with the r.v. which has distribution function $F(t) \wedge G(t)$.

To summarize we can say that for every preference relationship there exists a unique SSB functional φ and that a unique conditional probability corresponds to every SSB functional, but this does not imply the uniqueness of the associated benchmark $V(X, Y)$. Conversely it is true that a unique function φ corresponds to every random benchmark. In this framework we note that also when the decision rules seem to be different (i.e. they are based on different benchmarks), they may produce, or derive from the same preference relationship.

8 Conclusions

The SSB utility theory is very suitable to describe real decision processes: in fact, very often, common choices do not satisfy the usual rationality assumptions. Literature is rich in paradoxes and counter–examples, supported by empirical evidences, which show the failure of independence axioms and/or the transitivity of preferences. The SSB theory overcomes other well–known approaches in modelling reality and, in our opinion, stresses how choices are mainly done through a pairwise comparison. Nevertheless, to apply the Fishburn's model, one has to select his own SSB utility function and this implies a full knowledge of the "regret measure" existing between two alternatives, mutually exclusive. It is difficult to say how this kind of knowledge can be reached. In this sense the proposed probabilistic interpretation can be of some help: if a decision maker realizes that his preferences are well described by a pairwise comparison relatively to a third random variable, depending of the pair considered, then the quantitative aspect can be extimated by means of a set of bets on the possible outcomes.

Anyway, the matching between the utility and the probability language, guaranteed by a correct use of a "subjective" conditional probability instead of a "subjective" utility function, allows one to face the decision–making problems from different points of view. Of course this does not mean that we have to argue only in a probabilistic way but simply that we can do it whenever this may be helpful.

To complete this study we believe that it could be interesting to face the stochastic relationships between the r.v.'s V and the pair X, Y using the powerful tool provided by the copula concept.

Furthermore, one might deepen the study of the mechanism to generate the set $\mathbf{V}$ of random benchmarks for a given functional φ and viceversa.

References

P. Billingsley, 1986, *Probability and Measure*, Wiley & Sons, Chichester.

L. Bondesson, 1992, *Generalized Gamma Convolutions and Related Classes of Distributions and Densities*, Springer Verlag, New York and Berlin.

E. Castagnoli, 1990, "Qualche riflessione sull'utilità attesa", Ratio Mathematica, 1, 51–59.

E. Castagnoli and M. Li Calzi, 1993a, "Expected Utility without Utility", presented at the Colloquium Decision Making: Towards the 21th Century, Madrid, June 2-5.

E. Castagnoli and M. Li Calzi, 1993b, "Expected Utility without Utility: Constant Risk Attitude", Rendiconti del Comitato per gli Studi Economici, 30-31, 145–160.

E. Castagnoli and M. Li Calzi, 1994, "Expected Utility without Utility: A Model of Portfolio Selection", Operation Research Models in Quantitative Finance, R. L. D'Ecclesia and S. A. Zenios (eds.), Physica -Verlag, 95–111.

G. Dall'Aglio, S. Kotz and G. Salinetti (eds.), 1991, *Advances in Probability Distributions with Given Marginals*, Kluwer Academic Publishers, Dordrecht.

W. Feller, 1966, *An Introduction to Probability Theory and Its Applications*, Wiley & Sons, Chichester.

P. C. Fishburn, 1982, "Nontransitive Measurable Utility", J. Math. Psych., 26, 31–67.

P. C. Fishburn, 1984a, "SSB Utility Theory and Decision-Making under Uncertainty", Math. Soc. Sci., 8, 253–285.

P. C. Fishburn, 1984b, "SSB Utility Theory: an Economic Perspective", Math. Soc. Sci., 8, 63–94.

P. C. Fishburn, 1984c, "Dominance in SSB Utility Theory", J. Ec. Theory, 34, 130–148.

P. C. Fishburn, 1988, *Nonlinear Preference and Utility Theory*, J. Hopkins Un. Press, Baltimore.

G. Loomes, R. Sugden, 1982, "Regret Theory: an alternative theory of rational choice under uncertainty", Ec. Journ., 92, 805-824.

A. Rényi, 1970, *Probability Theory*, North–Holland, Amsterdam.

B. Schweizer and A. Sklar, 1983, *Probabilistic Metric Spaces*, North-Holland, New York.

T. Tjur, 1980, *Probability Based on Radon Measures*, Wiley & Sons, Chichester.

C. Wrather and P. L. Yu, 1982, "Probability Dominance in Random Outcomes", J.O.T.A., 36, 315–334.

Proper Risk Aversion in Presence of Multiple Sources of Risk

Luisa Tibiletti

Dipartimento di Statistica e Matematica Applicata alle Scienze Umane
Università di Torino, I-10122 Torino, Italy

Abstract. A risk-averse agent finds each of two *independent* risky assets undesirable. If he is imposed to take one, will he continue to evaluate the other undesirable one? In other words, can an undesirable lottery be made desirable by the presence of another undesirable lottery? In the negative case, the agent is said to have a *proper risk aversion*. This notion has been introduced by Pratt and Zeckhauser (1987) and a weaker version has recently been proposed by Gollier and Pratt (1993). Families of utility functions displaying the properness and weak properness properties for *all* couples of undesirable lotteries have been found (Kimball (1993), Gollier and Pratt (1993, 1995)). The aim of this note is to face the problem from a different point of view. Conditions to guarantee properness and weak properness properties are no longer stated for *all* couples of undesirable risks, but are formulated by means of a characterisation of the utility function (in terms of the coefficients of risk-aversion, of prudence and temperance) and by imposing restrictions on the marginal distributions of the risks involved. An extended notion has also been proposed for *non-independent* risks and sufficient conditions for properness are provided. Proper risk aversion should have important consequences in applications. For example, properness guarantees that the demand in insurance and in other forms of hedging does not decrease as the number of independent unfavourable risks increases.

Journal of Economic Literature Classification Numbers: D80, D81, D83.

Keywords. Proper-Risk Aversion, Multiple Risks.

1   Introduction[*]

A debated question in recent literature concerns the behaviour of a rational agent facing the following problem. Let X and Y be two undesirable *independent* risky assets. If the agent is required to take one, let it be Y, then will he continue to evaluate the other undesirable one? In other words, with the introduction of an

---

[*] *Acknowledgments*
The Author is grateful to J.W. Pratt for some helpful comments and suggestions. However, she remain the only responsible for any remaining errors.

unfavourable background risk Y in the portfolio will the agent be induced to modify his evaluation on an *independent* unfair risk asset X ? At first glance intuition suggests a negative answer: firstly, because X is unfair, secondly, because the independence hypothesis does not induce a decreasing of the portfolio variance.

In spite of what our intuition can suggest, a number of counter-examples (see Gollier-Pratt, 1993 and the Appendix of the present paper) show that even for very simple concave utility functions the above answer can be positive. These counter-intuitive situations were originally investigated by Pratt and Zeckhauser (1987), who introduced the concept of *properness* in order to eliminate the above mentioned "paradoxical" results. Sufficient conditions for properness have been investigated: one is that the utility function u be analytical (Pratt and Zeckhauser, 1987), another is that both absolute risk aversion and absolute prudence be decreasing in wealth (Kimball,1993). Recently, Gollier and Pratt (1993) have introduced the concept of *weak-properness* which induces the same comparative static results as the properness assumption. Risk aversion is said to be weak-proper if an undesirable risk can never be made desirable by the introduction of a background risk Y, such that $E(Y) \leq 0$. A sufficient condition for weak-properness is that the absolute risk aversion is decreasing and convex.

Our aim is threefold. The first one is to show how the above mentioned behaviour is only apparently paradoxical and an intuitive explanation can be provided. The answer lies in the fact that the higher order derivatives of u can be interpreted as the "weights" that have to be attributed to the higher order moments of the risks under discussion. Therefore, an unfavourable shift in a particular moment (for example an increase in variance) can be compensated for by a favourable one in another moment (for example an increase in skewness for a prudent agent).

The second aim concerns the search for conditions guaranteeing the weak-properness properties no longer valid for *all* couples of unfavourable risks, but formulated by means of relaxed conditions on both the utility function (in terms of the coefficients of risk-aversion, of prudence and temperance) and on restrictions on the marginal distributions of the risks involved.

The third one is devoted to extending the properness concept to *not necessarily independent* risks.

Implications of properness in the insurance economics are also pointed out.

The plan of the work is as follows. In Section 2 preliminaries and definitions are settled. In Section 3 an explanation of the "paradoxical" behaviour is suggested. In Section 4 sufficient conditions to guarantee weak-properness are stated. Section 5 concerns the case of dependent risks. Applications are listed in Section 6. A summary concludes the article.

2 Preliminaries and Definitions

Consider an expected utility maximizer endowed with a von Neumann-Morgestern utility function u.

In what follows the probability distributions are assumed to have finite moments until the n-th order $(n>1)$. In addition, it is necessary to restrict the set of utility functions to those ensuring that the expectation exists. For example, that is fulfilled by the class of infinitely differentiable functions u for which a (negative) integer k exists such that $\left(1+x^2\right)^k \partial^n u/\partial x^n$ goes to zero at infinity for every n.

In order to make the note self-contained, we will recall a set of definitions.

Definition 1. A risk X is said to be *undesirable* for individual u with random background wealth W if

$$\mathrm{E}u(W+X) \le \mathrm{E}(W).$$

Let us consider some subsets $\Sigma_i(w,u)$ of random variables which satisfy some specific properties related to characteristics of u. In the following we define the concept of "properness" with respect to Σ_i.

Definition 2. The von Neumann-Morgenstern utility function u is *proper* at w with respect to Σ_i, $i = 1,2,3$ if any undesirable risk given background wealth w can never be made desirable by the introduction of any independent risk Y:

$$\mathrm{E}u(w+X+Y) \le \mathrm{E}u(w+Y) \quad \text{whenever} \quad \mathrm{E}u(w+X) \le u(w) \text{ and } Y \in \Sigma_i(w,u). \quad (1)$$

where
$$\Sigma_1(w,u) \equiv \{Y : \mathrm{E}u'(w+Y) \ge u'(w)\}$$
$$\Sigma_2(w,u) \equiv \{Y : \mathrm{E}u(w+Y) \le u(w)\}$$
$$\Sigma_3(w,u) \equiv \{Y : \mathrm{E}Y \le 0\}$$

Properness with respect to Σ_1 is what Kimball (1993) calls *standardness*; with respect to Σ_2, it is called *properness* by Pratt and Zeckhauser (1987) and that with respect to Σ_3 is called *weak-properness* by Gollier and Pratt (1993).
It can be demonstrated that *standardness* implies *properness*, and *properness* implies *weak-properness* (see Gollier-Pratt, 1993).

3 An intuitive explanation for local behaviour

Taking the Taylor expansion of u in the expected values involved in (1), we obtain

$$\mathrm{E}u(w+X+Y) = u(w) + u'(w)\mathrm{E}(X+Y) + \frac{u''(w)}{2!}\mathrm{E}(X+Y)^2 + \qquad (2)$$

$$+\frac{u'''(w)}{3!}E(X+Y)^3+...+o\big(E(X+Y)^n\big)$$

$$Eu(w+Y)=u(w)+u'(w)E(Y)+\frac{u''(w)}{2}E\big(Y^2\big)+\frac{u'''(w)}{3!}E\big(Y^3\big)+...+o\big(E\big(Y^n\big)\big)$$

$$Eu(w+X)=u(w)+u'(w)E(X)+\frac{u''(w)}{2}E\big(X^2\big)+\frac{u'''(w)}{3!}E\big(X^3\big)+...+o\big(E\big(X^n\big)\big)$$

In the case that X and Y are *independent*[1], *properness at w with respect to* Σ_i, is equivalent to

$$u'(w)E(X)+\frac{u''(w)}{2}\Big[E\big(X^2\big)+2E(X)E(Y)\Big]+$$

$$+\frac{u'''(w)}{3!}\Big[E\big(X^3\big)+3E\big(X^2\big)E(Y)+3E(X)E\big(Y^2\big)\Big]+ \tag{3}$$

$$\frac{u^{(iv)}(w)}{4!}\Big[E\big(X^4\big)+4E\big(X^3\big)E(Y)+6E\big(X^2\big)E\big(Y^2\big)+4E(X)E\big(Y^3\big)\Big]+...\le 0$$

subjected to the conditions

$$u'(w)E(X)+\frac{u''(w)}{2}E(X)^2+\frac{u'''(w)}{3!}E(X)^3+...\le 0 \qquad \text{and} \quad Y\in\Sigma_i(w,u) \tag{4}$$

Formula (2) displays the meaning of the higher order derivative $u^{(i)}(w)$: they exhibit the importance which is to be attached to the i-th moment of the random amount under discussion. Therefore, the positiveness of $u^{(i)}(w)$ displays the agent's preference (aversion) towards the positiveness (negativeness) of i-th moment.

That provides an intuitive explanation for the apparently paradoxical behaviour of a "non-proper" agent: a shift in an addendum in (3) can be compensated for by concomitant shifts in the other addenda.

---

[1] If the random variables X and Y are independent, therefore for any borel functions g, h the random variables $g(X)$ and $h(Y)$ are still independent.
Therefore, for example, the third moment of the sum of two independent random variables we have

$$E(X+Y)^3=E\big(X^3\big)+3E\big(X^2Y\big)+3E\big(XY^2\big)+E\big(Y^3\big)=$$

$$=E\big(X^3\big)+3E\big(X^2\big)E(Y)+3E(X)\big(Y^2\big)+E\big(Y^3\big)$$

So, for example, a penalising shift in the second moment $E(X+Y)^2$ can be compensated for by a favourable shift in the third moment $E(X+Y)^3$. In other words, an unfavourable increase in variance can be counterbalanced by a favourable one in skewness. So, for example, an agent endowed with a positive third derivative prefers positively skewed random amounts: he appreciates lotteries with low probability to lose large amounts, and, on the other hand, high probability to lose small amounts. In this situation, an increase in skewness produces a natural hedging to make significant losses (for a detailed analysis on this subject see Tibiletti (1994)).

Let us now investigate the analytical support of this intuitive thesis. Condition (3) is equivalent to

$$u'(w)E(X)+\frac{u''(w)}{2}E(X^2)+\frac{u'''(w)}{3!}E(X^3)+\frac{u^{(iv)}(w)}{4!}E(X^4)+...\le$$

$$-\left\{u''(w)E(X)E(Y)+\frac{u'''(w)}{2!}\left[E(X^2)E(Y)+E(X)E(Y^2)\right]+\right.$$

$$\left.+\frac{u^{(iv)}(w)}{4!}\left[4E(X^3)E(Y)+6E(X^2)E(Y^2)+4E(X)E(Y^3)\right]+...\right\}$$

where the left-hand-side term in the above inequality is negative and is equal to $Eu(w+X)-u(w)$. Therefore, we have

$$Eu(w+X)-u(w)\le$$

$$-\left\{u''(w)E(X)E(Y)+\frac{u'''(w)}{2!}\left[E(X^2)E(Y)+E(X)E(Y^2)\right]+\right.$$

$$\left.+\frac{u^{(iv)}(w)}{4!}\left[4E(X^3)E(Y)+6E(X^2)E(Y^2)+4E(X)E(Y^3)\right]+..\right. \tag{5}$$

This result offers an intuitive explanation: properness is guaranteed whenever the risk X is sufficiently disliked, $i.e.$, the difference $Eu(w+X)-u(w)$ is not greater than a barrier determined by the higher order utility function and the moments.

Moreover, condition (5) shows that properness can be guaranteed in different manners: (i) imposing restrictive conditions on the relative values of the derivatives of u, or (ii) after having fixed the values of the derivatives of u, finding out restrictions on the moments of the random variables involved. The former research line has been followed in above mentioned literature, the latter one will be chosen in the following.

Below strictly increasing and concave utility functions u will be treated. Moreover, as the above mentioned authors, we will assume that u can be satisfactorily described by a fourth degree polynomial.

4 Conditions for local weak-properness

Suppose $E(Y) \leq 0$. It is immediate to see that (5) can be satisfied by both a negative-mean variable X and by a positive-mean one.

- Let $E(X) \leq 0$. In this case, a sufficient condition is that the right-hand-side of (5) is positive, so

$$\begin{cases} E(X) \leq 0 \\ u''' \geq 0 \\ u^{(iv)}\left[2E(X^3)E(Y) + 3E(X^2)E(Y^2) + 2E(X)E(Y^3)\right] \leq 0 \end{cases}$$

this last condition depends on the sign of $u^{(iv)}$, if $u^{(iv)} \leq 0$ and u is analytical, then weak-properness is guaranteed (see Gollier-Pratt, 1993); vice versa if $u^{(iv)} > 0$, the object can be reached by imposing conditions on the moments of X and/or Y, for example:

$$\begin{cases} u^{(iv)} > 0 \\ E(X^3) > \dfrac{-3E(X^2)E(Y^2) - 2E(X)E(Y^3)}{2E(Y)} \end{cases}$$

- Let $E(X) > 0$. A sufficient condition is given by the positiveness of the right-hand-side of (5),

$$E(X)\left[u''(w)E(Y) + \frac{u'''(w)}{2}E(Y^2)\right] +$$

$$+ E(Y)\left[\frac{u'''(w)}{2}E(X^2) + \frac{u^{(iv)}}{3!}E(X^3)\right] + \frac{u^{(iv)}}{4!}\left[6E(X^2)E(Y^2) + 4E(X)E(Y^3)\right] < 0$$

Therefore, sufficient conditions are

$$\begin{cases} p < 2\dfrac{E(Y)}{E(Y^2)} \\ tE(X^3) > 3E(X^2) \\ u^{(iv)}\left[3E(X^2)E(Y^2) + 2(X)E(Y^3)\right] < 0 \end{cases}$$

where $p=-u'''/u''$ is the *coefficient of prudence* introduced by Kimball (1990,1993) and $t = -u^{(iv)}\big/u'''$ is the *coefficient of temperance* (see Eeckhoudt and Schlesinger (1991), Gollier and Pratt (1993, 1995)).

So, it results that once the derivatives $u^{(i)}(W)$ are chosen on the basis of the importance attached to the *i*-th moment of the agent 's random wealth, then *properness* can be guaranteed by restrictions on the moments of X and/or of Y.

5   Properness for dependent risks

A different problem is now faced. In the following, the risks involved are *not necessarily independently* distributed. Then we say that the utility function u is "proper" at w for the couple of risks X and Y if

$$\mathrm{E}u(w+X+Y) \le \mathrm{E}u(w+Y) \text{ whenever } \mathrm{E}u(w+X) \le u(w) \text{ and } \mathrm{E}(Y) \le 0$$

The question is: whenever the risks X and Y become "more positively dependent", does the agent continue to reject X? The intuitive answer is affirmative.

Let us formalise this concept. From the above discussion on formulas (2) it follows that properness-condition involves *all* the moments of the random sum $(w+X+Y)$. Therefore, it is foreseeable that the Pearson correlation coefficient could not be a suitable tool for our object since it *only* displays the influence of the dependence structure between X and Y on the variance of the sum $(w+X+Y)$.

Above idea of "more positive dependence" can be captured by the notion of more concordance. The intuitive idea underlying this notion is that: X and Y are concordant when large values of X go with large values of Y. The concordance is a matter of association of X and Y along any (strictly) monotone function, taking into account the kind of monotonicity (whether increasing or decreasing). So, the maximum is attained when a strictly increasing relation exists between the variables, vice versa the minimum is attained when the relation is strictly decreasing. A qualitative idea of concordance was first expressed by Gini (1915-1916) and furthermore, many attempts have been made to formulate this concept more precisely (see Tchen (1980), Marshall-Olkin (1988), for a general definition in terms of copula see Scarsini (1984)).

Definition 3. Let (X_1,Y_1) and (X_0,Y_0) be two pairs of random variables with same marginals F and G and distribution function $H_0(x,y)$ and $H_1(x,y)$, respectively. Then H_1 is said to be *more concordant* than H_0 if $H_1(x,y) \ge H_0(x,y)$, for all $x,y \in \Re$.

In these circumstances we also say that (X_1, Y_1) is *more concordant* than (X_0, Y_0).

Without loss in generality from an application point of view, we will consider random vectors with finite support. We can state now the following

Proposition 1. *Let (X_0, Y_0) and (X_1, Y_1) be two pairs of random variables with same marginals F and G. Let (X_1, Y_1) be more concordant than (X_0, Y_0). Therefore for any risk-averse agent endowed with utility function u, it results*

$$E\big(u(w + X_0 + Y_0)\big) \geq E\big(u(w + X_1 + Y_1)\big).$$

Proof. Let H_i be the distribution function of (X_i, Y_i), $i = 0, 1$. Denote by $[a, b]$ and $[c, d]$ the intervals containing the supports of X_i and Y_i, respectively. It results

$$E\big(u(w + X_i + Y_i)\big) = \int_a^b \int_c^d u(w + x + y) dH_i(x, y)$$

Integrating by parts in the bivariate integral above (see Young (1917) or, for example, Picone-Viola (1952)), we obtain

$$= \Delta_a^b \Delta_c^d \big[u(w + x + y) H_i(x, y) \big] - \Delta_a^b \int_c^d u'(w + x + y) H_i(x, y) dy +$$

$$- \Delta_c^d \int_a^b u'(w + x + y) H_i(x, y) dx + \int_a^b \int_c^d u''(w + x + y) H_i(x, y) dx dy =$$

$$= u(w + b + d) - \int_c^d u'(w + b + y) G(y) dy - \int_a^b u'(w + x + d) F(x) dx +$$

$$+ \int_a^b \int_c^d u''(w + x + y) H_i(x, y) dx dy.$$

Compare now $E\big(u(w + X_0 + Y_0)\big)$ with $E\big(u(w + X_1 + Y_1)\big)$. By negativeness of u'' coupled with the more concordance condition $H_1(x, y) \geq H_0(x, y)$, we have

$$\int_a^b \int_c^d u''(w + x + y) H_0(x, y) dx dy \geq \int_a^b \int_c^d u''(w + x + y) H_1(x, y) dx dy$$

and our claim turns out.

Proposition 2. *Let* (X_0, Y_0) *and* (X_1, Y_1) *be two pairs of random variables with same marginals* F *and* G. *Let* (X_1, Y_1) *be more concordant than* (X_0, Y_0). *If the utility function* u *is "proper" at* w *for the couple of risks* X_0 *and* Y_0, *i.e.,*

$$\mathrm{E}u(w + X_0 + Y_0) \le \mathrm{E}u(w + Y_0) \text{ whenever } \mathrm{E}u(w + X_0) \le u(w) \text{ and } \mathrm{E}(Y_0) < 0,$$

then, u *will also be "proper" at* w *for the couple of risks* X_1 *and* Y_1, *i.e.,*

$$\mathrm{E}u(w + X_1 + Y_1) \le \mathrm{E}u(w + Y_1) \text{ whenever } \mathrm{E}u(w + X_1) \le u(w) \text{ and } \mathrm{E}(Y_1) < 0.$$

Proof. Since (X_0, Y_0) and (X_1, Y_1) have the same marginals, we have

$$\mathrm{E}u(w + Y_0) = \mathrm{E}u(w + Y_1)$$
$$\mathrm{E}u(w + X_0) = \mathrm{E}u(w + X_1)$$
$$\mathrm{E}(Y_0) = \mathrm{E}(Y_1)$$

By Proposition 1, we obtain

$$\mathrm{E}\big(u(w + X_1 + Y_1)\big) \le \mathrm{E}\big(u(w + X_0 + Y_0)\big) \le \mathrm{E}u(w + Y_0) = \mathrm{E}u(w + Y_1)$$

and the desired statement comes out.

6   Properness in Application

The analysis of the behaviour of a risk-averse agent acting under the presence of multiple sources of risk has recently received a considerable amont of attention with reference to insurance demand. In this context pioneering works of Mayers and Smith (1983), Doherty and Schlesinger (1983) are to be mentioned (see for example Eeckhoudt and Kimball (1992) for an ample references).

As already pointed out by Pratt and Zeckhauser (1987), offering insurance for one risk (i.e. rejecting the "background" risk Y) the agent could be only more encouraged to accept new risks X. Consequently, the opening of new options and futures markets could stimulate activities on competitive markets. Clearly, that is not ensured if the agent is *not* proper. In fact, if his wealth is random and equal to $(w + Y)$, then he can be prone to accept the new risk X, viceversa if the initial wealth is non-random and equal to w, he refuses X.

7   Conclusions

Proper risk aversion is investigated along three different research lines. Firstly, an intuitive explanation of a non-proper behaviour is provided. It relies on the fact that an unfavourable shift in a moment of the random amount under discussion can be counterbalanced by a favourable one in another moment.

The second line concerns the investigation of sufficient conditions for properness by relaxing the restrictive conditions on the utility function and, on the other hand, introducing restrictions on the moments of the random amounts involved. The last line concerns an extension of the properness concept to the case of *not necessarily dependent risks*: sufficient conditions are therefore achieved. Application in insurance economics are also suggested.

Appendix

Examples of utility functions which violate the property of properness are reported below.

The following concerns a non-differentiable utility function. The example is due to Gollier and Pratt (1993).

Example 1.   Let

$$u(w) = \begin{cases} w, & w < 100 \\ 50 + w/2, & w \geq 100 \end{cases} \tag{6}$$

if the agent's initial wealth is 101, then he dislikes the lottery

$$X = \begin{cases} -11, & p = 1/2 \\ 14, & p = 1/2 \end{cases} \tag{7}$$

because $Eu(101 + X) = 98,75$ and $u(101) = 100,5$.

But, if the undesirable *independent* "background risk"

$$Y = \begin{cases} -20, & p = 1/2 \\ +20, & p = 1/2 \end{cases} \tag{8}$$

is added, then the agent will find X desirable, in fact we have $Eu(101 + X + Y) = 96,875$ while $Eu(101 + Y) = 95,75$.

A naïf explanation of this "irrational" behaviour is suggested by means of the following calculations.

$$E(X) = 1,5 \quad E(X^2) = 158,5 \quad E(X^3) = +706,5 \quad E(X^4) = 26528,5$$

$$E(Y) = 0 \quad E(Y^2) = 400 \quad E(Y^3) = 0 \quad E(Y^4) = 160000$$

$$E(X+Y) = 1,5 \quad E((X+Y)^2) = 558,5$$

$$E((X+Y)^3) = +2506,5 \quad E((X+Y)^4) = 566928,5$$

So the introduction of X produces a disliked increase in the second moment, nevertheless that can be compensated for by the increase in the third and fourth moments[2] if the third and the fourth derivatives of the agent's utility function are positive.

The above utility function u is *not* differentiable, so we can *not* check condition (5). An example of differentiable utility function which approximates (6) is reported below.

Example 2.   Let

$$v(101+x) = 100.5 + v'(101)x + \frac{v''(101)}{2}x^2 + \frac{v'''(101)}{3!}x^3 + \frac{v^{(iv)}(101)}{4!}x^4$$

where
$$v'(101) = +0,1093, \qquad v''(101) = -0,02875, \qquad v'''(101) = +0,0016583,$$
$$v^{(iv)}(101) = +0,0015$$

be the agent's utility function. In analogy with the function u, it results

$$Ev(101+X) = 98,75 \text{ and } v(101) = 100,5$$

therefore X is undesirable.

But, X becomes a desirable asset whenever Y is in the portfolio, because $Ev(101+X+Y) = 96,875$ is greater than $Ev(101+Y) = 95,75$.

Straightforward calculations show that condition (5) is violated.

The relevance of Example 2 is twofold:

- firstly, because it provides a simple approximation of u such that the properness-condition (5) can be checked;
- secondly, it shows that the violation of the differentiability of the utility function is *not* the cause of the agent's non-properness (for a detailed study on the implications of the utility function non-differentiability in the "coward" behaviour *à la* Ulam-Samuelson see Segal-Spivak (1990)).

References

Doherty, N. and H. Schlesinger, 1983, 'The optimal deductible for an insurance policy when initial wealth is random', *Journal of Business* 56, 555-565.

---

[2]It is worth noting that   in our context $E(X+Y)^3 > E(X^3) + E(Y^3)$ and $E(X+Y)^4 > E(X^4) + E(Y^4)$.

Eeckhoudt, L. and M. Kimball, 1992, 'Background Risk, Prudence and the Demand for Insurance', in *Contributions to Insurance Economics,* Georges Dionne ed. , Kluwer Academic Publishers, Dordrecht, 239-254.

Eeckhoudt, L. and H. Schlesinger, 'A Precautionary Tale of Risk Aversion and Prudence', presented at the FUR VI, Paris, July.

Feller, W., 1971, *'An Introduction to Probability Theory and Its Applications',* vol. II, New York, John Wiley & Sons.

Gini, 1915-6, 'Sul criterio di concordanza tra due caratteri', *Atti del Reale Istituto Veneto di Scienze, Lettere ed Arti,* Serie 8, 75, 309-331.

Gollier, C. and J.W. Pratt, 1993, 'Weak Proper Risk Aversion and the Tempering Effect of Background Risk', Cahier de Recherche HEC School of Management n.494/1993, Paris.

Gollier, C. and J.W. Pratt, 1995, 'Risk Vulnerability and the Tempering Effect of Background Risk', manuscript.

Kimball, M.S., 1990, 'Precautionary saving in the Small and in the Large', *Econometrica* 58, 53-73.

Kimball, M.S., 1993, 'Standard Risk Aversion', *Econometrica* 61, n.3, 589-611.

Mayers, D. and C.W. Smith, 1983, 'The Interdependence of Individual Portfolio Decisions and the Demand for Insurance', *Journal of Political Economy.* 91, n.2, 304-311.

Marshall, A.W. and Olkin, I. 1988, 'Families of Multivariate Distributions', *Journal of American Statistical Association* 83, 803-806.

Picone, M. and T. Viola, 1952, *'Lezioni sulla teoria moderna dell'integrazione',* Einaudi ed., Torino, Italy .

Pratt, J.W. and Zeckhauser, 1987, 'Proper Risk Aversion', *Econometrica* 55, 143-154.

Scarsini, M., 1984, 'On Measure of Concordance', *Stochastica* vol. VIII, 3, 201-218.

Segal, U. and A. Spivak, 1990, 'First Order versus Second Order Risk Aversion', *Journal of Economic Theory* 51, 111-125.

Tchen, A., 1980, 'Inequalities for distributions with given marginals', *Annals of Probability* 8, 814-827.

Tibiletti, L., 1994, 'Risk Premium for Higher Order Moments', *Atlantic Economic Society,* Anthology section vol. 22, n.3, 82.

Young, W.H., 1917, 'On Multiple Integration by Parts and the Second Theorem of the Mean', *Proceeding of the London Mathematical Society* 16, 271-293.